A RITUAL
GEOLOGY

A RITUAL GEOLOGY

GOLD AND SUBTERRANEAN KNOWLEDGE IN SAVANNA WEST AFRICA

Robyn d'Avignon

DUKE UNIVERSITY PRESS
Durham and London 2022

© 2022 DUKE UNIVERSITY PRESS
This work is licensed under a Creative Commons
Attribution-NonCommercial 4.0 International
License, available at https://creativecommons.org/licenses
/by-nc-nd/4.0/.
Printed in the United States of America on acid-free paper ∞
Designed by A. Mattson Gallagher
Typeset in Garamond Premier Pro
by Westchester Publishing Services

Library of Congress Cataloging-in-Publication Data
Names: d'Avignon, Robyn, [date] author.
Title: A ritual geology : gold and subterranean knowledge in
Savanna West Africa / Robyn d'Avignon.
Description: Durham : Duke University Press, 2022. | Includes
bibliographical references and index.
Identifiers: LCCN 2021049254 (print)
LCCN 2021049255 (ebook)
ISBN 9781478015833 (hardcover)
ISBN 9781478018476 (paperback)
ISBN 9781478023074 (ebook)
ISBN 9781478092674 (ebook other)
Subjects: LCSH: Gold mines and mining—Africa, French-
speaking West. | Gold miners—Africa, French-speaking West. |
Geology—Africa, French-speaking West. | Mines and mineral
resources—Africa, French-speaking West. | Ethnology—Africa,
French-speaking West. | BISAC: SOCIAL SCIENCE /
Anthropology / Cultural & Social
Classification: LCC HD8039.M732 A3545 2022 (print) |
LCC HD8039.M732 (ebook) | DDC 338.2/741096—dc23/
eng/20220110
LC record available at https://lccn.loc.gov/2021049254
LC ebook record available at https://lccn.loc.gov/2021049255

Cover art: "Miner descending to the bottom of the placer."
Bambala, Siguiri, Guinea, 1953. Photograph by Savonnet.
Courtesy of the Institut Fondamental d'Afrique Noire.

This book is freely available in an open access edition thanks
to TOME (Toward an Open Monograph Ecosystem)—a collaboration of the Association of American Universities, the
Association of University Presses, and the Association of Research Libraries and the generous support of New York University. Learn more at the TOME website, which can be found
at the following web address: https://openmonographs.org.

This book is dedicated to my parents,
Linda Pegg d'Avignon and Dana André d'Avignon

CONTENTS

Acknowledgments ix
Orthographic Notes xv
Abbreviations xvii

Introduction. Geology and West African History 1

1. A Tale of Two Miners in Tinkoto, Senegal, 2014 29

2. West Africa's Ritual Geology, 800–1900 58

3. Making Customary Mining in French West Africa 86

4. Colonial Geology and African Gold Discoveries 108

5. Mineral Mapping and the Global Cold War in Sénégal Oriental 129

6. A West African Language of Subterranean Rights 153

7. Race, Islam, and Ethnicity in the Pits 177

Conclusion. Subterranean Granaries 201

Glossary 207
Notes 211
Bibliography 259
Index 295

ACKNOWLEDGMENTS

It is an honor to thank the people, institutions, and places that have nurtured my scholarship, and my soul, in a journey that has spanned three continents and fifteen years.

My deepest gratitude extends to the people of Kédougou. In many ways, I became an adult in this place, forged by the grace and humor of friends and strangers. For countless meals, for teaching me Pular, and for caring for me when I was ill, I thank my family in Togué: Manga and Aliou Kamara and their children, Ndiogou, Fatoumata, Mamadou, Mawdo, Dienabou, and Sanoumou. I have been enriched by the friendships of Idi Diallo, Mamadou Diallo, Balaal Kamara, Malaal Kamara, Khalifa Kébé, Aissatou Keita, and Sokhana Keita. In Kédougou town, I cannot adequately express my gratitude to the generosity of Pape Mamadou Aliou Diallo and Adji Marieme Seck. For hosting me in their home, I thank Baba Amadou Woury and Nene Fatoumata Bineta Diallo, and their children, Mamadou Kaninou, Petit Amadou, Papa Hamidu, Elhaj Abdourahmane, Ibrahima, Sophie, Awa, and Nenegale. Doba and Harouna Diallo welcomed me into their families in Kédougou and Daandé. Over the years, I have learned much about the history of Kédougou and Senegal in conversation with Aliou Bakhoum, Abdoulaye Balde, Bocar Diallo, Mamadou Diallo, Modou Khouma, Aliou Monékheta, Filé Sadikaho, Khalidou Cissokho, Yousseph Diallo, Aruna Diop, and Abdoul Karim Keita. From Antwerp to Toronto, my friend El Hadj Mamadou Cissé showed me how transnational business, and politics, are made. I have sharpened my thinking in dialogue with the work of the Kédougou-based journalists Famakhan Dembélé, Adama Diaby, Pape Diallo, and Adama Diop. I write in the memory of two dear friends who passed during the writing of this book: Djiba Diallo and Manga Kamara.

Many of the individuals I interviewed are acknowledged in the text and in the endnotes; others requested anonymity. I thank them all for sharing their time and stories. Families in the following villages hosted and humored me: Bambaya, Bambaraya, Bantaco Dimboli, Duuta, Fongolimbi, Kanoumering, Kerekonko, Linguekoto, Kharakhena, Mako, Mamakono, Niéménéké, Sabodala, Sambaranbugu, Saraya, Tambanoumoya, Tinkoto, and Tomboroncoto. I thank Bambo Cissokho for a permanent entryway to Tinkoto. Elements of this project emerged in conversation with Gassimou Cissokho, Mamadou N'Dionge, Mamadou Dramé, Bliesse Kamara, Yonko Camara, Diba Felix Keita, Salioum Soaré, Soriba Keita, and El Hadji Alpha Diby Souaré. Alex MacKenzie generously invited me to Bassari Resources, in Dakar and in Duuta, and shared his personal history in gold exploration.

I benefited from the expertise and friendship of several research assistants in Senegal. Maciré Diallo and Khouddouse Diallo assisted me in archival research in Dakar. Pape "Dayo" Diallo made crucial introductions in Kédougou town, the Jakha, and in Niokolo. Madi Camara generously shared his knowledge of the juura and his family's rich history. I cannot adequately express my gratitude for the friendship and intellectual companionship of Falaye Danfakha during field research in Kédougou and in the years that have followed. Falaye's intellectual curiosity and commitment to social justice shaped every facet of the research and writing of this book. Falaye, thank you for enduring hardships of the heart and body to bring this history to light.

Senegal's Ministère de l'Education et de la Recherche and the Gouvernance de Kédougou authorized my research in Senegal. Mariane Yade and Professor Ousmane Séne of the West African Research Association assisted with visas and gave me an intellectual home in Dakar. Ousmane Cissé and Diene Rokhaya Samba facilitated my access to the archives of Senegal's Direction des Mines et de la Géologie. For their expertise at every turn, I thank the staff of the Archives Nationales du Sénégal, and in particular Boubacar Ndiaye. Saokho Mame Diarra shared her lunch tickets and time at the Service d'Archives et de Documentation du Soleil. I thank Anta Demba Thiam of the audiovisual division of the Institut Fondamental d'Afrique Noire. At the Université de Cheikh Anta Diop in Dakar, I thank the staff and faculty of the Département de Géologie and the Institut des Sciences de la Terre. I am grateful to the many earth scientists in Senegal who shared their time and experience with me, including Mababa Diagne, Dina Pathe Diallo, Moussa Diba, Cheikh Diop, Babacar Diouf, Abdoulaye Aziz Ndiaye, Hamidou Sow, and Lamine Sy. In Guinea, I thank Abdoulaye Diallo; the staff at the Archives

Nationales de la Guinée, Mörike Sidibé at the Université de Kankan; Djiba Kaba in Kankan; and Khalifa Diallo in Labé. In Barcelona, I thank Taouda Djiguiba and Younkoun Kamara. In Paris, Cheikhou Saouré and Siré Danfakha opened their homes to me and shared insights about Kédougou's diaspora. For hosting me in Dakar and Paris, I thank my friends Cara Haberman, Jedidiah Fix, John Paul Fortney, and Julie Roddier.

This project grew up in a special place: the Interdepartmental Program in Anthropology and History at the University of Michigan. I could not have asked for a more fearless adviser and friend than Gabrielle Hecht. At a key moment, she told me to trust myself and never look back. I took her advice and crossed a border. In ways you will never know, Gabrielle, you helped me bring this project, and my career, to fruition. Stuart Kirsch tirelessly supported this project and gently guided it back to where it belonged: in the agrarian world. He models engaged anthropology at its very finest. Nancy Rose Hunt, one of the most elegant historical thinkers and writers I know pushed me to think comparatively and to take joy in the creativity of this path. Rudolph Ware III understood this as a spiritual as much as an intellectual pursuit. Friday afternoons with Butch and Amir Syed on North Campus transformed my understanding of Islam and West Africa. Mike McGovern's feedback on my dissertation, and my ongoing engagement with his work, guided key revisions on the road to a book. Derek Peterson's generous reading and mentorship have shaped my practice as a historian and my ethics as a historian of Africa.

Judith Irvine introduced me to the study of language as social action in Africa. Thanks also to Howard Brick, David William Cohen, Alaina Lemon, Matthew Hull, Paul Johnson, and Elisha Renne. I was surrounded by incredible colleagues at Michigan, including Cameron Gokee, Sara Katz, Doreen Kembabazi, Adam Fulton Johnson, Amanda Logan, Benedicto Machava, Lamin Manneh, Pedro Monaville, Davide Orsini, Tasha Rijke-Epstein, Jonathan Shaw, Nafisa Essop Sheik, Stephen Sparks, Amir Syed, Edgar Taylor, Christopher Tounsel, and Daniel Williford. Liz Harmon shared Cornwell Place, laughter, and long walks. I am not at all sure where I would be without the brilliance and friendship of Adriana Chira.

New York University (NYU) brought wonderful new people into my life and sharpened my mind. Jane Burbank and Fred Cooper have shared meals, conversation, and a commitment to intellectual community. Julie Livingston models everything I aspire to become as a scholar. Thank you, Julie, for showing me how to bridge Africa and New York, and anthropology and history. I am grateful to Michael Gomez for his support, mentorship, and commitment to African history. This manuscript was greatly improved by a workshop with Fred, Mike, Julie, and Andrew Sartori. For supporting my scholarship in myriad ways, I thank Karl Appuhn, Edward Berenson, Karin Burrell, Liz Ellis, Ada Ferrer, Rozy Fredericks, Rebecca Goetz, Stefanous Geroulanos, Yanni Kotsonis, David Ludden, Jennifer Morgan, Andrew Needham, Guy Ortolano, and Chelsea Rhodes. I have learned from a talented group of graduate students at NYU, including Folarin Ajibade, Danielle Beaujon, Brendan Collins Jordan, Daniel Cumming, Zachary Cuyler Davis, Tanvi Kapoor, and Melissa Levkowitz. Hannah Leffingwell's deft eye saw this manuscript through final revisions. Mamadou Diouf, Gregory Mann, and Rhiannon Stephens welcomed me at Columbia. Ananda Burra and Ashley Rockenbach shared a move from Michigan to Manhattan. New York gave me the artist and historian Kamau Ware and the rich community of the Black Gotham Experience. Anoordha Siddiqi, Asif Siddiqi, and Betty Banks taught me the joy of collaboration. I have shared book writing, and worries of the heart, with Monica Kim and Anne O'Donnell. Cecilia Márquez transformed New York, disarmed me with laughter, and gave me Annise Weaver.

Glenn Davis Stone knows that the questions animating this book began with contract chicken farming in southern Missouri. Glenn, thank you. I hope you find merit in this work and see the signature of your mentorship in the career I have made. Ongoing conversations with my friends Jeremy Dell, Kevin Donovan, Emma Park, and Nikolas Sweet have sharpened my thinking about African history, writing, and ethics. For reading portions of this manuscript with great care, I am deeply grateful to Robert Blunt, Coleman Donaldson, Cameron Gokee, Jeremy Dell, Emily Riley, and Daniel Williford. Peter Andrew Kannam read this manuscript with an eye to geology. Thanks to my Peace Corps family: Cameron Fink, Jedidiah Fix, Cara Haberman, Erin Hayward, Andrew Jondahl, Sarah Lee, Ashleigh Lovett, Matthew McLaughlin, Kay Stones, Nikolas Sweet, Amy Truong, and Jordan Welty. The wise Sasha Dimant helped untether my past from my future. From Togué to New Haven, I have been sustained by the friendship of Stephen Wood, and now Jillian Bell and Henry. To the crew, I thank Animale, Pierreba, Al, Benjy Bunnoit, Charles, Frankie, Martino, M. Eloise, Marcos, and ever Tuna and Larry. Some of my oldest friends—Lindsay Brill, Maya Buchanan, Alexandra Reisman, and Emily Warming—supported this book, against their better judgment.

This research was made possible by generous funding from the National Science Foundation, the Wenner-Gren Foundation, and the Social Science Research Council. At the University of Michigan, I received financial support from the College of Literature, Science, and the Arts, the Eisenberg Institute for Historical Studies, the African Studies Center, the International Institute, the Department of Afroamerican and African Studies, the Department of Anthropology, Rackham Graduate School, the Sweetland Writing Center, and the Graham Sustainability Institute. The NYU Department of History and the Center for the Humanities contributed to book production costs. I am appreciative of the Leonard Hastings Schoff and Suzanne Levick Schoff Memorial Fund at the University Seminars at Columbia University for their help in publication. The ideas presented here benefited from discussions in the University Seminar on Studies in Contemporary Africa.

I presented early drafts of this work at the Colorado School of Mines, Columbia University, the École Normale Supérieure, the University of Edinburgh, Emory University, the University of Florida, Harvard University, New York University, Northwestern University, the Block Museum at Northwestern University, Yale University, and the Mellon-funded Michigan-Wits collaborative. Many ideas in this book were generated in dialogue with scholars at these institutions and other workshops and conferences. Thank you to Emmanuel Akyeampong, Jody Benjamin, Keith Breckenridge, Emily Brownell, Brenda Chalfin, Barbara Cooper, Jean Comaroff, David Conrad, Clifton Crais, Joshua Grace, Kathryn de Luna, Maria Pia Donato, Barbara E. Frank, Mary E. Hicks, David Kneas, Abby J. Kinchy, Roderick McIntosh, Fiona McLaughlin, George Paul Meiu, Emily Lynn Osborn, Abena Dove Osseo-Asare, Tom Özden-Schilling, Roopali Phadke, James Scott, Jessica M. Smith, Benjamin Soares, Alioune Sow, Helen Tilley, Pablo D. Herrera Veitia, Luise White, Martha Wilfahrt, Alden Young, and the Mande Studies Association listserv. A W. E. B. Du Bois Research Institute McMillan-Stewart Fellowship at the Hutchins Center for African and African American Studies at Harvard gave me the time and resources to finish a draft of this book. I thank Henry Louis Gates Jr., Krishna Lewis, and Cornel West and the 2018–19 fellows.

I am fortunate for the collaboration with Duke University Press and its immensely skilled editorial team. Elizabeth Ault deftly guided me through each stage of publishing. I thank Benjamin Kossak and Susan Albury for close reading and timely feedback. It was a true gift to work with Tim Stallman, who designed the maps that grace these pages. Two anonymous reviewers, who read the manuscript during the height of the COVID-19 pandemic, helped make this a far better, and shorter, book.

No one has sacrificed more to see this book to completion than my family: the McNairs-Shermans, Oforis, Quarshies, and d'Avignon-Kriegs. I thank Matekwor Ofori for inviting me into her family in the United States and Ghana and for investing her time and resources in helping our family grow and flourish. I am grateful for James Quarshie's curiosity, sense of humor, and warm welcome in Ghana. My desire to explore the world took root in the modest central Illinois ranch house of my late maternal grandmother, Ruthellen Kettler Pegg. In their own ways, Deborah d'Avignon and Sue d'Avignon modeled a life that traversed continents but always returned to the Adirondacks. Every day, I strive to be more like my sister, Sonya Kannam, and brother, Peter Kannam. Thank you for your love and energy and for reminding me of the ways of the Booble. Peter Andrew, Zachary, and Cole Kannam grew up alongside this book, happily diverting me to trails, ice-cream stands, and soccer games. This book is dedicated to my parents, Linda Pegg and Dana André d'Avignon, who have enriched my life beyond measure. They traveled half-way around the world to meet new friends and encouraged a life of the mind even when it took me far from them. As an artist and a scientist, my dad taught me to see research as a creative pursuit on a journey for knowledge that will span my lifetime. I would never have completed this book without my best friend and my editor, my mom. She read, and reread, every page of this book, every grant proposal, and every paper along the way. She taught me to listen to the quiet voice of my soul and to keep an eye upward, on the skies. This book was forged in the grace of her boundless love.

Nana Osei Quarshie, how many nights have I sat down to thank you? But the words fail me, so inseparable is this journey from your love. On laptops and crumpled papers, this book has traveled with us to Accra, Dakar, Marseilles, New York, and New Haven. From rat park to the crew, you made me laugh and helped me to see this project, and the world, anew. I thank you from the bottom of my heart for sharing Jude Tawia, our greatest pride and joy. You two have brought me more happiness than I ever thought possible. As I close this book, I am overwhelmed with gratitude and awe for what I have learned. Those I have mentioned briefly, or not at all, I thank you. In closing, my recourse is to a Pular tradition of leave-taking: please forgive me (*accanan hakke*).

ORTHOGRAPHIC NOTES

Maninka and Pular are the language varieties most commonly spoken on the goldfields of Senegal, Mali, and Guinea. *Maninka* (Malinké in French) is the Manding dialect spoken in eastern Senegal, western Mali, and Guinea. *Maninka* is also an ethnonym used by speakers of this variety, many of whom claim heritage from the thirteenth-century Malian empire. Manding is a language continuum of the Mande language family spoken by more than thirty million people in West Africa, from Senegal to Burkina Faso. I use the term *Pular* to refer to the dialect of Fula spoken in southern Senegal and northern Guinea. Fula (Fulfulde, Fula, Fulani, Pular or Peul) is a language continuum of the West Atlantic branch of the Niger-Congo language family spoken by more than fifteen million people from the Atlantic coast in Senegal to the savannas of East Africa.

I have italicized non–English-language words in their initial usage in the book. Italicized words are in Maninka unless indicated (by context or explicitly) as Arabic, French, Pular, or Wolof. For words derived from Arabic commonly used in English, such as *jihad*, I use established Latin spellings without italics. I worked with Falaye Danfakha to translate interviews from Maninka into French. Falaye and Mohamadou "Pape" Diallo helped with some translations in Pular, and I completed others independently. French translations are my own. Any consistent approach to orthography in this book proved elusive due to the diversity of languages, time periods, and national alphabetic conventions at play. This heterogeneity reflects the linguistic diversity of the region and the uneven legacies of colonial languages, and Arabic language instruction, on linguistic norms. In transcribing African languages, I use a combination of simple phonetic and the official orthography of Senegal, where I conducted most of my interviews. For ease of reading, I do not use special characters or tonal diacritics. Whenever possible, I have avoided the use of plurals.

For the names of people and places, I generally followed French spellings and accents according to common usage in the West African country in question or as spelled by individuals and published authors. I have chosen to use the phonetic spellings of common words that begin with the sound "j," such as juura and jalan. I retain the French spelling of "dia" for patronyms, such as Diallo and Diaby. When writing on the colonial era, I have kept the French names of colonies, such as "Soudan."

All dates are Common Era (CE).

ABBREVIATIONS

AOF	Afrique-Occidentale Française/French West Africa
BPS	Bloc Populaire Sénégalais
BRGM	Bureau de Recherches Géologiques et Minières
BRP	Bureau de Recherche de Pétrole
BUMIFOM	Bureau Minier de la France d'Outre-mer
CEA	Commissariat à l'Énergie Atomique
CFA	Communauté Financière Africaine
CSR	Corporate Social Responsibility
DFMG	Direction Fédérale des Mines et de la Géologie (French West Africa)
DMG	Direction des Mines et de la Géologie (Senegal)
FAC	Fonds d'Aide et de Coopération
IFAN	Institut Fondamental d'Afrique Noire
ILO	International Labour Organization
IST	Institut des Sciences de la Terre
KKI	Kédougou-Kéniéba Inlier
MDL	Mineral Deposits Limited
NGO	non-governmental organization
OECD	Organization for Economic Cooperation and Development
RDA	Rassemblement Démocratique Africain
SAP	structural adjustment program

SEIS	social and environmental impact studies
UCAD	Université de Cheikh Anta Diop
UDRSO	Union Démocratique des Ressortissants du Sénégal Oriental
UN	United Nations

Introduction
Geology and West African History

On a cloudless afternoon in June 2017, three Senegalese geologists visit the edge of the exploration permit of their employer, the small Australian gold-mining firm Bassari Resources.[1] The permit sits in the region of Kédougou, in southeastern Senegal, bordering Guinea and Mali. More than three-quarters of the region's surface area, which stands at over 16,000 square kilometers, is covered by gold-exploration permits and mining concessions. These geologists spent nearly a decade modeling the scope and concentration of gold within a dense basalt rock gold deposit known as Makabingui. Formerly a Maninka place name for a small stream, Makabingui now names a roughly one-million-ounce gold deposit lying directly underfoot. The geologists oversee the work of a Canadian firm subcontracted to diamond-drill core samples to reveal the mineral profile of soils hundreds of feet underground. The field is ochre red from iron-laden soils oxidizing in the savanna heat. Stripped of all foliage, the earth looks exposed and moonlike.

The muddy field is all that remained of the "battle for Makabingui," a conflict that waxed and waned between the Australian firm and so-called artisanal miners—known as *orpailleurs* in Francophone West Africa—for several years.[2] The battle reached a crescendo in 2011 as the firm intensified its exploration of Makabingui. At the time, orpaillage was expanding to unprecedented scales in Kédougou. The region has a history of seasonal gold mining, excavating shallow pits with iron picks, dating to the medieval period. In the 2000s, orpaillage in Senegal was becoming more capitalized and mechanized. Emigrants from Senegal living in Spain and France sent gold detectors and hydraulic drills to brothers back home. With mortar pickers and dynamite, multiethnic teams of orpailleurs excavated deposits, such as Makabingui, that were impervious to hand tools. Bassari Resources lobbied the Senegalese state to expel the orpailleurs from their permit, claiming

Figure I.1 A portion of Makabingui after it was bulldozed. Sambaranbugu, Senegal, 2014. Photograph by the author.

that "illegal miners" were "eating away" at its mining prospect. In late 2012, the Senegalese army bulldozed Makabingui (figure I.1). Months later, orpailleurs reoccupied the deposit. In 2014, the state directed a second fleet of bulldozers to Makabingui and installed a gendarme post in a shipping container to guard the field.[3] As of this writing, the Senegalese state has approved a concession to exploit Makabingui as an open-pit mine, the third of its kind in Senegal. Meanwhile, orpailleurs have turned to other deposits in Kédougou.

The Australian firm won the battle for Makabingui, but the war for the future of hundreds of goldfields in West Africa is ongoing. Senegal sits on the western edge of a geological formation known as the Birimian Greenstone Belt. Created between 2.2 billion and 2.1 billion years ago, Birimian rocks contain many of the region's gold, iron, and diamond deposits. Since the late 1990s, a gold-mining boom has been gaining speed across West Africa's Birimian rocks. It was born of a conjuncture of rising gold prices, the widespread adoption of pro-market mining codes, and new mining technologies that reduced reliance on local labor and infrastructure. Mining firms based in former British settler colonies—the United States, Canada, Australia, and

South Africa—sought new outlets for their skills and capital in Africa. By the early 2000s, Guinea and Mali were among Africa's top gold producers, with Burkina Faso close behind. Senegal opened its first open-pit mine in 2008.

In promotional films targeted to investors, exploration firms and mining companies promote savanna West Africa as an "emergent" and "virtually underexplored" gold belt. Such phrases are paired with descriptions of the region as "sparsely populated," suggesting the possibility of extraction with minimal human interference. This is an aspiration to removal from the social world in which these gold deposits are embedded.[4] But talk of undiscovered riches lying in wait maps poorly onto a region where men and women have been mining, processing, and trading gold for more than a millennium. Kédougou occupies a Birimian formation that geologists call the Kédougou-Kéniéba Inlier (KKI).[5] The KKI aligns with an ancient gold-producing province known in medieval Arabic chronicles as Bambuk (map I.1). By the ninth century, gold from Bambuk was sold to camel caravans across the Sahara Desert, fueling the rise of West African empires and furnishing the mints of Mediterranean city-states until the European encounter with the Americas in the fifteenth century.

Gold is also integral to the histories of lineages and clans that settled Bambuk in search of fresh gold deposits of their own. When famine and war depleted granaries, gold was bartered for grain. In the fifteenth century, hope of accessing the fabled goldfields of Bambuk enticed Portuguese sailors to navigate down the West African coast. Decades later, this seaborn encounter set the transatlantic slave trade in motion. In the nineteenth century, the French empire united the goldfields of the West African savanna under a new foreign power. French ambitions to transform Bambuk into the "Californie" of France motivated conquest campaigns and shaped imperial mining policies. This is not a new mining frontier. It is a very old one, carved open by generations of West Africans.

A Ritual Geology situates what economists have coined the "twenty-first century scramble for Africa's resources" within two intertwined histories.[6] The first thread documents how the French colonial state, and its postcolonial successors, regulated orpaillage while also profiting from the gold discoveries of West African miners. African mining economies, I argue, were central to the emergence of modern exploration geology in West Africa. This claim inserts struggles over mineral discovery into the history of mining capitalism in Africa, a field that has studied African miners as laborers and victims of land alienation, but rarely as intellectual actors. The second thread of this book concerns how West African societies have cultivated

GEOLOGY AND WEST AFRICAN HISTORY   3

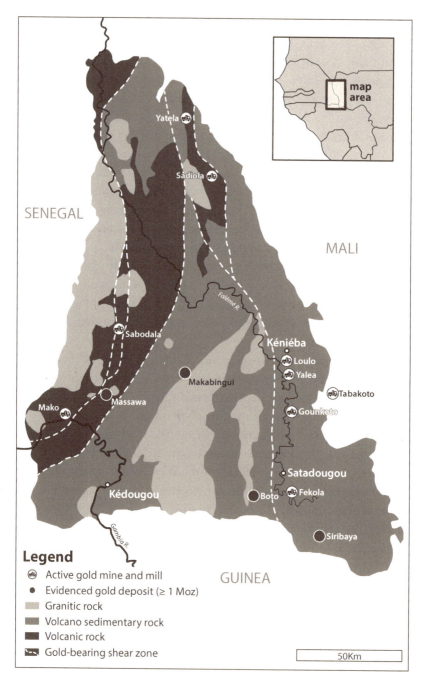

Map I.1 Major gold mines and prospects on the Kédougou-Kéniéba Inlier, which aligns with the historical gold-producing region of Bambuk.

knowledge about the underground, made claims to mineralized land, and managed gold mining and trade. By the time of French colonial conquest, orpailleurs elaborated a "ritual geology" across the Birimian rocks of savanna West Africa. I define a ritual geology as a set of practices, prohibitions, and cosmological engagements with the earth that are widely shared and cultivated across a regional geological formation. I draw my concept of "ritual" from the work of the late religious studies scholar Catherine Bell, who understood ritual as a category of practice that can be sacred or nonsacred in form. Orpaillage shares a number of attributes that Bell identified for rituals in other contexts. They include an organized set of expressions or gestures or a code of communication; the attempt to demarcate, and to make activities consistent with, preceding cultural practices; rules that are imposed on, and meant to restrict, human action and interaction; and shared symbolism that is sacred in nature.[7]

West Africa's ritual geology is neither monolithic nor static. It is similar to a language family with many varieties: some are mutually intelligible, others share only core vocabularies and grammatical forms. Languages shift over time from the innovations of their speakers, encounters with new languages and ecological change, among other factors. West Africa's ritual geology has also evolved and adapted to different corridors in response to shifts in regional markets, migration, and the arrival of tools from elsewhere on the globe.[8] In its various iterations, this ritual geology has shaped how Africans governed mineralized land and people, including miners, traders, state makers, and earth scientists. Scholars have glimpsed the edges of this ritual geology. But studies bound by region, colony, ethnic group, or nation-state have failed to capture the spatial and temporal breadth of this regional phenomenon. By placing data from my research in dialogue with historical, archeological, and ethnographic studies from across the Sahel and savanna, this book models a new regional approach to African history: one centered on geology.

I also explore how different groups in West Africa mobilize the past to make claims to gold-bearing land to the state, to one another, and to corporate capital. To demonstrate precisely how the past resonates in the present, I move across several temporal and geographic scales. My account begins and ends on the goldfields of Kédougou in the 2010s, when I carried out ethnography, oral histories, and archival research. I weave these sources together to explore the history and active life of orpaillage in southeastern Senegal, a region that is central to the history of gold in West Africa.[9] The book's middle chapters open onto the goldfields of modern Guinea, Mali, and Senegal from the medieval period to the Atlantic age through the French occupation of the western savanna in the late nineteenth century. I then track attempts by the French colonial state, and independent West African states, to profit from orpaillage as a source of revenue and subterranean knowledge, while excluding agrarian residents from durable rights to minerals.[10] This project is framed by the ongoing corporate enclosure of West Africa's goldfields, which threatens the future of one of the world's oldest indigenous gold-mining economies. Thus, this book is also an account of the meaning of history in an urgent present.

Making "Artisanal Miners"

For centuries, orpaillage has been an engine of trade, a famine resource, and the platform for a multiethnic, seasonal urban form in agrarian West Africa. Orpaillage was also the largest mining industry of France's West African empire until the 1950s. Yet until recently, it was the subject of only a handful of articles.[11] Orpaillage has been occluded from the historical record by enduring representations of African-controlled mining economies—by states, international agencies, and the media—as backward, primitive, and criminal. This problem has long haunted the study of technology in Africa. Two decades ago, it was possible to claim that Africa had been excluded from global histories of technology except as a victim of European technological imperialism or as a recipient of technology "transfers" from elsewhere.[12] Fortunately, this is no longer the case. Studies of uranium mining, oncology, car repair, moneylending platforms, firearms, hunting, and healing plants have placed Africa at the center of global networks of innovation.[13] This scholarship resonates with decades of archeological research documenting the sophistication of African metallurgy, plant domestication, and food processing over the past two millennia.[14] While scholars have refuted assumptions of primitivism in African technological practice, we have only begun to interrogate how "technical" categories themselves may perpetuate these characterizations. It is precisely because technical categories appear natural—and thus beyond the realm of public debate—that they are such powerful instruments for shaping the world in their image.[15] "Artisanal mining" is one such category.

What is artisanal mining? States, international agencies, and mining firms define the term according to different characteristics: techniques ("low tech"), labor requirements ("no mechanization" or "labor-intensive"), or legal status ("absence of formalization," "illegal," or "lack of adequate regulatory framework").[16] A World Bank report released in 2009 describes it as mining that relies on "low investment, labor intensive local production, informality, as well as no or low levels of mechanization."[17] These reports are not transparent accounts of technological practice. Rather, they define the artisanal miner in relationship to an implied counterpart: the industrial miner. In colonial Africa, the industrial miner was racialized as a white European and gendered as male. This colonial binary is perpetuated in contemporary policies and descriptions of mining practices around the globe.

artisanal miner = third world, illegal, primitive, local, customary, Black/Brown

industrial miner = first world, legal, technologically advanced, global, modern, white

The precise terms attached to these categories have shifted across time, inflected by new laws and linguistic norms. In much of Africa, the category of the artisanal miner emerged from colonial-era laws regulating "customary mining," a racialized legal framework applied only to the extractive activities of African subjects.[18] In the mid-twentieth century, as African states were gaining independence, the term *artisanal* replaced *customary* in mining. Many twenty-first century media and policy reports still describe artisanal mining as "primitive" and "simple," evoking tired colonial tropes of technological backwardness and primordialism. This is not a coincidence. Artisanal mining remains concentrated in the formerly colonized world: Africa, Southeast Asia, the Eurasian Steppe, Oceania, and Latin America. While artisanal mining is certainly associated with enduring agrarian poverty in these regions, it is also the outgrowth of an unfinished struggle over mineral rights that began with the colonial enclosures of mineralized land. Similar to poaching, artisanal mining is a category of technological practice produced by property laws that sought to legitimize certain uses of nature and to criminalize others.[19]

Artisanal mining forces difficult questions onto the table. Unregulated labor-intensive mining contributes to deforestation in the Amazon; child trafficking in coltan mines in the Democratic Republic of Congo; and the methylmercury contamination of groundwater around the globe.[20] At the same time, artisanal mining offers a pathway out of poverty for many rural citizens, an alternative to soil-depleting cash cropping or migration to megacities (figure I.2).[21] Artisanal mining is unlikely to go away anytime soon, a fact recognized by the World Bank and the United Nations. After decades of

Figure I.2 Orpaillage team in Tinkoto, Senegal, 2014. Photograph by the author.

funding programs designed to discourage or to create alternatives to artisanal mining, these organizations now pledge millions of dollars to formalize the sector in the global South.[22] In a sign of just how far the negative media image of artisanal mining has come, in 2017 *The Economist* published the article "In Praise of Small Miners," which celebrated artisanal mining for creating jobs in "some of the poorest places on earth" at a pace that far outstripped jobs generated by corporate mines.[23] Some scholars even suggest that artisanal mining, as a citizen-led counterpart to corporate mining, is a democratizing political force.[24]

Reassessments of artisanal mining as democratic and innovative—in contrast to the destructive forces of corporate mining—reverse the values of the artisanal-versus-industrial binary while leaving the binary itself intact. This binary is reinforced by scholars who tend to study either industrial or artisanal mining. Ethnographies of extraction in twenty-first-century Africa illustrate this point. On one hand, there is a rich stream of ethnographic literature on the technical, fiscal, and moral arrangements of corporate mining in Africa.[25] Meanwhile, a separate group of ethnographers examine forms of economic subjectivity, consumption, and masculinity in unregulated mining sites.[26] However, beyond a handful of articles on conflicts between artisanal and corporate gold miners, these studies do not address the historical relationship between artisanal and industrial mining.[27] The result is a problem of representation, to extend a critique the historian Steven Feierman once waged against studies of capitalism and Christianity in Africa.[28] Studies of corporate and artisanal mining in one African locale or another are often aggregated only on the basis of their shared relationship to neoliberal market reforms, a rise in global consumer demand for minerals used in smartphone manufacture, or the vertical integration of multinational mining corporations. The "African" side of the equation remains local and fragmented: a case study, but not the heart, of a global story.

This book challenges the reification of industrial and artisanal mining through the work of history. It does so by situating colonial and contemporary Euro-American mining ventures within the unfolding cultural and technical practices of orpaillage, a regional mining tradition that has flourished on the West African savanna for two millennia. The term *tradition* is a contested one in African history. Colonial officials often described African traditions, more often glossed as "customs," as static practices tied to rural, ethnic spaces. I draw on a very different concept of tradition, defined by the historian Jan Vansina as "a collective body of cognitive and physical representations shared by their members."[29] Drawing on a deep time study of the "Rainforest Tradition" of Bantu-speakers in the Congo basin, Vansina argued that traditions are a dynamic constellation of practices and beliefs inherited and transmitted from one generation to the next through narratives, political institutions, rituals, and bodily praxis. Far from preserving a set of timeless or rote practices, traditions require autonomy and the capacity to change. Once born, traditions can endure for millennia. But they can also die when the fundamental principles of the tradition are abandoned by its carriers in favor of another one.[30] Vansina's formulation provides a framework to compare traditions from around the globe in a meaningful, nonhierarchical fashion. We can, for example, compare elements of the Abrahamic religious traditions to those of Congo's Rainforest Tradition, which flourished from 500 to 1900, when the cumulative effects of the Atlantic slave trade and colonialism led to its demise.

While Vansina's Rainforest Tradition incorporated many dimensions of productive and ritual communal life, my notion of a mining tradition is more constrained in scope. It refers to the collective body of cosmological engagements, epistemic orientations, and physical practices tied to prospecting, extracting, and processing minerals. A mining tradition is a scientific tradition—one that entails, as all historical scientific traditions do, distinctive ritual and cognitive engagements with the physical world.[31] I have chosen the

French word *orpaillage* to describe this West African mining tradition despite the term's colonial origins. In the eighteenth and nineteenth centuries, French explorers and traders plying the Senegal River used the term to gloss the diverse activities relating to prospecting, excavating, and processing gold carried about by African miners in Bambuk. By the beginning of the twentieth century in metropolitan France, the term *orpailleur* referred to what is known as gold panning in English: the separation of gold flakes from soil by hand.[32] In French West Africa, however, the term was racialized. Colonial officials called Africans orpailleurs and Europeans miners (*mineurs*), even when Africans excavated underground tunnels and Europeans panned for gold. However, in recent decades in Francophone West Africa, the valence of the term has shifted as men and women have adopted it to describe their work. Today, the male-gendered term *orpailleur* is used by men (and many women) who consider orpaillage their occupation. Following their lead, I use the term *orpaillage* to refer to the dynamic West African mining histories of which these individuals are part.[33]

I have identified five broad characteristics that constitute the mining tradition of orpaillage in West Africa as it has been practiced over the past several centuries. First, orpaillage is carried out geographically on gold-bearing Birimian rocks on the savanna, a bioclimatic zone to the south of the Sahel. Much of this region came under French colonial rule in the late nineteenth century. Second, orpaillage is organized around a loose set of political and ritual organizations that are understood by its practitioners as ethnic Maninka in origin. Maninka is a language variety of Manding, a language continuum spoken by upward of thirty million people in West Africa that includes Bambara, Maninka, Mandinka, and Jula.[34] *Maninka* is also an ethnonym used by speakers of this variety, most of whom claim heritage from the thirteenth-century Malian empire. By the eighteenth century, Maninka was a lingua franca in gold-bearing regions of Senegal, Mali, and Guinea.[35] Third, gold is considered the property of underground spirits. This is a central tenet of West Africa's ritual geology, which I return to later. Fourth, orpaillage is a spatially extensive mining tradition based on seasonal mobility. Archeological evidence of alluvial gold mining confirms that contemporary spatial practices of orpaillage are of some antiquity.[36] Communities of miners have tended to mine a given deposit for several weeks, or months, before moving to a new goldfield. Orpailleurs often returned to abandoned deposits in later years after heavy rains redistributed gold flakes in the substrata. This practice mirrors the logic of shifting cultivation, an agricultural system practiced widely on the savanna, whereby farmers clear forest and cultivate a plot of land for several years before leaving it fallow for seven years or more.[37] The extensive character of orpaillage contrasts with capital-intensive mining, which aims to deplete gold entirely from a parcel of the earth.

Fifth, orpaillage is an incorporative institution adapted to cyclical drought. Mining sites across the savanna have long welcomed strangers, and hosting was a reciprocal expectation. Many West African societies place a high value on strangers, one ideological repercussion of the fact that labor, rather than land, was often the limiting factor to production.[38] But hospitality on the goldfields was also tied to the importance of gold as an agrarian resource during times of drought and famine.[39] Gold was an open resource, available to anyone willing to mine it. If goldfields near home became depleted, one could migrate to a distant goldfield and expect to be welcomed. While some lineages specialized in orpaillage, it was never the exclusive purview of a single craft, ethnic, or religious group.[40] This distinguishes orpaillage from iron smelting, wood carving, and leather-working: occupations carried out exclusively by craft specialists in savanna West Africa since the medieval period. Orpaillage did attract particular segments of the population and not others. It was, and remains, physically arduous and dangerous labor performed during the hottest time of the year, when temperatures can reach 120 degrees Fahrenheit. Elites opted out of mining, and so did Muslims, for reasons elaborated later. The poor, practitioners of African religions, and the formerly enslaved dominated orpaillage because they lacked the capital to pursue other activities. The importance of orpaillage to agrarian life in West Africa has waxed and waned with shifting regional ecological circumstances and fluctuating prices for gold on global markets (figure I.3).

Neither orpaillage nor the mining techniques of visitors to West Africa's goldfields were a hermetically sealed system. For centuries, orpailleurs have incorporated efficacious techniques from other global mining traditions they encountered. These include metal balances and numismatic systems from medieval North Africa; river-damming techniques from colonial-era French prospectors; and cyanide heap leaching from chemists working for multinational mining operations in the early 2000s. West African miners have also exchanged techniques with one another across vast geographies. During the Atlantic period, mining techniques from the southern forests of modern Ghana spread into parts of Burkina Faso, just as Muslim measuring systems for gold dust and Manding-derived mining vocabulary appeared in Akan language varieties spoken in Ghana's gold-rich southern forests.

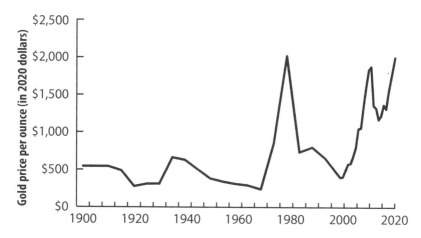

Figure I.3 Gold prices, ca. 1900–2020.

Scholars tend to frame mining corporations as transnational, operating at a more encompassing spatial scale than artisanal mining, which is described as community-based, grassroots, and local.[41] But the technological and financial networks of orpailleurs span the globe, similar to those of corporate miners. Since the ninth century, West Africa's gold has reached across the Sahara and into the Arabian Peninsula. Today, orpaillage is supported by manufacturing hubs and trading diasporas in Dubai, Delhi, and Amsterdam.

Much of the knowledge produced and transmitted by orpailleurs is embodied. This includes techniques of digging, winnowing, and smelling the earth for gold. It also entails embodied philosophies of human-spirit interactions, such as stories of the bones of suffocated miners turning to gold underground (chapter 7). Orpaillage invites comparisons with modes of knowledge embedded in African art—the subject of a rich scholarship in its attention to skill, form, and knowledge transmission.[42] Approaching orpaillage as both an economy and an art allows us to see how orpailleurs creatively combined dynamic West African techniques and ritual complexes tied to Birimian rocks with innovations from elsewhere. The result, to quote the art historian Chika Okeke-Agulu, are "messy, fraught, and inevitably distinctive" forms of extractive practice and political subjectivity.[43]

The material distribution of gold in West Africa has facilitated the emergence of widespread ritual and social institutions tied to orpaillage.[44] In Birimian rocks, gold is found in either secondary or primary deposits. In primary deposits, gold is amalgamated to other minerals in lode ore. The weathering of primary deposits creates secondary ones as gold flakes are dislodged from ores, transported through the water table, and redistributed as "free" particles among sands, silts, and sediments. African farmers and hunters glimpsed gold flakes in plant roots and along streams after a hard rain. For much of the past millennium, orpailleurs excavated placer deposits on riverways or desiccated paleo-channels covered by a few meters of sterile rock and sand. Mining alluvial gold requires minimal processing, making the activity accessible to men and women, the elderly, the young, and the disabled. The ubiquity of gold prevented a single sovereign or state from monopolizing this resource. Control over goldfields was decentralized, and gold was incorporated into the aesthetics and cosmologies of diverse West African societies.

My approach to orpaillage—as a regional mining tradition with considerable historical continuity—is not one-size-fits-all for studies of artisanal mining economies. In India and Mongolia, for example, most artisanal mining is recent, with few linkages to historical modes of income generation.[45] There are important distinctions within Africa, as well. In South Africa and Central Africa, where industrial-scale mines have operated for over a century, scholars have analyzed the recent growth of artisanal mining through the lens of postindustrial ruination and post-wage work.[46] By contrast, there was very little capital-intensive mining in savanna West Africa until two decades ago. Wage work has always been the exception, not the norm. African-controlled orpaillage was the dominant mode of extraction. Such divergent historical trajectories require different genres of narration. Indeed, any activity that more than one hundred million people around the globe rely on as their primary source of income has many stories to tell. This book is not a universal tale; it is a regional one grounded in West Africa's Birimian rocks.

Searching for Subterranean Knowledge

A Ritual Geology trains its focus on the decades—centuries, in some cases— of mineral exploration that precede the opening of a mine, whether corporate or artisanal in scope. This approach departs from most scholarship on mining in the global South, which examines the extractive process itself or the social life of decline "after the rush."[47] It is during exploration, I argue, that the expectations and grievances for future extractive projects take shape in the political imagination and in modes of storytelling.[48] Resource exploration is uneven and time-consuming, contingent on capricious

GEOLOGY AND WEST AFRICAN HISTORY   13

market conditions and luck. Geologists can spend decades studying a zone before a mine is established, and most exploration projects never identify a mine-worthy prospect. This uncertainty, paired with the latent potential of discovery, shapes the sociology of the spaces where mineral research is concentrated.

Southeastern Senegal is a place where histories of mineral research have accumulated on the landscape, in individual biographies, and in the settlement narratives of villages. The search for gold in this region has unfolded on multiple temporal horizons. Maninka lineages have searched for gold for generations, transmitting techniques for gold prospecting to their children. Knowledge of surface and subsurface gold mineralization is recorded through bodily praxis, the deft manufacture and use of locally forged tools, and storytelling embedded in features of the landscape and family genealogies. As early as the seventeenth century, European explorers traveled to Bambuk to document the location of "native mines" and observe the techniques of African miners. During French colonialism, and after West African states gained independence, geologists hired by states and private companies continued to shadow orpailleurs to generate baseline data for geological maps (see chapters 4 and 5). Shadowing rarely produced immediate discoveries. Resource exploration was slow and cumulative. Rising metal prices attracted new generations of geologists who updated old maps with geochemical and aeromagnetic techniques. Some villages in Kédougou have hosted mineral exploration camps for six decades. While the personnel and names of firms have changed, exploration has continued, animating expectations for a future mine.

This book is one of the first sustained accounts of the central role of African mining expertise in geological exploration in colonial and postcolonial Africa (figure I.4).[49] In recent years, the history of science has expanded beyond its conventional geographic focus of Europe and North America to document the contribution of non-Western experts to scientific discoveries formerly credited to the "West." We have learned that many technical innovations passed off as European were, in fact, the hybrid product of cosmopolitan "contact zones" populated by Asian, Indigenous North American, Caribbean, and African healers, traders, farmers, and blacksmiths.[50] For colonial Africa, it is now well established that European agronomists, ethnographers, botanists, and cartographers garnered methodological and conceptual insights from African healers, assistants, hunters, and translators "in the field."[51] In a parallel vein, scholars of the Atlantic world have documented that Africans contributed not only brute labor to plantations

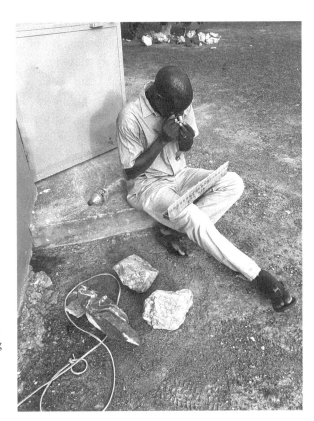

Figure I.4 Moussa Diba, geologist-engineer and exploration manager of Bassari Resources, examining a rock specimen. Duuta, Senegal, 2017. Photograph by the author.

in the Americas but also expertise in pharmacotherapies, rice farming, and animal pasturage.[52] A similar consensus is emerging in studies of how African healers shaped medical practice on a global scale through their work on slave ships and in ports across the Atlantic world.[53]

While historians have shown that Africans were always part of global scientific production, they have attended less to how laws determined the benefactors of epistemic exchange under conditions of sustained inequality.[54] An exception to this in African history are studies of the exchange and appropriation of botanical knowledge, or "bioprospecting." Patents have enabled some scientists and corporations, including African ones, to claim ownership over healing formulas to the exclusion of others.[55] Questions of discovery are rarely straightforward. For example, in tracing the journey of healing plants from Africa into pharmaceutical formulas, the historian Abena Dove Osseo-Asare contrasts the "fragmented, synchronous stories of shared creation" of plant knowledge produced through the interactions of African healers, scientists, and corporations with narratives of "priority" that insist with certitude that "we know the time of each discovery."[56]

The parallels with mineral discovery in Africa are remarkable. Most European mining enterprises in colonial Africa began as "takeovers" of African mines, followed by an investment in capital. This was the case for gold-mining industries in nineteenth-century South Africa and Ghana and tin mining in the early twentieth century on the Jos Plateau of Nigeria.[57] Despite the ubiquity of these practices, political struggles over mineral discovery are largely absent from histories of mining in Africa, which are focused on capitalist expansion, the exploitation of land and labor, and the emergence of collective and ethnic politics in mining towns.[58] Of course, many Africans were exploited workers in colonial-era mines. But others generated scientific knowledge on which industrial mines depended—a fact elided in the historiography. Regional divergences in mining developments and mineral laws may account for this oversight. Many southern African colonies outlawed mining by Africans and alienated land, forcing Africans to labor on European-owned mines. But not all colonial regimes criminalized mining by Africans. Colonial officials in French West Africa encouraged orpaillage, relied on African authorities to manage gold mining, and profited by taxing the gold trade and exports.

In tracking how orpaillage shaped exploration geology, this book also examines how West African societies give political form to geological processes.[59] Historians and archeologists have shown how African societies managed two-dimensional geographic space. Examples include accounts of road making by the Asante kingdom and the organization of sacred space in the stone architecture of medieval Zimbabwe.[60] Studies of cartography reveal how colonial and postcolonial African states used maps to rationalize landscapes for taxation, to segregate European settlers from Black Africans, and to fix pastoralists and mobile agriculturalists into place-bound "ethnic groups."[61] By contrast, there are few accounts of how African polities, lineages, or individuals managed three-dimensional resources, such as water, mineral reserves, and airspace. Historians of Africa could benefit from engaging with an emergent literature in critical geography on "vertical geopolitics."[62] Research on "volumetric" qualities of state territory—the management of aquifers and underground tunnels; the mapping of subterranean minerals—challenges the horizontal orientation of most theories of state and corporate power.[63] These issues are of particular interest in Africa, where the capacity of the state to conduct geological surveys was historically weak. At the same time, the continent is home to rich regional traditions of mining and well digging that have rendered the subsoil knowable, calculable, and subject to competing use rights. The history of how African societies have come to know the underground remains to be written.

I use the term *geology* in this book in two registers. For one, I discuss geology as a scientific discipline and geologists as trained professionals in this field. As an academic field that coalesced in Europe in the eighteenth and nineteenth centuries, geology deals with the history of the earth and its life, especially as recorded in rocks and sedimentary strata. Second, I use the terms *geology*, *geologic*, and *geological* to describe the actual physical formations and processes of the earth. Examples includes the "geology of Senegal" or the "geologic maps of West Africa." The concept of a ritual geology falls into this category. Of course, the two meanings of *geology* are interrelated. As the geographer Kathryn Yusoff argues, the nomenclature used by the discipline and practice of "White geology," as Yusoff calls it, took shape in racist imperial formations, where geology was built on the idea of the inhuman that "doubled as a notion of property." Yusoff calls on scholars to develop a "different economy of description that might give rise to a less deadly understanding of materiality."[64] I heed this call by centering how West African orpailleurs themselves named and modeled the underground. In so doing, they shaped the methods of what became known as the discipline of geology, though often not on terms of their own choosing.

Pagans, Muslims, and Birimian Rocks

Another conceptual thread of this book concerns the sacred engagement of West African societies with geological formations—in this case, Birimian rocks (map I.2). Despite a renewed interest in the role of West Africa's gold in early globalization and trade, we have few accounts of what gold and gold-bearing land meant to the region's miners.[65] The diverse communities who mined gold over the past two millennia practiced ancestral religions, Islam, and blended religious traditions. But by the eighteenth and nineteenth centuries, a set of practices, prohibitions, and cosmological notions were shared broadly by gold miners that formed a regional "ritual geology." Since the medieval period, there is evidence that orpaillage was predicated on a sacrificial exchange relationship between orpailleurs and territorial spirits, considered the guardians of this metal (see chapter 2). Another tenet of the ritual geology of West Africa's Birimian rocks is an ideological opposition between gold mining and Islam. By the eleventh century, many ruling dynasties on the Sahel had converted to Islam, strengthening bonds of trade,

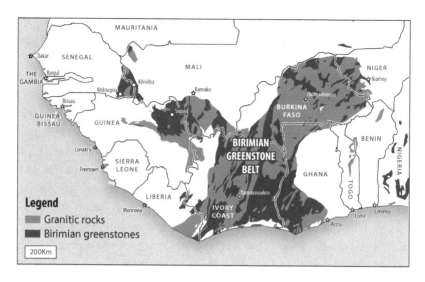

Map I.2 West Africa's Birimian Greenstone Belt.

scholarship, and law across the Sahara. However, for centuries—and well into the twentieth century in some corridors—gold miners on the savanna resisted Islam and overrule by Muslims. This earned orpailleurs a reputation as *pagans*, a term I use in this book to gloss the views of African and non-African Muslims toward practitioners of *ancestral religious traditions*.[66]

Geology played a role in the religious history of gold-producing zones. The same geological processes that injected gold veins into quartz rock generated rocky soils and rock escarpments. This land was undesirable to centralized states that relied on agricultural surplus. Birimian formations resembled what the political scientist James Scott calls "shatter zones:" isolated and hostile terrain settled by people fleeing state-making projects.[67] Goldfields became dominions of ancestral religious traditions and spaces of ritual innovation as refugees fleeing Muslim overrule settled on Birimian rocks, intermingled, and created new religious traditions.[68] Opposition to Islam on the goldfields may have been grounded in a desire for religious autonomy, a mode of resistance to becoming an economic subject of the state, or both. While the ritual cosmology of orpaillage was marked by opposition to Islam, the two deeply influenced each other.

Attention to the dialogical relationship between geology and religious practice generates new spatial units of analysis for environmental history.[69] Oceans, archipelagos, and river basins feature prominently in the subfield.[70]

But historians of the environment have yet to explore how geological formations shape political and religious life. Scholars of mining have long documented the saturation of mining tunnels and quarries with ritual protocols.[71] For much of recorded history, mining has been associated with risk, luck, and proximity to the underworld of the Abrahamic tradition and other "earth-beings" who occupy mineral-rich mountains.[72] But studies of mining have tended to center on a single mining site, ethnic group, or urban center. A focus on narrow spatial corridors can miss broader regional patterns. Do geological formations generate a material platform for the exchange of sacred engagements with the earth? Are some ritual practices tied to mining shared across geological belts as ideas and practices are passed from one mineral deposit to another? I address these questions by framing orpaillage as a regional institution that developed in dialogue with Birimian rock formations.

In narrating this history, I draw inspiration from Walter Rodney's work on the Upper Guinea Coast and Boubacar Barry's on Greater Senegambia. These historians pioneered regional approaches to West African history by tracing the spatial connections forged by African traders, political and religious movements, and the social sinews formed across river basin ecology.[73] The scale of their work was political. It challenged the tendency of ethnographers to study individual "tribes" in relative isolation from one another and of historians to project the borders of colonial and independent African states onto the precolonial past. Following Rodney and Barry, the geographic scope of this book emerges from tracking the movements of orpailleurs, their rituals, and their techniques across the savanna.

West Africa's ritual geology challenges the common historiographical framing of ancestral religious practices in West Africa as more localized than their implicit counterparts: Islam and Christianity.[74] Over the past decade, scholars of Islam in West Africa have adopted broader regional and temporal scales to demonstrate how West African Muslim clerics, Qur'anic schoolteachers, and empire builders shaped the broader Islamic world and created expansive Islamic-based religious movements and forms of embodied knowledge.[75] But Islam was not the only religious tradition that traveled in medieval or Atlantic-era West Africa. By the Atlantic age, and likely earlier, ritual institutions tied to orpaillage were spread along goldfields from Senegal in the east to Burkina Faso in the west. These ritual complexes were not "local," even though local conditions shaped dimensions of their practice. Jean Allman and John Parker argue a similar point in their history of Tongnaab, an ancestor-deity of Tallensi origin. In the early twentieth century, Tongnaab spread southward from the savanna to the Akan forest and trading towns of the Gold Coast, where it became a powerful witch-finding deity. As Allman and Parker argue, indigenous African gods and their congregations, far from being a "localized phenomenon rooted in a fixed ritual landscape," evolved across "great distances and transcended a variety of political, cultural, and ecological frontiers," as did Christianity and Islam.[76] A similar dynamic of "trans-regional ritual dialogue" was at play on the goldfields. However, in contrast to Tongnaab's spread over several decades, this ritual geology spread piecemeal across centuries and left sparse records. West Africa's ritual geology fell short of constituting a "religion" in its own right, as it was never united by a single prophet, medium, shrine, or liturgical tradition. Orpailleurs, blacksmiths, and traders participated in it, but they did not identify with gold mining as a religious category of belonging. The ritual geology of the savanna was eclectic, adapted to different gods and social circumstances.

Kédougou, Senegal

The goldfields of Kédougou, Senegal, are the vantage point from which I narrate this regional history of struggles over mineralized land.[77] Situated in the country's southeastern corner, Kédougou is a geological and cultural anomaly within modern Senegal. Much of Senegal sits less than three hundred feet above sea level. Senegal's landscape is sparse and flat, covered in young sedimentary depositions of silty gray soils spread from the Atlantic coast across the middle belt of the country, known as the peanut basins. These silts supported the peanut export economy of colonial Senegal and make up the cultural heartland of Wolof-speakers and the Muslim Sufi order of the Muridiyya, or "Mourides."[78] By contrast, Kédougou occupies ancient gold-bearing Birimian rocks and is bordered to the south by the foothills of the Fouta Djallon mountains. It also occupies the headwaters of the river basins of the Gambia and the Falémé, a tributary of the Senegal River that marks Senegal's border with Mali (map I.3).

Though Kédougou is Senegal's most sparsely populated region, its population is as diverse as the most vibrant multiethnic neighborhoods of the cosmopolitan capital of Dakar. It is home to speakers of Pular, Jakhanke, Soninke, and Maninka and to several of the country's smallest ethnic groups, including the Beliyan-Bassari, Bedik, and Jallonke.[79] This diversity is a legacy of Kédougou's position as a crossroads between Guinea and Mali and its Atlantic-era history as a refuge for ethnic and religious minorities who sought cover from slave raiders in the region's rock escarpments, thick bam-

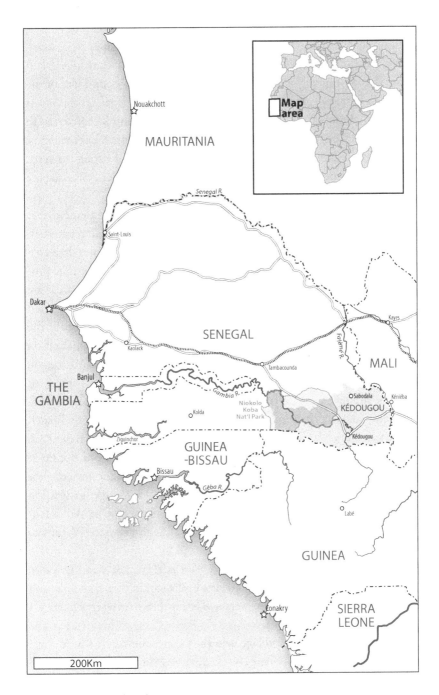

Map I.3 Senegal and Kédougou region, ca. 2020.

boo forests, and maze of rainy season rivers. Senegal's population is overwhelmingly Muslim, with some estimates running as high as 95 percent. While Muslims have lived and traded in Kédougou for centuries, Islam did not become widely adopted in the region until the second half of the twentieth century, late compared with the rest of Senegal. In the 1960s and 1970s, a number of Beliyan-Bassari, Bedik, and Maninka converted to Christianity through a Catholic mission based in the region. Since the 1970s, conversion to Islam has expanded, even among former Christian converts. Today, most residents of Kédougou are Muslim, but outsiders still associate the region with ancestral religious traditions (see chapter 7).

Rooting this book within the histories of interethnic settlement that characterize Kédougou's agrarian landscape generates an alternative to what Mamadou Diouf calls the "Islamo-Wolof" model of Senegalese civilization.[80] This model refers to the long-term cultural and economic processes that have privileged the coast and the peanut basin. These areas are dominated by ethnic Wolof and the Muridiyya, who are over-represented in the national media and in scholarship on Senegal. As Diouf argues, the Islamo-Wolof model was built, in part, on the exclusion and marginalization of non-Muslim and non-Wolof groups from national narratives. Kédougou is one such exclusion. During French rule, Kédougou was weakly tethered to the economy and infrastructure of colonial Senegal. Young men from Kédougou engaged in annual rainy season migrations, known by French officials as the navètane, to cultivate peanuts in central-western Senegal. The navètane helped to spread the Wolof language to Kédougou, but Pular and Maninka remained the region's lingua francas. It was not until the late 1990s that Wolof became the preferred language of a younger generation in Kédougou, one expression of "Wolofization," the spread of Wolof language and cultural hegemony across regions of Senegal where Wolof was not historically dominant.[81]

Situated at the edge of Senegal and West Africa's gold-bearing rocks, Kédougou offers a critical, peripheral view of the region's ritual geology and of Senegal's history. It is also my personal entry into writing this history. I first moved to Kédougou in 2006 as a US Peace Corps volunteer. For one year, I lived in a small Pular village near the Guinea border. The next year I moved to Kédougou town, where I worked at a women's technical school and with urban gardeners. During this time, Senegal's budding mining industry was confined to a string of rudimentary exploration camps and a single mining concession, known as Sabodala, which was then under construction. Kédougou was a sleepy town, known for its relaxed and multiethnic sensibility. The Gambia River wove through the heart of town, flanked by verdant green market gardens sprouting okra, cherry tomatoes, cabbage, and banana trees. Fishermen plied the Gambia in small dugout canoes that doubled as local ferries. Soaring dry season temperatures pushed people outside. Young men gathered under mango trees to drink sweet green tea over charcoal. At nightfall, families hauled foam mattresses outdoors, falling asleep to Argentinian soap operas dubbed in Wolof or Pular. Women sat in plastic chairs along the exterior walls of homes, selling fried balls of pounded river fish.

Kédougou's social energy gathered around the central market. Concrete stalls spilled their wares—aluminum marmites and cooking utensils, imported soap and lotions, and a spread of bright plastic basins—onto packed dirt walkways. A row of Guinean men sat under beach umbrellas, selling fresh kola nuts from rice sacks lined with banana leaves. Traveling Wolof merchants sold sunglasses displayed on cardboard planks. Across from the market sat a cluster of aging administrative buildings, a public radio station, and a crumbling colonial-era park. Kédougou's two oldest neighborhoods fanned outward from the marketplace, one dominated by ethnic Maninka and the other by ethnic Pular. Brick fences encircled single-story concrete buildings. Hand-dug wells supplement piped water from the municipal grid. The outskirts of town were dotted with piles of brick that demarcated the claims of their owners, awaiting funds to build exterior walls. Car ownership was rare. Bicycles and motorcycles were the primary mode of transit.

Toward the end of my stay in Kédougou in 2008, an Australian company completed construction of the Sabodala gold mine and mill. For several months I worked with an organization of Senegalese farmers who were trying to sell vegetables to Sabodala and several other gold exploration camps. I served as an interpreter with the catering managers of these camps, many of whom spoke only English, and farmers from Kédougou, who spoke French, Wolof, Pular, or Maninka. Companies were eager to purchase local produce, but they followed international food safety standards that regional farmers could not meet. The fragile supply chain fell apart, my first glimpse at how difficult it was, even when goodwill was ample, for residents to capture opportunities around the formal mining economy.

For several years after leaving the Peace Corps I returned annually to Kédougou for short visits. Each year, the impacts of Senegal's growing mining industry became more evident in Kédougou town and in the countryside. Truck traffic intensified along Kédougou's main roads, churning up clouds of dust that covered air-dried laundry and bowls of shared rice.

Men from across Senegal moved to Sabodala to seek work in the mine. Subcontracting services for the mining industry—chemical warehouses and diamond-drilling camps—multiplied in dusty workshops on the road linking Kédougou town to the Malian border. Local entrepreneurs began leasing secondhand dump trucks and bulldozers to exploration firms. Rates of HIV/AIDS rose as a result of increased trucking. The sharp influx of foreign capital led to inflation in prices for meat, vegetables, fish, and housing. Faced with growing costs, families who had once reserved rooms for relatives from remote villages to visit the hospital began leasing out spare bedrooms to strangers.

Meanwhile, the effects of Kédougou's growing orpaillage economy appeared in intimate realms among Senegalese friends and colleagues. Rural households expanded seemingly overnight with migrant orpailleurs from Mali and Guinea.[82] Motorcycles multiplied in rural villages, purchased by young men who had struck it lucky in the mines, flush with cash to pay bridewealth, a goal that took their peers years of savings from modest bumper crops of peanuts. Others were less fortunate. A sixteen-year-old I knew from a Pular village joined an orpaillage team as a rope-pulley operator near the border with Mali. He returned home three months later severely ill with a bacterial infection, carried home on a lorry truck by a friend. His cousin returned from the mines having lost the use of three fingers, the nerves severed by the misplaced blow of an iron pick in a poorly lit mining shaft. The expansion of orpaillage also inspired concerns about the moral status of money produced by gold. Rumors circulated that successful orpailleurs conducted human sacrifices and trafficked with the devil to earn the favor of the territorial spirits who haunted underground mining shafts and the gold placers of riverbanks. Muslim clerics opined that orpaillage pulled the young from the path of Islam and Qur'anic school.

Many of the worries about gold mining relayed to me in household foyers resonated with those of mining frontiers around the globe. Other grievances were regional in scope. While corporate mining was new to Kédougou, geological exploration and gold prospecting had been ongoing in the region for decades. Some elderly men I knew worked as guides and laborers for Soviet and French geologists in the 1960s and 1970s (chapter 5). Time and again I was told by residents of Kédougou that they and their ancestors—not geologists—had discovered gold deposits slated to become open-pit mines. As I learned, competing historical claims to gold discovery generated expectations in rural communities for the returns they, and their children, should receive from corporate gold mines.

Anthropology and History

In January 2013, I returned to Senegal for eighteen months as a doctoral student in anthropology and history to conduct the intensive field research on which this book relies.[83] I divided my time among Kédougou (thirteen months), Dakar (four months), and France (one month). In Kédougou town I kept a room in the concession of a large Pular family I had known since the Peace Corps. I also lived intermittently in the household of Bambo Cissokho, the chief of Tinkoto, Kédougou's most celebrated orpaillage village (see chapter 1). I met Bambo Cissokho in 2008 while distributing bed nets for an antimalaria campaign. While living in Tinkoto, I accompanied orpailleurs as they prospected for gold with detectors and excavated gold-bearing rock from mining shafts. At night, I attended an extralegal "court" convened by Cissokho to mediate disputes that emerged by day on the goldfields. I conducted interviews in eighteen other villages in Kédougou, situated within and beyond the region's central gold-mining corridor. As the opportunity arose, I visited the camps of numerous exploration and mining firms.

Ethnography and oral history were my research methods in Kédougou, and the two frequently blended together. As a Peace Corps volunteer, I spent many days leisurely assisting farmers sowing cornfields and practicing Pular phrases with women as they prepared meals. As a researcher, I was in constant motion, tacking between orpaillage sites and agricultural villages on the back of motorcycles and pickup trucks. My movements mirrored the intensely busy lives of the men and women I sought to interview. They traveled to freshly discovered gold deposits; consulted with ritual practitioners in Mali and Gambia; and recruited workers for their mining teams. Whenever possible, I worked through my networks of friends and former colleagues in Kédougou to arrange interviews. In time, I adopted an informal snowball method that relied on serendipity and the generosity of near-strangers who afforded me their time. In total, I conducted more than 150 oral histories for this project with orpailleurs, farmers, historians, imams, healers, politicians, geologists, and gendarmes. I also initiated dozens of informal interviews with state bureaucrats, police officers, lawyers, and nongovernmental organization (NGO) workers. I traveled to Dakar to conduct interviews with geologists, mining company personnel, bureaucrats, and representatives of NGOs who worked in the mining sector.

I carried out interviews in Pular, French, and Maninka or a mixture of these languages. I speak Pular and French. I studied Maninka for six years through a combination of formal training and two summers in West Africa, but I never gained conversational fluency in the language. In southeastern Senegal, many Maninka-speakers are also fluent in Pular or French. To bypass my halting Maninka, they would frequently switch to a language we both spoke with ease. It was to address my limitations in Maninka that I sought out a research assistant in Senegal, which led me to Falaye Danfakha. A talented teacher of Pular and Maninka, with deep personal connections to Kédougou, Falaye became a close intellectual partner and friend. We conducted dozens of interviews together, traveling by bush taxi and motorcycle to reach remote orpaillage villages. In the final month of my stay, we spent hours a day transcribing interviews from Maninka to French in a concrete room we rented as our office in Kédougou. We continued this work remotely over the course of several years. Many of the ideas in this book emerged from our conversations during a research period that cemented an ongoing transatlantic friendship and multiple visits—him to the United States and me to Senegal—as our families have grown and careers have taken new directions.

I complemented field research in Kédougou with archival research in Dakar, Conakry, and Paris, which I conducted during the summers of 2010 and 2011 and for two months in 2014. In Dakar, I consulted collections at the Archives Nationales du Sénégal, the Institut Fondamental d'Afrique Noire, and Senegal's state-sponsored *Le Soleil* newspaper. The geological maps featured in this book are drawn from the archives of Senegal's Direction des Mines et de la Géologie, which include those of the geological service of colonial Afrique-Occidentale Française (French West Africa). I took shorter research trips to the Archives Nationales de Guinée in Conakry, Guinea, and the Archives Nationales d'Outre-mer in Aix-en-Provence, France. These collections enabled me to tell a regional history of orpaillage under French colonial rule. I deepened my knowledge of the social and ritual worlds of orpaillage prior to colonialism by analyzing oral traditions; archeological reports; European travelogues; songs and chants; and published primary source materials on gold miners, traders, and dynasts who lived on the historical goldfields of Bambuk (western Mali and eastern Senegal), Buré (Guinea), Gaoua and Poura (Burkina Faso), Hiré and Yaouré (Côte d'Ivoire), and Akan (Côte d'Ivoire and Ghana).[84]

A Ritual Geology is part history and part ethnography. This structure reflects my personal entry into this project, first as an observer of Kédougou's gold-mining boom and later as a scholar who inquired about the past. It also reflects my approach to history as a material set of structures and events that create conditions of possibility for the present—and as a resource for contemporary claims making. Residents of the West African savanna are distinctively self-conscious about their region's historicity. Family genealogies and theories of ethnogenesis are common topics of everyday conversation. Many of my interlocutors traced their heritage to medieval empires and tested my credibility as a historian by quizzing me on the region's precolonial history. The same individuals draw on historical narratives to argue with neighbors, state officials, and mining firms over who has the right to mine regional gold deposits. For them, history is a polyvalent resource for asserting cultural belonging and ownership of natural resources.

My doctoral training in the Interdepartmental Program in Anthropology and History at the University of Michigan primed my attention to the political work of history in oral and written forms. I was immersed in a community of "anthro-historians" interested in how different societies produced history.[85] I also studied models of historical anthropology in African studies, a field that pioneered the use of oral and archeological sources as portals to the past where documents are sparse.[86] Methodologies for interpreting oral traditions, in particular, created an evidentiary base for African history, which became incorporated into the academy in the 1960s after most African states gained independence.[87] Oral sources, which could "'talk back' in a way that documents do not," inspired rich reflections on African epistemologies of history and the ways in which "the past" became filtered through the politics and projects of the present day.[88] Several threads of this scholarship inspired my historical and ethnographic practice. First, I attended to how history was relayed through rumors of spirits, ritual practice, and the embodied praxis of gold mining.[89] I often gained access to these unconventional repositories of historical consciousness when I accompanied men and women through landscapes attached to spirits and departed relatives. They included abandoned mines, rock gullies, fallow millet fields, and the entryways to sacred groves.[90] Second, I noted how my interlocutors "assembled" histories in the space of formal interviews and in casual conversations. As the historians David William Cohen and E. S. Atieno Obhiambo observed in their research in Kenya, history does not exist out there to be collected by an impartial researcher. Rather, history is produced in dialogical settings.[91] If the assemblage of history is particularly visible in the retelling of oral traditions and oral histories, this is true of all genres of historical production, anywhere in the world, in and beyond the academy.

Whenever possible, the chapters to follow weave oral and archival sources into a single narrative fabric. But this was not practical for the entire book. Some chapters rely largely on oral testimony and ethnography, while others are drawn from archival data. The historical chapters present new empirical material on orpaillage in West Africa. The ethnographic chapters do so as well, but they are more concerned with how different members of West African societies have debated and constructed "facts" about gold discoveries and claims to mineralized land. Thus, this book both tells a history of orpaillage and interrogates how histories of orpaillage are made in family genealogies, village settlement narratives, and state and corporate archives.

My status and privilege as a white woman from the United States shaped, at every turn, the questions I asked and my narrative choices. I am an outsider to West Africa who, through serendipity and choice, has made this part of the world central to my career and my family. While my subject position limited my access to some forms of knowledge, it facilitated my entry into other realms and sources of funding from which many of my African colleagues are excluded. At times, I found these inequities paralyzing. But they also motivated me to leverage my privilege to tell the history of a West African mining tradition that has been racialized, denigrated, and portrayed as static by powerful actors. The global hierarchies in which this subject and I are embedded were on glaring display when, at numerous times during my research, I was accused of covertly prospecting for gold. While I was not searching for minerals, I was seeking knowledge about the region's past as generations of geologists had before me. I came to see these suspicions as evidence of the political economy of knowledge on a resource frontier, a central theme of this book. They remind us that seeking and producing subterranean knowledge is never neutral.

1
A Tale of Two Miners in Tinkoto, Senegal, 2014

Situated thirty kilometers northeast of Kédougou town is Senegal's most celebrated orpaillage village: Tinkoto. Motorcycles whir along its dirt paths, weaving among concrete shops selling imported rice, dried milk, and tarp. Tinkoto sits on an ancient volcanic rock plateau, its edges framed by scrubland. The village is the central spoke of a rhizomatic network of dry season mining sites, known as *juuras*, spread along the Birimian rocks of eastern Senegal. Work in Tinkoto is organized around the deployment of men, machines, and chemicals across the landscape. Orpailleurs dig for gold in multiple juuras, bringing gold-bearing rock back to Tinkoto, where it is processed and sold as gold dust. Young men from Burkina Faso, known as Burkinabe, operate diesel-powered machines that pound buckets of auriferous rock into powder.[1] Households are gold refineries in miniature, where women sort, wash, and chemically isolate gold (figure 1.1). In the dry season, from November to April, more than fifteen thousand people live and labor in Tinkoto and on its juuras. When rains arrive in May, dry-season migrants return to Mali, Guinea, Burkina Faso, and coastal Senegal. For them, Tinkoto is a site of wealth accumulation for futures located elsewhere. But for a growing number of men and women, Tinkoto is a permanent home.

Tinkoto began its life in the Atlantic era as a juura mined by Maninka-speaking residents of the small-scale provinces of Bélédougou, Sirimana, Niokolo, and Dantila. For generations, people refused to pass the rainy season in Tinkoto because it claimed the lives of dozens of infants. Oral traditions locate two causes of this infant mortality: "sleeping sickness," a parasitic disease transmitted from animals to people by the tsetse fly, and a powerful infertile female spirit.[2] Embittered by her inability to have children, the spirit demands blood sacrifices—of chickens, goats, cows, and even, it is rumored, people—to release gold to human hands. When orpailleurs

Figure 1.1 Women washing gold by sluice. Tinkoto, Senegal, 2014. Photograph by the author.

did not meet these sacrificial demands, the spirit took her own sacrifices, burying miners under collapsed tunnels and bringing illness to newborns. In 1984, the crescendo of a multiyear drought, a small group of orpailleurs from Senegal, Gambia, and Guinea stayed in Tinkoto to farm while they continued to mine. Children survived past their first birthdays for the first time in living memory, overcoming both sleeping sickness and the wrath of the spirit. "In the past, spirits were thick here," recounted Telli Diallo, an elderly resident of a neighboring village. "Now it is better. People worked the land and made sacrifices to release gold. You would hear cows and babies crying, but there was no one there. Now many children live there."[3]

Today, the Senegalese state recognizes Tinkoto as a village, but its robust commercial sector and cosmopolitan sociability are decidedly urban. Its urban form is seasonal and cyclical, shaped by the rains, shifting gold prices, and discoveries of new gold deposits in neighboring villages and states. Maninka is the primary lingua franca of Tinkoto, with Pular a close second. But conversations in Bedik, Susu, Wolof, Kpelle, and Bambara can be overhead in Tinkoto's multilingual marketplace. Makeshift dwellings of palm fronds and split bamboo, called *nyafa*, dominate Tinkoto's construction. Farmers historically crafted nyafa in distant agricultural fields, where they guarded crops from hyenas and baboons. Because many of Tinkoto's residents never planned to stay, few built fences or planted shade trees. Concessions spill into one another, creating an ambiance of exposure. In the mid-2010s, this architecture of impermanence intensified when Burkinabe migrants imported Western-style camping tents to Tinkoto to sleep adjacent to rock-crushing machines.[4] Tinkoto's growth materializes broader changes in West African orpaillage over the past two decades as new machines, chemicals, and migrants extend what was once a seasonal activity deeper into the rainy season.

At the heart of Tinkoto sits Bambo Cissokho's concession, a sprawling collection of concrete buildings, huts, hangars, and workshops. Cissokho's name is synonymous with gold in southeastern Senegal. In the early 2000s, he became the first *dugutigi* of Tinkoto, a Maninka term for "master of the land," commonly translated as chief.[5] Cissokho grounds his authority over Tinkoto's juuras by appealing to the historical prominence of ethnic Maninka on the goldfields of the savanna and of the Cissokho clan, over orpaillage in Senegal (see chapter 2). "My father and my grandfather worked gold in Tinkoto, and then they went home to farm. Every juura from here to the Falémé was opened by the hand of Cissokho," he relayed in one of our many exchanges.[6] Generous but quick-tempered, Cissokho spends his days in motion, transiting the juuras of Tinkoto and visiting orpaillage villages elsewhere in Senegal and Mali in his tinted-glass Cadillac Escalade. Cissokho has close to thirty children and more than a dozen grandchildren. He speaks fluent Maninka and Pular, broken Wolof, and little French. Unlike many men of his generation, he did not migrate to the peanut farms of west-central Senegal or to the coast. His life is rooted in the goldfields of southeastern Senegal.

While Cissokho's four wives occupy concrete buildings, he resides in a modest mud-and-thatch hut. His hut opens onto a massive concrete hangar, shaded by an awning of bamboo stalks, from which Tinkoto—"stream of palms" in Maninka—derives its name. Two brown velour recliners flank the door, facing rows of white plastic chairs arranged in a semicircle. Cissokho occupies one recliner; the other is reserved for special guests. This is Cissokho's self-described "tribunal," where he adjudicates conflicts on Tinkoto's juuras. A row of motorcycles rust in the far corner of the hangar, abandoned by those unable to reconstitute their debts with the chief. West African migrants, merchants, and widows gather at the tribunal to ask Cissokho's permission to open a new boutique or to join his mining team. Suspected gold thieves are brought to the tribunal by men wearing matching blue shirts emblazoned with "Tinkoto Sécurité" across the back. These are *tomboluma*, the traditional

A TALE OF TWO MINERS   31

security force of juuras across much of savanna West Africa. Cissokho recruits tomboluma from across Senegal, Mali, and Guinea in a nod to Tinkoto's history as a gathering point for regional migrants, a place open to anyone willing to dig for gold. Cissokho works with the tomboluma to mete out punishments and fines at the tribunal. They have no legal authority to adjudicate a tribunal, and most of Tinkoto's juuras are illegal. But the state tolerates these activities because they have found in Cissokho a willing partner in managing Senegal's complex and dangerous gold-mining frontier.[7]

Cissokho's recliners reveal the material and political workings of gold exploration and mining in twenty-first-century West Africa. On a Monday, the guest recliner is occupied by the chief of a neighboring village, who is searching for a man who stole gold-bearing rock from one of his mining teams. On a Tuesday, an officer of the gendarme, the militarized police, occupies the recliner. He investigates a complaint that orpailleurs from Tinkoto snuck onto a portion of the exploration permit of Randgold, a South African–based mining firm.[8] By Wednesday, the chair is occupied by one of Randgold's geologists, a Senegalese man who has worked in the Kédougou region for nearly two decades. Several children in Tinkoto are named after him, a testament to the intimate, though tumultuous, relationship between the village and gold-mining capital.[9] "You have your parts, and we have ours," the geologist pleads with Cissokho, asking him to direct orpailleurs away from Randgold's mining prospect.[10]

This chapter offers an ethnographic angle—based on research conducted in 2013–14 and 2017—on core themes of this book. I argue that the rotating cast of characters who occupy Cissokho's guest recliner blur the line between licit and illicit economies and artisanal and industrial extraction. Tinkoto and Randgold are entangled components of a single extractive economy across which family histories and cyanide solution circulate. Cissokho's engagements with corporate and state authorities speaks to the multilayered histories of law and the production of subterranean knowledge that animate this book. In the fast-paced world of Tinkoto, orpailleurs from across West Africa and geologists working for multinational mining corporations collaborate and conflict in a competitive search for gold. Cissokho's recliners engage with several temporal scales of regional history, including communal sacred engagements with the spirit forces of gold-bearing Birimian rocks—a component of West Africa's ritual geology. Tinkoto is part of Bambuk, a region that once furnished medieval West African empires with gold and attracted Portuguese ships to Senegal's shores. African authorities have managed gold mining in this zone for centuries and continue to do so in the present day. But Cissokho's tribunal is far from a precolonial relic or survival. Many of the customs practiced on Tinkoto's juuras are of recent vintage, forged through encounters with corporate mining capital.

Exploration Camps and Corporate Enclaves

In 2008, Senegal's national television station broadcast a ribbon-cutting ceremony for Sabodala, the gold deposit after which Senegal's first gold mine and mill was named. For most Senegalese, Sabodala's opening marked the beginning of the country's gold-mining boom. On the ground in Kédougou, however, the boom had been gaining speed for years, and its actors were far more diverse than the barbed wire fences of the Sabodala mining camp, which then occupied only twenty square kilometers. Sabodala was encased in dozens of gold exploration permits spanning hundreds of kilometers, held by Canadian, Australian, South African, and Senegalese firms. And every exploration permit contained dozens of villages, like Tinkoto, engaged in their own search for gold.

Mineral exploration, rather than mining as such, is the primary activity that structures relationships between villages and corporate capital in Senegal, as in many mineral-rich regions of the global South. Tinkoto is a case in point. Beginning in the 1950s, Tinkoto was used as a base camp for geologists, then working for Senegal's French colonial government, who prospected for lead, nickel, and gold. They were drawn to Tinkoto by its reputation as a seasonal gathering point for orpailleurs from across southeastern Senegal. In the 1990s, "junior" exploration firms—small outfits operating on slim budgets with minimal staff—began exploring for gold in and around Tinkoto. In 2003, Randgold acquired permits that encompassed Tinkoto and its juuras. It established a base camp adjacent to Kanoumering, a Pular village several kilometers from Tinkoto. In 2007, Randgold announced the discovery of Massawa, a three-million-ounce gold deposit named after a local mountain range. Roughly fifteen years later, Massawa has yet to be mined, but it has changed corporate owners at a dizzying speed. In 2018, Randgold merged with the Toronto-based Barrick Gold, one of the world's largest gold producers. Two years later, Teranga Gold, which operated the Sabodala mine, acquired Massawa. In 2021, Teranga was acquired by Endeavor Mining, a Britain-based firm that is the largest gold producer in West Africa. As I write, Massawa is slated to be excavated and milled at Sabodala.[11]

Extreme time lags between discovery and development are common in the gold industry. So is the sale of gold discoveries. By the time this book goes to press, Sabodala-Massawa may be owned and operated by yet another firm. Such turnover is generated by the progressive vertical integration of the gold-mining industry and the ubiquity of juniors in gold exploration. Some juniors convert their discoveries into mines, but most sell their findings to larger firms and move on to new exploration prospects elsewhere in the region.[12] Few of the juniors I encountered in Kédougou are still active in Senegal. Their stock options have disappeared, and new firms have absorbed their old permits. For orpailleurs, however, Massawa is not a speculative stock-market option. Corporate realignments force orpailleurs to forge new relationships with geologists, camp managers, and private security guards on which their ongoing access to gold deposits depends.

Relationships between exploration camps and communities such as Tinkoto are far more porous and intimate than those between corporate mining enclaves, such as Sabodala, and surrounding villages. Like most open-pit mining operations, Sabodala is based on the so-called Angola model, a reference to the spatial geography of "offshore" oil rigs that proliferate along the coast of West Africa and the Gulf of Mexico. As the anthropologist James Ferguson argues, the gold industry became more "oil like" in the 2000s with the adoption of global logistical services and open-pit mining techniques, which replaced local laborers with bulldozers and a small fleet of (mostly white) engineers. These changes enabled mining firms to operate on more narrow pockets of land fortified with barbed wire and armed security forces.[13] Extractive enclaves, such as Sabodala, are provisioned with private air strips allowing mining executives to come and go while bypassing interregional road infrastructure and interactions with residents of surrounding communities (figure 1.2). The Sabodala concession includes a gargantuan open-pit mine, dug out by bulldozers, and a mill where gold-bearing rock is crushed, washed, and run through several chemical refinements. Connected by a labyrinth of roads to the mine and mill is a camp composed of management offices, geological laboratories, and employee housing. Similar to corporate mining facilities around the world, Sabodala's camps are multiethnic and stratified according to different skill and pay grades, which largely align with divergent racial and national groups.[14] Senior management consists primarily of itinerant white workers from Europe, North America, Australia, and other Commonwealth countries.[15] Mid-level staff, including engineers, geologists, and accountants, are white, African, and Senegalese. They sleep in air-conditioned bedrooms and work in shared offices. Semiskilled workers and laborers, mostly Senegalese, stay in bunk-style housing. Local laborers, chauffeurs, and technicians may sleep at home. Private security guards and a Senegalese gendarme station regulate entry and exit from the camp.

34   CHAPTER ONE

Figure 1.2 Airstrip at the Sabodala mine. Sabodala, Senegal, 2014. Photograph by the author.

Exploration camps are smaller and less fortified than mining camps. Some are fashioned from shipping containers molded into dining halls, offices for geologists, and hangars for storing equipment and geological samples (figure 1.3). Many exploration camps rely entirely on food purchased from local farmers and markets, whereas mining camps import most of their food by refrigerated trucks or planes that comply with international catering standards. Exploration camps are usually built directly adjacent to a village to facilitate access to local labor for building and cleaning the camp. The geologists, cooks, and technicians in Kédougou's exploration camps are largely Senegalese, recruited in Dakar. Many mechanics, electricians, and chauffeurs are from the region, as are "unskilled" laborers and cleaners. Though camps are surrounded by barbed-wire fences the boundary between the camp and the village is fluid. Women come to wash laundry for a wage and return home to nurse children. Young men pull up to the gates on motorcycles, seeking day labor or assistance in transporting sick relatives to Kédougou.

Exploration teams work to insert themselves into the social fabric of the villages surrounding their camp. Even though they carry state-issued permits, geologists accommodate to local pressures and social formalities. But the rapport between camps and villages can transform overnight when a

Figure 1.3 Exploration camp of Bassari Resources. Duuta, Senegal, 2017. Photograph by the author.

junior exploration firm sells its discoveries. A geologist may maintain a sincere friendship with local political leaders, such as Bambo Cissokho, but this relationship can shift with new corporate strategies and distant market forces. Within months, a merger agreement signed in Dakar or Melbourne could transform a modest exploration camp into a mining enclave with strict visitor policies and gates. Cissokho is keenly aware of the shifting temporal horizons of exploration geology. In his words, "When Randgold came here, they told us they were small, just searching for gold. They had no power because they were searching. They asked us for assistance. They asked us to leave them alone while they were searching. But small boys can grow into big men."[16]

"Every Place Has Its Master"

When I was living in Tinkoto in 2014, the most popular juura within Cissokho's customary jurisdiction—a slippery and contested geography—was Juuraba, which translates as "big mine" in English. Randgold's geological team uncovered Juuraba. They dug exploration trenches along its hillside, employing local men as prospecting assistants and trench diggers. Geologists abandoned the prospect, but orpailleurs followed in their wake, deepening the firm's trenches and transforming this jagged hillside into a latticework of hand-dug mining shafts. For a fee, Guinean chauffeurs ferried orpailleurs in pickup trucks to and from Juuraba and Tinkoto, ten kilometers down an access road, also built by Randgold.

The base of Juuraba was lined with a row of woven raffia huts. Inside, women fried eggs in sizzling pans of oil on single-burner petroleum stoves. Children slept on blankets. Men huddled on narrow wooden benches to eat egg sandwiches. In an open-air workshop, a blacksmith (*numu*) stoked a fire burning at the juncture of three acacia logs, where he sharpened pickaxes (*soli*). Teenage boys sit astride Styrofoam coolers that concealed soda cans swimming in pools of melting ice, transported from Kédougou town—the closest source of reliable electricity—each morning. Young girls wove among the crowd, carrying plastic basins on their heads filled with snacks of sliced mangos and roasted peanuts.

The juura collects people on the margins: the poor, the widowed, the unemployed, and eldest sons responsible for aging parents. Yaya Touré fell into the last category. He grew up in a village outside Tambacounda, the eldest of seven siblings. "I came in 2003 to Tinkoto when I was still a student," he said. "I came to stay with my uncle, who was in orpaillage. I started by working the pulley."[17] The following year, Touré left school to work in the juura. When I met Touré nearly a decade later, in 2014, he was a "master of the mining shaft"—a *damantigi* in Maninka—coordinating the labor and financing of a mining shaft (*daman*) at Juuraba. Touré's daman was covered by a tarp, propped up by bamboo poles that shaded workers from the sun. Eight to twelve male diggers, *damansinna*, share the labor of digging. Yaya leased a mortar picker to break the thick crust of volcanic rock before his men used pickaxes and shovels to deepen the shaft. Two men work underground at a time, descending on ladder rungs dug into the earth. Flashlights flank their ears, bound with thick cotton bands. They dig vertically until they strike a vein of gold-bearing rock. When they hit gold, they carve open a cavern large enough for two men to stand underground. The gold excavated from this cavern is known as "rocks in hand" (*ken bulu*). "The ken bulu is only for the workers," Touré explained. "It is for when the times are difficult. The workers take their share to their house and treat the rock to cover their expenses."[18]

Once the ken bulu is removed, Touré recruits a "placer of wood" (*balandula*) to reinforce the mining shaft with wood beams. Because the work of the balandulas is specialized and dangerous, they are remunerated with a

Figure 1.4 Guardian watching sacks of gold-bearing rock. Tinkoto, Senegal, 2014. Photograph by the author.

handsome share of auriferous rock. After the wood is placed, the damansinna pursue the seam of gold, digging at a horizontal angle until they meet their neighbor's daman. At the mouth of the mine, two team members operate pulleys to evacuate rock dug out by miners underground. Historically women known as *juulusabala* performed this task, and some continue to do so for otherwise all-male mining teams. Today, it is an entry into orpaillage for young and inexperienced men, who observe the techniques of damansinna before descending themselves.

Orpailleurs load gold-bearing rock and gravel into empty rice sacks, sewn shut with chicken wire. Guardians, employed by mining teams, watch the sacks around the clock until the daman is depleted of gold (figure 1.4). Most damans are no deeper than thirty meters due to the release of methane, carbon dioxide, and carbon monoxide underground. Proximity to other damans is a geophysical exigency. As damans conjoin, they create a natural aeration system, lowering the risk of asphyxiation. Run-ins with neighboring teams underground can also generate disputes over where the rock of one team ends and that of another begins. Profits and conflicts go hand in hand.

I frequently traveled to Juuraba with Gassimou Cissokho, the eldest son of Bambo Cissokho's third wife, who was also a damantigi of several teams working in Tinkoto in 2014. Like Touré, Gassimou left school at a young age and entered orpaillage by operating the pulley. He later apprenticed with his father and a balandula from Mali. Gassimou now spends days on and off his motorcycle, shuttling tea, cigarettes, and jugs of fresh water from Tinkoto village to his teams, mostly male migrants from Guinea and Mali. He covers the cost of two meals a day for his team, any medications, and raises the capital needed to finance ropes, buckets, rice sacks, and generator-powered machinery from friends and acquaintances. Each investor will receive a share of harvested gold rock. Such investments are risky. Some teams never strike gold, while others quadruple their investments. Two years earlier, one of Gassimou's damans filled fifty rice sacks with rock. His share of the proceeds financed his marriage and the construction of a concrete house. But in 2014, one of Gassimou's damans barely filled ten rice sacks. Gassimou's success is shaped by his luck and his knowledge of the earth. To determine where to sink a daman, Gassimou spends hours scouring the juura for indications of the orientation of gold-bearing rocks underground: slight land depressions, the direction of acacia tree roots. Once the daman is opened, Gassimou descends underground at each meter to test and smell the earth. As gold approaches, the soil smells like a freshly fired traditional hunting rifle.[19]

Beyond holding knowledge of soils, rocks, and plants, damantigi must engage with the whims and desires of the owners of gold subterranean spirits. "Gold is in the hands of the spirits" (*Sanu ye jinne le bulu*) is a ubiquitous phrase on the juuras of southeastern Senegal. In this region, the most common term for spirit is *jinne* (*djinn* or *jinn*), derived from the Arabic word for spirit (*jinn*) used in the Qur'an. With the growing Islamization of the region over the past century and a half, spirits of diverse nomenclature have been reinterpreted within Qur'anic cosmology.[20] Jinne are preternatural, mortal, and gendered. Like humans, they display a full range of personalities and desires. But they outlive people by hundreds of years and can move at the speed of light, making them valuable allies for those skilled in divination or the arts of the occult. As relayed in the Qur'an, the Almighty God conferred ownership over land to jinne. As a result, accessing arable land, minerals, and wild animals involves exchange relationships with these spirits. Jinne prefer cool and dark places: mountains, rivers, waterfalls, crevices, boulders, and rock escarpments. These natural features coincide with geologically active Birimian-age shear zones where gold deposition is common. Jinne of diverse genealogies haunt the gold deposits of southeastern Senegal. They include spirits bound to specific tracts of land—such as the female jinne of Tinkoto's juuras—and mobile serpent spirits that move underground through the earth and haunt the region's major waterways. Today, the most famous of the serpent spirits is Nininkala or Ningiri (see chapter 2). In the words of Moussa Cissokho, an experienced orpailleur in his sixties from the historical province of Sirimana: "The wealth of the underground is for Ningiri. In Bélédougou, a daman once reached the hole of Ningi. With your flashlight, you could see her path in the daman. She lives from gold."[21]

Responsibility for cultivating relationships with jinne falls on different actors. The master of the mines, the *juurakuntigi*, is the most encompassing ritual authority on the goldfields. Historically in Tinkoto, orpailleurs elected the juurakuntigi based on his—or, more rarely, her—perceived affinity with the occult forces of the juura. Mamadou Sagna, an elderly resident of Mamakono whose ancestors mined Tinkoto, explained that "anyone can become a juurakuntigi. It is a question of their luck with gold. The juura reflects the juurakuntigi. If the juura was not good, sometimes we would change the juurakuntigi until we found the right person."[22] Juurakuntigis made sacrifices to territorial jinne, Nininkala, and other spirit guardians of gold at shrines (*jalan*) constituted at the base of sacred trees or on the juura itself. Many oral traditions suggest that the most lucrative juuras of the western savanna are based on the sacrifice of a person.[23] With the Islamization of gold-bearing regions, long home to ancestral religions, most sacrifices on the juura are made in lineage compounds and mosques, not on the goldfields or on shrines. Yet accusations abound that fertile juuras emerge from sacrifices on jalans (see chapter 7). In the words of Fanta Madi Cissokho, an elder from Bambaraya, a village east of Tinkoto, "The juura is land sacrificed to the jalan."[24]

In 2013, Tinkoto's residents elected a new juurakuntigi, Idi Diallo. Diallo's parents were among the early founders of Tinkoto, and Diallo was raised on the juura. For this reason, it is rumored, Diallo is a person mystically allied with gold, known as a *sanumogola* in Maninka.[25] Diallo maintains the ritual fertility of all juuras managed by Tinkoto village. He spends weeks on the road, traveling to Senegal, Guinea, and Mali to consult with Muslim clerics, diviners, and practitioners of ancestral religious traditions. Diallo opens every new juura discovered within Tinkoto's territory. Sacrifices differ from one juura to another. During my time in Tinkoto, Diallo slaughtered chickens, goats, sheep, and cows in his family compound for Tinkoto's juuras according to halal protocols. To cover the costs of these sacrifices, mining teams give Diallo a portion of rock dug from each daman.

The juurakuntigi also enforces a set of ritual taboos on the goldfields, known as *tana*.[26] Many clans or lineages in West Africa share tanas: commonly a ritual avoidance of killing or consuming animals considered sacred to the group. Juuras are unique in that they are a place, rather than a group of people, with tanas. Some of the tanas enforced on the juura are arbitrary: they work simply by binding members of a community together. Other restrictions please spirits, such as a tana—found on goldfields across the savanna—against the presence of onions, dogs, whistling, and military boots on the juuras. Mining after sunset and on Mondays is also prohibited. These are times when spirits roam on the earth's surface. Because most orpailleurs in Senegal are Muslims, they do not work on the juura on Friday, the day of rest in the Islamic calendar, or Monday, the day of rest for jinne.

The most controversial tana enforced on goldfields in Senegal, Guinea, and Mali is the prohibition against leatherworkers (*garanke*) working in juuras.[27] One regional theory for this restriction is that garanke were once used as human sacrifices in the juuras. For this reason, garanke are entitled to a share of gold without having to to mine it, and their presence as workers in the juura angers jinne. As Gassimou Cissokho explained, "If a garanke comes to the village, we will give them a portion of gold, but they cannot go underground. If a garanke goes underground and we find out, we will tell everyone to leave the mine because it is poisoned."[28] Others argued that their ancestors cut the ears of garanke who entered the juuras, allowing their blood to seep into the soil to appease angered jinne. Over the past decade, garanke lineages have challenged this tana, leading to conflicts that have landed in regional court. One case involved two Soninke women of garanke descent who panned for gold along the Falémé River. Several Maninka men pulled the women from the river and beat them. The men, who received a jail sentence of close to a year, defended their actions in court on the grounds of "custom."[29]

While it is a communal responsibility to uphold the tanas of the juura, each mining shaft is haunted by its own constellation of spirited inhabitants. It falls on individual orpailleurs and the master of the mining shaft, the damantigi, to discern the sacrificial needs of these spirits. Diviners, practitioners of ancestral religions or African/Black knowledge (*farafin londo*), and Muslim religious specialists (*mori, marabouts* in French) offer their services to orpailleurs on a fee-for-service basis.[30] Orpailleurs often consult multiple religious practitioners, bathing in herbs that are pleasing to spirits and donning protective amulets based on the Islamic esoteric sciences. Orpailleurs or damantigi struggling to find a gold seam often travel with samples of sand from their damans to consult with renowned religious practitioners in rural Mali, Gambia, and Guinea. Some offer advice on which direction to dig underground, others recommend sacrifices to free gold from spirits. As damans deepen, the search for knowledge intensifies on the surface of the earth. Abdou Sangare, a Malian mining team leader (*chef d'équipe*) explained. "Jinne seek wealth, like us. And if I want to take your place, I will have to give you something in exchange, right? That is why you can cut a rock [underground] and see lots of gold, but when you take it to the surface you will see nothing. In this case, you emerge from your daman and start your research. Gold, you cannot work it without money. You have to make sacrifices. You have to seek knowledge. And knowledge will cost you money."[31]

Like so many aspects of social life in West Africa, digging for gold is predicated on an exchange relationship with people and with the unseen world. To descend underground is to risk death by an ill-placed wood beam or an angered jinne. Some orpailleurs report feeling the presence of jinne—laughter, dancing, or the "ping-ping-ping" of spirits digging for gold of their own—beneath them as they work.[32] Some find this presence comforting, a sign that they will soon reach gold. For others, it is an unwelcome reminder that they are in the domain of capricious spirits and proximate to death. As I was often told on the juura, "Every place has its master" (*Dulo woo dula, a tigo be kelen*). Knowing the master of one's daman can determine whether you emerge from the underground enriched or as a corpse.

Washing Sand and Raising Children

> It was 1984. The year of the drought. I came here [Tinkoto] and realized that in doing orpaillage along the river, I could feed my family. And I have stayed for twenty-nine years. Now we mine the rock, before it was the sand. I live from gold and I raised my children on gold.[33]

I first met Yonko Camara, the father of a friend, in late 2013. A slight man, sparse with words, Yonko is a respected damantigi. During the dry-season, he oversees the labor of close to a dozen men—mostly migrants from Guinea and Mali—who work on Tinkoto's juuras. Yonko and his first wife, Coumbouna Camara, maintain two households: one in their native village of Bantata, a Maninka settlement in the historical province of Niokolo, and the

42 CHAPTER ONE

other in Tinkoto. Their compound in Tinkoto is a collection of machines and people, with tentacles reaching into labor markets across West Africa and factories in Shenzhen, China that manufacture mining equipment.[34] A half-dozen concrete buildings house their six children and some of the migrants who work on Yonko's mining teams. In the far corner of the courtyard, Coumbouna oversees two sluices, where she washes auriferous sand excavated by her husband and his workers. Opposite her workshop, two young Burkinabe operate a rock-crushing machine. In exchange for the security of lodging in their household, the men offer Yonko and Coumbouna a discounted rate for crushing rock. By day, Yonko and his workers fan into the savanna on motorcycles to dig for gold at one of the mining shafts he oversees as a damantigi. At night, they share rounds of sweet tea prepared on charcoals. Some wander into Tinkoto's streets for grilled lamb skewers and cold beer sold at clandestine bars, "clandos," with diesel-powered refrigerators.

Yonko and Coumbouna's family has grown alongside the expansion of orpaillage in Senegal. Married in the 1970s, both were raised in farm families in the village of Bantata. As a young girl, Coumbouna joined women in her family to pan for gold with calabashes along the Gambia River, where women convened in February and March. Along the riverbanks, women mined alluvial gold deposits, known as *nara* in Maninka, which are found in a number of regional villages along ancient paleo-channels covered by sterile sediment and gravel. Before panning, they spilled prepared beans, cereals, corn, and millet into the river as an offering to Nininkala, the serpent spirit who brokers access to the river's fish and gold-bearing sands. As recounted by Coumba Keita, an elderly woman who practiced orpaillage near Coumbouna's natal village, "We also slaughtered red chickens and goats there on the river. We made our jalan on the river to appease the jinne."[35] In the 1980s, Yonko worked as a farm laborer, a *surga*, near Tambacounda. He cultivated peanuts for his Senegalese host four days a week and farmed two days a week for his own profit. In the dry season, he mined nara at a juura near Kerekonko, a small village on the Gambia. Older women from neighboring villages were credited with discovering this juura, which men only began to mine during the onset of drought in the late 1970s.[36]

In 1984, Yonko and Coumbouna joined a small group of migrants in establishing Tinkoto as a year-round village. In their early years in the village, they excavated nara as a team. Yonko dug shallow damans (up to two meters deep) while Coumbouna washed auriferous sand in nearby streams. Yonko retained two thirds of the gold they mined while Coumbouna kept one third for herself. Mining nara covered the cost of clothing and school fees for their children and enabled the couple to purchase, rather than cultivate, most of their food. In the 1990s, Yonko mined lode-ore rock—*sanukuru* in Maninka; *filon* in French—in a juura in Tinkoto known as Walila Filon. The juura was named after Wali Danfakha, a regional orpailleur who discovered the juura. Yonko was close friends with Wali and the two worked together for several years until their mining shafts flooded with water. Yonko returned to mining nara until the early 2000s, when he, along with dozens of other orpailleurs from Tinkoto, recommenced lode-ore mining.

Lode-ore mining expanded rapidly on Kédougou's juuras in the early 2000s, spurred by rising gold prices and the discovery of new lode-ore deposits by orpailleurs and corporate exploration firms. Lode ore, which is often found at greater depths than nara, requires teams of men to excavate. Nara can be washed directly after it is mined, but lode ore must first be pounded into dust. Historically, the added labor of mining lode ore limited its profitability. However, the rising price of gold attracted to Senegal's juuras poor migrants, who performed the grueling labor of *kuru taki*: pounding gold-bearing rock in cast iron mortars and pestles. In the 2010s, Burkinabe merchants began importing rock-crushing machines to Senegal, which mechanized this labor for a fee. But many orpailleurs continued to hire laborers to crush rock by hand because they suspected machine operators of stealing gold.

Lode ore also carried social advantages. In Yonko's words, "Sanukuru is more beneficial than nara. You can give some of the sand of nara to someone, but they can only treat it once in the river and it's finished. But with rocks, you can bring it to your house. Your wife will have some, your children will have some, and other people in your household can have some rock."[37] The divisibility of rocks enabled Yonko to share rock along a chain of dependents, incorporating more children, workers, and clients into the mining and processing of gold in his family concession.[38] In a region where labor was long the limiting factor in production, the expansion of a household with dependents is a sign of wealth and prestige.[39] The unpredictable returns of mining lode ore confers both advantages and risks. Nara mining returns a reliable quantity of gold per unit of auriferous sand, while lode-ore rocks are more variable. A bucket of rock with no visible gold veins may produce four ounces of gold, while rocks richly marbled with gold may yield only two. The uncertainty of how much gold will be recuperated from washing rocks makes lode ore a potent form of social exchange, one embedded in the ritual life of luck.

44 CHAPTER ONE

While still mining nara, Yonko married a second wife, close in age to Coumbouna and also from Bantata. She bore seven children, including two sets of twins. In 1997, Yonko began mining for gold in Bantaco, a village close to Bantata in the historical province of Niokolo, where lode ore was discovered in Anmericosa's exploration trenches. Bantaco's residents at the time were unfamiliar with orpaillage beyond gold panning carried out largely by women on the Gambia. Yonko and several other orpailleurs from Tinkoto demonstrated techniques for mining lode ore to the population of Bantaco. Yonko eventually established another household in Bantaco, now the primary residence of his second wife. With proceeds from lode-ore mining, Yonko purchased a motorcycle and replaced his family's mud-and-thatch huts with concrete buildings. In 2007, he married a third wife. Yonko became a sought-after damantigi, deft at pairing investments from Senegalese emigrants and businessmen with skilled teams of orpailleurs. In any given year, Yonko mines gold in Tinkoto, Bantaco, or in both villages. Similar to a multinational mining company, he maintains multiple prospects in his portfolio, mining those that are most profitable based on market and labor conditions.

As Yonko's success grew, Coumbouna took charge of an increasingly complex gold-processing workshop in their family concession based in Tinkoto. Not far from her cooking hut she maintains two wooden sluices lined with a strip of coarse green rug. Plastic buckets, brimming with powdered rock, line the sluice. Two buckets glisten with water freshly pulled from a well. Coumbouna runs the auriferous powder through the sluice a total of three times. As the water carries lighter minerals and silt down the sluice's slope into a runoff bucket, the coarse rug traps the heavier gold flakes. Coumbouna lifts the rug strip and submerges it in a bucket of fresh water. Gold flakes settle to the bottom of this bucket. Once the excess water is filtered off, a brackish mixture of gold and mineral particles remains. The gold recuperated from the first two washes of sand is considered Yonko's share of the gold. Coumbouna reserves the third washing of the sand as her profit. In theory, this gendered division of proceeds mimics the historical partitioning of nara mining (one third for women and two thirds for men). But there is a key difference: with nara, women received a third of the auriferous sand before it was washed, whereas with lode ore they receive the remaining gold after it has been washed three times, which is far less than one third of the overall gold recuperated from underground. Men justify the diminishing returns of women's share of gold by the fact that the fee for pounding rock—by machine or hand—eats a portion of the proceeds.[40] Another ambivalent outcome for women of the growth of orpaillage in Kédougou is that goldfields historically controlled by women, particularly nara sites, have come under the control of men. Sajoh Madi Kamara, the chief of Linguekoto, an agricultural hamlet on the Gambia, described the transition: "In the time of our grandmothers, gold did not have much value. The juura was largely for women. When the price for gold went up, men began to search."[41] Or, in the words of Mariama Bâ, who began mining nara on the Gambia in the 1960s: "In the past it was women who searched for gold, but now men start to have machines, so they are searching for gold."[42]

Just as women have lost control over goldfields, the gendered task of washing gold has also become profoundly more toxic. In the mid-2000s, women began adding a drop of methylmercury to the final auriferous mixture that remained after manually disaggregating gold from silts and metallic sands. Malian gold merchants introduced mercury to Senegal in the mid-1990s, but it did not become widespread until the transition to lode-ore mining in the 2000s. Mercury binds to gold, creating a slippery silver amalgam. Women use Bunsen burner–style stoves to burn off the mercury, leaving behind the molten gold. This process pollutes the adjacent air and soil.[43] Because lode ore contains lower-karat gold than nara, mercury recuperates fine-grained gold particles from pounded rock that are invisible to the naked eye. Mercury poisoning is now an acute public health concern on juuras in Senegal. Like many women I spent time with, Coumbouna is aware of the danger of methylmercury. Nongovernmental organizations (NGOs) have led dozens of trainings on the toxic effects of mercury and have distributed machines that contain most of the mercury emissions. But there is no recourse for repairing a broken machine after the NGO departs. Even though most mercury sales are illegal, mercury is effective, inexpensive, and accessible: it does not break down, and it can be easily stored. Orpailleurs purchase mercury in small amounts from the same merchants to whom they sell gold dust. Today, gold merchants—known for centuries in West Africa as juula—operate out of the back rooms of boutiques located in large orpaillage villages. Orpailleurs often sell gold in small quantities (anywhere from one-tenth of a gram to ten grams) shortly after processing it. Merchants weigh out gold dust or amalgam on electronic balances and offer prices determined by global market prices for gold and the relative isolation of the mining site from a major gold market. In 2017, Senegal created a gold dust sales board. Before then, most gold transactions were illegal. Gold mined on Senegal's juuras was smuggled through Bamako and onward to gold markets in the United Arab Emirates and India.[44]

The growth of orpaillage, particularly of lode-ore mining, has enabled Yonko and Coumbouna to finance their children's education and expand their household far beyond the bounds of their native villages. At the same time, the adoption of new machines, migrants, and chemicals into their family compound has transformed the rhythm of their labor and ecology of the soil and water on which they—and their children—also depend.

The Wealth of Strangers

> You must respect strangers, because you do not know their value in the future. They can come here today on a bicycle, and the next time you see them they are driving a four-by-four.[45]

Aruna Sawadogo, who shared these words with me, has made a lucrative living as a stranger on Senegal's juuras, with his own story of social mobility through machinery. Raised in a small village outside of the city of Bobo-Dioulasso in Burkina Faso, Sawadogo now employs more than one hundred men who operate rock-crushing machines and mechanical jigs on juuras in the Kédougou region. He has resided in Senegal for more than fifteen years; his children attend school in Senegal and speak fluent Wolof, Maninka, French, and broken Mooré—his mother tongue. Broad-shouldered and quick to smile, Sawadogo planned to become a school-teacher but left his studies when his father, a cashew farmer, fell ill. He tried his hand at orpaillage and discovered that his "luck was in gold." Gold paid for his father's hospital bills and financed his marriage. In 2004, on the advice of a cousin, Sawadogo traveled to Senegal, his first time in the country, with a mechanical jig he purchased in Burkina Faso. Sawadogo befriended the chief of a small orpaillage village along the Gambia River, two dozen kilometers from Tinkoto. The village hosts a nara juura that orpailleurs excavate like an open quarry rather than digging mining shafts. The village chief invited Sawadogo to install his mechanical jig within the village. Sawadogo purchased auriferous sand, mined by local orpailleurs, and transported it by donkey cart to the Gambia, where he passed the sand through the jig, powered by river water and a diesel generator. By the time I met Sawadogo in 2014, he owned more than a dozen jigs and employed fifty Burkinabe migrants to operate them. Sawadogo paid his workers a salary of 50,000 West African CFA francs, roughly equivalent at the time to the base salary for elementary-school teachers in Kédougou.[46] The monthly payments Sawadogo made to the village chief paid for medicines at a local health clinic and school supplies for children. Sawadogo also financed weddings, baptisms, and funerals. Sawadogo's wealth and that of the village grew in tandem.

In the early 2010s, Sawadogo began to derive a new income stream from purchasing orpaillage tailings—the sand accumulated in the workshops of women after they finish washing gold—and treating them in cyanide heap-leaching (figure 1.5). Sawadogo's employees bought tailings from dispersed household workshops, loaded them into donkey carts or onto three-wheel motorcycles, and drove to distant agricultural fields that Sawadogo leased from local farmers. They dumped the tailings into rectangular pits, lined with thick black tarps, that contained a cyanide-water solution. Cyanide breaks down and reacts with organic elements, binding to gold and silver particles. This makes it one of the most important elements used in the industrial gold-mining industry.[47] Cyanide entered juuras in Senegal from Burkina Faso in the mid-2000s, when some corporate mining firms began selling cyanide through extralegal networks and mining engineers employed in the "formal" sector began moonlighting in orpaillage. Sawadogo's team left the tailings in the tarp-lined pits for several weeks, until the cyanide solution evaporated into a gaseous state, leaving a gold-silver-cyanide amalgam. Sawadogo smuggled this mixture back to Burkina, where a business partner used a zinc-derived compound to disaggregate silver from the gold amalgam. This system ensured that Sawadogo's workers could not steal gold, since his Burkinabe business partner retained a monopoly on the chemical compound to distill gold.[48] In the summer of 2014, the Senegalese government catalogued and closed most of these illegal cyanide pits, including a number in Tinkoto. But for a period of time they generated enormous profits for Sawadogo and other entrepreneurs like him.

During my fieldwork, Senegalese government officials targeted regional migrants from Burkina Faso, Mali, and Guinea as the source of disease, chemical pollution, and crime on Senegal's juuras. Migrants, they argued, accrued more benefits from orpaillage than Senegalese because they were more skilled in mining than their Senegalese hosts and had access to cheap machinery and chemicals in their countries of origin that were subjected to stricter regulation, and thus more expensive, in Senegal. It is true that many migrants to Senegal have a comparative advantage in orpaillage, but these arguments also obscure the economic and social value that migrants generate for Senegalese households. Senegalese orpailleurs locate the value of strangers in several historical precedents. For one, they place the origins of orpaillage in "Manden," the heartland of the medieval empire of Mali, in what

Figure 1.5 Cyanide heap-leaching pits. Tinkoto, Senegal, 2013. Photograph by anonymous.

is today northern Guinea. In the words of the orpailleur Moussa Cissokho: "Mining came from Manden. It started in Guinea, and went from Guinea to Mali, until it reached us. The people of [Manden] helped us understand the benefit of the juura. They taught us how to make a juurakuntigi and the secrets of the mines. It all started with Manden."[49] Orpailleurs also credit Malians and Guineans for recent technological innovations. In the 1980s, Bambo Cissokho recruited Malians from across the border to introduce lode-ore mining techniques to Tinkoto. "Strangers brought the sanukuru to Tinkoto," he explained. "It is the Malians who know the work of the rocks. They showed us the technique of balandun. They showed us the veins of gold in the bedrock. If [they hadn't], we [would] not know gold was found in the rocks."[50] This account is intriguing because orpailleurs in Tinkoto did mine for lode ore prior to the 1980s. Many of my interlocutors spoke of male twins from Bélédougou who mined lode ore in Tinkoto in the 1940s. Despite this, so valued are strangers on the juura that Senegalese orpailleurs credited them with this discovery. These statements reveal a regional logic of the juura as a famine resource: a place where strangers are welcome. In the words of Yonko Camara, the juura is a place where "everyone received

A TALE OF TWO MINERS   49

something; [whether] it was small or a lot, no one left here without earning something."[51]

The Maninka and the Geologists

"I've always said the Malinké [Maninka] were the first geologists," Hamidou Sow recounted over coffee at a bakery in Les Almadies, a neighborhood in Dakar that is home to the corporate offices of many mining companies working in Senegal. At the time of our meeting in 2017, Sow was the chief geologist of ToroGold, a British firm (later acquired by Resolute Mining) that opened the Petowal/Mako mine, Senegal's second open-pit mining project and mill.[52] Equally at ease in a Friday kaftan in Dakar or in steel-toed boots in a ravine, Sow is passionate about field geology and Kédougou, where he met his wife and has spent most of his career over the past two decades. Senegalese geologists who work on the Birimian rocks of Kédougou are historians of orpaillage in their own right, keenly aware of the prominent role ethnic Maninka have played in the discovery of regional gold deposits. Gold mineralization in Kédougou region is concentrated near Maninka villages, many of which were settled by people in search of gold deposits (see chapter 7).[53]

As Sow built his geological career, he also became familiar with the histories of villages and juuras in southeastern Senegal. As part of his geological training, Sow learned to map and sample the pits of orpailleurs during baseline geological mapping.[54] While in the field, he also spent time with village elders who led him to juuras and other natural features of interest in structural geological mapping. Exploration geologists often name gold deposits after local villages and place names for valleys, agricultural basins, and hunting grounds. Most multimillion-ounce gold deposits evidenced in Kédougou since the early 2000s are named for Maninka place names, such as Petowal, Massawa, and Makabingui. Geologists incorporate regional genealogies of settlement and sacred engagements with the landscape into the scientific literature by naming geological features after a fusion of place names and scientific terms, such as the Tinkoto pluton, the Mamakhono pluton, the Badon granodiorite, and the Laminia Kaourou plutonic complex. Just as regional histories and cultural practices shape geology, the biographies of Senegalese geologists are grafted onto those of family lineages in Kédougou. Sow learned Maninka while working in Kédougou. His relationship with his in-laws, who are from Kédougou, have strengthened his ties to the landscape and local family lineages.

The relationship between geologists and orpailleurs is fraught. Orpailleurs argue that geologists have located many regional gold deposits by co-opting the gold discoveries of orpailleurs. Geologists counter that they are not searching for the same type of deposits as orpailleurs, who historically mined alluvial gold deposits (*nara*), whereas geologists are primarily interested in locating lode-ore deposits (*sanukuru*). In practice, however, the distinction between these two depositional types is murky. For one, today orpailleurs do mine lode ore—and at increasing depths—with mortar pickers and dynamite. Second, geologists often discover lode-ore deposits by studying alluvial ones, including those mined by orpailleurs. The discovery of Petowal (currently mined by Resolute Mining) underscores the ambiguities of discovery. Sow first explored for gold near Petowal in the late 1990s while working for an exploration firm based in the United Kingdom. He sampled alluvial deposits on the northern bank of the Gambia, including the juuras of Linguekoto and Tambanoumouya. These juuras were primarily mined by women who panned for gold in the Gambia or dug shallow shafts, up to a meter in depth, along the damp silts of the riverbanks. Sow suspected that these low-lying deposits were created by gold disaggregated from lode ore lodged in a mountain ridge to the north. But his employer lost interest in the prospect. More than a decade later, Sow returned to the region while employed by ToroGold. By retracing his previous itinerary, he was able to confirm the presence of Petowal, a more than one-million-ounce deposit north of the Gambia. Juuras guided Sow's research, but he also discovered lode ore that was not mined by orpailleurs.

Orpailleurs also shadow geologists, digging out their exploration trenches to create new juuras. This practice led to the opening of several of Tinkoto's famous juuras: Juuraba, Gulf, and Tambabiri. Geologists employ local men, who moonlight as orpailleurs, as laborers: to cut roads and to dig exploration trenches that reveal a cross-section of the sedimentary strata of the earth. If trenches reveal promising concentrations of gold, geologists' subcontract Rotary Air Blast–drilling and diamond-drilling teams to extract deeper samples. These subcontractors also employ local men to bag and to sort samples. If local workers can glimpse gold mineralization with the naked eye, they report these indexes to brothers and uncles, who return to trenches after geological teams have moved on to explore other portions of their permit. This rotating door of personnel, and mutual pirating of discoveries, is another means by which the line between corporate gold exploration and orpaillage is blurred on the Birimian rocks of the West African savanna.

A Sharia, a Social License

West Africa's twenty-first-century gold-mining boom has conferred greater power on local authorities such as Bambo Cissokho, as exploration and mining firms look to these figures to represent the communities in which their camps, mines, and mills are located.[55] Cissokho's tribunal is an obligatory passage point for companies, such as Randgold, which want to maintain positive relationships with local residents and keep orpailleurs away from their primary gold prospects. It is impossible for exploration firms to police the entirety of their permits, which for Randgold alone stretched to 1,650 square kilometers in 2014. The most economical way to ensure that orpailleurs do not "eat" corporate mining prospects is for geologists and camp personnel to negotiate directly with figures such as Cissokho.

Exploration firms refer to the relationships they cultivate with villages within their permits as their social license to operate or simply their "social permit."[56] Social permits lack the formality of Corporate Social Responsibility (CSR) programs, which are often based on written agreements between mining companies and the communities in which they operate.[57] Social permits are extralegal, ad hoc agreements that refer to the general acceptance of a mining project by local stakeholders. Exploration firms cultivate buy-in by employing local laborers, meeting with community leaders, and investing in humanitarian projects. The websites of extractive firms in Senegal are peppered with verdant green snapshots of children watering vegetable gardens and clutching new school supplies. In Tinkoto, for example, Randgold financed a women's garden, latrines, deep-bore wells, solar panels, and a new classroom for the elementary school. When a grease fire burned much of the village in 2008, Randgold distributed food aid and clothing. Solar panels and school supplies produce more than glossy photographs for corporate websites. They are the operating costs of camp security: they contain the potential of violence from orpailleurs.

Securing a "social license" for gold exploration in West Africa also entails allowing orpailleurs to mine portions of state-issued exploration permits. Randgold, for example, brokered with Cissokho to avoid "no-go" zones where their active prospects were located while allowing orpaillage elsewhere on the permit. This social license evolves as exploration advances and the needs of local orpailleurs shift. Negotiations with mining firms also shape how Cissokho governs juuras located within the customary jurisdiction of Tinkoto—itself a blurry and contested territory (see chapter 7). In addition to enforcing ritual prohibitions, tana, on the juuras, each orpaillage village in southeastern Senegal maintains a so-called sharia—a set of rules and regulations enforced by village chiefs (*damantigi*) and the juura police force (*tomboluma*). *Sharia* is the term for Islamic canonical law based on the teachings of the Qur'an and the traditions of the Prophet Muhammad. The sharia of the juura does not align with Islamic law; rather, the term references a set of socially recognized rules and prohibitions not legally sanctioned by the state. Every juura has its own sharia. Tinkoto's includes, for example, a prohibition against cooking fires after noon (introduced after the 2008 grease fire) or driving motorcycles after dark (introduced after a motorcyclist killed a child). Violators pay fines to Cissokho.

Tinkoto's sharia has shifted along with the exploration activities of mining firms. In 2002, Randgold was carrying out gold exploration from its base in the village of Kanoumering, from where it employed men from Tinkoto and Kanoumering as laborers. At the time, Tinkoto's population was growing overnight, and orpailleurs were increasingly mining lode ore, in part due to discoveries made within Randgold's exploration trenches. One night, several of Randgold's local Senegalese employees organized an expedition to the firm's trenches shortly after the geological team had moved its activities to another portion of the permit. For several nights, they dug out Randgold's trenches until the firm's private security guards surprised the diggers. The guards brought the orpailleurs to the gendarme station in Kédougou, where the accused were later tried in regional court and given jail sentences of several months. This conflict between Randgold and Tinkoto's orpailleurs became known in Tinkoto as the "Gulf Wars," a name derived from action movies depicting US combat forces in the Gulf Wars that were popular in southeastern Senegal in the early 2000s. Following this turmoil, Cissokho called a meeting of Tinkoto's long-term residents. As one attendee recalled, he appealed to the crowd: "The government does not support us, and we are at war with Randgold. I need force so I can fight with the company. I pray to you for help. Every time you dig a shaft, I need a portion of your rock, so I can afford to go to Kédougou to negotiate with the state."[58]

Historically, orpailleurs in Kédougou did not allocate a portion of their mined rock to the village chief—only to the chief of the mines and the group of tomboluma. A council of senior male residents of Tinkoto agreed to give Cissokho a share of auriferous rock from their damans to finance his negotiations with state authorities and with Randgold.[59] With early proceeds from his new share, Cissokho purchased a truck to travel on the unpaved, and often flooded, roads linking Tinkoto to Kédougou and to Randgold's exploration camp in Kanoumering. Cissokho earned a reputation as a deft mediator with regional government officials and representatives of Randgold. The company apologized for jailing Tinkoto's residents and offered increased employment for local men at its exploration camp. This marked the opening of a golden era in Randgold's social license to operate in Tinkoto. Meanwhile, the practice of allocating a portion of auriferous rock to the dugutigi—known as "Cissokho's sharia"—was adopted by chiefs of villages across southeastern Senegal. In this instance, corporate strategy incited a new "custom" on the juura.

Many orpailleurs saw the spread of Cissokho's sharia as bloating the proceeds of chiefs and their allies at the expense of workers. In the words of an experienced orpailleur based in Tinkoto, "In the past, gold was for the workers. We gave the juurakuntigi and the tombolomon a share out of respect. Today, everyone comes to claim gold, and the workers, those who have sacrificed their bodies, are left with little."[60] In his view, Cissokho's opulence was signaled by his purchase of a Cadillac Escalade to replace an aging Toyota pickup truck. Cissokho also built a new home in Kédougou, where he stays when he is meeting with the gendarmes to plead the case of orpailleurs from Tinkoto who landed in jail. These visits double as opportunities for Cissokho to meet with merchants and politicians in Kédougou who invest in Tinkoto's mining shafts. Like the orpailleurs who work on Tinkoto's juuras, Cissokho accumulates wealth and alliances through strategic mobility. The Escalade not only provides transportation: it projects Cissokho's prestige as he travels across the region.

Tinkoto's sharia evolved again when market prices for gold spiked in 2011, which led to an uptick in migration to Tinkoto and violence within the village. Cissokho began assigning individual tomboluma, dubbed *sécurité privée* (private security), to each mining shaft to represent their interests and to protect members of the mining team. This departed from the historical practice of orpailleurs' giving a share of mined rock to the group of tomboluma, not individual ones. Beginning in 2011, Cissokho forced orpailleurs to pay two levies: one to the group of tomboluma and one to their sécurité privée. Cissokho contended this new tax would decrease violence on the juura. But orpailleurs saw the fee as a cynical move by Cissokho and his tomboluma to extract a greater share of auriferous rock from laborers. Despite their protests, Cissokho's new rule became a norm across the region.

Because orpaillage is illegal in most contexts, orpailleurs rely on figures such as Bambo Cissokho to negotiate collective usufruct resource rights. The social license and the sharia are the extralegal agreements that enable orpailleurs and geologists to engage on mutually agreed-on terms. The social license is just as customary as the sharia, and the sharia is just as shaped by transnational mining capital as the social license. Both agreements are fragile, stitched together by shared will and the threat of force. They bind artisanal and corporate miners together in a dense, and volatile, set of reciprocal obligations.

"Men Divide Rocks, God Divides Gold"

Midnight approaches on Juuraba. An eerie silence descends on this rubble of rock and frayed tarps after the daytime whir of motorcycles and mortar pickers ceases. A new moon casts feeble light on two dozen men and a few women who encircle a mound of rock and gravel, the spilled innards of dozens of rice sacks stuffed with gold-bearing rock. This is the day of the division of rocks (*kuru tala luno*), a ceremony that brings together the workers and investors who purchased the food, machines, supplies, and ritual sacrifices for the daman. They await their share of the proceeds from Gassimou Cissokho's daman at Juuraba. Gassimou's father, Bambo Cissokho, takes part in most kuru tala luno. Two tomboluma and the guardian of the rice sacks are also present.

The workers reflect the diversity of the juura: young men from Guinea working for their first season on Senegal's juuras, seasoned Malian balandula. An elderly man opens the ceremony in a Qur'anic prayer. Gassimou reads aloud a list that indicates the share of rock each member of the team will receive. The shares are measured in piles of rock. The division of rock differs from one team to another; it is based on a collective agreement among the team. This night, the proceeds are divided into three categories:

3 piles

Damantigi
Chef d'équipe (Fr.)

2 piles

Balandula
Tomboluma "sécurité privée"

1 pile

Juulusabala
Gardien (Fr.)
Investisseur (Fr.)
Damansinna

Dugutigi
Juurakuntigi
Numu
Tomboluma

A twelve-year-old girl, the daughter of a local family, walks into the middle of the circle. Children, less vulnerable to corruption than adults, serve as the master of ceremonies (*kalakuntigi*). While her back is turned, each team member places an object in the circle: a piece of plastic, metal, an amulet. The object stands in for the person's share in the mine. The kalakuntigi turns around and begins pointing to rocks. Two tomboluma, armed with picks, retrieve and split the rocks she selects as she indicates the division of each piece among the objects. The concentration of gold in any given rock is indiscernible from the glance of a child under the cover of night. The public nature of the kuru tala luno is designed to eliminate human bias. It is also a ritual arbitration shaped by the whims of the spirit world. Jinne reward some with more gold than others. As the saying goes in Tinkoto: "Men divide rocks, God divides gold" (*Moxo le se kuru tala, Allah le se sano tala*).

Once the largest rocks are divided, the tomboluma use plastic buckets to mete out the remaining gravel and sand into piles. Their work is slow and methodical; the ceremony stretches until dawn. The chef d'équipe and the damantigi give some of their rock to workers as a bonus, an incentive to join a future team under their leadership. Each team member places handfuls of gravel on a pile set aside for those who cannot work in the mines: the debilitated, the blind, and the destitute. This offering of auriferous rock parallels a common practice by regional farmers, who leave piles of millet, sorghum, or rice alongside their fields after the harvest for those in need to recuperate at their discretion. This is an agrarian expression of *zakat*: obligatory almsgiving of the Islamic tradition. It is thought to bring blessings onto the harvest of rock and grain that is retained.

Each team member fills empty rice sacks with their rocks, strapping their proceeds onto the back of motorcycles or into the beds of pickup trucks rented for the occasion. Back home in Tinkoto, the division of rocks continues as workers and investors share a portion of their proceeds with wives, brothers, friends, and ritual intercessors. In the days following the ceremony, orpailleurs will host collective meals in their family concessions or those of their hosts. Goats and chickens will be slaughtered in the name of Allah; others, in the names of subterranean spirits as thanks for blessing their families with gold. As rock is divided into smaller pieces, it moves from the hands of spirits to orpailleurs, investors, tomboluma, chiefs; to machines and pounders of rock; to wives and daughters who wash gold; and to Burkinabe who chemically leach gold flakes in basins of cyanide.

The kuru tala luno has the appearance of a time-worn custom. But like many practices on the juura, it is a new tradition that accompanied the expansion of corporate capital and the rise of lode-ore mining on Kédougou's juuras in the early 2000s. When men and women mined nara from desiccated streambeds in Tinkoto, workers divided gold-bearing sand among themselves at the end of each day. Still, it carries echoes of older practices. In the past, the juurakuntigi of Tinkoto was selected in a similar manner to the kalakuntigi of today. Each man or woman eligible for the office placed a stick in the circle. A child selected one of the objects, and the corresponding owner became the juurakuntigi. The selection appeared random, but it was understood that spirits guided the child's hand.

In recent years, as disputes between gold exploration firms and orpailleurs have intensified, customary authorities have increased the share they draw from damans to finance their meetings with mining companies, gendarmes, and bureaucrats. These relationships are tenuous, based on conflict and mutual dependence, as state agents struggle to police a dual mining frontier: one corporate, one artisanal. In the next chapter, I situate Tinkoto in a far older time than that of corporate capital, when medieval West African traders and states vied for control over the gold markets of Bambuk, where Kédougou region was then situated. By turning to this deeper past, we can better understand how a mineral lodged in the hands of spirits became crucial to the sacred engagement of generations of West Africans with the Birimian rocks of the savanna.

2
West Africa's Ritual Geology, 800–1900

Situated thirty kilometers northeast of Tinkoto is the village of Mamakono. Founded roughly six hundred years ago, Mamakono is one of the oldest known settlements in southeastern Senegal and a reference point for the region's history of orpaillage. In the Atlantic era, Mamakono was the seat of a small province known as Bélédougou, which then consisted of a cluster of villages, each numbering several hundred residents of mixed Pular, Maninka, and Soninke heritage. Like residents of provinces scattered along the Birimian rocks of the savanna, Bélédougou's people farmed, hunted, and engaged in orpaillage. Today, Mamakono sits in the heart of Senegal's corporate mining corridor. Mamakono is encompassed by the exploration permits of Endeavor Mining, a Britain-based gold company that now operates the Sabodala mine. Some young residents of Mamakono work as truck drivers and mechanics in Endeavor's camp. But most labor as orpailleurs in surrounding villages. Mamakono is prosperous compared with many villages in the region. Since the early 2000s, concrete buildings have replaced mud huts with funds from the expansion of orpaillage and corporate gold mining. Boutiques stocked with rice, onions, and sugar line neat dirt pathways that wind between lineage compounds and two mosques.

Roughly ten kilometers west of Mamakono, it is reported, sits a tomb covered in a pile of porous laterite rocks. A shrine marks the foot of the tomb—an assemblage of splintered iron scraps, strips of cloth, and the dried blood of slaughtered chickens. The shrine is dedicated to Taubry Sidibé, an infamous tyrant who briefly ruled as a "slave king" over Mamakono, likely in the eighteenth century. Oral traditions recounted in Kédougou region today speak to the alliances Taubry Sidibé forged with territorial spirits to exercise control over two crucial subterranean resources: gold and water. The precise period of Taubry Sidibé's reign, and the circumstances of his life, are mysterious.[1] The name Sidibé, a common Pular patronym, suggests that he may have been a former captive of a Pular lineage. He earned fame by overthrowing the Soumaré clan, then the Soninke overlords of Mamakono. Taubry was ritually cunning. Every Monday—considered a day of rest for spirits—he ordered men to lower him with ropes into Mamakono's only water well. Taubry remained underground until village residents mined enough gold dust to fill a goat's horn. According to some versions of the story, Tinkoto was discovered during Taubry's reign, as orpailleurs ventured farther and farther in search of gold (map 2.1).[2] After the Soumarés were deposed, they attempted to kill Taubry, but a spirit allied to the "slave king" shielded him from their attacks. Desperate, the Soumarés called on Soro Cissokho, a Maninka hunter from western Mali, for assistance with Taubry. Soro sent two of his sons, Siriman and Moussa Cissokho, to Bélédougou. Their cousin, a stunning woman named Dan Mania, accompanied the brothers.

While crossing the Falémé River, Siriman remarked on the fish darting in the fresh water and the rich land lining the riverbanks. He decided to stay and farm along the Falémé, founding Sirimana, a province that bordered

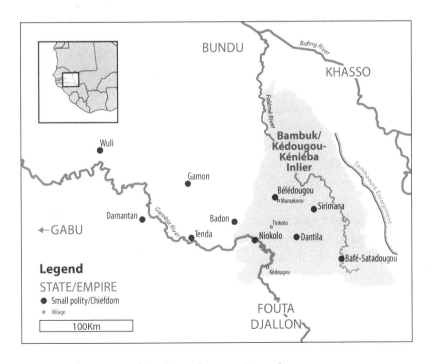

Map 2.1 Atlantic-era polities in southeastern Senegal, ca. 1700–1900.

WEST AFRICA'S RITUAL GEOLOGY

Bélédougou to the south. Moussa and Dan Mania continued their journey. Upon arriving in Mamakono, Moussa hid in the Soumaré clan's household, and Dan Mania approached Taubry's compound. She declared her desire to marry Taubry. Compelled by her beauty, Taubry prepared a marriage. On their wedding night, while she braided his hair, Dan Mania asked Taubry to reveal the secret to his ritual power. Taubry replied, "Nothing can overcome me unless you slaughter a white rooster and throw it on the roof of my dwelling."[3] Dan Mania relayed Taubry's secret to Moussa Cissokho, who prepared the sacrifice. Taubry cried out as the rooster descended onto the roof, his occult power severed. Dan Mania seized Taubry's braids and decapitated him with a cutlass. She carried Taubry's head to the Soumarés.[4] The Soumarés placed Taubry's head on a metal balance and piled gold dust on the other end until the balance leveled. They offered the gold to the Cissokhos and announced, "You liberated us. We could do nothing against this slave. Now, to show our gratitude, we give you the land of Bélédougou. In exchange, we ask that you do not harm us."[5] In oral renditions of the Taubry narrative, this offering is an origin story for the transfer of political power over Bélédougou from the Soumaré (ethnic Soninke) to the Cissokho (ethnic Maninka). While the Cissokhos became the masters of the land (*dugutigi*) of Bélédougou and Sirimana, descendants of the Soumaré retained a ritual office as masters of shrines (*jalantigi*): to cultivate relationships with territorial spirits. In one account, the Soumarés prepared sacrifices at Taubry's tomb to appease the spirit guardians of gold, with whom Taubry had a privileged relationship.[6] Until the present day, male descendants of the Cissokho clan occupy the office of the dugutigi in all but one village within the historical province of Bélédougou.[7] Bambo Cissokho, the dugutigi of Tinkoto (see chapter 1), also traces his ancestry to Moussa Cissokho.

Taubry Sidibé is remembered as a tyrant because he breached a cultural ideal of the savanna: that distinct authorities should manage ritual power over gold and political power over the land. In recent centuries, this division was maintained by the separation of the dugutigi from the juurakuntigi: the former managed rights to land; the latter, rights to the subsoil. Taubry monopolized both offices. By overthrowing the Soumaré clan, he became the dugutigi of Mamakono and harnessed occult power over gold. Today, Bambo Cissokho is similarly criticized for overstepping his jurisdiction as dugutigi by claiming a share of all gold mined within Tinkoto, a privilege once exercised exclusively by the juurakuntigi. Separated by centuries, the stories of Taubry Sidibé and Bambo Cissokho speak to competition for

CHAPTER TWO

power over gold-producing polities and of tempestuous alliances between ritually attuned persons and spirit guardians of gold. Such themes are not isolated to southeastern Senegal. They belong to the spatially and temporally expansive history of gold-producing communities that have occupied West Africa's Birimian rocks over the past millennium. As previewed earlier, I call this phenomenon a ritual geology: the set of material and ritual practices, prohibitions, and ideological engagements with the earth and its spirited inhabitants shared widely across a geological formation.

This chapter traces three elements of West Africa's ritual geology that took shape sometime between the ninth century, when we have the earliest evidence for regional gold production, and the nineteenth century, when the French army conquered much of the savanna. The full expression of this ritual geology comes firmly into view only in the early nineteenth century, when the documentary record for the region thickens. But features of this ritual geology are evident as early as a millennium ago in the oral traditions attached to the expansion of medieval polities; village settlement narratives; migrations of blacksmiths and gold merchants; and the narratives of the spirit snakes Bida and Nininkala that traveled along historical trade routes and disparate goldfields. For one, during this millennium of history, small, non-centralized societies retained control over gold production. At different junctures, hierarchical states situated on the Sahel and the savanna controlled the trade in gold but not gold mining itself.[8] Second, since the medieval period, Muslim outsiders, who wrote many of the early accounts of gold mining and trade in West Africa, denigrated and racialized African miners as pagans.[9] The ideological opposition of gold miners to Islam was partly cultivated by the rock escarpments and poor agricultural soils of geologically active zones, where gold is often found. These landscapes served as a natural refuge for generations of men and women who wished to practice and innovate ancestral religious traditions beyond the reach of slave raiders and Muslim states. Third, West African societies of the savanna and the Sahel regarded gold as a dangerous occult substance tied to spirits, including malevolent ones. This may account for why gold producers on the savanna preferred copper over gold for jewelry, ritual affairs, and burials. Ritual concerns about gold in West Africa do not reflect a generalized concern with accumulation, greed, or usury, qualities associated with gold in medieval and Renaissance Europe. Rather, I argue, they emerged from a regional ritual geology that predated, and evolved alongside, cultural critiques of gold and mining capitalism elsewhere on the globe.

My account of the emergence of West Africa's ritual geology complements a growing scholarship on medieval and early Atlantic-era West Africa that highlights the region's participation in early globalization through the gold trade and Muslim scholarly networks.[10] The historian Toby Green offers a compelling theory for why West African polities, from thirteenth-century Mali to sixteenth-century Asante, sold so much gold dust to Europeans on the cheap. At the dawn of the Atlantic age, Green argues, a variety of materials were valued for currency in Europe and in Africa. Africans sold gold dust, which was ubiquitous in the region, in exchange for materials they valued as currencies on regional markets: imported cloth, cowries, copper, iron, and silver. Over time, capital imbalances between the two regions emerged as most of the materials imported from Europe lost their value as currencies beyond West Africa, while gold and silver retained their value and European city-states backed their credit systems with these metals.[11] West Africa remained disadvantaged in its access to capital as the region's gold dust accumulated in the coffers of European and North African states at the same time that the labor value of African war captives, sold into the Atlantic economy, benefited New World plantations.[12]

I offer a parallel suggestion: ritual concerns also motivated gold producers to part with gold. This remained the case even as it became clear that the middlemen of the Sahara and European traders were benefiting far more from the trade in African gold than their trading partners south of the Sahara. Green hints at the ritual powers associated with gold mining.[13] But he does not specify the content of these powers and how they evolved alongside markets for currencies and enslaved persons. Though West African societies have long considered gold a commodity—an abstracted token of generalizable exchange—gold has also remained a ritually fraught object attached to occult forces, territorial spirits, and mobile spirit snakes. To build this argument, I triangulate archeological reports, Arabic manuscripts in translation, French and British archival sources, oral narratives, oral histories, and songs from across West Africa. My entry point are the goldfields of Bélédougou: the realm of Taubry Sidibé and his successors, the Cissokho clan. In prior centuries, outsiders lumped Bélédougou into Bambuk, the name given to gold-producing territories located between the Senegal River and its tributary, the Falémé.[14] From Bambuk, I widen my spatial lens to cover events in what is today modern Mali, Guinea, Burkina Faso, Côte d'Ivoire, and Ghana. The history of orpaillage in Bambuk must be placed within the vast territorial and temporal reach of West Africa's ritual geology.

Spirit Snakes and Gold in West Africa, 800–1200

A millennium prior to Taubry Sidibé's reign over Bélédougou, gold mined from Bambuk was used to mint coins in North Africa and Europe. While the antiquity of gold mining in West Africa is debated, there is clear evidence for a far-western trans-Saharan trade route in gold by the ninth century.[15] The gold trade coincided with the introduction of Islam into Saharan trading diasporas. Islamic conquests in North Africa further integrated the region into Muslim mercantile networks of the Sahara to Mediterranean port cities and the Arabian Peninsula. Gold fueled the expansion of city-states and centers of Islamic learning across West Africa, including Gao, Timbuktu, Tadmekka, Takrur, Silla, and Mali. In its reputation and influence in the wider Muslim world, none of these trading centers rivaled Wagadu, known in Arabic sources as Ghana, the name of its dynasts. As Al-Ya'qūbī wrote in 872–73, the king of Ghana is "very powerful.... In his country are the gold mines."[16]

The ancestors of today's Soninke peoples, who speak a variety of Mande languages also known as Soninke, established Wagadu as early as the year 600.[17] From the ninth through the thirteenth century, Wagadu appears to have held a monopoly on a western Saharan trade route stretching from its presumed capital, Koumbi Saleh, in southeastern Mauritania, to the northern Saharan entrepôt of Sijilmasa, in southern Morocco. Though historians have long described Wagadu as an empire, it more likely operated as a loose "over-kingdom" that incorporated Soninke provinces and multiethnic trading centers into a sphere of Soninke commercial and ritual influence.[18] Centuries prior to the rise of a regularized Saharan gold trade, urban societies on the Sahel forged dense regional trade networks in West Africa (map 2.2).[19] However, what distinguished Wagadu from its predecessors was the power its Soninke dynasts exercised over the trade in gold mined on the savanna against salt and copper from the Sahara desert.

Despite the growing scholarship on medieval West African empires and trade, little is known about gold-producing communities and their relationship to mineralized land. Sources are a limiting factor. Early mining concentrated on alluvial gold deposits, which leave few traces in the archeological record.[20] Gold objects recovered from burial mounds on the Sahel and the savanna and recently excavated gold-processing sites are key sources of data.[21] Most Arabic sources on the gold trade are second- or thirdhand accounts, compiled by diplomats and traders based in North Africa and Andalusia. And the few Arab travelers who visited West Africa were prohibited from

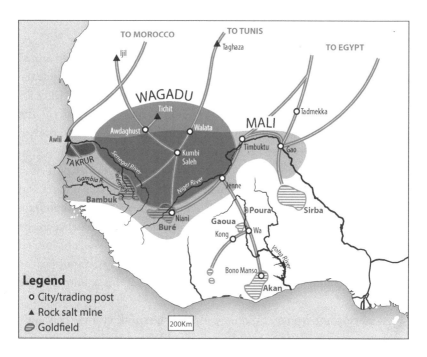

Map 2.2 Medieval West African empires and trade routes, ca. 900–1500.

visiting the gold mines. Chroniclers imagined that Wagadu's dynasts oversaw huge open-pit mines powered by slave labor. The reality was far different. Wagadu built its wealth on the gold trade, but control over gold-bearing land and mining remained in the hands of small-scale villages and provinces dispersed along the savanna to the south of Wagadu's capital. Bambuk was likely the earliest source of Wagadu's gold.[22] While regional oral traditions credit ancestral Soninke and Maninka peoples as the earliest miners of gold in Bambuk, the precise cultural and ethnic makeup of early orpailleurs are unknown.[23] As shown by the archaeological work of Ibrahima Thiaw, by the early second millennium there is evidence for Soninke influence on the gold trade, and on pottery styles, to the north of Bambuk.[24] This is suggestive of the growing reach of a Soninke trading diaspora with roots on the Sahel, known as the Wangara, into gold-producing regions of the savanna.

Wangara traders were crucial to the rise of Wagadu's monopoly over the trade in gold. The Wangara converted to Islam shortly after its introduction to the Sahara in the first two centuries after the Prophet Muhammad's death in 632.[25] They were predecessors to the *juula*, a generic Maninka term for long-distance traders in use by the thirteenth century. Wangara linked disparate geographies: savanna and forest zones where gold was mined and kola nuts collected, city-states of the savanna and Sahel, and Saharan copper and salt mines. Wangara traders established autonomous Muslim settlements among gold-producing pagans, with whom they exchanged rock salt, copper, cloth, and glass beads for gold dust, elephant tusks, animal skins, and the occasional war captive.[26] Wangara also nurtured relationships with Berber and Arab clans who controlled copper and rock salt mines on the Sahara, which occupies a distinct geological formation from gold-bearing Birimian rocks.[27] Bambuk's residents derived ample salt for dietary needs from plant ash, but they sought rock salt for seasoning, animal pasturage, healing preparations, and cultural prestige. Gold producers valued copper, a metal revered for warding off malevolent spirits, in contrast to gold, which attracted them. Copper and copper alloys were also desired for aesthetic and tonal qualities that changed in different climates.[28] These qualities may explain why many medieval West African societies preferred copper ingots and rods as currencies. While Arab chroniclers marveled at the high price, in gold, that orpailleurs paid for copper, gold miners appeared eager to rid themselves of a metal controlled by spirits for one that offered protection from occult forces.

The archeologist Susan Keech McIntosh proposes that a "royal ideology," shared between Wagadu's pre-Islamic kings and gold producers, could have provided a ritual incentive for gold miners to sell gold to Wagadu.[29] This royal ideology may express West Africa's medieval ritual geology. Evidence for this theory emerges from Soninke oral traditions that recount the fate of Bida, Wagadu's guardian spirit snake. Bida was one of the twin sons born to Dinga, the purported founder of the Soninke clan who migrated to West Africa from biblical lands. Dinga acquired ritual power by vanquishing the guardian spirits and beasts of the land and waterways he traversed. He married the three daughters of one such spirit. One of Dinga's wives gave birth to male twins: Diabé (a human) and Bida (a spirit snake). Diabé founded Wagadu, guarded by Bida who became the Soninke clan's totem. In some accounts, Bida guarded the gates of Wagadu wound in seven great coils; in others, he haunted a subterranean aquifer. Bida protected the fertility of Wagadu's land and its people by calling forth a rain in gold three times a year. In exchange, Bida demanded a yearly sacrifice of a young woman. Preceding the sacrifice, Bida raised his head three times from his aquifer before seizing the offering and retreating underground. One year, on the heels of a costly war, Bida chose the beautiful Sia Jatta Bari as his sacrifice. Sia's lover resolved to challenge the snake. When Bida emerged from the well, the crowd bade farewell to Sia. The second time Bida emerged, Sia's lover decapitated the snake with his sword. With a second blow, he severed the serpent's tail. Bida hurtled through the air, cursing Wagadu and depriving it of gold and rain. The snake's trisected body rolled southward. Where each section landed, a goldfield emerged. In some versions of the narrative, Bida's entire body created the goldfield of Buré in northeastern Guinea. In other accounts, his trisected corpse nourished three gold-bearing territories: Bambuk, Buré, and Akan. Cursed by killing its totem, Wagadu suffered a drought, and its residents migrated southward.[30]

Scholars have interpreted Bida's death through various registers: as a climatic shift to drier conditions on the Sahel that favored migration toward the savanna; the possible invasion of Wagadu by the (alleged) Berber Muslim Almoravid dynasty around the year 1076; or the emergence of a more reformist Islam among the Sahel's ruling elite.[31] Bida's story can also be read as a template for a shared ritual geology in which rain, gold, and fertility are materialized in the body of spirited snakes who broker among the underground, the earth's surface, and the sky. Bida's golden rain and the movement of his severed corpse bound Wagadu's Soninke residents and dynasts with southern-lying goldfields. Bida's death may have marked the end of a ritual ideology shared by Wagadu's pre-Islamic kings and the gold producers of the savanna. The breach could have been rooted in the conversion of Wagadu's dynasts to Islam in the eleventh century, following a trend among the Sahelian ruling classes.[32] Earlier in the century, the Andalusian geographer Al-Bakrī described the religion of the king of Wagadu as "paganism and the worship of idols." The king presided over sacred groves "where the sorcerers of these people, men in charge of their religious cult, live. In them too are their idols and the tombs of their kings." Was Bida's aquifer concealed in these sacred groves, guarded by the king's soldiers so that "none may enter them and know what is there?"[33] Did this "religious cult" propitiate Bida? If so, the conversion of Wagadu's dynasts to Islam may have severed this sacred tie, pushing Bida and his followers southward toward the savanna.

Bida's spirit continued to haunt the living, traveling through subterranean tunnels and aquifers, appearing at gold-mining sites across the savanna's Birimian rocks. Spirit snakes were also bound to the ritual iconography of iron smelting in medieval West Africa. Iron-smelting technology, widespread in West Africa by 500, was embedded in concerns with fertility and abundance. Smelting kilns were modeled on pregnant women; the iron bloom represented a fetus.[34] Blacksmiths brokered with spirits attached to iron ore and channeled occult power by smelting iron from rocks. Spirit snakes aided in the ritual and technical labor of blacksmiths. Early West African blacksmiths may have doubled as rainmakers, as suggested by some Maninka creation myths.[35] A blacksmith shrine, possibly a ritual device tied to rainmaking, was found at the archeological site of Jenne-Jeno along the Niger River in modern Mali. Dating to roughly 1000, it features a large sandstone basin with a pot lid rimmed in a serpent.[36] Around the same period, oral narratives from Guinea and Mali suggest that Maninka blacksmiths adopted the python as their occult totem.[37] Spirit snakes, revered for connecting the physical and the spirit world, emerge in other accounts of medieval West Africa. Al-Bakrī described the "Zāfqū"—likely a clan of Soninke origin—making offerings of alcohol, milk, and garments at the mouth of a "cave in the desert" that housed a monstrous snake. When one of their rulers died, Al-Bakrī reported, the snake selected his successor by prodding one with his nose.[38] Centuries later, spirit snakes and ritually cunning people harnessing the occult forces of the underground re-emerge in the oral narratives of speakers of Maninka and Pular language varieties. Recall that Taubry Sidibé—the "slave king" of Bélédougou—descended into Mamakono's sole water well until villagers paid a tribute in gold. Taubry's descent parallels that of Bida, who surfaced from his aquifer for an annual sacrifice. Spirit snakes provide a glimpse of the edges of a medieval ritual geology shared by Muslims and non-Muslims alike.

During the early first millennium, the tension between pagan gold producers and Muslim dynasties also emerges as a central tenet of West Africa's medieval ritual geology. Beginning in the eleventh century, many African dynasties on the Sahel converted to Islam. Arabic sources began to draw a distinction between Muslim urban centers in West Africa and non-Muslim gold-producing groups to the south of these polities. Chroniclers described gold producers as animal-like, cannibals, and stateless fish eaters.[39] These characterizations likely expressed an ideological justification for slave raiding by Muslim dynasts who sold pagans in small numbers across the Sahara. In medieval Muslim theology, resistance to Islam was considered grounds for enslavement. Facing pressure to convert to Islam or risk enslavement, some residents of the Sahel may have migrated southward into the mountains of Bambuk, where they could practice ancestral religious traditions. By the thirteenth century, external sources identified Bambuk as a land of pagans and a potential source of slaves for Muslim states and traders. By then, several elements of West Africa's early medieval ritual geology had taken shape: the association of gold with malevolent spirits; an opposition between gold mining and Islam; and the role of spirited snakes in maintaining fertility, goldfields, and iron smelting. These themes reemerged, and took new directions, with the rise of the Malian empire.

Blacksmiths and Muslim Kings, 1200–1500

A century after the demise of Wagadu, the Maninka empire of Mali rose to prominence on the savanna plains of the Upper Niger River. This shifted the locus of power in the trans-Saharan gold trade from the Sahel to the savanna. From the thirteenth to the sixteenth century, Mali expanded its influence into the southern forests of Guinea and Sierra Leone and toward the Atlantic Ocean, establishing vassal states as far west as modern Gambia. Manding language varieties and institutions spread across this broad geography during and after Mali's reign. A growing demand for gold in North Africa and Europe fueled the empire's success. The goldfields of Buré—situated several days' walk from Niani, one of Mali's presumed capitals—was a key source of Mali's gold.[40] Goldfields in Burkina Faso, Niger, Côte d'Ivoire, and Ghana also likely entered production during Mali's reign.

Mali's rise is recounted in the oral epic of Sunjata Keita, the most famous of its genre in West Africa reported by a specialized class of Maninka griots, known as *jeli*.[41] Sunjata was born in the early thirteenth century to an illustrious hunter, Magan Kon Fatta, on the savanna plains of Manden, a landscape of decentralized Maninka polities in the Upper Niger River. Magan's second wife and Sunjata's mother, Sogolon Kejou, was prophesied to bear the next leader of the Keita clan. But Sunjata, Sogolon's only son, was born with a severe disability for which he was ridiculed. After the death of Magan Kon Fatta, Sunjata's half-brother Dankaran Tuman seized the crown. Fearing assassination, Sunjata and Sogolon fled Manden and sought refuge in the Soninke polity of Mema, to the west. While in exile, Sunjata overcame his disability and became a revered hunter and warrior. Residents of Manden called on Sunjata to return home to fulfill his birthright when Dankaran Tuman was overthrown by Sumanguru Kante, the blacksmith king of the Sosso people. Sosso was a successor polity to Wagadu, and Sosso/Susu is a Mande language variety closely related to Soninke. In some versions of the epic, Kante transformed into a monstrous forty-headed snake. In others, he kept a massive snake in an earthenware vessel in his chamber.[42]

Sunjata returned to Manden, recruiting an army along the way, to battle Sumanguru. In the oral epic, Sunjata's power derives from a combination of ancestral religious traditions and Islam. By contrast, Sumanguru is depicted as pagan, his powers channeled through a mystical serpent. With the help of his sister, Sogolon Kolokon, Sunjata severed Sumanguru's ritual power, symbolized by the death of his snake. Sunjata was crowned the "king of kings" (*mansa*) of Manden, which became known to outsiders by the Pular name of Mali. Sunjata's descendants ruled over Mali until its demise. The death of Sumanguru and his serpent marked the end of a political epoch, echoing Bida's death and the dissolution of Wagadu. Sumanguru was one of many blacksmith kings who ruled polities in West Africa prior to Mali's rise.[43] With Sunjata's thirteenth-century victory over Sumanguru, blacksmiths exited political office and became techno-ritual specialists known as *nyamakala*.[44] *Nyama* is a Maninka term that refers to an occult force or energy that "flows through all animate and inanimate things."[45] Nyama is contained by all sentient beings, objects, and landscapes. Nyamakala, the "handle (*kala*) of nyama," specialized in manipulating this force. Blacksmiths (*numu*) are likely the early prototype for nyamakala, which later incorporated leatherworkers (*garanke*) and griots (*jeli*).[46]

The emergence of the occupational category of the nyamakala was part of a trend toward social stratification that crystallized under Mali into a tripartite division among slaves (*jon*); freeborn farmers and nobles (*horon*); and craft specialists (*nyamakala*). Over time, these social categories came to be understood as embodied differences—channeled through saliva, blood, and semen—and inherited through descent. They also acquired a geographic character. By the early first millennium, blacksmiths at Jenne-Jeno had moved their homesteads and kilns to the hinterland of the core settlement. This separation was likely motivated by ritual concerns, as there is no clear material justification for it.[47] By the time of the Malian empire, nyamakala lived and worked at a physical remove from slaves and nobles.[48] The geographic segregation of the dwellings of competing ritual powers is also evidenced in the considerable physical distance between Muslim and non-Muslim neighborhoods in medieval Wagadu, Gao, and Mali.[49]

Respect for complementary ritual powers in medieval West Africa, regulated through spatial segregation, may explain why Muslim rulers left pagan polities to oversee gold mining. A reported exchange from Cairo in 1324 sheds light on this pattern. According to an account by the chronicler Al-Dawādārī, Qadi Fakhr al-Din asked Mansa Mussa—a descendent of Sunjata, then king of Mali—about the "place where gold grows" back in Mali. Mansa Mussa was passing through Cairo en route to Mecca, a voyage that left a mark on medieval maps and North African currency markets as

Mansa Mussa gave gifts of enormous quantities of gold to his hosts along the way.[50] Mussa reported that gold "is not in that part of our land which belongs to the Muslims, but in the land which belongs to the Christians [pagans] of Takrūr."[51] The qadi asked Mussa why he did not take this land by force, to which Mussa replied: "If we conquer them and take it, it does not put forth anything. We have done this in many ways but seen nothing there; but when it returns to them it puts forth as usual."[52] Nearly a decade later, Al-'Umarī offered another version of this exchange that speaks to the relationship of gold to different ritual authorities: "If the sultan wished he could extend his authority over them [gold producers] but the kings of this kingdom have learnt by experience that as soon as one of them conquers one of the gold towns and Islam spreads and the muezzin calls to prayer there the gold there begins to decrease and then disappears, while it increases in the neighboring heathen countries."[53] Al-Dawādārī's and Al-'Umarī's accounts both suggest that Mali's kings shared at least one belief with gold miners: Muslim overrule made gold disappear. Gold preferred pagans.

The goldfields in these accounts likely refer to those of Buré (map 2.3). Similar to Bambuk, Buré was a non-centralized and multiethnic political landscape, dominated by speakers of Maninka and Jallonke, a Mande language variety related to Susu and Soninke. Residents of Buré paid tribute to the mansa of Mali, but they enjoyed political and religious autonomy from Mali—similar to the structural relationship of Bambuk to Wagadu.[54]

By the time of Mansa Mussa's reign, there was a clear divergence in the metal value system of West African dynasts, on one hand, and gold producers, on the other. The former embraced gold as a sign of prestige, wealth, and power, whereas the latter continued to privilege copper and copper alloys. This divergence is on display by the eleventh century, when Al-Bakrī described the king of Wagadu wearing gold necklaces "round his neck and [bracelets] on his forearms, and he puts on a high cap decorated with gold and wrapped in a turban of fine cotton." The king held audience in a "domed pavilion around which stand ten horses covered in gold-embroidered materials" while pages held shields and swords decorated in gold. Dogs, guarding the doors, wore gold and silver collars studded with "balls of the same metals."[55] Centuries later, Ibn Battūta described the gold regalia donned by the mansa of Mali, his elite military cavalry, and royal dogs.[56] Al-Bakrī also observed elite women wearing small rings twisted into a torque-like shape along each ear, in the nose, and as a forehead ornament.[57] By contrast, there is no evidence for a tradition of gold regalia or jewelry among non-Muslim populations of the savanna, where gold was mined, until the Atlantic period.

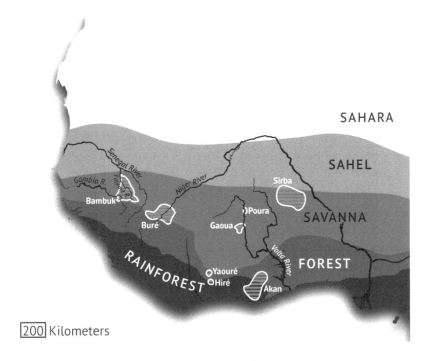

Map 2.3 Bioclimatic zones and historical goldfields in West Africa.

It was not until the twentieth century that a goldsmithing trade, separate from blacksmithing, emerged on the savanna. By contrast, in the forests of modern Ghana, where gold was first mined centuries later than on the savanna, goldsmithing was a specialized craft by the seventeenth century, and there was a rich aesthetic tradition of jewelry and artistic objects crafted from gold.[58]

Did gold producers abstain from wearing gold because of its ties to the occult? We can only speculate. But intriguing new archeological evidence suggests that although Muslim rulers—and populations on the Sahel more oriented to the Muslim north—wore gold, they rarely chose gold to accompany them in death. Excavations of tumuli dating from the eighth to the fifteenth century in contemporary Senegal and Mali have unearthed only a scattering of gold objects—the odd pendant, ring, earring, bead, or ingot fragments—embedded in much larger caches of ornaments in copper, stone, and silver (which is not native to West Africa).[59] An excavation at Koï Gourrey, Mali, dating to the eleventh or twelfth century, revealed that a man was buried with bronze animal figurines, objects alloyed with high levels of zinc to mimic the patina of gold. Gold was ubiquitous at the time of the burial, so the choice of copper was not strictly economic. Rather, the brass figurines signal the metal system of the Muslim north while suggesting a reluctance to bury the dead with gold.[60] In a burial at Kael, Senegal, dated to the twelfth or thirteenth century, a man in his forties was interred with a bracelet composed of two bands—one of silver, and the other of a gold alloy fabricated with gold that did not originate from a West African source. The bracelets evidence a previously undocumented southward traffic of gold into the Sahel while reinforcing a possible ritual avoidance of burying the dead with gold mined in West Africa.[61] When paired with evidence from other burials, the bracelets point to a possible ritual avoidance of incorporating pure gold mined in West Africa in burials. This is a suggestive prong of a ritual geology shared by Sahelian elites and gold producers on the savanna. While gold generated considerable wealth for some West African merchants and kings, they shared a concern with gold producers about gold's ritual dangers.

The realm of Mali's influence expanded in the thirteenth and fourteenth centuries as its Muslim trading diaspora, the juula, opened new routes for trade in gold and kola nuts as far east as Worodugu, in Côte d'Ivoire, and Hausaland, in northern Nigeria. Village settlement narratives from modern Burkina Faso suggest that speakers of Manding language varieties, potentially juula traders themselves, introduced mining to the goldfields of Poura and Lobi.[62] As juula spread into new ethnolinguistic landscapes, many took on the languages and ethnonyms of their hosts. They became the Maninka Mori of Kankan, the Marka of Niger, the Dyula of Côte d'Ivoire, and the Jakhanke of the Senegal River Valley. Under Mali's rule, juula reached the goldfields of the Akan forest, establishing trading centers at Bono-Mansu, Wa, and Wala of modern Ghana that were linked to Sahara-bound trading routes.[63] Juula traders, mobile gold miners, or Manding-speaking blacksmiths in search of fresh iron deposits may have introduced gold mining to Côte d'Ivoire and Ghana as they encountered Birimian rocks that reminded them of gold-bearing landscapes back home.[64]

In the fifteenth century, Tuareg and Pular raids along the Niger River, and the rising power of Songhay to the east, fissured Mali's dominance. But the cultural legacy of the Malian empire was only beginning to take root across the territories of its former influence. In the centuries to follow, Manding-speaking polities consolidated in modern Gambia, Senegal, and Guinea-Bissau. Origin narratives for the kingdoms of Niumi, Wuli, and Gabu report that their settler-founders migrated from Manden during the time of Sunjata and his generals, conquering local populations through violence. Though migration from Manden cannot be ruled out, these stories may also be allegories of a far more gradual transfer of Maninka language and political institutions into multiethnic spaces over centuries.[65] The spread of *komo*, a male power association of the Manding-speaking world, occurred in tandem with growing Maninka influence to the west and south. Blacksmiths led komo societies, which adopted the python as their totem, a key sacral element of West Africa's medieval ritual geology. Komo became known as komorang, jankaran, and kankarang as it adapted to local conditions in Guinea, Guinea-Bissau, Gambia, and Senegal.[66]

The settlement narratives of speakers of western Manding language varieties are also replete with references to another mystical snake: Nininkala (Nikinanka, Ningi-nina, Ningiri), the female guardian serpent of ethnic Maninka. Echoing the ancient movements of Bida, Nininkala dwells underground and in waterways. She presides over water, rainbows, springs, waterfalls, earthquakes, and two metals: iron and gold. Nininkala ate iron and secreted gold in her wake or produced gold from shedding her scales and skin. In the Casamance, Nininkala's head was covered in gold. In Guinea, she took the form of a lamb with golden fleece. Maninka migrants encountered Nininkala when they crossed the Gambia or the Senegal River. Blacksmiths made offerings to Nininkala before mining iron ore.[67] Nininkala was also central to the origin stories of Pular-speakers, having been sent to earth by an omniscient god under the name of Tyanaba, the serpent guardian of cattle, the historic wealth and livelihood of Pular pastoralists. Tyanaba emerged from the Atlantic Ocean accompanied by twenty-two cows that were confided to a young man named Gueno. The cattle traversed the savanna plains to the east until they reached the source of the Niger River. There Tyanaba changed his name to Nikinanka and guided the mythic fourteenth-century migration of Pular herders and farmers from Fouta Toro to the Fouta Djallon by the warrior Kolli Tenguela.[68] Well into the twentieth century, some Pular-speakers in the Fouta Djallon of Guinea took part in a cult called Ningiri dedicated to this spirit snake.[69]

Stories of Nininkala may have merged with or reinforced those of Bida. Both spirits dwelled underground, their bodies performing alchemy: the conversion of iron into gold and tears into springs. Bida's corpse fertilized new goldfields on the savanna, while Nininkala's excrement created gold veins. Both Bida and Nininkala guided migrants across foreign landscapes, discouraging settlement in territories haunted by malevolent spirits. Rumors of Bida's spirit moving along a north–south-trending paleo-channel along the Middle Niger—known as the "Vallée du Serpent" in Mali—may have warned people against settling in this corridor. In recent memory, as reported by the archaeologist Roderick McIntosh, the Vallée du Serpent is understood as "the manifestation of a subterranean pathway taken by the great snake, Bida, on his transverse from Wagadu southwards toward the Niger River."[70]

Spirit snakes offered humans metals and rain in exchange for the sacrifice of loved ones. These exchanges cemented the claims of people to natural resources. Oral traditions from the polity of Gabu relate that the power of its ruling dynasty was based on making a human sacrifice to Nininkala.[71] Though separated by centuries from the time of Wagadu, this story resonates with the yearly sacrifice given by the Soninke people to Bida, their guardian snake. Across the Gambia, Senegal, and Niger river valleys, human-spirit pacts, forged in violence and demanding constant renewal, generated the claims of empires to political power and of lineages to land, gold, iron, and water. Stories of the underground movements of Bida and Nininkala bound gold-bearing Birimian rocks across the savanna into a unified ritual geology.

The Devil's Workshop: Europeans in Search of Bambuk, 1500–1880

In the 1440s, the Portuguese monarch financed ships to navigate around the West African coast in search of the fabled goldfields of Bambuk. By then, Mediterranean city-states had minted coins with gold mined in West Africa for centuries. But Saharan traders mediated access to the West African gold dust trade. Portugal sought to bypass North African middlemen by creating a seabound trading relationship with West African traders and miners of gold. Portuguese mariners were searching for a direct corridor to Bambuk when they entered the mouth of the Senegal River in 1446. While no records remain of this voyage, the Portuguese left a rich documentary trail of their interactions farther south.[72] Along the Gambia River, the Portuguese encountered "Mandingo" traders, who traveled under the orders of the mansa of Mali. Farther south, along the coast of modern Ghana, Portuguese sailors established trading partnerships for gold with Akan chiefs and traders dressed in gold regalia. By 1482, the Portuguese had completed the fort of Elmina, "the mine," named after the large amounts of gold mined by Akan-speaking groups in the forested interior. In a few short decades, however, the Iberian encounter with the vast gold and silver working traditions of the Americas, and the opening of new mines in South America, reduced demand for West African gold. Over the next two centuries, the sugar plantation economy of the Caribbean and Brazil created an insatiable demand for a new trade—one in war captives—from the West African coast. The Elmina fort, and dozens of others constructed along the Atlantic, became portals for the trade in slaves.

As Afro-Portuguese trade thickened on the coast, juula traders in Senegambia began to redirect their caravans from the Sahara toward European riverine trading ports and the Atlantic coast.[73] By the mid-seventeenth century, British, French, Danish, and Dutch merchants were competing with the Portuguese for control over West African coastal markets. By 1700, the British Royal African Company had established a stronghold on the Gambia River, while the French Compagnie des Indes (later the Compagnie du Sénégal) monopolized trade along the Senegal River. For the next two hundred years, the primary preoccupation of the rival trade networks of the British and the French in Senegambia was the commerce in African captives, which they encouraged through the sale of firearms. But Europeans never stopped speculating about the riches they could derive from controlling either the gold trade, firmly in the hands of the juula, or mining itself.[74] Throughout the 1700s, trading companies attempted to bypass juula by creating direct trading relationships with gold producers. The French built forts along the Senegal River's upper reaches to divert the trade in gold dust to their ships. Juula traders and religious leaders from the Soninke state of Gaajaga thwarted these efforts by attacking forts and seeding rumors that people at the headwaters of the Gambia and Senegal were "ferocious and savage."[75]

The trickle of European travelers who reached Bambuk described it as a former Maninka "kingdom" fractured by war, where the lingua franca was a variety or creole of Maninka (Malinké in French travelogues; Mandingo in English accounts). In fact, Maninka cultural dominance likely emerged in the Atlantic period, when Bambuk became a refuge for those fleeing enslavement by mercenaries and Muslim polities. Immigrants integrated into Maninka lineages through marriage or by changing their patronyms. Even today, many ethnic Maninka in southeastern Senegal claim their ancestors migrated from the Malian empire. But settlement narratives suggest a far more recent history of blended, multiethnic societies, drawn from a mixed heritage of speakers of Mande (Jallonke, Soninke, and Maninka), Pular, and Tenda (Beliyan-Bassari and Bedik) language varieties. These groups may have adopted Maninka institutions as a form of cultural authentication.[76]

By the eighteenth century, Bambuk was surrounded on three sides by Pular Muslim states: Fouta Djallon to the south, Bundu to the north, and Khasso to the east. These states grew from their involvement in markets tied to the transatlantic slave trade. Fouta Djallon and Bundu waged jihad against practitioners of ancestral religious traditions who refused conversion to Islam. These states sold war captives to juula intermediaries and kept enslaved people as domestic servants and agricultural laborers. Bundu and Fouta Djallon occupied rich agricultural and pasturage land. By contrast, Bambuk's igneous volcanic formations contained only narrow corridors of arable land. In this inhospitable terrain, people of diverse backgrounds created an inland maroon society.[77] As a French explorer remarked in 1818, Bambuk's "elevation proves a defense to the country, constantly exposed to the invasions of the Poulas of Bondou and the Bambaras."[78]

While Bambuk was geographically isolated compared with neighboring states, it was deeply entangled in regional commercial networks through the gold trade. Mining alluvial gold enabled its residents to access salt, cloth, and other imports. In 1846, Anne Raffenel, a French explorer, described women panning for gold dust along the Falémé:

> This is how they do it: the products of the mine, made up of large fragments of shale, pebbles and sandy soil, are placed in a calabash full of water and kneaded by hand until they are crushed; the pebbles, a large part of the sandy earth and very large fragments of shale are thrown away after this first operation.... The calabash contains only a muddy sand which, subjected to repetitive washes, ends up producing a very fine black sand, in which is found gold, in the form of molecules and flakes, sometimes very fine.[79]

Only men dug for gold underground. They dug circular mining shafts with iron picks that doubled as farming tools. Most mining was focused on alluvial deposits, known as nara.

Long-distance Manding-speaking traders—the juula—visited dispersed goldfields to purchase gold dust or thin gold wire smelted by blacksmiths. Juula organized caravans of donkeys and human porters who traveled through Bambuk to trade for gold, ivory, beeswax, animal skins, and shea butter. Residents of Bambuk exchanged these products for strips of cotton cloth, copper bars, salt, rifles, and gun powder.[80] Some gold-producing communities in Bambuk organized their own overland caravans, bound for British forts on the Gambia, where they traded gold for alcohol, cloth, and salt. But much of the gold trade from Bambuk was organized by overland juula caravans that traveled through Muslim Jakhanke villages along the Gambia River. Jakhanke, an ethnic group who trace their ancestry to the Soninke, were followers of the pacifist teachings of Al-Hajj Salim Suwari, a thirteenth-century Islamic scholar. By renouncing involvement in political affairs, the Jakhanke lived and traded peaceably with non-Muslim neighbors while presiding over autonomous Muslim villages of their own.[81]

The boundaries of political belonging were narrow in Atlantic-era Bambuk. The authority of chiefs rarely extended beyond a single settlement of several hundred souls. Villages occasionally federated for defensive purposes. But they also raided one another for war captives, a symptom of the growing violence and militarization of life in the region. Young men with rifles guarded villages encircled by *tatas*, stone walls built for defense.[82] Armed warriors and hunters accompanied men and women to distant agricultural fields and mining sites, where they were vulnerable to roaming mercenaries seeking captives. In 1729, a French traveler remarked that most villages were populated by women and children. Men had departed for warfare or long-distance caravan trade or had been captured for the slave trade.[83] "Bamboukains" earned a reputation as "ferocious and mean," known to "kill travelers and pillage their merchandise under the slightest pretext."[84] Gold miners chased away European travelers and often refused their requests to take samples of gold-bearing soils.[85] The suspicion of African miners toward outsiders was so well established that the Scottish explorer Mungo Park feigned a lack of interest in the "riches of their country" to earn trust from local chiefs.[86]

European explorers commented on the lack of Muslims in Bambuk and glossed the region's diverse residents as pagans or fetishists (*fétichistes*), as did earlier generations of Arab chroniclers.[87] These terms elided the heterogeneity of ancestral religious traditions, and the emergence of new ritual forms, practiced in the region. Most non-Muslim Maninka residents of Bambuk believed in a world presided over by a Supreme Being who confided elements of the natural world to spirits. Malevolent demons, witches, and ancestors also haunted the world of the living. Bambuk's ritual landscape was shaped by the presence of lineage shrines (*jalan*) erected by the founders of villages to consecrate their relationship with territorial spirits, who brokered access to the natural world for humans. The foundation narratives of villages in Bambuk align with a template for establishing land claims found across West Africa. The village founder-settler, a distant ancestor, stumbles upon land propitious for hunting, iron mining, or cultivation. Many oral traditions present landscapes as uninhabited with the exception of spirits, the real autochthons of the land.[88] Village founders ask the permission of spirits to settle the land. In many accounts, the founder-settler offers a sacrifice, often a child, to the spirit. By accepting the sacrifice, the spirit accords the right to the founder-settler to hunt, mine, and farm in the spirit's territory.

The founder-settler consecrates this pact by erecting a jalan to the patron spirit.[89] His male descendants claimed autochthony, or first-comer status, and occupy the office of dugutigi, charged with allocating land to newcomers and hosting strangers.[90]

The territory of the first-comer group was configured as a field of power that radiated outward from the jalan. Over time, clearing land for farming extended the boundaries of the traditional territory of the village.[91] Descendants of the founder-settler lineage slaughtered animals at the jalan to renew the human-spirit pact the shrine consecrated.[92] The jalan presided over the fertility of the land and productive activities that marked the alteration of the savanna's distinct seasons. During the annual rains, life was bound closely to the village. Women tended plots of tobacco, okra, and tubers near their cooking huts. Men cultivated millet, sorghum, and fonio at fields within walking distance of the village. Harvest ceremonies opened the dry season—a time of mobility and adventure, when boys and girls underwent puberty rites; hunters tracked elephants for the caravan trade; and women collected shea butter nuts and medicinal plants.[93]

Excavating gold from nearby riverways and alluvial placers was also a dry season activity. Gold-bearing lands were ritually charged landscapes, haunted by two categories of spirits: those bound to the territory and spirited snakes who traveled across space. Oral narratives gloss both categories of spirits by the term *jinne*.[94] Dwarf-like goblins, *goto* in Maninka, also haunted gold deposits, mountains, and caves. The proliferation of spirits on Bambuk's goldfields may explain why Maninka lineages retained a special politico-ritual office to manage relations with these spirit forces: the juurakuntigi (master of the mines).[95] *Juura*, the Maninka term for a gold mine, referred to any expanse of land, a hill, or a riverbank that contained gold.[96] The geography of a juura aligned with the territory of a resident spirit. Each juura had a primary patron spirit, though other classes of spirits traveled through it. The juurakuntigi ritually opened the juura to the broader community. They were aided in their ritual functions by young men who prospected for fresh gold deposits on behalf of their lineage or village. Washing in ablutions of leaves that pleased spirits, these men searched the savanna landscape for signs of gold. Some tree species coincided with paleo-channels lined with ancient alluvial gold deposits.[97] Men learned from their fathers how to taste and smell soils for the presence of iron, pyrite, and gold. Prospectors sampled termite mounds for traces of gold dust. Because termites burrow hundreds of meters underground in search of water and carry soils to the surface through their digestive tracts, termite mounds generated a cross-section of the composition of underlying soils.[98] When they discovered a new goldfield, the juurakuntigi slaughtered a chicken, goat, or lamb on the goldfield in the name of the patron spirit of the underlying geobody. The animal carcass was buried up to its neck underground. Spirits signaled their acceptance of the sacrifice by retracting the carcass into the earth. If the carcass remained at dawn, the spirits rejected the sacrifice and refused to release gold.[99]

Once a juurakuntigi opened a gold deposit, anyone could putatively mine the juura as long as they submitted to the ritual authority of the juurakuntigi and respected a set of ritual prohibitions or taboos (*tanas*). The key exception was a prohibition against leatherworkers (*garanke*) entering the goldfield (see chapter 1). By the late nineteenth century on some of the large goldfields in Bambuk, a group of young men known as the tomboluma—a portmanteau of the Maninka terms for "prohibition" (*tom*) and "handle on" (*boluma*)—enforced the juura's tanas.[100] The origins of the tombulama are unclear, but the institution may date to the Atlantic era. In oral histories, the term *tomboluma* was used interchangeably for hunters or warriors who accompanied miners to seasonal juuras for protection.[101] Generations of sacrifices performed on mineralized land transformed the juura into a shrine, a jalan, dedicated to its spirited owners. The juurakuntigi also made offerings to Bida and Nininkala—the spirit snakes (*jinn saa*) that haunted the goldfields and paleo-channels of the savanna and the Sahel in medieval West Africa.

The accounts of European travelers to Bambuk are saturated with references to the occult power of gold and animal sacrifices. Europeans likely learned about ritual practices on the goldfields from their African guides, porters, and translators. Atlantic-era travelogues filtered accounts of blood sacrifice through Christian frameworks, but they captured the edges of the ritual geology, one built on the precedents of earlier centuries but taking on new features with the violence of the Atlantic era. French accounts, for example, are peppered with stories of a Maninka "belief" that the devil was the "true master of the mines."[102] In 1729, Claude Boucard, an officer of the Compagnie des Indes, described the "common opinion" that "he who discovers a mine invariably dies if there is not within eight days a black cow burned for the gold that they say is a sorcerer."[103] Jean-Baptiste Durand, a director of the Compagnie du Sénégal, wrote that Maninka miners were "certain that gold is a malignant being who delights in tormenting those who loved it, and for this reason it often changes place."[104] Europeans were particularly vexed by mines that were "no longer worked because of a superstition of the country."[105] Such reports suggest spirits making sacrificial demands—likely of humans—that miners were unable or un-willing to meet (see chapters 4 and 7).

Many chroniclers interpreted the "beliefs" of Bambuk's gold miners as a shield for their ignorance of "the art of excavating mines."[106] As early as the 1680s, European travelers argued that massive profits could be drawn from Bambuk's soils by replacing the "wasteful" techniques of Africans with ladders, pumps, and machines.[107] But due to ongoing warfare in the Senegal River Valley, it was not until the 1850s that the French tested the long-circulating theory that Europeans could transform Bambuk into the "Californie d'Afrique." At the time, the coastal colony of Senegal was under the governorship of General Louis Faidherbe, who had fought a series of battles against Al-Hajj Umar Taal. The descendant of a Pular Muslim clerical family from Fouta Toro, Taal led a massive Muslim reform move-ment in the Senegal River Valley that critiqued the African Muslim clerisy that was aligned with the French. Like many Muslim leaders before him, Taal raided Bambuk's non-Muslim population for war captives under the banner of jihad.[108]

In 1857, the French narrowly defeated Taal at a battle at the French fort of Médine. Taal ceded the Senegal River to France. To signify his victory over Taal and to prove the region's potential to generate wealth for France, Faidherbe initiated a mining project in the village of Kéniéba of modern Mali.[109] Gold production was low, however, and the mine was closed in 1860. Faidherbe attributed the project's failure to a lack of capital and appropriate machinery. But mystical theories also circulated. Africans abandoned the mining site because they were "horrified by the pits."[110] Were they terrified because the French did not make adequate sacrifices to territorial jinne and Nininkala? The death rate alone was cause for terror. Roughly eighty African workers were ill at any given time, and dozens died. Three French technicians died within weeks of their arrival. Yellow fever and malaria took its toll, but there are suggestive parallels with oral traditions of the angered spirit of Nininkala who seized miners for making inadequate sacrifices. The lead French engineer of the mine expressed fears of a breach with the occult when, bedridden for five months, he wrote to Faidherbe that the Kéniéba mine was "cursed."[111]

European travelogues presented two hermetically sealed and diamet-rically opposed worlds of mining: one French, one West African. In fact, mining in Atlantic-age Bambuk was the shared product of an evolving Afro-Atlantic encounter that shaped the Upper Senegal Valley for roughly four hundred years prior to colonial rule. Mining techniques and notions about geology were exchanged at this interface, as were ideas about gold and spirits. Bambuk's spirits had much in common with those haunting underground mines in France. For example, seventeenth-century residents of France's Midi region reported that "evil spirits sought to prevent men from entering the mines" in the Pyrenees. The inhabitants of Couzeran recounted "terrible and awful noises and the lightning and thunder that befell anyone who tried to open mines in the mountains of Poueg and Gouas." In Alsace-Lorraine, a goblin-like gnome, the petit mineur, played tricks on miners by extinguishing lamps.[112] Despite obvious parallels between the petit mineur of Alsace-Lorraine and the jinne of Bambuk, French travelers to Atlantic-era Bambuk framed the "beliefs" of West African miners as an exotic and primitive foil, distant in time and space from their own.

European accounts of Bambuk became a privileged ground for the emergent European conviction that Africans were technologically backward and mired in "superstitions," frozen in an earlier epoch of human history long surpassed by Europeans.[113] Reports from Bambuk merged with efforts by eighteenth-century French and British naturalists to expunge the demons, angels, and gods long associated with mining in Europe from the new "scientific" discipline of geology.[114] As European naturalists worked to distance themselves from geology's origins in biblical creationism and Christian demonology, they located the presence of spirited mines overseas. These two processes were related and part of a much broader constellation of discursive and legal contrasts that Europeans invented in the Atlantic age to emphasize their distinctiveness from Africans, which became a justification for the transatlantic slave trade and later colonialism.

The multiethnic landscape of Bambuk created new conditions for ritual practices that Europeans interpreted as time immemorial and static. A key prong of the ritual geology described in this book—the notion of gold as the property of spirits—likely solidified in the Atlantic era, a time when new notions of territory and people circulated across the Atlantic world.[115] That "spirits own gold" (*sano ye jinne le ti*; *ko jinne jey kanye* in Pular) is a ubiquitous phrase in twentieth- and twenty-first-century Bambuk. The Maninka and Pular verbs in this phrase are the same as those used to describe the historical "ownership" of slaves by masters in these languages. The lexicon of property is also evident in accounts of French explorers who described spirits jealous of a "metal that is his property" or "the devil, who is the master of the gold mines."[116] Spirits may have become owners of gold as notions of people as commodities that could be exchanged against metals solidified along the West African coast in the seventeeth and eighteenth centuries.

WEST AFRICA'S RITUAL GEOLOGY **81**

Sylvain de Golbéry, a French geographer who traveled to West Africa in the 1780s, spoke to the metonymy between people and metals in a rumor of the fate of miners buried underground. Golbéry reported that cave-ins in Bambuk's mines were created by "the devil," who "occasions these accidents in order to procure slaves for himself":

> The Bamboukains suppose that the devil fabricates gold at an immense depth in subterraneous caverns; that he causes this rich metal to be worked by slaves; that the number of these slaves employed in this manufactory is very great; that a certain quantity of them perish every year; and that the falling in of the pits is only a trick of the devil's, who wants to get some new slaves to replace those he has lost. Impressed with this opinion, they are afraid to help the unhappy sufferers, they would displease the devil if they were to try to save them, and thus deprive him of his slaves, besides running the risk that his highness would carry the gold out of the country, and establish his workshop in some other place.[117]

Golbéry couches this stunning account of the "devil's workshop" in a broader exegesis about the technical incompetence of "simple and mindless" African miners who think fallen pits are the "work of the devil" rather than "the effect of their own stupidity."[118] If Golbéry assumed metropolitan readers would interpret this as an account of fantastical African beliefs, the devil's underground traffic in African slaves was an all-too-realistic interpretation of current events. Golbéry's travelogue was written in 1802, many years prior to the criminalization of the slave trade. At the time, thousands of Senegambian war captives were sold off the Atlantic seaboard to Caribbean Islands, Brazil, and the United States. Golbéry wrote about a subterranean "slave trade" in Bambuk that "takes more than 10 to 12 men a year in the most productive mines." At the time, mercenaries took hundreds of men and women from Bambuk in raids each year, targeting isolated mining sites. Logged and marched in caravans bound for the coast, they were sold as domestic slaves to wealthy African merchants or shipped across the Atlantic.

In 1855, more than a half-century after Golbéry penned his account, two French agents wrote about the fate that befell a miner "surprised by a landslide that filled his pit." The land would be set aside for the family of the deceased, who would wait seven years before unearthing the cadaver. At this time, the "pores of the bones will be filled with gold flakes."[119] The disturbing conflation between the bones of miners and gold, between an unspeakable tragedy and extraordinary gains, reemerges in oral narratives, colonial-era reports, and present-day rumors on the goldfields of Bambuk. It recalls the alchemy performed by Nininkala, who consumes iron and excretes gold, or the transformation of Bida's slayed body into the goldfields of Bambuk and Buré. But while this account echoes medieval concepts of metal and ritual conversions, it also points to inventions of the Atlantic-era, such as the practice of paying for war captives with mineral currencies: gold flakes, iron bars, copper rods, or so many cut slabs of rock salt. The fate of a young man buried alive in Bambuk, his bones turned to gold, is not distant from the very real possibility that the same person could have been sold for iron bars on the Gambia River. Far from fantastical African "beliefs," these narratives reveal how the ritual world of Bambuk was shaped by Euro-African trade relationships based on converting people into metals.

Mining Gold in the Realm of the "Slave King"

We do not know when Taubry Sidibé reigned as the slave king of Bélédougou, the small gold-producing province in western Bambuk. Taubry likely lived in the eighteenth century, as his name does not appear in the accounts of nineteenth-century travelers to Bélédougou. In 1881, Ernest Noirot, a French artist traveling with the lieutenant-governor of Senegal, wrote about his passage through Mamakono, a "Malinké" village surrounded by bamboo forests with a "king" named Kié-Kié-Mahadi. Kié-Kié-Mahadi's patronym was Cissokho, indicating that the transition from Soninke to Maninka rule in Mamakono was already underway. Like other French travelers of his day, Noirot described a landscape devastated by slave raiding and displacement.[120] For decades, mercenaries from the Pular Muslim states of Fouta Djallon and Bundu, and the Maninka state of Konkodougou to the east, had pillaged small provinces to the west of the Falémé River for war captives. Militias from the small provinces of Bélédougou, Sirimana, and Niokolo partook in this economy of violence, raiding neighboring polities for captives. Noirot estimated that of Mamakono's roughly five hundred residents, as many as three hundred were captives. Slave labor contributed to Mamakono's relative prosperity. It boasted dense fields of sorghum, millet, cotton, and tobacco. Women mined gold from placers on the Falémé's tributaries. After the November harvest, men from the village sacrificed a "red goat and a white hen. They eat half and throw the other half here and there so that the devil will not bother the workers."[121] Following a drumming ceremony, as Noirot casually mentioned, Kié-Kié-Mahadi signed a treaty "permitting the French to settle in Bélédougou and to exploit gold there."[122]

By the 1880s, despite the tepid results of earlier mining ventures in Bambuk, there was renewed optimism in French circles for the prospect of turning a profit from Bambuk's gold. Across much of Africa, Victorian rumors of hidden mines and unexplored "El Dorados" proved illusory. But competition for access to natural resources, real and imagined, shaped growing European ambitions to control land, and not just riverine trade, in West Africa. In the decades to follow, the French army led conquest campaigns in the Senegal and Niger river valleys. They faced their staunchest opponent in Samori Touré, a Maninka empire builder with a base in the Guinean highlands. In the 1870s, Touré controlled territories along the Niger River, including the goldfields of Buré. Touré requisitioned gold dust to purchase rice, millet, and rifles for his army from British posts in Sierra Leone. In 1884, the French captured Bamako, prohibiting Touré's movement northward, and in 1892, the French pushed Touré out of Buré—claiming this goldfield for imperial France.

Meanwhile, the French were gaining a foothold in the Fouta Djallon from the south. In 1893, desperately clinging to power, Alpha Yaya, the prince of the Fouta's northern province, expanded his power to the north. His soldiers pillaged Bélédougou, Sirimana, Dantila, and Niokolo for captives and tribute in what is today southeastern Senegal. In 1894, representatives of these provinces appealed to the French for assistance against attacks. The French agreed to protect these small states (*petits états*), which they saw as a bulwark against large Muslim states with standing armies, in exchange for their allegiance to France.[123] It was at this time that the French began referring to the small polities stretching west of the Falémé as Haute-Gambie (Upper Gambia). In 1886 and 1887, the French army invaded this region in pursuit of Mamadou Lamine Dramé, a Jakhanke Muslim reformer calling for Islamic renewal. The French killed Lamine in 1887, an event commonly interpreted as the end of French conquest in the Senegal Valley.[124] During the same mission, officials of the French army signed treaties with the chiefs of Niokolo, which included the future base for French officials in the region: the town of Kédougou.

By the close of the nineteenth century, the French army had claimed a West African landmass nine times the size of metropolitan France—a large corner of the European "scramble" for Africa that accelerated across the continent in the 1880s and 1890s. The petits états to the west of the Falémé were first administered from the post of Satadougou in French Soudan. In 1907, the French constituted the circle of Upper Gambia, with a French commander resident at Kédougou, and made the provinces of Niokolo,

84 CHAPTER TWO

Dantila, Sirimana, Bafé-Satadougou, Bélédougou, Badon, and Tenda into cantons with French-appointed African canton chiefs. Colonial rule was most keenly felt by the imposition of a yearly head tax collected by African canton chiefs. Residents of gold-producing provinces in eastern Senegal and western Mali—historical Bambuk—turned to regional goldfields to meet these tributary demands. In an unknown year early in the new century, swarms of locusts decimated the millet and sorghum crop. As famine loomed, men and women from across southeastern Senegal packed bundles of clothing and tools and walked to Tinkoto, situated in the borderlands of Bélédougou and Niokolo. Tinkoto was then a dry season gold-mining site, a juura. Its patron spirit, childless and angered, demanded the sacrifice of a dozen young men to release gold to human hands. Makhan Keita, an elderly man from Kanoumering, a village neighboring Tinkoto, recounted: "Some years, she asked for a man or a woman. But that year, she demanded the sacrifice of twelve young men. And so, we dug twelve mining shafts in a line, and we buried our children up to their necks in soil. We told the jinne: 'Look this is your share. In taking this sacrifice, may you liberate our share.' When they returned the next day all of the bodies had disappeared into the earth. Gold was abundant. No one was hungry that year."[125]

This stunning tale of human sacrifice is likely apocryphal, a metonym for the loss of young life to famine, violence, and slave raiding. But the account also articulates with a regional idiom of exchange between humans and the otherworldly owners of minerals. It recalls the annual sacrifice made by Wagadu's residents to Bida to secure water and gold. It is a blueprint for dozens of human-spirit pacts forged by confiding a beloved child to the spirit world. These stories speak to the very high price West African societies situated along the Birimian rocks of the savanna paid to gain access to gold. The ritual geology elaborated by generations of West African miners, traders, kings, and blacksmiths reframes French colonial conquest of Bambuk in the late nineteenth century as a question not only of the economic value of land but also of the ongoing presence of subterranean spirits.

3
Making Customary Mining in French West Africa

"Siguiri has become absolutely worldly within the decade," remarked a French mining engineer in 1934. He was returning to Dakar from the placer mines of French Guinea.[1] It was the height of the global Depression, and Siguiri was the epicenter of the largest indigenous gold-mining boom in colonial Africa. With the onset of the financial crisis in the late 1920s, prices for peanuts, palm oil, and cotton plummeted across the colonial federation of French West Africa (Afrique-Occidentale Française [AOF]). Gold dust was one of the few commodities with stable market prices at French merchant houses. To meet colonial head tax demands, thousands of residents of the historical gold-producing territories of Bambuk and Buré—now divided among the French colonies of Senegal, Soudan, and Guinea—mined gold in kin-based groups with locally forged iron tools. Between the two world wars, West African households produced no less than twenty tons of gold, constituting more than 90 percent of the AOF's mineral exports.[2] French officials called the diverse activities associated with West African gold mining *orpaillage indigène*. During the colonial period, orpaillage in the AOF was concentrated in placer mines, secondary gold deposits created by ancient drainage systems covered by meters of laterite rock. The most popular placers attracted migrants from across Senegal, Soudan, Mali, and British-controlled Sierra Leone. During the dry season, villages in historical Buré and Bambuk mushroomed into cosmopolitan seasonal cities that attracted the young, the poor, and the marginal. On multiethnic goldfields, descendants of former slave lineages earned bridewealth and remade their lives beyond the bounds of their natal villages.

The fluorescence of orpaillage in the colonial AOF reveals a set of forces that were apparent everywhere on the African continent during colonialism but that historians of Africa are only beginning to uncover: the role of long-standing African expertise and technological practice in the expansion of colonial mining economies. Until the 1950s, orpaillage was the AOF's largest mining industry (map 3.1). It thus challenges the dominant narrative of colonial mining as the displacement of indigenous mining economies, the primitive accumulation of land, and the transformation of Africans into a proletariat locked into migratory labor cycles.[3] This narrative emerges from South Africa and other colonies with large white settler populations, where mining by Africans was criminalized outright. In West Africa, where white settlers were few, the alienation of land was rare.[4] Rather, through the imposition of head taxes and forced labor requirements, colonial officials forced Africans to "self-exploit" the labor of their own kin and regional migrants to cultivate and collect cash crops and forest products for metropolitan industries.[5] In West Africa, the French profited from orpaillage as an economic enterprise (the subject of this chapter)—and as a source of gold discoveries for future mining enterprises (chapter 4).

Orpaillage suited the neo-mercantile economy of the AOF, which was among the least industrialized of France's overseas territories. Like their counterparts in British West Africa, the French made few investments in infrastructure in the AOF prior to World War II. The AOF's economy was based on controlling markets that tied rural producers of tropical commodities to

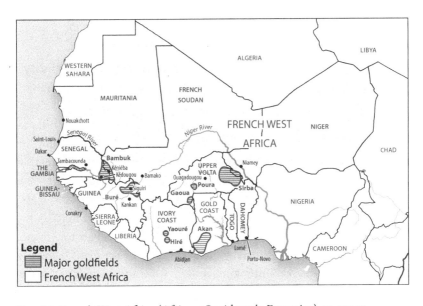

Map 3.1 French West Africa (Afrique-Occidentale Française), ca. 1930s.

MAKING CUSTOMARY MINING IN FRENCH WEST AFRICA

colonial trading circuits dominated by merchant houses from Bordeaux and Marseille. French merchant houses purchased raw materials produced by Africans at suppressed prices set by the colonial state, while colonial officials compelled African farmers to sell their labor by imposing an annual head tax. The colonial state ensured a market monopoly for French merchants by severing the power of African juula, the Muslim traders who controlled the Afro-European trading interface for centuries prior to colonialism.[6]

Orpaillage had more in common with the cash-crop farming of peanuts in Senegambia and cocoa trees in Ghana than with capital-intensive gold-mining operations on South Africa's Witwatersrand. Colonial cash-crop farming in Senegambia and Ghana are the subject of a vast historical litera-ture. Yet the history of colonial orpaillage is largely untold.[7] In demographic terms alone, the number of migrant orpailleurs working on the placers of interwar Guinea rival that of the *navétane* migrants from Senegal, Soudan, and Guinea who spent the rainy season farming peanuts in west-central Sen-egal during the same time period.[8] Placers were spaces of concentrated labor that nurtured a seasonal, mobile, and multiethnic urban form. In contrast to the European-controlled mining hubs of Johannesburg and Kitwe, Africans controlled the AOF's goldfields. The expansion of orpaillage under French rule activated older patterns of mobility tied to the medieval gold trade and the expansion of Manding cultural hegemony over the Birimian rocks of the savanna. Colonial officials glossed orpaillage as a "Malinke profession" and reinforced the association of gold mining with Manding language and culture by relying on Maninka authorities to manage goldfields, even in zones where diverse groups mined for gold.[9]

Officials of the AOF created the regulatory category of the "customary" African miner—a precursor to the postcolonial figure of the "artisanal" miner—by regulating orpaillage through a "customary rights" (*droit cou-tumier*) legal clause.[10] This clause was incorporated into numerous mining codes adopted by the federation from 1896 until the AOF's dismantling in 1956. Customary mining rights gave Black African residents of the AOF seasonal and communal rights to mine gold and salt in select territories. French mining regulations did not transform orpailleurs into criminals, but they marked the boundary between the technological status of colo-nial subjects and citizens. Customary laws applied exclusively to African subjects (*sujets, indigènes*), whereby French citizens or nationals (*citoyens*) were eligible for multiyear mining concessions similar to those issued in the French metropole. Customary mining rights materialized the legal racism of French colonialism. In the AOF, civil codes governed French citizens and nationals, while African subjects were regulated by native or customary policies, mandatory labor requirements, and the *indigènat*, a discretionary legal clause that gave European officials summary powers to imprison, punish, arrest, and requisition labor from colonial subjects.[11] Beginning in 1848, a small number of permanent Black and métis residents of Senegal's coastal cities were classified as colonial citizens and granted the right to elect a representative to the National Assembly in Paris. However, most Africans were classified as subjects and had few political rights.[12] For colonial officials, orpailleurs were the quintessential indigènes: rural peasants governed by "ancient customs."[13]

This chapter tracks the expansion and regulation of orpaillage across colonial Soudan, Senegal, and Haute-Volta (Burkina Faso), but it is rooted in the goldfields of northeastern Guinea. While Africans mined gold in most of the territories that became incorporated into the AOF, the circle of Siguiri in Guinea was the undisputed center of orpaillage.[14] Siguiri encompassed the historical territory of Buré, several days' walk from the medieval empire of Mali. Developments in Siguiri shaped policies toward orpailleurs working throughout the federation. French officials created an unusually dense archive of orpaillage. In a bid to better tax orpaillage and regulate customary mining rights, colonial governors commissioned dozens of studies of gold mining and markets from circle commanders.[15] Geologists working for the AOF's Service of Mines produced hundreds of maps and reports on African gold workings in their quest to understand the region's geology and to map the federation's mineral deposits (see chapter 4). Colonial reformers and social scientists, including the French sociologist George Balandier and early African ethnographers, also documented the "cosmopolitan society produced on the placers."[16] Few of these studies resulted in policy changes, but the granular attention to the ritual, social, and technical life of orpaillage under colonial rule offers a rare glimpse into how this African-controlled mining tradition brought the fabric of French empire to its doorstep.

Making Customary Miners

French officers who led conquest campaigns in West Africa in the late nineteenth century wrote popular accounts of their travels for metropolitan audiences that described "natives mining gold a little bit everywhere."[17] Drawing on these reports, colonial boosters marketed the goldfields of Senegal, Soudan, and Guinea to French investors who, they argued, could easily replace the "primitive methods" of the natives with "scientific techniques."[18]

By 1895, when France folded its West African territories into a confederation, French financiers were submitting dozens of requests for gold concessions in the historical territory of Bambuk.[19] Officials in Paris also promoted gold mining in France's overseas colonies. In 1873, the French franc was repegged to the gold standard, yet France controlled only a fraction of global gold production. The Colonial Ministry in Paris commissioned a French engineer, Maurice Barrat, to draft a mining decree for Senegal and Soudan: historical Bambuk. The presence of orpaillage presented unique legal challenges. Barrat argued that while gold-bearing lands in French Guyana and Caledonia "could be considered vacant," in Soudan "the mines are currently exploited by the natives, belonging to a race of a relatively developed order, possessing a certain civilization, the notion of law and a set of customs we are obliged to take into consideration.... [T]his primitive industry constitutes their only means of existence, their only resource to pay taxes, it therefore appears impossible to dispossess them of this customary right."[20]

Barrat aimed to design a mining law for the AOF that would preserve the so-called customary rights of orpailleurs while creating legal mechanisms for Europeans to invest in mining operations.[21] Surprisingly, the customary rights of African miners was also framed as a matter of military honor. When the French army invaded the goldfields of Buré—in pursuit of the Maninka empire builder Samori Touré—they promised to protect the right of Buré's residents to mine gold. This concession was meant to distinguish French rule from that of Samori, who requisitioned gold to purchase rifles from British forts in Sierra Leone.[22] While French military officers regularly broke agreements made with African intermediaries, generations of colonial officials upheld the promise to defend customary rights of orpailleurs.

But what, exactly, constituted the custom of orpaillage? And how would the rights of African miners to gold-bearing land be differentiated from those of Europeans? Barrat assumed that European firms would discover and exploit gold hundreds of meters underground, as British firms did in the capital-intensive gold mines of Witwatersrand.[23] Africans, meanwhile, could stay at the surface, digging "to the depth they can reach with their current procedures." Barrat codified this vertical segregation of mining rights—Africans on the surface, Europeans at depth—in an 1896 "mining regime" for Senegal and Soudan. In 1899, this mineral regime was transformed into a "mining code" applied to the entire federation. This mining code transformed orpaillage into a legal category of technological practice.

Over the next six decades, competing actors within the French colonial sphere debated whether to define African mining custom based on a vertical or horizontal division of rights. The vertical limited the rights of orpailleurs based on assumptions of African technological inferiority: Africans could mine only as deep as their "traditional" mining tools, iron picks and calabashes, allowed. The horizontal defined custom in geographic terms: Africans could mine only in territories where they historically mined. Both versions framed African mining techniques as static. Modifications to the AOF's customary mining clauses reflected a selective hybrid of actual African mining techniques and administrative efforts to shape those practices to suit the state's shifting economic and political goals. Similar to colonial customary laws in other domains, some forms of custom were "invented," while others mapped more directly onto preexisting practices.[24] In a federation of 4.6 million square kilometers, there was not one African mining custom, there were many, and they were dynamic. Colonial agents acknowledged this fact, but the federation's mining codes only recognized a singular, static definition of mining custom.[25]

In the 1890s, colonial officials imagined that the AOF's customary mining rights clause would be a temporary stopgap, an evolutionary stepping-stone on the path to establishing "modern" European-owned mines that would eliminate the need for customary rights altogether. "In several years," Barrat mused, Africans would cease to work "blindly for themselves" and join "well constituted companies, overseen by geologists."[26] This technological transition would never come to pass in the AOF. Rather, over the next six decades of colonial rule, orpailleurs used the precedents established in the AOF's first mining code to defend their customary rights to mine gold in flexible kin-based groups across the Birimian rocks of savanna West Africa.

Customary Conflict

Orpaillage was largely abandoned during French conquest in the late nineteenth century as African military leaders, desperately clinging to power, raided the non-centralized provinces of goldfields for captives and gold dust to finance their militaries.[27] Africans slowly returned to orpaillage as the French expanded their monopoly on violence and imposed a head tax (*l'impot de capitation*). By the beginning of the twentieth century, the French demanded payment of the tax in francs. Because coins were not minted in the colonies, Africans could obtain French francs only by selling raw materials for export to the metropole. In Buré and Bambuk, orpailleurs sold gold dust to juulas who, barred from accessing export licenses for gold, worked as intermediaries for French and "Syrien" merchant houses. *Syrien* was a gloss for immigrants from the Ottoman Empire who established a commercial presence in French West Africa in the late nineteenth century. Syriens had an early stronghold in Guinea's wild rubber boom, focused on Siguiri.[28] The boom withered after rubber from Southeast Asia flooded global markets in the 1900s. For the remainder of colonial rule, households in Buré relied on gold dust to pay head taxes.

As orpaillage expanded in Guinea, Soudan, and Senegal, the Colonial Ministry in Paris issued hundreds of permits to French firms for gold exploration in Buré and Bambuk. Most permits were purchased on a speculative stock exchange designed to extract value from European investors rather than from the gold of West Africa.[29] The few French firms that ventured into the AOF lacked sufficient capital and knowledge of regional climatic conditions. These operations did not prospect for deep lode ore; rather, they requested permits that mapped directly onto mines "dug by the natives."[30] Conflicts ensued, leaving a paper trail that reveals orpailleurs were well aware of their customary rights to mine gold just years after those rights became law. In 1898, for example, African residents of the village of Dialandiri, in southern Soudan, complained to the commander of Satadougou that a French gold prospector was violating their customary rights by exploiting a deposit mined by the village for generations (figure 3.1).[31] French officials sided with the orpailleurs and annulled a permit issued to the French prospector, stating that it was dangerous to "dispossess" Africans from their "gold mines" in a region that was "barely pacified."[32]

Orpailleurs in Siguiri also appealed to their customary rights in conflicts with European miners. By 1909, thousands of orpailleurs were mining for gold alongside roughly 115 Europeans in the circle of Siguiri.[33] The largest European operation was a French firm, the Compagnie des Mines de Siguiri, which secured a permit to mine Fatoya, a mountain Africans had exploited intermittently for decades. In 1910, the company installed rock-crushing machines and a light rail on the southern edge of the mountain. Orpailleurs mined on the northern half of the mountain, but by 1914 they had encroached on the central "corridor of the company's concession with their picks and shovels."[34] The company called on the commander of Siguiri to intervene. Once again, African chiefs defended their "customary rights" to exploit "superficial deposits" to the company.[35] As in Soudan, the governor of Guinea and the governor-general of the AOF came to the defense of orpailleurs and forced the company to close. As the commander of Siguiri observed:

> In considering things more closely, one remains convinced that almost all of the permits accorded [to French companies] contain in their

Figure 3.1 "Miner descending to the bottom of the placer." Bambala, Siguiri, Guinea, 1953. Photograph by Savonnet. Courtesy of the Institut Fondamental d'Afrique Noire.

perimeters old and recent shafts dug by the natives, and one is tempted to conclude that the permits were requested because the natives mine for gold within their perimeter, or because they are close to native work sites. And one could judge that it was unnecessary, in most cases, for the permit holders to undertake laborious research. It was the work of the natives that attested to the presence or the proximity of the precious metal.[36]

The closure of the Compagnie de Siguiri sounded a death knell for French mining investments in West Africa. Engineers working for the Colonial Ministry in Paris charged that the customary rights clause prevented the "rational exploitation of the subsoil" by French outfits made vulnerable to the "invasions of native miners."[37]

Back in West Africa, however, officials worried that harsh restrictions on customary rights would create political instability in regions far from European coastal enclaves. William Ponty, then the governor-general of the AOF, was eager to reduce conflicts between orpailleurs and future European miners without eliminating customary mining rights outright. The commander of

Siguiri proposed a creative solution to this problem. After dipping into the circle's archives and consulting with village elders about the history of orpaillage, he concluded that the AOF's mining code of 1899 had misinterpreted the customs of African miners. This initial code allowed any African subject to mine anywhere in the federation "to the depth they can reach with their current procedures." At the time the code was drafted, Siguiri was emerging from the "foreign rule" of Samori Touré, who had forced strangers to mine Buré to furnish his army with gold.[38] This, the commander argued, gave the false impression that "strangers" were allowed to mine freely on goldfields when, prior to Samori's rule, the custom had been to restrict orpaillage to the residents of neighboring villages. The commander's revision of African mining custom is dubious, given that West Africans had migrated to goldfields in times of drought for centuries before Samori's rule. Nonetheless, his account inspired William Ponty to redefine the customary rights of orpailleurs not by the depth to which they could dig with their customary tools, but by the traditional territories in which Africans mined.[39] Ponty proposed modifying the AOF's mining code to a horizontal, rather than vertical, segregation of mining rights: orpailleurs would be restricted to mining within a system of native reserves (*réserves indigènes*), whereas Europeans could request permits outside of these reserves. Though justified in the language of custom, this new law was designed to eliminate conflict between European and African miners for the same parcel of mineralized land.

World War I, and a reconfiguration of the AOF, slowed Ponty's mining reforms. But the native reserves policy was incorporated into a new federal mining decree adopted in 1924. According to the new law, only registered occupants of the canton in which the reserves were demarcated could mine within the reserves. This excluded both Europeans and "stranger" African migrants.[40] Prior to each dry season, the governor of each colony would determine the location and expanse of native reserves for the year. On the ground, however, neither French officials nor the African residents of Buré enforced the legal exclusion of "strangers" from the goldfields. By the 1930s, the de facto policy in the AOF was to promote orpaillage by any means necessary, by circle residents and migrants alike.

"Native Industry"

Between the two world wars, orpaillage expanded to unprecedented scales in the colonial AOF, while European-owned mining firms largely shut their doors. Siguiri emerged as the epicenter of the African-led gold boom. Small farming villages transformed into massive placer gold mines, hosting between five thousand and fifteen thousand dry season migrants.[41] In Paris, the Colonial Ministry embraced this "native industry" (*industrie indigène*) as a pathway to rebuilding metropolitan gold stocks depleted by World War I. Colonial officials requisitioned labor to build roads to freshly discovered gold deposits and coordinated with French merchant houses to transport migrants and rice imported from French Indochina to Siguiri's most popular placers.[42] French officials in Guinea began referring to the mining season as the gold campaign (*campagne de l'or*), an expression that echoed the peanut battle (*bataille d'arachide*) in Senegal, where French officials organized transportation for migrant laborers to African-owned farms.[43]

As orpaillage became the AOF's primary mining industry, colonial officials reassessed nineteenth-century appraisals of orpailleurs as "wasteful" and "primitive." In 1934, the governor of Guinea applauded the "incontestable rapidity and productivity" of orpaillage, stating he would not be surprised to "learn of the ingenuity of our miners to retrieve the best part of the auriferous sands."[44] In the same year, the assistant director of the AOF's Service of Mines was "brought to conclude that the natives, drawing on an ancient experience, practice an excellent method adapted to the conditions of the gold deposits, to their conditions of life, and to their customs."[45] "This industry is not anarchic," wrote a French geographer several years later, as "the organization and administration of the placers is regulated by ancient traditions."[46] Such statements echoed the growing appreciation of colonial technicians of African agronomic, healing, and forestry "wisdom" between the wars.[47] The celebration of African mining was also pragmatic. Orpaillage produced receipts for the state while costing little. In 1935, Henri Labouret, an administrator in Côte d'Ivoire, put it plainly: "Orpaillage represents, in contrast to overcapitalized European mining, a very economical mode of development of local wealth, for it does not involve any immobilization of capital or outlay of general expenditure."[48]

Yet orpaillage was a double-edge sword for the colonial state. Colonial officials from across the political spectrum idealized Africans as farmers and opposed plans for industrialization in the AOF that could transform the black peasant (*le paysan noir*)—a figure of imagined rural stability—into an urbanized black proletariat (*le prolétariat noir*) that would be harder to control.[49] Like agriculture, orpaillage was viewed as a traditional activity carried out in kin-based groups. But it was also dependent on a large migrant population (*la population flottante*) that concerned colonial officials, even as the colonial economy encouraged these migrations. Moreover, the urban atmosphere of placers attracted "young people" escaping "familial discipline" and nurtured cross-ethnic political alliances.[50]

With growing numbers of migrants trickling into Guinea's placers, colonial officials relied on African authorities to manage orpailleurs. French officials buttressed the authority of the damantigi—the master of the mines in Buré—who appointed a group of tomboluma to police multiethnic placers.[51] While the damantigi and tomboluma were historical offices in Buré, colonialism transformed the form and function of these positions. Prior to colonial rule, the damantigi was an ephemeral authority, elected by communities of orpailleurs based on their affinity with the spirit guardian of goldfields. Backed by the colonial state, the damantigi became more political and began to requisition a share of gold from each mining shaft, commodifying what was once a discretionary contribution of orpailleurs to cover the cost of animals for sacrifices.[52] Colonial officials sanctioned tomboluma to carry rifles on larger placers, a privilege otherwise reserved for the African guards of canton chiefs. Tomboluma brought orpailleurs accused of theft or indiscipline before the French commander of the circle, mediating between the workaday world of the placers and the armed violence of the colonial state.[53]

From January to March, entire families from neighboring circles in Guinea and Soudan migrated to Siguiri to generate their annual head taxes in gold dust.[54] Young and unmarried men also came to the placers individually or in small groups. Some joined "family" mining teams as paid workers. Others forged seasonal bonds of fictive kinship with other migrants.[55] Strangers were rarely refused on the mines. They found hosts among male lineage heads in Siguiri, who allowed migrants to build seasonal huts (*nyafa*) adjacent to their compounds. Orpailleurs slept and prepared meals in villages. At dawn, they walked or rode bicycles to nearby placers, returning before nightfall. Men carried iron tools: a short pickaxe (*soli*) and a long pick (*sonbe*). Female gold washers (*sanukuula*) balanced nested calabashes (*filen*) on their heads that doubled as bowls for cooked grain and basins for washing auriferous sand (figure 3.2). These lightweight tools could be easily packed and carried to a newly discovered placer mine. Blacksmiths (*numu*) crafted and repaired these tools in workshops established on placers and in surrounding villages.

Migrant mining teams sought the permission of resident damantigi to dig mining shafts. "Seers of gold" (*sanu londilalu*) were consulted on the placement of mining shafts. Religious practitioners included Muslim religious leaders—known as marabouts to colonial officials—and those who relied

Figure 3.2 "Returning from the placer." Siguiri, Guinea, 1942. Photograph by Labitte. Courtesy of the Institut Fondamental d'Afrique Noire.

on ancestral religious traditions to mediate with the unseen world (*féticheur* in French).[56] Conversion to Islam spread rapidly between the wars in Guinea, Soudan, and Senegal. On Senegal's peanut fields, the Muridiyya brotherhood gained adherents among migrants and former slaves who joined the expansive spiritual community of Amadou Bamba.[57] Muslim juula and marabouts were important figures on Siguiri's placer mines too, but the goldfields remained pagan spaces, dominated by Maninka religious practitioners: the damantigi. As in Atlantic-era Bambuk, mining was strictly prohibited on Mondays, a day of rest for underground spirits.[58] Colonial officials commented on the ubiquity of blood sacrifice on placer mines, echoing European explorers of earlier generations. "Gold is the property of devils that can move it from one space to another," reported Siguiri's French commander to the governor of Guinea. Sacrifices were made "if not to force the hand of the spirits, at least to make them abandon their gold so it can be exploited."[59] Damantigi determined communal sacrifices of chickens, goats, sheep, or cows. Mining teams also conducted sacrifices of their own.

One of Guinea's most celebrated writers, Camara Laye, wrote about the ritual world of interwar Guinea's goldfields in his first novel, *L'enfant noir*, a semiautobiographical account published in 1953. In it, Laye describes his father, a Maninka goldsmith based in Kouroussa, smelting gold earrings from dust "collected in the placers of Siguiri" by a woman who, "crouching over the river for months on end..., had patiently extracted grains of gold from the mud."[60] "What words did my father utter?" Laye asks. "I do not know. At least I am not certain what they were. No one ever told me. But could they have been anything but incantations? On these occasions was he not invoking the genies of fire and gold, of fire and wind, of wind blown by the blast-pipes of the forge, of fire born of wind, of gold married to fire? Was it not their assistance, their friendship, their espousal that he besought? Yes. Almost certainly he was invoking these genies, all of whom are equally indispensable for smelting gold."[61]

If the will of spirits (genies, jinnes) saturated the forge and the placers, as suggested by Laye, some ritual prohibitions were loosening on the goldfields of interwar Guinea. In 1937, Denise Savineau, a Frenchwoman commissioned to study the conditions of women in the AOF, wrote about the placers of Sindougou in Siguiri. "In the past," she wrote, orpailleurs departed from the placers together "for fear of incurring the wrath of the spirits and of seeing their luck run out. This healthy fear protected the extracted soil and the active mining operation against thieves. But the belief in spirits is being lost, greed is increasing: the daring linger, the ill-intentioned as well, and the spirits seem indifferent."[62]

While some orpailleurs challenged the prohibitions of the spirit world, others troubled traditional gender hierarchies and labor relations on the mines. For women, the large number of unmarried men working on Guinea's interwar placers created new economic opportunities. Women sold services historically performed for husbands and male kin: meal preparation, laundry, transporting rock, and washing gold-bearing sands (figure 3.3).[63] Paid in gold dust, women purchased cloth, imported rice, and condiments. Some unmarried women entered contracts with men for the exclusive exchange of sex and companionship known as a mine marriage (*juurafura*).[64] Other women worked exclusively with kin. A typical family mining unit, fictive or real, was composed of at least two men and one or two women. Men dug cylindrical shafts anywhere from seven to twenty meters deep. When they reached the auriferous layer, they carved out underground caverns and dug horizontally until they met the shafts of neighboring teams. As the tunnels grew, miners used chunks of auriferous rock to hold up the weight of the earth above. At the surface, women operated pulleys to evacuate the rock mined from below.[65] Although the techniques used to excavate placer deposits

Figure 3.3 "Series of mining shafts in a placer." Bambala, Guinea, 1953. Photograph by Savonnet. Courtesy of the Institut Fondamental d'Afrique Noire.

have changed considerably from the interwar period to the present day, the basic gendered division of labor remains similar on twenty-first century orpaillage sites in Guinea, Mali, and Senegal (see chapters 1, 6, and 7).

Savineau reported that men controlled the proceeds of family mining teams, which was used to cover head taxes for the entire group and any adults back home.[66] When orpailleurs met their tax demands, remaining profits went to bridewealth and to the purchase of salt, cloth, and brandy. Successful orpailleurs purchased bicycles, which facilitated travel across placer miners. Griots visited the huts of those who discovered a rich gold vein—named the master of gold (*sanutigi*) for a week—singing the praises of their family genealogies in the hopes of a share of gold. But the cost of life on the placers was highly inflated, eating sharply into these profits. Juulas from Guinea, Senegal, Soudan, and Côte d'Ivoire converged at Siguiri, where they sold miners rice imported from French Indochina, often on credit, as well as millet, fonio, and condiments. In exchange, juula purchased gold dust that was measured on metal balances against the brown seeds of tamarind fruit or calibrated metal weights (figure 3.4).[67] The names of successful juula gold traders circulated across the AOF's goldfields: Doko Sako of Sieke,

Souleymane Camara of Kentinian, and Wara Fama of Falama.[68] Young juula wore richly embroidered boubous and babouche shoes fashioned from gold-tinted leather. Many famous juula were based in Siguiri and Kankan, vibrant entrepôts for the centuries-old gold and kola nut trade. Between the wars a popular praise-song musical genre called *mamaya* developed in these cities. Mamaya songs, written and performed for juula, spread their fame across the goldfields of the savanna.[69]

The dense populations on Siguiri's placers encouraged technical as well as social innovations. French geologists estimated that between the wars roughly ten thousand to fifteen thousand men worked in the "profession of orpaillage" year-round. Some men became specialists in digging subterranean caverns (*kurumogo*). Kurumogo earned roughly half of the share of gold from a shaft for carrying out this dangerous work.[70] A new category of miner, the *sukunbalila*, emerges in the archival record in the 1920s. Sukunbalila descended into mining shafts that had been abandoned when depleted or deemed unsafe and dismantled the pillars of rock erected underground by orpailleurs. Constructed of rock from the auriferous layer, these pillars were guaranteed to contain gold. Sukunbalila earned roughly five times as

Figure 3.4 "Gold merchants near a placer." Bouremfaï, Siguiri, Guinea, 1942. Photograph by Labitte. Courtesy of the Institut Fondamental d'Afrique Noire.

much as a "family miner" during the same season. They traveled on bicycles in search of recently abandoned pit mines not yet inundated with early spring rains or erosion. "They are easy to recognize," remarked a Belgian gold prospector working in Soudan, because they "travel on bicycles."[71]

Sukunbalila were the first to use kerosene lamps to light their work underground, replacing the use of shea butter candles. They donned amulets that they placed around the opening of mine shafts to propitiate underground spirits.[72] Elegant and audacious, these men wore white boubous in the style of canton chiefs and strapped gramophones to the back of their bicycles to animate their work. Sukunbalila smoked English cigarettes and bought beaded jewelry from France for their lovers.[73] In 1945, a young Fodéba Keïta—who later founded the Ballets Africains de Guinée—published an ethnographic article on the sukunbalila. Keïta describes his friend, Siami, a sukunbalila who in a half-hour could "come back with 8 to 15 grams of gold" and "up to 20 grams a day on certain placers."[74] While such gains made these men wealthy in local terms, hundreds of sukunbalila died under collapsed mines. In 1936, it was reported near the town of Siebala in the circle of Siguiri that no fewer than twenty-two sukunbalila lost their lives in three different accidents.[75]

The emergence of new specialties of miners and opportunities for women to earn independent wealth on the placers troubled gendered and gerontocratic hierarchies. By the close of the 1930s, unmarried migrants were as numerous as family mining teams. Women left husbands who did not earn enough gold and insisted on receiving a portion of the family revenue for their own needs.[76] Savineau transcribed an interview with Naman Koumba Konaté, a chief of a village in Siguiri, who described these changes:

> In thirty years, says Naman Koumba, I collected more than a kilo of gold for my father. He never gave me back a decigram of it. I received, from that gold, only my portion of the inheritance, which was small, because the inheritor was not only his eldest son but all of his sons. Naman Koumba has hardly anything to live on but the gold collected by his children. In the past, he also took the gold of his nephews. Still, his sons don't give him all their gold. At one time, he would have beaten them for this act. One can no longer do this. Naman Koumba regrets this.[77]

Koumba expressed nostalgia for a time when elder men could claim the full proceeds of the labor of sons, daughters, wives, and even nephews. It is unclear how historical such a vision ever was, considering that orpaillage was largely the purview of women on the eve of colonial rule in Bambuk and Buré (see chapter 2). Regardless, Koumba's concerns resonated with those of French officials, who located political stability in the gerontocratic power of elder men, chiefs, and other male African authorities. Orpailleurs were not wage laborers, but French officials understood that the marketplaces of Siguiri fostered the same multiethnic political communities that challenged colonial authority in the port of Conakry and the railway hub of Thiès. These anxieties were prescient. In the aftermath of World War II, African politicians in the AOF would take up orpaillage and customary rights for African miners as a cause for party politics.

Orpaillage and the Union du Mandé in Postwar Guinea

World War II exposed the fragility of French power and sharpened African demands for greater parity with metropolitan citizens. France had been humiliated, occupied by the Germans and the collaborationist Vichy regime. African soldiers fought alongside French troops, and African peasants labored without pay to cultivate crops for the war effort. The Free French framed the war as a struggle for freedom against fascism and authoritarianism. The irony of this discourse was not lost on colonized populations. After the war, Africans demanded greater voting rights, equal pay for equal work, and an end to forced labor in the French empire.[78] In 1944, Charles de Gaulle initiated a process of reform that resulted in the adoption of the constitution of France's Fourth Republic in October 1946. Colonies were renamed overseas territories, the French empire became the French Union, and colonial subjects became citizens of the French Republic. Africans could now organize political parties and elect representatives to serve on Grand Councils (later called Territorial Assemblies) in West Africa and in the National Assembly, the Council of the Republic, and in the Assembly of the French Union in Paris.

The AOF's early political parties were modeled on metropolitan parties or based on ethnoregional affiliations. The Union du Mandé, formed in 1946 in Upper Guinea, was based on the latter model. Composed largely of ethnic Maninka, the union drew its core membership from Kankan and Siguiri.[79] Its early campaigns focused on reforming gold markets and reinforcing the customary rights of African orpailleurs. Questions about who had the right to work placer mines—and who had the right to buy and sell gold—took on new importance after the war.[80] In 1940, after the collaborationist Vichy regime gained control over the federation, Britain blocked maritime trade with the AOF. The loss of rice imports from French Indochina made it impossible to serve the large population of seasonal miners. In 1942, the governor-general outlawed orpaillage, redirecting seasonal labor toward peanut production in Senegal. In 1946, the administration reopened Guinea's placer mines, but the price of gold remained suppressed—a holdover from wartime commercial regulations. Officials offset the low gold price by allocating cloth to juulas to supplement what they paid orpailleurs for gold dust. But with inconsistent shipments of poor-quality cloth, juulas smuggled most of Guinea's gold to neighboring Portuguese and British colonies, where the price of gold was double that in the AOF.

In 1946, the Union du Mandé pressured the governor of Guinea to lift wartime restrictions on the gold trade.[81] Framoi Bérété, a founding member of the union and the first African from Siguiri elected to Guinea's Territorial Assembly, spearheaded a campaign to liberalize the AOF's gold market.[82] Sékou Touré, the future president of independent Guinea, and Mamba Sano joined Bérété's campaign. Sano was a teacher in Siguiri before he was elected as the first Guinean-born African to serve in the French National Assembly in 1946.[83] Sano had a personal stake in Guinea's gold as the descendant of a successful Maninka juula who likely worked in the gold trade. Bérété and Touré argued before the General Council in Guinea and the Grand Council in Dakar against the injustice of the suppressed gold price. In the National Assembly in Paris, Sano mobilized a coalition to "free" the AOF's gold commerce, framing it as a concern of "our national budget."[84] French merchants in Guinea, who suffered losses from gold leaking to neighboring states, also joined the coalition. In 1949, the French Parliament voted to allow gold to be bought and sold in the AOF as on the free market for gold in Paris. The campaign to liberalize the gold trade galvanized Upper Guinea's gold placers as a political constituency as African-led political activity was gaining momentum across the AOF. In 1950, Sékou Touré led a general strike in Conakry over the minimum wage. By then, he had left the Union du Mandé for the Rassemblement Démocratique Africain (RDA), an anticolonial political coalition that was gaining adherents across the AOF, to the detriment of ethnoregional parties such as the Union du Mandé.[85] It was also in the dry season of 1950 that the Bureau Minier de la France d'Outre-mer (BUMIFOM) launched a scheme to improve African mining techniques in Siguiri. Created as a public enterprise in France in 1948, BUMIFOM conducted targeted mineral prospecting in overseas territories to generate private-sector interest in key mineral resources. In 1950, BUMIFOM sent André Blouin, an engineer, to the village of Kentinian in Siguiri circle to demonstrate techniques for evacuating water from orpaillage shafts. Initially, the damantigi of Kentinian agreed to provide labor for two pit demonstrations at the expense of the BUMIFOM. But the damantigi never dug the shafts and began to evade Blouin's visits. "They are showing a certain hostility to me," Blouin wrote to his superiors. "The damantigi told me the elders would not work with me because they 'were fearful.'"[86] Blouin later discovered the source of this fear: a letter by Framoi Bérété published in the biweekly journal *La Voix de la Guinée*.[87]

Bérété pointed to the coincidence of Blouin's trip with a request, submitted by a French man to Guinea's General Council, for a gold exploration permit extending across Guinea's native reserves. Bérété suspected Blouin was in Siguiri not to improve African mining techniques but to locate and market gold deposits discovered by orpailleurs to European firms. "For several months," Bérété wrote, "the engineer is sent to study, interview, and observe in the circle. 'Is it really to improve our methods of exploiting gold?' the natives ask with suspicion. 'Or is it to delineate new gold mining areas for capitalists?'"[88] Within weeks of the publication of Bérété's letter, damantigi from across Siguiri signed a petition to expel Blouin from the circle.[89] They suspected that the engineer's maps were part of a design to "seize" Siguiri's goldfields for French investors and to dispossess orpailleurs of their customary rights.[90]

Bérété's support for the native reserves of Siguiri was effectively a defense of customary mining law. However, his letter expressed tensions faced by African politicians across the continent who, with few choices on hand, defended customary land and resource laws in an effort to resist land expropriation by white settlers and miners.[91] Bérété defended Siguiri's goldfields as a communal resource that was open to all West Africans, regardless of their region of origin. For Bérété, Siguiri's gold constituted a "natural patrimony" that BUMIFOM was obligated to protect for the future benefit of "thousands of Africans coming from Senegal, Guinea, Soudan, and Côte d'Ivoire." African mining supported the livelihoods of thousands, Bérété contended, while a company would "simply put this gold in hermetic boxes addressed to the metropole, if not to Canada or America."[92] Yet Bérété was aware that customary law was built on a racialized technological distinction: the notion that orpaillage was inferior to "modern" European mining industries. "If we are really French," Bérété went on to argue, "we have the right to believe that our sons and grandsons could become engineers, trained at the Polytechnique, and capable of unearthing gold wherever it is found."[93] For Bérété, membership in the French Union should bring an end to the political and technical disparities between residents of the metropole and those of overseas territories.

Customary mining rights in the AOF were a double-edged sword. They protected the right of Africans to mine gold, but they were seasonal and usufruct rights that territorial administrators could rescind. Moreover, because Africans were consigned customary rights, they were effectively barred from accessing more stable mineral property rights, such as multi-decade mining concessions. Africans therefore could either be customary miners with unstable usufruct rights or wage laborers at European-owned mining firms. But Bérété's vision was more radical: that Africans could work as engineers on African-owned capital-intensive mines. While French officials had long resisted industrialization in the AOF, by the 1950s they were acknowledging the need for increased investments in overseas territories in the name of "development," the postwar justification for European colonialism in Africa. Bérété pried open this distinct historical moment—in which anticolonial politics converged with the defense of customary mining—to reinforce the protection of gold-mining rights for West Africans.

As the political climate in Upper Guinea grew tense, the commander of Siguiri assured damantigi that Blouin aimed to "help the natives" and "not to dispossess them of their rights."[94] But Siguiri's orpailleurs were suspicious of this claim. Roland Pré, then the governor of Guinea, also expressed concerns about the extension of a European exploration permit over the "orpaillage zone in the region of Siguiri." In Pré's words:

> I will take this occasion to draw your attention to the subject of this request for a general permit, a significant portion of which concerns a region that the inhabitants of Upper Guinea consider as having been formally reserved for them by the agreements passed between them and the representatives of France at the moment of the country's occupation.... [T]he granting of this exclusive research permit would have the inevitable consequence of prohibiting to the natives of these regions, within a vast perimeter, the prospecting of new deposits they traditionally undertake when old deposits run out.[95]

Writing in 1950, Pré harked back to the promise made by the French army in the 1890s to protect the customary mining rights of the residents of Buré. Pré and the General Council of the AOF rejected the permit request by the French financier. This decision appeared to side with the interests of orpailleurs and their African representatives in the AOF's Territorial Councils and in Paris. In truth, French officials were motivated more by "political concerns" than by Bérété's radical vision of technological modernity led by African-trained engineers. As Pré put it, the "sheer size of the number of gold miners in the Siguiri region (more than 100,000 people work in the placers during the operating season)" justifies taking every precaution to avoid inciting complaints from "political agitators" in the region by awarding unfavorable permit requests.[96] Pré's support of orpailleurs was strategic. While projects for petroleum, uranium, and bauxite mines in the AOF were on the horizon, in 1950 the AOF's most important mineral export was gold, and orpailleurs produced the majority of it. Appeasing orpailleurs also contained the potential for violence from a large migrant population working far from the gaze of village elders.

Profiting from Orpaillage

Scholars have overlooked both the importance of orpaillage to the AOF's economy and the emergence of orpailleurs as an organized political constituency under colonial rule. Orpaillage was central to the colonial economy of the historical gold-producing territories of Buré and Bambuk, where gold dust was a preferred means of meeting head taxes. Gold mined by Africans was the primary mineral export of the AOF until the late 1950s, when bauxite and phosphate mines were opened in Guinea and Senegal.[97] Technicians working for the colonial state tried to eliminate the customary rights clause of the AOF's mining code but orpailleurs successfully defended this right across six decades of colonial rule. In 1954, the Ministry of Overseas France elaborated a single "modern" mining decree, applicable to all overseas territories.[98] The decree included one clause applicable exclusively to the AOF: it granted African residents of the federation the right "to exploit by traditional procedures" deposits of gold and other mineral substances in zones as defined by lieutenant-governors of individual colonies since 1924.[99] This was almost a verbatim rearticulation of the customary mining clause that had been incorporated into every mining code or regime adopted in the AOF since 1896. The expansion of orpaillage in the AOF, and its legal protection in mining codes, is a testament to the political influence of orpailleurs and their African representatives in shaping the French colonial state.

French officials profited from orpaillage, and the African institutions that managed it, because they lacked the finances to mount industrial-scale mines. Orpaillage was well suited to the political economy of indirect rule, which exploited African productive economies while making minimal investments in infrastructure and production. In West Africa, indirect rule is commonly understood as the retooling of indigenous institutions for colonial governance. The French did something similar with orpaillage by leaning on the damantigi to manage cosmopolitan urban placer mines on behalf of empire. Orpaillage in the AOF challenges a received narrative of the temporal progression of mining in Africa: that Europeans supplanted African mining economies, expropriated mineralized land, and reduced Africans to migrant wage laborers. While colonial head taxes encouraged orpaillage, African authorities controlled labor and life on goldfields, as they had for centuries. In this respect, orpaillage is a compelling case of what Richard Roberts describes as the strength of "local processes ... to withstand empire and ultimately to shape the experience of colonialism."[100] Yet orpaillage was anything but local. Under colonial rule, this regional mining tradition expanded through the movements of orpailleurs, juulas, geologists, and colonial officials. Across the Birimian rocks of savanna West Africa, an indigenous gold-mining industry with roots in the medieval period drew the French empire into the seasonal rhythms of placer mining.

The story of orpaillage bottlenecks into something more familiar by the 1950s, with African independence on the horizon. When newly independent African states nationalized their mining industries, they also criminalized orpaillage, a policy that departed from that of their colonial predecessors (see chapter 5). But the legacies of orpaillage in the AOF echoed far beyond the colonial period. Several decades following independence, orpailleurs in West Africa emerged as a powerful political lobby to make sophisticated defenses for their rights to minerals, including those based on their customary right to mine (see chapter 6). The next chapter turns to a temporally parallel but distinct story about orpaillage: the entanglement of this African mining economy with geological research and mineral prospecting. It lays the groundwork for a second, troubled legacy of the colonial period: the appropriation of African gold discoveries.

4
Colonial Geology and African Gold Discoveries

In 1935, Alexis Chermette, a French geologist working in French West Africa (Afrique-Occidentale Française [AOF]), descended into the "old native workings" of a lode-ore gold deposit in Hiré, a village in south-central Côte d'Ivoire. Chermette worked with two African research assistants from nearby villages: Niango, a veteran of World War I from Oumé, and Beriabou, the chief of Dibikro. These men, Chermette wrote, knew the location of all the "native [gold] pits."[1] In this forested region, the earth's substratum was revealed only along river gullies or by historical mine shafts, carved open by long-deceased orpailleurs. As Chermette descended into these abandoned mine shafts, he interpreted two histories inscribed in the rock: one geological, one social. Gold deposition at Hiré was lenticular, shot through with veins that ran parallel to one another like the sinuous fibers of celery.

Samples chipped from the rock revealed that gold likely entered the surrounding granite as an injection of a greenstone amalgamate during a major geological event. Hiré's rocks also told a story of human labor. The mines were the work of ethnic Baoulé, Akan-speaking people who mined gold across southern Côte d'Ivoire and Ghana. The Baoulé shafts (*puits Baoulé*), as the AOF's geologists called them, were twenty meters deep and irregularly distributed. Most orpaillage workings in the basin of Siguiri in Guinea were of secondary or placer deposits. At Hiré, however, orpailleurs had splintered gold-bearing quartz from the surrounding granite with fire and pulverized the quartz with rock stones before washing the powder.[2] Chermette remarked on the "very important native works," in his final report, "which denote such skill on the part of Baoulé miners."[3]

Chermette was one of dozens of European geologists, prospectors, and mining engineers—employed by the AOF and private firms—who mapped and sampled African gold workings over the course of French colonial rule. In 1935, with gold prices still high from the global Depression, orpaillage flourished in Guinea, Soudan, and Senegal. In Côte d'Ivoire, by contrast, orpaillage was largely abandoned in favor of wage labor on French-owned coffee plantations or migration to African-owned cocoa farms in southern Gold Coast (Ghana). The AOF's Service of Mines and Geology sent geologists to track new gold discoveries made by orpailleurs and to study abandoned orpaillage sites to evaluate whether a European firm could profitably exploit the "former workings of the natives."[4]

Between the 1910s and the 1950s, the AOF's Service of Mines developed insights into the federation's structural geology and mineralization through the techniques, political and ritual institutions, and skilled labor of West African orpailleurs. Because funding for scientific research in colonial Africa was sparse, collaboration with African experts was common in field-based sciences, including geology, agronomy, botany, cartography, and anthropology. As the historian Helen Tilley argues, by the end of World War I, British technicians in Africa had critiqued earlier pejorative views of African environmental practices as backward and primitive and begun to seriously study "Africans' subaltern, or orally transmitted, knowledge" of the natural world. African assistants, Tilley shows, shaped the epistemology of the field sciences in colonial Africa to a degree unparalleled elsewhere in the imperial world.[5] If this argument holds for the sciences in British Africa, an even more forceful case could be made for geology in French Africa.

By the turn of the twentieth century, the British financed extensive geological research in South Africa, Ghana, and Rhodesia, colonies with capital-intensive gold and copper mines.[6] By contrast, the AOF marginalized the Service of Mines and dismissed plans for industrialization out of fear they would "proletarianize" African peasants.[7] In this policy framework, the AOF's geologists focused on the future, generating geological surveys and mineral inventories to locate deposits for exploitation by future European enterprises. Working across a vast federation with few preexisting geological maps, geologists asked African elders and guides to lead them to abandoned orpaillage workings and iron kilns: sites with known metal deposition. Though geologists forged relationships with individual orpailleurs and blacksmiths, they were interested in the aggregated gold discoveries of men and women over the course of decades. Just as customary law recognized Africans as members of groups, the AOF's geologists and mining engineers saw orpailleurs as a "mass" of specialists, not as individuals. In this respect, studies of orpaillage articulated with the broader impulse of colonial states in

Africa, which were less focused on producing knowledge about individuals, than knowing their populations on a collective scale.[8]

Colonial-era geologists mapped dozens of hard metal deposits in the AOF. Due to the federation's anti-industrial policies, however, most of these discoveries were shelved for future development. But studies and maps of African mines did accelerate scientific understanding of the West African Craton, the Precambrian basement rock that contains gold-bearing Birimian rocks in its southeastern portion. Studies of Birimian rocks made the careers of dozens of French and British scientists in the early twentieth century. British geologists working in Ghana coined the term *Birimian* after the Birim River in the gold-producing zone of Akyem.[9] French geologists deepened knowledge of regional Birimian formations through scientific publications and, by the 1930s, *Birimian* (*Birrimien* in French) became the accepted scientific term for Precambrian basement rocks found in West Africa and South America—two continents once conjoined as part of the supercontinent of Pangea.[10] Because most of West Africa's gold is found in Birimian rocks, mapping orpaillage sites was crucial to the aggregation of regional scientific knowledge about the geology of the AOF's basement rocks, which were significantly older than those of Western Europe.

In the AOF, regional geological knowledge was forged through the encounters of geologists with regional ecology—savanna scrubland, deserts, and rain forests—in addition to a millennium of human mining history.[11] As geologists began to aggregate data from orpaillage sites into a regional view of geological formations, they also glimpsed the edges of West Africa's ritual geology that spread piecemeal across gold-bearing Birimian rocks. In their field reports and publications, geologists commented on the cosmology of orpaillage and ironworking kilns that harnessed the occult forces of volcanic rock. Hand-drawn maps of abandoned orpaillage workings created a visual archive of human-spirit relationships, some turned malevolent from inadequate sacrifices. To conduct geological surveys on the AOF's Birimian rocks was to document a regional ritual formation in rapid transformation with the expansion of orpaillage. This chapter's account of geology in French West Africa invites historians of science to consider how the making of regional environmental knowledge may, in fact, be built on older concepts and practices of regional interconnection.

The dense entanglement of field geology with orpaillage in the colonial AOF is not a simple story of the colonial appropriation of indigenous mining knowledge, although this is an important thread. Just as French prospectors benefited from the labor and mineral expertise of generations of African miners, orpailleurs acquired new techniques from expatriate geologists. The dynamic exchange and pirating of mineral discoveries created an "open access" economy of subterranean knowledge that blurred any facile distinction between African and European mining practice.[12] At the same time, racist colonial mining laws ensured that the benefits of this fluid exchange of knowledge accrued largely to the colonial state and French mining firms. The documentation of African mining discoveries and the regulation of orpaillage were carried out by different colonial officials with divergent interests. When merged, however, colonial laws restricted the rights of orpailleurs while geologists accumulated subterranean knowledge they produced.

Geology in French West Africa

By the late nineteenth century, when European powers had colonized much of the African continent, the earth sciences in France, Britain, and Germany were tightly bound to industrial developments and mining of coal, iron, and copper ore.[13] The professionalization of field sciences, including geology, produced studies of the earth that made nature amenable to calculation and conscription into property regimes.[14] Dreams of turning easy profits from mineralized land motivated European colonization. As a result, geology was part and parcel of imperial expansion in India, Canada, Australia, and across the African continent.[15] European states conducted surveys of their national and imperial mineral resources as a means of measuring state power and making estimates of global mineral resources.

In the early decades of the twentieth century, geological exploration in the AOF was carried out primarily by one man: Henry Hubert, a colonial administrator with training in the natural sciences. Hubert traversed much of the federation by horseback, collecting rock and mineral samples that he sent for analysis to the Muséum National d'Histoire Naturelle in Paris.[16] In 1911, Hubert drew the AOF's first geological map, which remained the only one of its scope for decades. In the late 1920s, Fernand Blondel, director of the Service of Geology in French Indochina, campaigned to reverse the AOF's poor reputation in international mining circles. Blondel asked why "mineral riches appear, by virtue of an inexplicable phenomenon, to stop at the political frontiers" of French West Africa.[17] Citing major mining projects in the British colonies of Nigeria, Ghana, and Sierra Leone—which shared geological formations with French colonies—Blondel concluded there were undiscovered hard metal deposits in the AOF. For Blondel, orpaillage also evidenced the AOF's mineral potential. A federation, he wrote, where "the natives were able to extract with their own labor 2,900 kilos of gold in one year, should allow the possibility of profitable operations for others."[18] "Others" implied Europeans. In 1927, the Colonial Ministry financed a new Service of Mines in the AOF and hired a French mining engineer, Jean Malavoy, as its first director. Malavoy and Blondel expanded geological exploration in the AOF, recruiting young, athletic geologists who showed signs of "loving a life in the bush."[19]

Malavoy coordinated geological research from Dakar, where the Service of Mines occupied a single floor in a downtown office building that housed a chemistry and gold-smelting laboratory, a map-drafting room, and rock and map collections.[20] During the rainy season, Dakar was the stage for scientific exchange, when geologists wrote reports and collaborated with cartographers to visualize their observations in the field. During the dry season, geologists fanned across the federation on missions of eight to nine months to conduct geological reconnaissance over large expanses or more focused prospecting of specific minerals.[21] Most French technicians were unfamiliar with West Africa's rock structures and sedimentary deposits. Similar to nineteenth-century European explorers, geologists stayed in villages as guests of local chiefs, in huts constructed and set aside for the occasional visits of French commanders during the annual tax collection and census. But geologists became far more adept in local languages than most circle commanders. The AOF implemented a "turntable" principle, transferring commanders from post to post and colony to colony every few years. This policy was intended to prevent French officials from developing strong ties to any particular area.[22] Geologists, by contrast, returned to the same region year after year, sometimes over the course of decades. Geologists often provided local administrators with data about the terrain; the presence of natural curiosities, such as waterfalls; and the location of remote farming hamlets.[23]

Dozens of African porters carried equipment, tents, and provisions for geologists. Geological teams numbered anywhere from twenty to one hundred men. They began their journey by train, truck, or boat. In zones free of the tsetse fly, French technicians and African assistants traveled the final distance on horseback, camel, or donkey. In forested areas, porters traveled on foot and carried geologists in rope hammocks.[24] Geologists recruited blacksmiths and Maninka and Baoulé orpailleurs to accompany them on prospecting missions to regions with little history of orpaillage.[25] African men carried out the brutalizing labor of digging exploration trenches. This was similar to work Africans performed, often by force, to build colonial roads and railways. Figure 4.1, a photograph of a gold-prospecting mission

Figure 4.1 "Digging a trench in a gold-bearing placer." Côte d'Ivoire, 1950. From Michel Bolgarsky, *Étude géologique et description pétrographique du Sud-Ouest de la Côte d'Ivoire*, planche photographique 10.

to Côte d'Ivoire in the 1940s, displays the racialized exploitation of African labor in geological research that was characteristic of the colonial period.

While geologists wrote dozens of reports from the field and back in Dakar, little is revealed about the identity of the diverse West Africans who participated in their missions. Geologists credited African workers for identifying outcrops, locating abandoned placer mines, and for their knowledge of botany and its relationship to underground resources, including aquifers and the presence of tin, gold, iron, and zircon.[26] Given their intimacy with rural populations and African orpailleurs, it is no surprise that geologists took an interest in the social and political institutions of the African people they encountered in the field in addition to the geophysical landscapes they were commissioned to document.

Encountering a Ritual Geology

The AOF's early geologists read the earth's sedimentary strata as a palimpsest, correlating the fragments and arranging them in a sequence to develop theories of temporal causation.[27] In the absence of aerial mapping, and with geochemical techniques in their infancy, rock outcrops were the primary road signs for the earth's history. Outcrops are fragments of basement rocks that push through superficial deposits to appear on the surface of the earth, exposed through erosion or tectonic uplift. Outcrops may be single boulders, a cliff, or an entire exposed mountain range. By measuring the bedding planes and foliation of outcrops, geologists constructed a picture of how and when the underlying bedrock was formed. Outcrops are rare on the West African savanna and Sahel, where meters of laterite, sand, and volcanic basalt cover much of the earth. Farther to the south, dense tropical forests cover rock formations, providing few insights into the earth's terrane. Geologists complained about walking "tens of kilometers without finding a clean rock."[28] They walked along colonial railways, where dynamite blasting revealed the substratum, and along galley forests lining rivers, where water eroded the laterite to expose portions of bedrock underneath. Geological work was cumulative. Geological surveys generated baseline studies designed to develop insights into basic structural geological formations. Later generations produced more granular maps of regions that the Service of Mines deemed of interest to understanding the AOF's mineral potential.

Many West African communities living on the savanna in the early twentieth century also valued rock outcrops as portals to the domain of otherworldly forces and ancestors. In Côte d'Ivoire and Haute-Volta, outcrops were a common base for shrines, glossed in French as "fetishes" (*fétiches*).[29] Geologists recognized shrines and the entries to sacred groves "used for the initiation of children" by the smearing of chicken blood, strips of cloth, or the juice of mashed kola nuts on rocks or trees. In some sectors, geologists reported that nearly every visible outcrop adjacent to village settlements was a shrine. Geologists sought permission from local chiefs to sample rocks from these sacred platforms. In a memoir of his geological work in interwar Côte d'Ivoire, Alphonse Obermuller recalled the use of outcrops as shrines: "If, after 5 to 10 kilometers of the road, the only rare outcrops that were particularly interesting were fetishes, I would summon the village chief and explain to him that my job was to break rocks without any intention of trying to oppose their customs. The sample was taken in his presence." Many African field assistants and porters refused to eat food prepared in a village from which such samples were taken out of fear of retributive poisoning for disturbing the patron spirits of the shrine. For this reason, triple rations of rice were distributed to African staff before traveling to "fetishist sectors."[30]

Rock outcrops that doubled as shrines were one site through which French technicians engaged with the ritual geology of West Africa's Birimian rock formations. Ritual practices observed on goldfields, where generations of colonial geologists sojourned, provided another angle. J. Siossat, a private gold prospector working in western Soudan in the 1930s, reported that the blood of slaughtered animals was poured into mine shafts to "force the hand of the devil, to make him abandon his gold."[31] Geologists assigned to Guinea and Côte d'Ivoire learned that spirit animals haunted the underground. Geologists reported that Maninka-speakers in Bambuk referred to gold veins as "spirit snakes" (*jinn saa*), a reference to the mystical snake of Nininkala, who consumed iron and excreted gold in her wake.[32] In Siguiri, this spirit appeared as a white ram who circulated beneath the surface of the earth, birthing gold or shedding his golden fleece, which created gold deposits.[33] On the ethnically heterogeneous goldfields of Côte d'Ivoire, by contrast, an earth deity known as "Koyo" excreted gold veins.[34] These stories resonate with oral traditions of Bida, whose trisected body, slain by the lover of Sia in medieval Wagadu, nourished the goldfields of Akan, Buré, and Bambuk. Geologists and colonial administrators working among the Lobi reported that gold was "a dangerous living thing" that had to be "killed" before it could be processed or sold.[35] On the goldfields of Poura, shrine priests converted gold to a "dead" substance by making sacrifices of domestic animals on lineage shrines to the guardian spirits of gold.[36] In Siguiri, large gold nuggets were "killed" through prayers and incantations by ritual practitioners the French called wizards (*sourciers*), fetishists (*féticheurs*), and Muslim religious leaders (*marabouts*). Tomboluma, the indigenous police force of mining sites, fired at gold nuggets with rifles to "chase away the genies."[37]

Similar to other colonial personnel who frequented the AOF's goldfields, geologists took an interest in the cosmology of orpaillage as an object of intellectual curiosity and exoticism.[38] They also sought empirical correlations between African "beliefs" about gold and geological phenomena. In the 1910s, for example, the AOF commissioned Jean Méniaud, a natural scientist, to study the economic potential of Haut-Sénégal-Niger (divided after World War I into the colonies of Soudan, Guinea, and Haute-Volta). Writing about the goldfields of Bambuk and Buré, Méniaud drew correlations between the "superstitions" of orpailleurs and the mineralization of gold. He interpreted the widespread belief that "gold moved from place to place" as a practical explanation for the fact that many alluvial deposits were found in depressions along ancient waterways. Over time, as violent storms disaggregated laterite rock, gold flakes were newly distributed across the regional water-drainage system, creating new alluvial deposits and revealing others formerly buried under laterite and sedimentation. This, Méniaud concluded, explains the "belief of the blacks that gold 'walks' and that it can be found anew in exhausted mines, after two, three, or four years of neglect." In contrast to European travelogues of the eighteenth and nineteenth centuries, which denigrated the beliefs of African miners as "irrational," Méniaud argued that these "superstitions" were based on "considerable experience in the matters of the subsoil."[39] In a 1935 report, Rostislav Goloubinow, a geologist then working for the AOF in Siguiri, remarked that apart from "their particular superstitions" and "their sacrifices," Maninka prospectors have "good knowledge" of the subsoil. Orpailleurs, he described, prospected for gold by proceeding from a hillside along the downward sloping edge of a valley, where gravity caused the heavy metal to accumulate in the local water table.[40]

Just as colonial technicians studied the earth's topography for signs of the architecture of the terrain, African prospectors scanned the surface of the savanna for signs of underlying gold deposits. While anyone except leatherworkers could putatively prospect for gold, ethnic Maninka were specialists in the domain in Guinea, Soudan, and Senegal. Some deposits were discovered by accident as men dug water wells or women glimpsed gold in the roots of cassava plants. In some villages, orpailleurs organized prospecting campaigns toward the end of the dry season. West Africans drew on botanical knowledge, embedded in a ritual cosmology of its own, to guide gold prospecting. Geologists wrote about the importance of several tree species to prospecting. Trees known in Maninka as *congouroun* and *boure* (*Kigelia Africana*) were counter-indications for gold.[41] *Sounsoun* (*Diospyros mespiliformis*) and *so* or *soso* (*Berlinia heudelotiana*) grew in land depressed by the weight of underwater aquifers, often lined with alluvial gold deposits.[42] A French prospector working in Maramandougou, Soudan, remarked that orpailleurs there dug prospecting mine shafts perpendicular to the branches of sounsoun to test for the presence of gold. *Nyama* or *niomo* (*Bauhinia reticulata*) trees also grew along alluvial gold deposits. A shrubby tree with gray bark, nyama was considered favorable to spirits, which accounts for its name, nyama, the life force of Maninka cosmology.[43]

Orpailleurs bathed in the leaves, bark, and sap of certain trees to earn the favor of the spirits haunting ore bodies. Maninka-speakers considered plants—like all animate and inanimate objects from the natural world— charged with nyama. Certain plants were burned or steeped for fertility, to protect newborn babies from spirits, and for burials. When burned, the nyama of plants could be transferred onto people and animals. Maninka authorities, who presided over the ritual life of placer mines in Soudan, Guinea, and Senegal, erected shrines at the base of African mahogany trees

(*Khaya senegalensis*), known as *jala* (*diala, jalo*) in Maninka. The Maninka term for shrine—*jalan* (*jalang, jalano*)—is derived from the jala tree.[44] The jala is the most important tree of the Maninka spiritual world. After giving birth, women and their newborns were bathed in a poultice of jala leaves. Some mothers named their newborns after the jala to recognize the tree's power to intervene in fertility.[45] Jala bark was burned as incense when praying for the deceased. Gold prospectors conducted sacrifices at the base of the jala to guide their work and orpailleurs also washed in its bark as protection against malevolent spirits.

Dreams and guardian spirits also guided gold prospecting. It was reported in a 1946 article on the placer mines of Siguiri that a man named Siaba Kone had discovered a gold deposit by consulting with the Koma, likely a reference to komo, the historic Maninka power association and masking society. For several nights, Koma led Saba through the bush to a rich gold placer, later named "Siabala" after its founder.[46] In Guinea, a dream led a man named Bamba to the discovery of the placer of "Bambala," which he envisioned by a stream, afternoon sunlight streaming through the trees.[47] The names of seasonal placer deposits carried echoes of the circumstances of their discovery: the personal names of prospectors (Moussala, Niagalla), features of the physical landscape (Sondondiala, Tambaoura, Linguekoto), or the name of guardian spirits (Maimouna, Ningri).[48]

Orpailleurs, geologists learned, avoided mining some tracts of land altogether due to the presence of malevolent forces. Colonial reports from Soudan and Guinea are riddled with stories of people rendered blind, insane, or deaf by handling gold nuggets. In 1913, Méniaud reported an account of this genre circulating several years prior in Guinea.

> I heard it affirmed by the natives that Mount Didi contained considerable wealth in gold, but that the devil did not wish to relinquish it. They added, in their ardent faith, that there are mortars and pestles for millet made entirely of gold, which were hidden by the first inhabitants of the region. Those who have seen them or attempted to move them were stricken with madness. A woman who still lives in the village of Fatoya discovered them, on a day when she was looking for firewood in the bush. At the moment when she leaned down to gather the pestles, she was violently knocked down on the ground by invisible hands and showered with blows. She could not rise until she let go of the previous instrument and returned to the village after having lost the ability to hear.[49]

There are two plausible reasons for the retribution of spirits in cases such as these. First, gold nuggets presumably contain powerful concentrations of nyama that were harmful to those who did not take ritual protections against this occult force. Second, there is no mention that the woman offered a sacrifice to spirits in exchange for the large quantity of gold contained in the golden mortar and pestle. In other stories of this genre, territorial spirits asked for the sacrifice of people for gold (see chapter 7). If West Africans refused to meet this sacrificial demand, they avoided mining the mineralized tract of land altogether or did so at the risk of bodily and psychological harm at the hands of angered spirits.

West Africa's ritual geology was in rapid evolution under colonial rule, as orpaillage spread in some zones and dried up in others, and as head taxes encouraged the commodification of labor and ritual payments on large multiethnic placer mines. The AOF's geologists translated elements of this ritual geology into scientific correspondence by marking the locations of abandoned orpaillage sites and reporting rumors about guardian land spirits in their field reports. As they archived the sacred engagement of orpailleurs with the earth, they also gained insights into the structural geology of Birimian rocks and the distribution of gold across the West African Craton.

Gold Prospecting in Ancient Quarters

In June 1939, several months prior to the outbreak of World War II, Marcel Bardin, a contractual geologist employed by the AOF, was sent to carry out "a methodical and rational study of the work undertaken by the natives on the gold deposits of Upper Guinea." Bardin was instructed to establish "their [gold deposits'] intrinsic value, their yield, and the average profits made by the orpailleurs."[50] The reliance of geologists on orpaillage—as a source of geological data, labor, and techniques—reached its apogee between the wars. Geologists profited from the expansion of orpaillage during the global financial depression by prospecting for gold in the wake of gold deposits newly discovered by orpailleurs. During this time period, geologists and orpailleurs, working in each other's shadow, discovered several major gold deposits that, decades later, would become the region's most lucrative corporate open-pit gold mines. Geologists also documented iron, copper, phosphate, and bauxite deposits in the federation. But gold was favored in the short-term due to the lower upfront expense to mine it compared with these industrial metals, which required railroads, major roadways, and electricity production.

For geologists, the value of mapping orpaillage sites was indirect and deferred. Most Africans mined alluvial deposits, whereas the AOF's geologists were primarily interested in lode ore that, they hoped, could one day be exploited by capital-intensive mines controlled by Europeans. But since alluvial deposits were generally formed in proximity to lode ore, mapping the former could lead geologists to the latter. Goloubinow refined methods of using orpaillage workings to guide prospecting for lode ore. He spent years living and working in Upper Guinea, gaining fluency in Maninka. He published a doctoral thesis on Guinea's gold resources and methodological articles on how to conduct "rapid gold prospecting" on West Africa's old rock platforms.[51] He elaborated his method in a 1940 article:

> The only guide for prospectors is generally a large-scale geological map, demarcating [...] gold-bearing regions to eventually prospect and indicating a certain number of rudimentary native mining sites, when they exist. Traditional prospecting work which consists of pits and surveys reaching down to the bedrock is slow and costly; it is very difficult to extend this to the entirety of a zone demarcated by the geological map; one is obliged to make a choice before beginning actual prospecting. To give oneself the best chances, the prospector usually chooses the site of old native mines.[52]

Goloubinow went on to explain that "native miners tend to group around the mountains, where water runs down." By studying the secondary deposits exploited by orpailleurs, prospectors could determine whether the gold originated from the decomposition of quartz located farther uphill.[53]

Goloubinow's hand-drawn maps of his gold-prospecting activities in northern Guinea visualize his method of triangulating orpaillage workings with features of the landscape—ridges, depressions, and riverways—to identify the likely location of lode ore. Figure 4.2, "Bassin inférieur du Lélé," is one of a series of maps attached to a 1935 prospecting report on the Lélé River basin. The map shows how "the author's itinerary" (*itinéraires de l'auteur*) intersects with "native works, current or former exploitations" (*travaux indigènes, exploitation actuels ou anciens*). The names of villages are indicated on the map, along with a "former women's mine" (*anciennes mines de femmes*). Some mine workings are simply labeled "old" (*ancien*); while others are dated.[54] Clusters of dots indicate "prospecting shaft lines" (*lignes*

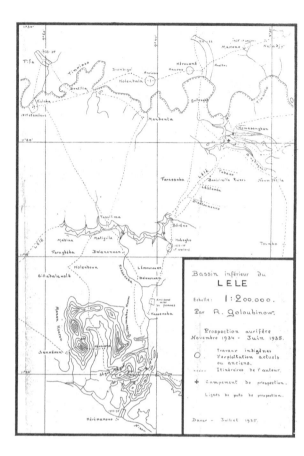

Figure 4.2 Map of the geological itinerary of Rostislav Goloubinow in the Lower Lélé Basin, Guinea, 1935. Courtesy of the Direction des Mines du Sénégal.

de puits de prospection) dug by Goloubinow's team to test gold concentrations. Many clusters align with "native works," revealing the extent to which Goloubinow's shadowed the prospecting activities of unnamed orpailleurs. Goloubinow also adopted orpailleurs' techniques—notably the use of the cylindrical "Maninka shafts" (*puits Malinké*), measuring three-quarters of a meter in diameter—as prospecting shafts.[55] Private gold prospectors in the interwar AOF also used the location of "indigenous gold exploitations" to determine if there were deposits "in their [orpailleurs'] former workings or in their proximity" of interest to European investors.[56]

Some technicians working in the AOF learned more indirectly from orpailleurs. This was the case for Eduard Julian, a French mining engineer who worked in interwar Guinea. In 1933, Julian piloted a model mine (*exploitation modèle*) in Kentinian, a village located in the heart of the circle of Siguiri. The goal of the project was to model "technically improved procedures" to orpailleurs to increase the quantity of gold they extracted from gold-bearing rock.[57] The governor-general financed the model mine on the grounds that, as long as "orpaillage substitutes for modern industry, we are morally obligated to improve the process of exploitation."[58] As Blondel put it in 1934, "To increase indigenous production ... reconciles both our moral duty and our material interest: to improve the well-being of orpailleurs and increase their buying power, which would benefit the colonial economy."[59] Julian demonstrated the use of wooden pillars to support subterranean mine caverns, designed to replace the rock pillars constructed by orpailleurs.[60] But Julian struggled to recruit workers, who preferred orpaillage to laboring for a colonial officer, and a flood rotted his wood supports.[61] In 1936, the Service of Mines closed the project, and Julian returned to France embroiled in a forced labor scandal.

Though Julian's model mine was a failure, he recorded numerous African gold discoveries while in Siguiri. While awaiting equipment shipments for the model mine, Julian passed the time by traveling to gold deposits recently discovered by orpailleurs. In 1933, for example, he visited a newly discovered mine near Kouroussa, where he tested orpaillage shafts. He recruited an elder to guide him to the "ancient quarter" of gold workings "abandoned more than 100 years ago," where he took more samples.[62] The overlap between Julian's efforts to improve orpaillage and his documentation of African gold discoveries was not lost on orpailleurs. Decades after Julian's departure, orpailleurs viewed any effort by French geologists to "improve" their techniques as a cover for French mining interests. This was the concern of Framoi Béréte, the postwar Guinean politician who accused French geologists of marketing gold deposits discovered by Africans to French financiers (see chapter 3).

With the onset of World War II, the AOF's Service of Mines retrenched its reliance on African mining economies as a source of subterranean knowledge and revenue. By August 1939, nonessential European personnel in the AOF, including most geologists, were enlisted in the French army. Within the year, the collaborationist Vichy regime had gained control over the south of France and most of the French empire, including the AOF. Marshal Philippe Pétain, leader of Vichy France, requisitioned peanuts, cotton, palm oil, and gold dust from the AOF to finance the war effort. The skeleton wartime staff of the Service of Mines scrambled to increase gold production to meet the demands of the governor-general of the AOF, who remained loyal to Vichy. Their strategy was twofold: to encourage orpaillage where it would not interfere with cash-crop production and to re-exploit orpaillage tailings.[63]

On the Poura goldfields of Haute-Volta, an important Atlantic-era center of gold mining and trade, the administration injected funds into a middling public-private partnership that dated to the mid-1930s to exploit a "large mass of rejected native exploitation of lode ore."[64] By processing the tailings of African mine workings at Poura, more than four kilograms of gold were recuperated in 1939, its first year of production. Encouraged by this success, the Service of Mines opened another state-run enterprise to exploit an African alluvial gold discovery: a deposit in Dahomey (now Benin).[65] Through the rest of the war, the AOF's sole mining industry was based on exploiting the tailings of earlier generations of orpailleurs. Ironically, just as the AOF's Service of Mines reached an apogee in its reliance on African mining economies, African orpaillage was criminalized outright. In 1942, the governor-general closed placer mines across the federation to funnel African labor toward agricultural production, deemed more important for the war effort.

L'Ingénieur and *l'Indigène* in the Postwar AOF

Subterranean knowledge did not flow in one direction in French West Africa. Orpailleurs also profited from the gold discoveries of European prospectors. As early as the 1890s, French prospectors working in Soudan complained to French commanders that Africans dug out their prospecting pits to create orpaillage sites.[66] This was the source of a controversy in the 1930s in the circle of Dabola, situated on Guinea's border with Sierra Leone, where orpailleurs "followed in the wake" of exploration trenches dug by a French firm. Local employees of the firm reported that, when the firm's "prospectors found interesting concentrations, the natives started working after the team had progressed 40 or 50 meters."[67] In 1949, a French company operating a dredge boat on the Falémé River began to prospect for gold in Soudan but was forced to abandon its permit when orpailleurs, having been informed "from the indiscretion of our own workers that there were rich deposits, used their usual methods to skim the richest parts of the deposit."[68]

Orpailleurs also learned new techniques from Europeans. In Siguiri of the 1910s, orpailleurs began damming rivers, based on observing French prospectors using this method, to reveal previously submerged alluvial deposits.[69] Orpailleurs readily adopted wooden sluices that were introduced by the AOF's Service of Mines in the 1930s. Orpailleurs' selective embrace of European mining methods built on centuries of technical exchange on the region's goldfields, including the adoption of Islamic weights; numismatic systems; and the spread of more angular, Akan-style mining shafts, well suited to wet climates, into other forested regions of West Africa. Africans also exchanged techniques with one another during the colonial period. Diamond digging, which became a boom industry in interwar Sierra Leone and in Guinea's forested region, drew heavily on gold-panning methods refined in Buré. And in the 1940s, orpailleurs in Kédougou recruited expert gold miners from Siguiri to teach them eluvial mining methods.[70] Far from two hermetically sealed mining "systems," European and African miners evolved their techniques, and made gold discoveries, in dialogue with one another.

The end of World War II in 1945 brought about a long-anticipated influx of funding for geological surveys and mining development in French West Africa. It also shifted the value geologists placed on orpailleurs from one focused on mapping their gold discoveries to an explicit attempt to integrate Africans into colonial knowledge production. At the Brazzaville Conference of 1944, a wartime meeting of European leaders, France and Britain embraced "development" as a renewed justification for imperial occupation. France ended a long-standing policy of self-financing in the colonies, which they renamed overseas territories, and invested in scientific research and industrial development. After the explosion of nuclear bombs in Hiroshima and Nagasaki, and with the metal demands of postwar reconstruction, France turned to its overseas territories as a source of "strategic" and "industrial" minerals. In 1945, France created an agency dedicated to prospecting for petroleum (Bureau de Recherche de Pétrole [BRP]) and one for uranium (Commissariat d'Energie Atomique [CEA]). In 1948, a final public organism, the Bureau Minier de la France d'Outre-mer (Bureau of Mines of Overseas France [BUMIFOM]), was created to develop mining projects for all other minerals in overseas France. Meanwhile, the AOF's Service of Mines became a major recipient of social and economic development funds financed in part by the US Marshall Plan. Under this new bureaucratic configuration, the AOF's Service of Mines would no longer operate mines. In theory, it would conduct geological surveys to orient mining projects that BUMIFOM organized as state or public-private mixed ventures.

After the war, the AOF's mining industry expanded from one based on African orpaillage and the exploitation of African gold mine tailings to include industrial phosphate and bauxite mines and the documentation of major deposits of uranium, petroleum, cassiterite, and iron. In 1944, after years of subordination to the Department of Public Works, the service became an independent federal department known as the Direction Fédérale des Mines de la Géologie (DFMG). Two years later, a three-story building was completed

COLONIAL GEOLOGY AND AFRICAN GOLD DISCOVERIES   123

in Dakar for the department. The building housed up to forty-five geologists and was equipped with modern laboratories, a mineral museum, dozens of offices, a mapmaking studio, and a library. With new scientific equipment and funding, the AOF's geologists undertook detailed studies of basement rock platforms and mineralization in Dahomey, Haute-Volta, Côte d'Ivoire, and Guinea. These studies generated data for dozens of doctoral theses completed when geologists returned to France. In these and other publications, the regional scope of West Africa's Birimian-age rocks came into view, previously seen on a more localized scale.[71] Exploration of younger sedimentary deposits near the Atlantic coast of West Africa led to discoveries of bauxite in Guinea and phosphate in Senegal. In the early 1950s, mixed state-private firms were created to exploit these metals, which replaced gold as the AOF's most important mineral exports until decolonization in the late 1950s.

Even as the mandate of the AOF's Service of Mines expanded to include other metals, gold prospecting remained a priority for the federation.[72] Due to the ubiquity of orpaillage workings, geologists argued, gold prospecting generated rapid insights into the region's Birimian rock formations, which could lead to the discovery of other hard metal or gemstone deposits of potential interest to the state or private firms. In 1946, the governor-general reopened the federation's placer mines, but orpaillage never reached its prewar levels due to suppressed gold prices (see chapter 3). Rising prices for agricultural products also made orpaillage less attractive. The Service of Mines saw the contraction of orpaillage as an opportunity for staff geologists to prospect for gold without attracting orpailleurs to their exploration trenches.[73] For them, the development of capital-intensive gold mines was finally within view, an industry that would supplant orpaillage and create jobs for Africans in industrial manufacture.

Geologists envisioned a role for orpailleurs in the transition to this industrial future, particularly in geological exploration. In the words of Gilbert Arnaud, the director of mines before and after the war, "Experienced miners, true specialists who have a deep experience with certain types of deposits and who conduct real prospecting..., probably more than 100,000 in number, already familiar with subterranean work and with recuperating gold, [are] immeasurable capital for the AOF that we must prudently manage."[74] Arnaud imagined that Africans would carry out the bulk of gold reconnaissance in the AOF, "at their risk but also to their entire benefit," with some technical assistance from geologists. The shortcoming of orpailleurs, he argued, was that they lacked "a general view of the geographic distribution of mineralized zones. They can therefore only extrapolate timidly beyond the quarters of former mines."[75] French geologists could eliminate this problem by offering an "aerial view" of gold distribution through maps. With the use of maps, geologists could collaborate with African prospectors to guide "African mining chiefs . . . to deposits they can extract with their empirical knowledge."[76]

André Marelle, who briefly directed the Service of Mines in 1948, also saw a dynamic role for "skilled Guinean shaft-diggers" in mineral research conducted in the federation.[77] Marelle recognized that "a problem very particular to the AOF is that of the insertion of customary orpaillage into the framework of mining development." He envisioned incorporating "this local craft into the gold industry" by encouraging orpailleurs to prospect for gold while restricting them from mining lode ore, which would be reserved for European enterprises. To implement this vision, Marelle drafted a plan to open a "school for prospectors and mining foremen" at the École Technique Supérieure de Bamako. The aim was to educate young men from gold-producing regions in French prospecting techniques.[78] The school in Bamako never came to fruition, but in the late 1940s geologists opened a school based on this model in Bas-Cavally, Côte d'Ivoire, where orpaillage was expanding.[79] In 1951, an École des Moniteurs des Mines was attached to Côte d'Ivoire's section of mines, at which engineers taught African orpailleurs how to read topographic maps, use a compass to mark their routes, and create a mineral profile based on soil sampling. African students with basic French fluency were taught to write reports and prepare documents for permit requests.

The École des Moniteurs des Mines, later renamed the École de Prospecteurs-Topographes, was an attempt to formalize the long-standing practice of European geologists and prospectors who sojourned in the AOF: to map, sample, and track orpailleurs to advance administrative knowledge of the distribution and concentration of gold. But Marelle's view departed from that of prewar colonial officials in that he envisioned orpailleurs as aides in a modern economy, not as people engaged in a traditional activity. Recognizing Africans as specialists enrolled in a "rational" organization of extraction articulated with a broader shift in the postwar AOF to seeing Africans as active participants in development.[80] Postwar colonial institutions and private firms trained Africans in scientific disciplines, including cartography, agronomy, medicine, and psychiatry. The AOF's Service of Mines took part in these efforts by training African assistants in the field and, after 1954, in the federal laboratories in Dakar.[81] Despite these changes, AOF's geologists did not see African miners as their equals. Postwar directors of the Service of Mines maintained a technical division between Africans—glossed in their reports as "natives" (*indigènes*)—and European "engineers" (*ingénieurs*). Africans would be trained as prospecting and geological aides, not as engineers and geologists.[82] Independence movements, which gained speed in the mid-1950s, troubled this vision, insisting that Africans be trained as scientists and managers of African-led mining enterprises.

Erasing Orpaillage

When the annual rains beckoned, the AOF's geologists returned to Dakar with dozens of hand-drawn maps and field reports and rock and soil samples. They had learned broken Wolof and Maninka while traveling with dozens of African porters on foot, on horseback, and in hammocks. They carried simple pencil drawings, sketched in journals and on parchment paper—a few embellished with watercolors. These sketches gave shape to the geological anomalies they encountered across the federation: granite rocks protruding like rotted teeth from the plains and waterfalls cascading along the cataracts of the Falémé. Other maps traced itineraries traveled by geologists on foot through abandoned orpaillage workings. Shaded pen marks on map legends corresponded to "old native mines" and farming hamlets. Geologists embedded these landscapes of human labor and settlement within more stable geophysical features of the land: depressions, streams, plateaus. In Dakar, field geologists collaborated with cartographers to draw formal maps to scale. They used blue and red pens to indicate the suspected location of lode-ore deposits in relationship to these data points. Some of the abandoned villages on these maps were once seasonal orpaillage sites, cosmopolitan hamlets of migrants congregated to mine for gold.

Across the roughly six decades of French colonial rule in West Africa, geologists shadowed orpailleurs, both living and dead, through the traces they left on the landscape: shafts, tunnels, caverns, and piles of discarded mine tailings. While many Atlantic-era European travelers to West Africa denigrated African mining traditions, by the turn of the twentieth century the AOF's geologists praised the skill and dexterity of male and female miners and marveled at "ancient [African] mines." In part, the reliance of geologists on the labor and knowledge of orpailleurs was an innovation born of necessity. Chronically underfunded until the postwar period, geologists tracked and mapped the gold discoveries of orpailleurs. Geologists also used technologies unavailable to orpailleurs: soil composition analysis and structural mapping. The search for subterranean knowledge in the AOF produced other kinds of knowledge: ethnographic, political, and ritual. Orpaillage was deeply embedded in the cultural and political history of West Africa. It was also enmeshed in the evolving ritual geology of the savanna, a centuries-old dialogue between diverse West African communities and the Birimian rock formations that geologists mapped for a global scientific community. For colonial technicians, engaging with this ritual geology was an obligatory passage point for acquiring insights into regional geology.

The exchange of techniques and gold discoveries between the AOF's geologists and orpailleurs shaped the methodology of geological research in overseas France. It also enabled colonial technicians to model the region's primary gold-bearing rock formations: Birimian rocks. An influx of funding after World War II enabled the AOF's Service of Mines to expand geological reconnaissance across the federation, gaining a more regional view of West Africa's structural geology and the place of Birimian formations within it. At the same time, two intertwined processes—one cartographic, the other temporal—erased the contributions of African orpailleurs to geological knowledge. Between the wars, maps drawn by geologists depicted the distribution of African placer mines in intimate relationship to the landscape, tracing the precise itineraries they walked and the location of every passing village. These maps were drawn on a large scale, where one centimeter equaled two hundred meters. Some maps encompassed no more than a single village and its farming hamlets; a cluster of settlements on a hillside; a row of mining shafts winding along a riverbed. As geological research accumulated over the decades, however, geologists drew maps at smaller scales, to depict geological formations across multiple colonies. While these smaller-scale maps were drawn from aggregating data from maps of African mines and settlements, the final product no longer signaled the presence of orpaillage on the landscape. Mineral discoveries made by orpailleurs were subsumed under colors that corresponded to auriferous zones on map legends. Geologists still included maps at larger scale in their field reports and doctoral theses based on research in West Africa. Figure 4.3 exemplifies the attention given to the location of African gold placer deposits in a geology thesis focused on southwestern Côte d'Ivoire. But concise publications on this research that appeared in international scientific journals offer only an "aerial view" of colony or federal-level mineral inventories that no longer included the mineral discoveries of orpailleurs—and the names of their villages and gold placers—on the ground.

Temporal delays between the mapping of gold mines and the opening of industrial-scale mines facilitated amnesia and the erasure of contributions by orpailleurs to colonial-era gold discoveries. The AOF's geologists documented

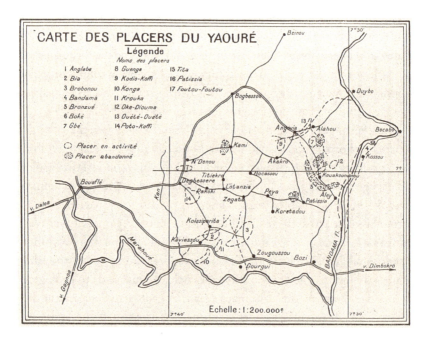

Figure 4.3 "Map of Yaouré Placers." Côte d'Ivoire, 1950. From Michel Bolgarsky, *Étude géologique et description pétrographique du Sud-Ouest de la Côte d'Ivoire*, 135.

dozens of gold deposits, many of them discovered by orpailleurs, over the course of six decades of colonial rule. But apart from short-lived private mining operations, and the Poura mining project in Haute-Volta, only orpailleurs exploited these deposits under French rule. Capital-intensive gold mines would not be opened in the former federation of the AOF until the late 1990s. In an ethnography of petroleum exploration in São Tomé and Principe, Gisa Weszkalnys describes the temporal "pauses" in mineral exploration as central to the contradictory processes entailed in the capitalist accumulation of nature. Pauses, Weszkalnys argues, are acute in "frontier regions" where "scientific knowledge is incomplete, and geological conditions challenging."[83] In the case of gold mining in the AOF, the delay between the colonial mapping of key goldfields and the industrial mining of these deposits spanned decades. The interim period was filled by the heady optimism and bitter disappointments of independence, the global oil crisis, structural adjustment, and the expansion of corporate mining across the formerly colonized world. In the next chapter, I turn to the social and scientific life of this pause on the goldfields of one independent nation-state: Senegal.

5
Mineral Mapping and the Global Cold War in Sénégal Oriental

When "the Russians" arrived in Kédougou in 1971, they requested El Hadj Mori Tigana's compound by name. In the early 1960s, just after Senegal's independence from France, Mori Tigana earned a reputation as a skilled prospecting aid in working with earth scientists from Switzerland, Poland, Canada, the Soviet Union, and from the Senegalese capital, Dakar. Tigana assisted Soviet scientists in establishing a base camp in Mamakono, home of the Atlantic-era "slave king," Taubry Sidibé.[1] In the 1970s, Mamakono's population hovered at several hundred. The village had already hosted four international mineral research missions, the products of cooperative research protocols signed between independent Senegal and the United Nations (UN), France, and the Soviet Union.

The 1960s was "the time of electricity in Mamakono," when geologists powered floodlights with diesel generators to sort soil samples at night and children played in the hazy glow of artificial light. Senegalese ministers visited elders in the village, urging them to support the work of mineral missions. Geological research, they were told, would transform Kédougou into an engine of industrial development for independent Senegal. The mineral missions did document major reserves of iron and gold. But prices for hard metals were low at the time, and Kédougou was distant from Dakar's ports. As a result, mineral prospects discovered by these missions became "shelf projects"—shelved in the archives of Senegal's Direction des Mines et de la Géologie (Department of Mines and Geology [DMG]).[2] Decades later, in the early 2000s, this geological research proved crucial to Senegal's emergence as a major gold producer. Many of the corporate-owned gold mines operating today in Senegal, Mali, and Guinea began as independence-era shelf projects.

This chapter shifts the geographic and temporal focus of this book from the goldfields of the AOF to the Birimian rocks of a single postcolonial state:

Senegal. Independence-era mineral missions offer a window onto a poorly understood chapter in the history of science in postcolonial West Africa. How did decolonizing African states generate knowledge about newly national subterranean resources? What role did rural citizens, such as Tigana, play in identifying and valorizing minerals? To address these questions, I turn to the political life of exploration geology: the slow and uncertain scientific labor required to transform fluids and rocks into operative mines. Like most African states, Senegal developed knowledge of its subsoil and expanded national expertise in the earth sciences in a context of financial austerity.[3] Senegal's DMG was a "bricoleur" of geological expertise, creatively combining competitive offers for cooperative scientific assistance with the environmental knowledge of its rural citizens. The French anthropologist Claude Lévi-Strauss conceived of the bricoleur as someone who is "able to perform a large number of diverse tasks" while "making do with the 'means on hand'" through the use of "heterogeneous tools and materials."[4] I extend the term to describe how Senegal navigated scientific cooperation during the global Cold War to conduct mineral surveys: a crucial component of scientific sovereignty.

Scientific ambitions figured prominently in the goals of African leaders at independence. Africa's independence generation demanded to be stakeholders in scientific work while advocating for equal access to scientific training and innovation conducted by Africans in Africa.[5] States across the continent pursued the Africanization of scientific staff, the building of national laboratories, and acquiring access to scientific education for African citizens. The expansion of laboratories at independence built on growing investments in scientific research in postwar Africa by the French and British.[6] Guinea's first president, Sékou Touré, opened Pharma Guinée, a pharmaceutical factory dedicated to "Guinean" plant-based formulas. In Ghana, Kwame Nkrumah began a quest to acquire a nuclear reactor and national expertise in nuclear physics.[7] Meanwhile, in Senegal, Léopold Sédar Senghor oversaw the opening of state toxicology, botany, and nutrition laboratories.

The history of science in postcolonial Africa is a nascent but growing field. In Francophone Africa, research has focused on the activities of French *coopération* in the urban laboratories of African capitals. The coopération was a series of formal contracts signed between the French Republic and its former colonies, in most cases, for institutional and technical assistance. Many French scientists converted jobs in the colonial service into careers as technical advisors, *coopérants*, who worked for the government and universities of independent African states. Guillaume Lachenal's study of the perpetual

130   CHAPTER FIVE

delay of the "Cameroonization" of the Pasteur Institute by coopérants, and Noémi Tousignant's account of how African scientists navigated the racist hierarchies of French coopération in a Senegalese toxicology lab offer a granular view on the fraught "Franco-African" relationship in scientific settings.[8] However, these studies treat the categories of African and European as the most salient divisions in postcolonial scientific practice.[9] This dichotomy may well apply to labor routines in urban laboratories of Dakar and Yaoundé. But a markedly different story emerges from geological field research in southeastern Senegal (renamed Sénégal Oriental at independence). Mineral missions conducted in the borderlands of the Senegalese state in the 1960s and 1970s materialized ethnic hierarchies among different groups of West Africans. By recruiting technicians in Dakar to manage local workers in Sénégal Oriental, independence-era mineral missions reinforced the French practice of placing coastal Senegalese in positions of authority over other ethnolinguistic groups. Ethnic and regional divisions defined hierarchies in colonial and early postcolonial scientific work as much as those between Africans and Europeans.

This chapter joins a growing effort to push studies of the global Cold War in Africa beyond a focus on ideological battles and formal diplomacy to examine how newly independent states leveraged competing offers for technical assistance to meet their own goals.[10] Senegal initially presents as a rather mundane country to study the politics of Cold War technical aid. Scholars have long echoed Senghor's critics, who accused him of neocolonialism and a stifling reliance on France.[11] This is an overly simplified view of Senegal's postcolonial history. While Senghor was cautious of Soviet involvement in Africa, he also accepted Soviet aid in key technical domains. From the perspective of scientific assistance and capacity building, Senegal was no exception to the rule that decolonization in Africa unfolded in a transnational, and not simply a postimperial, framework.

I also draw attention to the central role of the embodied praxis and expertise of orpailleurs from southeastern Senegal to the mineral discoveries made by independence-era mineral missions. Senegalese, Euro-American, and Soviet geologists sampled orpaillage workings, or juuras, and employed orpailleurs to lead them to active and abandoned juuras. Gender played a role in these exchanges. Due to low gold prices, orpaillage was largely a women's industry in the 1960s. Locally recruited men shared the location of juuras, which they viewed as women's work sites. The reliance of mineral missions on the discoveries and expertise of orpailleurs built on the precedent of colonial-era geology (chapter 4), although it was carried out in a postcolonial policy environment in which orpaillage was marginalized in favor of state-run enterprises. In the end, the missions did not lead to the hoped-for development of national mines in southeastern Senegal. The opening of the region's first industrial-scale gold mine was decades away. But the scientific groundwork for Senegal's neoliberal mining boom, and the grievances it produced over regional inequality and gold discovery, was laid in the early aftermath of colonial rule.

Orpaillage and African Socialism

While the AOF's colonial-era mining laws sanctioned orpaillage in certain corridors and seasons, orpaillage was effectively criminalized by independent Mali (formerly Soudan), Guinea, and Senegal, the states in which it had flourished under colonialism. African leaders viewed orpaillage as antithetical to the principles of African socialism and the goal of building modern, nationalized industries. By the late 1950s, West African states aimed to own and operate capitalized mines staffed by African engineers, managers, and workers. The political agendas of postwar international organizations reinforced this policy orientation, as did laws adopted by independence-era leaders in Africa that nationalized land and the subsoil, and emphasized the importance of farming to African socialism.

In 1958, Guinea became the first African colony to gain independence from France by voting "no" to French President Charles de Gaulle's referendum to join the French Community. In 1960, Senegal and Mali became independent through a power-transfer agreement.[12] Léopold Sédar Senghor, Sékou Touré, and Modibo Keita became, respectively, the presidents of independent Senegal, Guinea, and Mali.[13] All three men were active in the AOF's postwar politics. At independence they embraced African socialism as their guiding ideology, although what socialism meant in practice varied widely across these states.[14] Guinea and Mali expelled the French military from their territories, minted national currencies, and courted technical and financial assistance from the Soviet Union, the People's Republic of China, and the United Arab Republic.[15] Senegal declared itself an independent republic but remained linked to France by privileged trading policies, military assistance, and a shared monetary system. For Senghor, socialism had to be adapted to "African realities" rather than Marxist-Leninist–style communism.[16] He emphasized the importance of technological development—which he called *technicité*—but believed the country's future was primarily agrarian, grounded in the "communitarian" principles of farming and village life.

132   CHAPTER FIVE

Keita and Touré shared Senghor's conviction that farming was the core of African moral and economic development. This ideological commitment to farming shaped land-nationalization policies in all three states that reinforced state ownership of land, ocean resources off the coast, and of the subsoil.[17] Meanwhile, international organizations also encouraged African states to strengthen state control of natural resources. The Bandung Conference of 1955, attended by African and Asian participants, elaborated the concept of "resource sovereignty" as the right of states to use their natural endowments for public utility, security, and national interest. The Non-Aligned Movement adopted the principle of resource sovereignty. The UN General Assembly officially recognized this principle in 1960 and 1962 and encouraged African states to nationalize mines to restrict the access of private (former imperial) firms to minerals.[18]

The first mining codes adopted by Touré and Keita outlawed orpaillage. There was no room in the policy framework of decolonizing African states in the 1960s for a mobile extractive tradition that sustained seasonal cities and crossed national borders. Orpailleurs were neither industrial workers on state-owned industries nor year-round farmers rooted in fixed villages: two ideals of African socialism. Migration to goldfields posed obstacles to statist desires to control markets and secure borders against smuggling. The centrality of juulas, African Muslim traders, in gold collection also challenged state attempts to dismantle colonial trade monopolies over rural producers in which juulas played an intermediary role with French and Lebanese merchants. For Touré, curbing orpaillage would reduce what he described as the parasitic usury of African peasants by juulas.[19] In a show of force, Touré dispatched the Guinean military in 1960 to close the gold mines of Siguiri.[20] By the end of 1963, Keita had encouraged all citizens to farm by calling for a "return to the earth" (*retour à la terre*). He closed the placer mines of Kéniéba, a policy enforced by rural paramilitary organizations created by the government to "dissuade the departure of adventurers who put their interests before those of the state."[21]

Senghor took a less militant position. Like his counterparts in Mali and Guinea, he created national agricultural and commercial companies designed to cut out private traders, including juulas, as middlemen in rural commodity production.[22] But Senghor was careful not to alienate the patronage of the Muridiyya, the powerful Muslim religious order that coordinated migrant labor on Senegal's peanut fields under French colonialism. He also did not close the placer mines of Senegal, where orpaillage was limited to Sénégal Oriental. Yet the mining codes ratified by Senghor neither mentioned nor protected the practice. Beginning in the 1970s, a series of devastating droughts would force West African leaders to reconsider the criminalization of orpaillage adopted at independence.

Decolonization and Development in Sénégal Oriental

At independence, Senegal's leaders aimed to "reterritorialize" the country's rural economy to redress the unequal geographic legacies of French colonial rule. Senegal's infrastructure centered on roads, rails, and ports to cultivate and evacuate peanuts to the coast. As a result, regions peripheral to peanut cultivation were poorly integrated into the national territory. They were also culturally distinct from the coast and central-western peanut basin, which were dominated by ethnic Wolof and the Muridiyya brotherhood. An administrative bias toward ethnic Wolof developed under colonial rule due to the early recruiting of Wolof soldiers into the French army and the concentration of Wolof language and culture on the coast, the administrative seat of the AOF.[23] While Senghor himself was Catholic and ethnic Serer, his political base was built on alliances with the Muridiyya, who held sway over the votes of their followers (*taalibe*).

Senghor and Mamadou Dia, Senegal's prime minister and Senghor's right-hand man from 1957 to 1962, aimed to better integrate the country's geographic peripheries by encouraging regional economic specialties beyond peanut cultivation. They also worried that peripheral regions—including Kédougou, the Casamance, and the Fouta Toro—could become bastions of political resistance.[24] Indeed, in the late 1950s, politicians from these zones challenged Senghor's growing popularity in coastal Senegal and among the Muridiyya. Kédougou's leading political figure of the era was Mady Cissokho. Cissokho was born into a Muslim clerical family in Missirah Sirimana (also known as Sirimana).[25] He began his career as a clerk for the colonial state in Tambacounda and built a political following by visiting migrants from eastern Senegal at the railroad station in Tambacounda in transit from the navètane, the seasonal migration to cultivate peanuts on African-owned farms. While the navètane was putatively voluntary, many residents of the region were forced to undertake it to pay colonial head taxes and to meet state-dictated labor quotas. Cissokho assisted migrants who fell ill during this long voyage, which began and ended for residents of Kédougou with a 250 kilometer, week-long journey, often undertaken on foot.[26] Radicalized by these encounters, Cissokho created his own political party, the Union Démocratique des Ressortissants du Sénégal Oriental (UDRSO), which beat the candidate from Senghor's party, the Bloc Populaire Sénégalais (BPS), in the 1956 elections for Senegal's Territorial Assembly.[27] Senghor reportedly viewed Cissokho, who traveled with a private militia for protection, as a threat to unifying the country's southern regions.[28]

After Senghor became the president of Senegal in 1960, he persuaded Mady Cissokho to join his administration—a signature of Senghor's strategy of absorbing his political opponents.[29] Cissokho quickly rose in the political ranks. In 1961, he was elected the first deputy and mayor of the commune of Kédougou. In the same year, Senghor and Dia sent a special mission of Senegalese technical advisers, called Opération Kédougou, to study the economic and social life of Kédougou. The report described a circle that was "barely integrated into the Senegalese territory," echoing the concerns of colonial officials who reported that the circle was "isolated" from "Senegal properly speaking."[30] The mission underscored the unique developmental potential of Kédougou based on the mineral endowments of the region's Birimian rocks and the Niokolo-Koba National Park, an interwar colonial game preserve reclassified as a nature preserve in 1945.

Opération Kédougou was one of several missions that informed a new developmental cartography for Senegal in the 1960s. Mamadou Dia lobbied the Senegalese National Assembly to replace colonial administrative circles with larger regional units that could facilitate regional "developmental poles." They lumped the colonial-era provinces of Kédougou and Niani-Ouli (Tambacounda) into the single region of Sénégal Oriental, with a capital in Tambacounda.[31] In a bid to improve the productivity of household farming, Dia started a subsidy program for fertilizer, seeds, and draft plows alongside a program of rural technical and social assistance called Animation Rurale.[32] Senegalese field agents, or *animateurs*, extended both agricultural techniques and socialist principles to farmers.[33] Dia's left-leaning policies precipitated his political downfall. In 1962, Senghor accused Dia of planning a military coup and ultimately imprisoned him for more than a decade in Kédougou in a private jail designed for his detainment.[34] Dia's imprisonment solidified Kédougou's reputation as an exile for marginalized bureaucrats.

Despite the early attention given by Senghor and Dia to integrating peripheral regions into Senegal's national economy, the developmental goals for Sénégal Oriental remained vague in early planning documents.[35] Throughout the 1960s, the administration organized multidisciplinary research teams who proposed regional developmental specializations focused on a variety of export crops, animal husbandry, and subsidized agricultural schemes. By contrast, a very different group of scientists traveled to Sénégal Oriental: geologists, geochemists, and machine operators. They were commissioned to map the subsoil rather than human agrarian systems, and the research conducted by mineral missions worked to transform Sénégal Oriental into a natural reserve for the Senegalese state. During the same time period, Senghor also renewed investment in the Niokolo-Koba National Park. In both 1969 and 1975, he expanded the park to become the largest refuge for large mammals in former French West Africa. Senghor promoted the park as a safari destination for French and Senegalese tourists to view lions, hippopotami, chimpanzees, and elephants. To accommodate the park's expansion, the Senegalese army evicted and relocated more than a dozen villages.[36] These were the first in a series of displacements in Sénégal Oriental by state authorities hoping to generate revenues from the region's unique natural resource base. The park's expansion eliminated the possibility of linking Kédougou to Casamance by a southern route below the Gambia River. Kédougou would remain accessible to the rest of Senegal only by a northern road to Tambacounda, which was not paved until 1996.

Senegal in Search of Subterranean Knowledge

In the 1960s, a host of foreign governments and multilateral agencies extended offers of technical assistance to African states. Senegal's DMG accrued geological knowledge by patchworking cooperative research protocols for geological exploration, all of which carried divergent political expectations in the context of the Cold War. France remained the largest contributor to geological research in Senegal, but narrowly.[37] Protocols with the UN and the USSR also funded mineral exploration and trained the first generation of Senegalese geologists and mining engineers.

Geology was well adapted to the vagaries of international funding and lapses between projects. Research on agriculture and riverine ecology was quickly outdated with shifts in rainfall patterns, emergent parasites, or available fertilizers. But because geological formations are relatively static, knowledge of the subsurface could be aggregated piecemeal over time. The Senegalese state could complement geological research conducted by one mission with prospecting carried out by a different team of earth scientists' years after the initial study. The state's need to create a bricolage from divergent funding streams underscores the financial austerity in which scientific research was undertaken in the early decades of African independence.

As West African governments transformed colonial buildings into national ministries and laboratories, France converted its colonial institutions into public and parastatal organizations. A key component of French foreign policy after decolonization was maintaining a large technical aid program in former French colonies in Africa. In 1959, the Ministry of Cooperation, known colloquially as La Coopération, replaced the Ministry of Overseas France. That same year, two colonial institutions dedicated to geological research and mining—the AOF's Direction Fédérale des Mines et de la Géologie (DFMG) and the Bureau Minier de la France d'Outre-mer (BUMIFOM)—were absorbed into a single French parastatal: the Bureau de Recherches Géologiques et Minières (BRGM). One branch of the BRGM commercialized mining projects overseas; the other offered technical assistance. Both branches intervened primarily in France's former colonies. In many respects, the BRGM's activities in Senegal remained very colonial. For example, the bureau retained control of the palatial colonial DFMG building in Dakar, which housed state-of-the-art laboratories, a cartographic service, mineral collections, and a massive scientific library.[38] Meanwhile, the DMG of independent Senegal occupied a few sparse offices in an aging colonial building in downtown Dakar. The DMG's meager budget and laboratory made it reliant on foreign assistance and the BRGM.

The bald political calculations that characterized much of French aid in the 1960s and '70s were evident in accords signed between the BRGM and La Coopération with African states to finance geological research. In theory, these accords aimed to train Africans in the earth sciences and to generate baseline geological data of interest to building independent mining industries. But they also promoted the mining interests of the French state and private industries.[39] For one, the BRGM was a major recipient of money from the Fonds d'Aide et de Coopération (FAC), the funding branch of La Coopération, although the BRGM's research was primarily focused on locating minerals of interest to France rather than building national scientific capacity in Africa. Second, the BRGM primarily employed French (not African) scientists, most of whom had worked for colonial administrations. In their postcolonial "African careers" (*carrières africaines*), French geologists led a comfortable lifestyle in Dakar, with house servants, leisurely work schedules, and discretion over research agendas.[40] French influence also remained strong within the Geology Department at the University of Dakar. French coopérants staffed many of the key roles in the department, including the department chair, until 1980, when Ousseynou Dia became the first Senegalese chair. This transfer was part of a much delayed process of

Figure 5.1 Geomorphological sketch of Tinkoto region. Tinkoto, Sénégal 1961. Report prepared by Robert Giraudon for the Bureau de Recherche Géologique et Minière.

Senegalization of research staff, marked by the renaming of the University of Dakar in 1987 to the Université Cheikh Anta Diop (UCAD), after the Senegalese historian and physicist.[41]

The DMG acquired autonomy from French technical advisers by recruiting independent funding sources to pursue their own agendas for geological research. In the 1960s and 1970s, this agenda focused on the Birimian rocks of southeastern Senegal.[42] The presence of gold in the region was well known due to orpaillage and early French efforts to mine Bambuk. In the postwar period, several French geologists prospected for gold in the region by sampling active orpaillage sites, including the juuras of Tinkoto (figure 5.1), Mamakono, Khossanto, Laminia, and Sabodala.[43] A thriving precolonial blacksmithing industry and abandoned iron kilns had also drawn the attention of colonial geologists to the presence of iron on Senegal's border with Guinea. In 1962, the FAC funded an aerial magnetic survey of Sénégal Oriental. The survey detected magnetic anomalies, but field geology was needed to confirm whether those anomalies aligned with hard metal deposits that could be exploited economically. For this, the DMG appealed to the UN.

During the 1950s and 1960s, the UN extended considerable assistance to independent states in Africa for mineral mapping and prospecting. The UN's Special Fund, created in 1958, financed exploration geology in "developing countries."[44] It considered national geological surveys crucial for countries to evaluate the mineral potential of their territory for national defense and industrial development. The United Nations aimed to transcend Cold War political alliances by recruiting multinational teams of experts to deemphasize the political agendas of particular member states.[45] But politics seeped into UN missions, as it did into French technical assistance. In the 1950s, powerful UN member-states, including the United States and the USSR, saw Africa as a new market for metals to support their growing industrial sectors. The UN was also concerned about the outstripping of mineral resources by rapid global population growth. Mineral missions in Africa, Southeast Asia, and Latin America allowed the UN to support the national development of postcolonial states while acquiring a global view of available minerals.

In the early 1960s, Senegal signed accords for two major UN technical missions. One included a study of the technical feasibility of building a dam on the Senegal River. The other was for a broad "Mineral Survey of Sénégal Oriental" to test the anomalies detected in the 1962 aeromagnetic surveys of Senegal's Birimian rocks.[46] The second goal of the UN mission in Sénégal Oriental was to provide technical training to Senegalese personnel in the field and by the attribution of scholarships in geochemistry, geophysics, and geology.[47] The UN and Senegal signed an initial protocol for a general mineral survey from 1963 to 1965, and renewed the protocol for two phases: one focused on gold and diamonds (1966–69) and the other on copper (1970–71).

At first blush, the UN experts who arrived in Senegal in January 1963 embodied the organization's stated commitment to national diversity. Out of the initial group of ten UN personnel, two were French; two, Swiss; two, Russian; and one each from the Netherlands, Spain, Canada, and Belgium. But this apparent diversity belied continuities with French colonial expertise. Three of the four geologists assigned to the UN mission in Sénégal Oriental were former employees of the BRGM who had previously worked in Sénégal

Oriental (in some cases within the same year as the UN mission).[48] The UN also relied on the BRGM for laboratory services. Despite these continuities, the UN mission framed its work in Senegal as a break from colonial-era geology, which, it argued in its reports, had focused too much on basic geological questions rather than locating exploitable deposits.[49]

The UN covered the costs of research equipment, laboratory services, and the travel and salaries of its own technical experts from abroad. The Senegalese state, in exchange, furnished fuel and lodging in Dakar for experts, as well as the salaries of Senegalese employed for the mission (figure 5.2). Senegalese personnel were divided into three categories: scientists and technicians; mechanics and administrative assistants; and manual laborers. The first two categories were recruited in Dakar, the third in Kédougou. The Senegalese personnel recruited in Dakar included Ousseynou Dia, Pierre Diadhiou, Mouhamadou Sy, Mountaga Diallo, and Mamadou Yacine Fall. These men went on to occupy the most important posts within the DMG, the UCAD Geology Department, and Senegal's private mineral industry.[50] In Sénégal Oriental, the UN established a base camp in Mako, a Maninka and Pular village situated on the Gambia River in the department of Kédougou. From Mako, the mission split into teams that investigated smaller quadrants of the UN's 25,000 square kilometer research zone.[51] Teams consisted of a single UN expert, one to two Senegalese geological aides or prospectors, and anywhere from six to twenty-five local workers. Equipped with all-terrain vehicles, the teams worked relatively autonomously. Technical hierarchies emerged in the clustering of UN experts during field research. Soviet geologists specialized in gold prospecting. Some French and Swiss geologists returned to zones where they had worked for the French administration before independence. A number of field scientists were familiar with Birimian rock formations from cooperative technical research carried out in Ghana, which began hosting Soviet scientists in 1957. When the UN mission to Sénégal Oriental was renewed in the 1960s to focus on gold and diamond prospecting, Soviet geologists replaced the Francophones.

While the UN mission did not find diamonds in Sénégal Oriental, they did catalogue gold, chromite, copper, iron, lead, and uranium. But these deposits could not be profitably exploited at current market prices for hard metals. The distance of the region from coastal ports and obstacles to generating electrical power made mining too costly. The UN recommended that the DMG conduct more detailed prospecting of lode-ore gold deposits, particularly in the vicinity of Sabodala and Khossanto in the department of Saraya.

Figure 5.2 Research carried out by the United Nations prior to 1963. Map prepared for the United Nations' "Study of the Mineral Resources of Sénégal Oriental, 1970–71." Courtesy of the Direction des Mines du Sénégal.

The DMG carried through on the UN's advice and reached out to the USSR for cooperative assistance. In the 1960s, the relationship between Senegal and the USSR was guarded and tense. Despite the exchange of diplomatic missions in the early 1960s, diplomats from the USSR vocally characterized Senegal and Côte d'Ivoire as "semi-colonies."[52] Senghor, in turn, critiqued Soviet and Cuban involvement in Africa as a "reconquest from the east." These tensions did not stop the DMG from capitalizing on the USSR's offers of technical aid. In 1969, the DMG signed an accord with the USSR for assistance conducting gold and diamond prospecting in Sénégal Oriental.[53] Known colloquially as "Sénégalo-Sovietique," the mission lasted for three years, the longest Soviet mission in Senegal. Sénégalo-Sovietique was unique in that it was staffed exclusively by Soviets and overseen by a Senegalese geologist, Mouhamadou Sy, then the director of the DMG in Dakar.[54]

From 1971 to 1973, Soviets chose Mamakono as their primary base camp, with sub-camps at Wassangara and Mahina-Mine. In this time, roughly twenty-five Soviet experts, a dozen Senegalese technicians, and more than 220 local laborers worked for the mission. Sénégalo-Sovietique did not contract with the BRGM for laboratory services; it performed its own geochemical analyses in the field and at the DMG laboratory in Dakar, where Soviet geologists trained Senegalese counterparts in minerology. When the mission concluded in 1973, Russian geologists had mapped a massive lode-ore gold deposit they named Sabodala, after a village two kilometers to the south.[55] Sabodala was the most significant discovery of the independence-era mineral missions. The discovery of Sabodala was the collective labor of the DMG's bricolage of funding from the BRGM, the UN, and Sénégalo-Sovietique. Orpailleurs were also part of Sabodala's discovery, a fact that emerges only piecemeal in the reports of cooperative missions. It is to their stories that we now turn.

Sorting Out the Missions

> In the time of Charles de Gaulle, we migrated to farm peanuts. In the time of Senghor, we went into the bush. It was hard work. We slept and ate in the bush. We took samples of the earth, pounded and sorted them. All of this work went to Dakar.[56]

Telli Diallo, a resident of Kanoumering now in his late eighties, worked for eight seasons on mineral missions hosted by the BRGM and the UN. In the 1960s, work on these missions offered the first local alternative to navètane migration for earning a dry season wage. Missions employed regional residents as cooks, laborers, geological aides, and blacksmiths to repair tools used to dig exploration trenches. The missions paid a solid weekly wage, and many allocated a weekly food ration. Each Saturday, the UN paid local hunters to track antelope and divided the meat among the male workers. The allocation of food rations is remembered as an exemplary display of social solidarity.[57] Base camps for exploration were established adjacent to villages and consisted of tents and huts of local design and materials. In a single dry season, the UN employed between one hundred and two hundred workers from Kédougou, and the Soviets recruited close to one hundred. The BRGM and private French firms also signed a number of conventions with the Senegalese state for mineral prospecting in Sénégal Oriental that overlapped with the UN and Sénégalo-Sovietique. Senegalese prospecting aides

142   CHAPTER FIVE

recruited from Dakar and regional residents worked for multiple missions in the 1960s and 1970s. Toumanie Touré, whom I interviewed in 2014 in Mamakono, described a rotating door of employment: "They took me in 1962, '63, '64, '65. I worked all those years. [In] '62 I was with the BRGM, but in '63 it was [the UN] that took me on. In 1963 they divided. It was the same work, but there were different camps. The BRGM was to a side, and UN was to a side.... I knew geologists who worked for the BRGM. The next year they were with the UN. It was like us: one year with the BRGM, another year with the UN."[58]

Styles of labor organization, techniques for digging exploration trenches, and the social atmosphere of teams differed from one mission and year to the next. The unifying factor in the memory of the now elderly men who worked on these missions was a reliable cycle of dry season work. Sembou Danfakha, who worked for both the BRGM and the UN in the late 1960s, reflected on the stream of foreign scientists who visited villages near Saraya: "It is the research that never finished. Every time a group of *tubabs* [white people] arrived, we knew they had come to the mountain. I guided them. My father guided them. Now my son works for them. We dig for them. They take samples of rock back to Dakar, to Paris, to Moscow. Wherever they come from. For us, it was the white people who come."[59]

Mineral missions worked across different regions of Sénégal Oriental, where they prospected for iron, copper, molybdenum, cassiterite, monazite, gold, diamonds, and copper, lead, and uranium. The majority of work focused on the two major shear zones found in the Birimian rocks of the Kédougou-Kéniéba Inlier: historical Bambuk. Most of the magnetic anomalies detected in the 1962 aerial surveys of the region were located in these shear zones, which host the region's major gold deposits and historical orpaillage sites. For this reason, Senegalese, Euro-American, and Soviet earth scientists became frequent visitors to Kédougou's juuras, where they explored for gold and other minerals discovered by earlier geologists. The Sénégalo-Sovietique mission began its reconnaissance by sampling soils "from known metal-bearing prospects, of orpaillage sites." As its final report detailed, "[we carried out our work] in the most interesting part of the territory of Sénégal Oriental, including the main orpaillage centers (Kerekounda, Sambarabougou, Moura, etc....). In this territory are found the richest gold placers."[60]

In 1961, a BRGM mission led by the French geologist Robert Giraudon established a base camp in Tinkoto, which he described as an "old village abandoned for its insalubrity that remains frequented seasonally by orpailleurs from the North (Bambaraya)."[61] Giraudon prospected for lead and molybdenum, metals indexed by French geologists then employed by colonial institutions, who prospected for gold in the region several years prior to Senegal's independence from France. In the 1970s, Khossanto, today a large village and orpaillage site, was a favored base camp for the Commissariat à l'Énergie Atomique (CEA), a French parastatal that explored for uranium. French prospectors began working in Khossanto in the 1950s—then a "center of artisanal exploitation of gold"—where they observed residents exploiting lode-ore deposits, crushing gold-bearing quartz into a powder before washing it.[62] The UN's geologists frequented the juuras of Sambarabugu, Sabodala, Kerekounda, Daloto, and Sékoto-kô. From April to June, wrote Mohamadou Sy in a UN report, "there is a veritable swarm of gold diggers—some of whom come from elsewhere in the Malian territory."[63]

Mineral missions actively recruited orpailleurs for their expertise in the art of digging orpailleur-style shafts. As remarked in the final UN report, "The peasants come to work as manual laborers in the prospecting teams. Their traditions as orpailleurs make them dynamic shaft diggers."[64] By the 1960s, it was standard practice in mineral prospecting in former AOF states to dig exploration trenches in the style of orpailleur shafts (*puits type orpailleur*). Their diameter (roughly three-quarters of a meter) and cylindrical shape was stable in the sandy soils where alluvial deposits were found along regional riverways and in the denser laterite soils of geological shear zones.[65] Figure 5.3, drawn from a 1961 BRGM report on mineral prospecting in Kédougou, depicts a typical cross-section reference to orpailleur-style shafts.

Geologists asked Maninka orpailleurs to guide them to former and active juuras, a practice that was common in Guinea, Soudan (now Mali), and Senegal under colonial rule (see chapter 4). Sembou Danfakha, a resident of Saraya, dug prospecting trenches for the BRGM and for the CEA in the 1970s. He described the interplay between the prospecting techniques of geologists and those of orpailleurs:

> Yes, yes, of course when the missions came they had a map of the land. But they would also take a native from here. They would recruit an orpailleur to show them the points [*juuras*]. They [...] had maps and photographs. Then there were photographs taken from airplanes. But photographs and the land, they are not the same. You need someone to show you the place. On the map it looks one way, but on the ground everything can be different.[66]

As Danfakha infers, geologists drew on a range of tools to determine whether a zone contained hard metals of interest: aeromagnetic surveys,

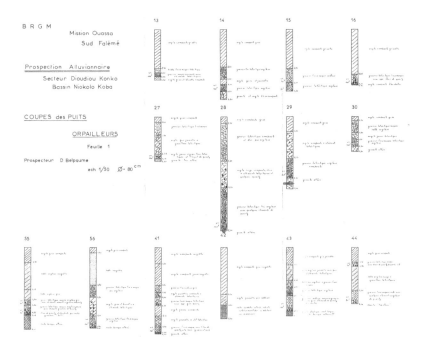

Figure 5.3 Cross-sections of orpaillage shafts. Ouassa-Sud Falémé Mission, Sénégal, 1961. Prepared by D. Belpaume for the Bureau de Recherches Géologiques et Minières.

structural geological maps, and techniques from geophysics, geochemistry, and hydrogeology. They also learned from mapping and sampling juuras, which provided direct indexes of gold. As described in a report from Sénégalo-Sovietique, reconnaissance often began with field surveys of large areas to create an "overview of different metallic indexes," including "gold workings of orpaillage, assemblages of rocks on the landscape, the outcrops of the region."[67]

Danfakha recounted why he and others were willing to lead geologists to local juuras: "We didn't see the problem in showing them our juura. It was not something that was kept as a secret among us. And no one was thinking that they would actually come and do anything with the juura. What we were concerned about, when we were young, was our *deux mille* [2,000 CFA francs] to meet our daily expenses."[68] Work as a laborer on the early missions was called "2,000 CFA of the Maninka" (*Maninkalu deux mille*), which indicated their weekly pay. Cissokho was motivated by a wage and he imagined his work on the missions as part of Senegal's national development and a future state-owned mine. In the 1960s, there were few signs that juuras were under threat of expropriation. The willingness of local men to guide geologists to local juuras was also gendered. Gold prices were at historic lows. Men had largely abandoned orpaillage in favor of more lucrative employment as guides or laborers on mineral missions or as migrant laborers in Senegal's coastal cities. Women, however, continued to mine alluvial deposits and discovered a number of new ones in Tinkoto and in Tomboroncoto in the 1960s and 1970s. Toumanie Touré recounted guiding geologists to women's juuras in the 1960s: "Often the missions wanted to see places where our mothers and grandmothers washed gold. We took them to the juura. For us, that was the work of women! And it was always into the river that the companies wanted to descend first. For us we could see no harm in this."[69]

Touré, like many of the men I interviewed, recalled his interactions with foreign and Senegalese scientists fondly. Base camps were cosmopolitan and exciting. Young men learned slang phrases in German, Russian, Bulgarian, and French. Others learned to operate rock-crushing machines and to sort and label strata of earth for laboratories in Dakar and Paris. Local laborers worked closely with Senegalese technicians recruited in Dakar. While a small number of local men were trained as prospecting aides and became team leaders, most retained the status of unskilled laborer and were overseen by a Senegalese boss.[70] During the rainy season, when scientists returned to Dakar for annual vacations and laboratory work, Senegalese technicians lived and worked with teams of local workers in bush camps for months at a time. A field team led by Mountaga Diallo was a typical arrangement. In 1964, after two years of work with the UN mission, Diallo led a team of thirty Senegalese workers on a campaign to prospect for alluvial gold during the rainy season. In his closing report of 1964, Diallo spoke to the intimacy of fieldwork: "My men and I have become like a family, and it is with great difficulty that I will leave these men behind at mission's end."[71] Toumanie Touré recalled a close friendship with Pierre Diadhiou, the Senegalese boss who oversaw his team in the field (Diadhiou was an ethnic Diola from Casamance, Senegal's other southern region): "He [Pierre Diadhiou] told me, 'Toumanie, you see that mountain, I can't say it will happen during the regime of Senghor, but this [iron] deposit will be exploited.... Even Sabodala, there is lots of gold there. If that gold is mined, it will serve all of Senegal. Not only Sénégal Oriental, but all of Senegal.'"[72] Touré's recollection of a decades-old exchange with Diadhiou glimpses a moment of shared pride and imagination. Two men from distinct cultural and educational contexts in a newly independent Senegal discussed how geology would shape the future of their country.

Older men in Kédougou also recalled tensions between local employees and their Senegalese bosses in mineral missions. In oral interviews, some remembered Senegalese technicians subjecting locally recruited workers to more severe work discipline than foreign staff. As recounted by one elderly Kédougou resident who worked for the BRGM and the Sénégalo-Sovietique in the 1970s: "We had no problem with European aid (*aide de toubab*). Our problem was with the northerners (*les nordistes*)."[73] *Les nordistes* is an inflammatory term used to emphasize the economic and cultural divides between the country's "north" (Dakar, St. Louis, the coast, and the central-western peanut basin) and "the south" (Casamance and Sénégal Oriental).[74] The term *nordistes* is affiliated with Wolof language and culture, although diverse groups live in the north. Stereotypes about the character of different regional and ethnic groups emerged sharply in some interviews. As Moussa Tigana put it, "The work of pit diggers? That is our history. We were at the base of the missions. It is from the sweat of our brow that we dug those ditches. We [Maninka] are not clever like the little Wolof and the little Pullo, but we know the work of force."[75]

Such stylized ethnic typologies map onto ethnoregional distinctions perpetuated by French colonialism. The colonial state assigned an ethnic Wolof, Abdoulaye Ndiaye, as the canton chief of the Oriental Provinces, where he requisitioned forced labor and taxes from ethnic Maninka, Pular, Beliyan-Bassari, Bedik, and Jallonke. This pattern of rule reinforced Sénégal Oriental's marginalization within a colonial economy that privileged ethnic Wolof and investments on the coast and in the central peanut basin. These historical divisions correlated with the categories of unskilled and skilled labor on the mineral missions.

Drought and the Birth of Artisanal Mining

The departure of Sénégalo-Sovietique in 1973 marked the end of an era in the history of state-sponsored geological research in Senegal. It also coincided with the global oil crisis of 1973 and falling prices for Senegal's two most important exports: phosphate and peanuts. The price of oil soared, and hard metal prices plummeted. A period of relative economic stability and state expansion in Senegal ended as the economy entered a crisis. The reports documenting the Sabodala gold reserve—the crown jewel of independence-era mineral missions—were shelved in the archives of the DMG. With only a modest operating budget and dwindling offers of technical assistance from abroad, Senegal's DMG could no longer fund exploration geology. It took on a strictly administrative role, operating as a "gatekeeper" for a trickle of permit requests, largely from French parastatals.[76]

Orpaillage began expanding in the early 1970s as a series of droughts struck West Africa, leading to severe famine in some regions. International media coverage of the "Sahel droughts," which peaked between 1968 and 1972 and, in 1983–84, made the region synonymous with poverty.[77] On the savanna plains of Sénégal Oriental, wells ran dry in the historical provinces of Bélédougou and Sirimana. Despite low gold prices, men and women turned to mining juuras, an intergenerational famine resource. Villages along the Gambia mushroomed as migrants populated the juuras of Kourounoto, Kerekonko, and Tambanoumouya. The population of Tinkoto, described as an "abandoned village" by French prospectors in the 1960s, swelled with migrants from Senegal, Mali, and the Gambia. In 1984, after years of drought and growing hunger, a group of migrants stayed in Tinkoto through the rains, transforming this juura into a village (see chapter 1).

The ritual cost of sustaining juuras grew as more people turned to gold as a livelihood. In Kédougou, rumors circulated of humans sacrificed to underground spirits. A group of nuns working for the Mission Catholique in Kédougou—which established a church and a missionary school in the department in the 1960s at the invitation of Léopold Senghor—reported rumors of "fabulous gains" in 1982–83 tied to "blood crimes," a euphemism for human sacrifice. French anthropologists, also working in the department of Kédougou in the 1980s, wrote that orpaillage was disturbing the "structure of the village" and leading to the "destruction of family life." They described the growing population of strangers on placer mines, the abandonment of agriculture for orpaillage, declining enrollments in school, and growing dependence on food imports, which encouraged an increase in "theft and criminality" in the region.[78] These accounts echoed the concerns of colonial and independence-era officials about the social dangers of orpaillage. These fears were short-lived, however. The rains recommenced in 1985, and many men and women returned to their natal villages to farm. Only a few families stayed on in Tinkoto year-round (see chapter 1).

The droughts of the 1970s and early 1980s also reconfigured the ethnic composition of orpaillage in Sénégal Oriental. As far back as oral memory serves, ethnic Maninka dominated dry season gold mining in Kédougou. Pular and Jakhanke avoided orpaillage, which they associated with paganism (see chapter 7). As crops suffered, however, Pular and Jakhanke men entered the juuras of their Maninka neighbors. Newcomers to orpaillage started in jobs historically occupied by women, such as the juulusabala: pulling buckets

148   CHAPTER FIVE

attached to ropes at the mouth of mine shafts to evacuate sand unearthed by Maninka men digging below. Bana Sidibé, a Pular resident of Kanoumering, recalled his entry into orpaillage. "It was 1984 the first time I worked in gold. It was only the Maninka in gold, Fulbe [Pulars] were not in gold. Fulbe only came to the juura to sell goats for sacrifices. Water was lacking. Some of the sorghum matured, some did not. I started out pulling the rope."[79]

Orpaillage also expanded on the historical goldfields of Mali and Guinea during the droughts, much as it had in the interwar period, when the prices for tropical commodities plummeted in the AOF. Moussa Traoré, who became Mali's president following a coup in 1968, initially shut down gold placers in Mali.[80] Sékou Touré dispatched the army to expel orpailleurs from any placer mines that had been opened illegally in Siguiri. But Touré and Traoré were swimming against a rising tide. State-run mining industries had not come to fruition at the scale and pace anticipated at independence. By the early 1980s, mounting years of drought forced these leaders to revise their criminalization of orpaillage.

Economic advisers working for the UN and the World Bank also reconsidered their policy recommendations for mining in Africa. In the 1970s, both organizations held international conferences evaluating the benefits of small-scale mining.[81] These meetings reflected a growing interest in "appropriate" small-scale technology in the global South in the face of mounting evidence that many large-scale projects—dams, mines, and intensive agricultural schemes—had failed to produce economic benefits. Publications issued from these meetings, attended by geologists and mining engineers from around the globe, included case studies from the United States, Canada, and Europe. But the central focus was on the *developing* world, a term born at midcentury to replace *colonies* in the parlance of aid and development organizations. It was also in these reports that the terms *artisanal* and *small-scale* mining gained currency as a catchall for labor-intensive and capital-poor mining methods that colonial states had previously glossed as customary.[82]

In the landmark publication *Small-scale Mining in the Developing Countries* (1972), the UN defined artisanal mining as involving the "application of human energy directly (as with a pick) on a one-to-one ratio to the physical production of minerals without multiplying that energy using mechanical means (jackhammer)." Evoking the language of technological evolution, these reports framed artisanal mining as a "primitive" and "archaic" form of extraction once practiced globally and now limited to developing countries.[83] Publications issued from these conferences detailed the nefarious dimensions of artisanal mining: barriers to regulation, inefficient depletion of ore bodies, and unsanitary conditions of some informal mining sites. At the same time, these reports argued, artisanal mining generated more employment than capital-intensive mines and discouraged young people from migrating to urban "shanty dwellings with their attendant high crime rate, malnutrition, and a preponderance of communicable diseases."[84] Some reports stressed the value of small-scale miners and "nomads" as producers of geological knowledge. A 1972 report recommended that developing countries formalize relationships with local miners by offering "free, possibly even subsidized, short courses in prospecting techniques" to train "nomadic herdsmen and other peripatetic persons" to look for unusual rocks and outcrops.[85] The report's authors promoted what geologists had done for decades in West Africa: using citizen miners (formerly colonial subjects) as indexes for mineral deposits.

In the late 1970s, several of the Senegalese earth scientists who had worked on the independence-era mineral missions, now employed by the DMG, returned to the villages where they had sojourned in southeastern Senegal. Funded by a discretionary budget for "small missions," they proposed to organize the region's orpailleurs into cooperatives.[86] This initiative was first proposed in the reports of independence-era mineral missions. In a 1965 report written for the UN, Mohamadou Sy described his gold-prospecting activities near a juura known as Kouloun-Tabalay. Concluding that it would be unprofitable to exploit Kouloun-Tabalay on an industrial scale, Sy proposed reserving it for "artisanal exploitation by village-level cooperatives overseen by the state."[87] If this experiment proved successful it "could have significant consequences for increasing the standard of living of peasants in Sénégal Oriental," a region that, in Sy's words, was "disinherited from Senegal."[88] In 1977, during the height of drought, the DMG organized cooperatives of orpailleurs at Sabodala and Mamakono. It equipped each group with "modern orpaillage tools."[89] In 1985, the director of the DMG approved a third and final orpaillage cooperative, based in the department of Saraya. Geologists hoped this effort "could bring about good results" in the country's most impoverished region.[90] Funding for this work, too, soon dried up.

In the end, the DMG's formal support of orpaillage was brief for reasons that had far more to do with plans devised for African mining policies in Washington, DC, than in Dakar. By the early 1980s, the World Bank and the International Monetary Fund were pressuring African states to adopt pro-market reforms and to clarify the rights of citizens to minerals in preparation for opening mining prospects to private bids. The policy window for orpaillage wedged open by drought would close again until the region's twenty-first-century gold-mining boom.

"A Man Who Searches with His Hands Will Find Dirt"

This chapter—one of the first histories of the earth sciences in postcolonial Africa—demonstrates how one newly independent African state deepened its knowledge of its subsurface in the context of scientific austerity. In the 1960s and 1970s, Senegal recruited scientists from home and abroad to map the mineral endowments of the Birimian rocks of Sénégal Oriental, a region that was geologically distinct from much of Senegal. Decolonizing states did not have the discretionary budgets to conduct national geological surveys, as was the norm by the mid-twentieth century in the Soviet Union and much of Western Europe, North America, and East Asia. Instead, Senegal's technical advisers—French and African—navigated Cold War politics to create a bricolage of geological knowledge from the UN, the Soviet Union, and France.

Maps, reports, and rock samples made the mineral potential of Sénégal Oriental legible to the Senegalese state and private capital. Combined with the expansion of the Niokolo-Koba National Park, also in Sénégal Oriental, the region's vocation as a natural reserve for independent Senegal was cemented. This generated a mixed legacy on the ground. The state's interest in Sénégal Oriental's unique minerals and wildlife created a pathway for citizens of this distant region to forge a relationship with a state apparatus centralized in Dakar. Yet regional residents found their own needs for land, animals, and minerals in constant threat of expropriation for the "public" good.

For foreign scientists, participation in mineral missions bridged employment in the late colonial service to international careers working for French parastatals or as coopérants for independent African states. The first generation of Senegalese earth scientists were trained on mineral missions. Many of these scientists went on to pursue doctorates in France, Canada, and the USSR. They became high-ranking officials, scientists, and professors in Senegal's private mining industry, at the DMG, and at the University of Dakar. By contrast, local employees of mineral missions recruited in Sénégal Oriental experienced little benefit from their work beyond seasonal wages. Though some men labored for decades on mineral missions, they did not receive pensions. These men are aging at precisely the moment when the region's mineral resources are more valued on global markets than ever before in their working lives.

It is only with the passage of time that the uneven benefits of the mineral missions of the 1960s and 1970s became clear to many men from Kédougou who labored on them. Today, mining corporations solicit men of his generation to participate as consultative "village elders" in meetings for Corporate Social Responsibility programs. But mining firms do not see these men as partners or experts. This bitter predicament has led some former employees of mineral missions to reinterpret their work as bush guides as a "theft of consciousness."[91] Moussa Tigana, who worked for the UN and Sénégalo-Sovietique put it in the following terms: "You see my hands. They are as rough as the sand. And you see my home. There is nothing to see here. Nothing. A man who searches with his hands will find dirt. Only a man who searches with his head will find riches."[92]

In the 1960s, there were few signs that residents of Sénégal Oriental would lose access to their juuras. In part, men from the region were willing to lead geologists to juuras because they imagined that their labor was contributing to future state-run mines, where they might one day work as salaried employees. The willingness to share gold discoveries was also gendered. When gold prices were low, men exited orpaillage, leaving juuras to women. When prices surged, men re-exerted control over gold-bearing land.

This chapter is not a straightforward account of scientists exploiting local labor and expertise. While this is part of the story, such a reading misses the unique historical opening of the independence-era in West Africa. The 1960s was a time of expansive possibility, of bold visions for the future. It was in this decade that Pierre Diadhou, an ethnic Diola recruited from Dakar, and Toumanie Touré, a lifelong farmer and orpailleur from Kédougou, stood on a hillside together and imagined a future in which their children, as citizens of the independent state of Senegal, might benefit from the subsoil. Their conversations, stitched together in broken French and Wolof, breathed new life into an unfulfilled colonial dream: industrial-scale gold mining on the savanna. Decades later, this long-deferred dream would come to pass, but under far different circumstances than either Diadhou or Touré imagined in the 1960s. The final two chapters of this book examine how the expectations and grievances accumulated during decades of geological exploration were reactivated with the unfolding of Senegal's twenty-first-century gold-mining boom.

152   CHAPTER FIVE

6
A West African Language of Subterranean Rights

In April 2014, Senegalese soldiers drove a fleet of bulldozers through the bustling town of Kédougou. One group diverted to the north, the other to the west. Over the next several days, soldiers bulldozed several of southeastern Senegal's largest juuras, or dry season mining sites.[1] Restrained at gunpoint, orpailleurs jeered as bulldozers shoveled dirt into hundreds of mine shafts. Some elderly women stripped naked to shame Senegalese armed forces. Senegal's President Macky Sall framed the juura closures as a security campaign (*campagne de sécurisation*) to restore public safety, protect the environment, and encourage farming in Kédougou.[2] National media coverage of the juuras marked a crescendo in a multiyear national news frenzy that presented Kédougou as a Wild West–style mining town characterized by crime, uncontrolled migration, and environmental degradation.[3] Journalists reported that the state was shutting down orpaillage in Kédougou. In fact, the army bulldozed only juuras approved to become corporate mines, leaving many other juuras untouched. In the next few months, the state legalized dozens of juuras by transforming them into orpaillage corridors (*couloirs d'orpaillage*), in which Senegalese citizens could mine for a nominal fee and with proof of citizenship status.[4] While juura closures accelerated the corporate enclosure of Senegal's goldfields, they also materialized a compromise: recognizing the claims of some orpailleurs to gold deposits.

Taking the 2014 juura closures as an entry point, this chapter tracks the emergence of a regional language of subterranean rights, centered on gold, that was innovated by Kédougou's residents in the mid-2000s. Some claims to gold were framed as "rights"; others, as moral entitlements. I place the word *rights* in quotes because orpaillage was almost entirely illegal during my fieldwork and remains so in many contexts. Behind closed doors, state officials expressed their desire to close all juuras, but they admitted it was untenable to eliminate the primary source of income for some of the country's poorest citizens.[5] Orpaillage was too established, widespread, and crucial to rural livelihoods to be criminalized altogether. Closing juuras is a risky enterprise for the Senegalese state. In the words of one official based in Kédougou, "When the hunger season hits, and people have no juura to mine, they will have nothing to lose."[6] The potential for violence on densely populated juuras forces the state and mining firms to make concessions to orpailleurs. I draw on the historian Gregory Mann's definition of *political language* to describe the "words, images, ideas, and expressions of sentiment that compose a common rhetoric animating uneven and inconsistent relations of power that exist between various parties."[7] While this chapter focuses on discursive elements of claims making, debates over subterranean rights are also waged by material means. Corporations speak through barbed-wire fences and security forces; the Senegalese state asserts its claims to gold with bulldozers and mining conventions. Orpailleurs, in turn, burn government property, block roads, and invade state-sanctioned permits. Orpailleurs may be the least powerful actors in these encounters, but they are an influential constituency that neither the state nor corporations can ignore.

In southeastern Senegal, a political language of subterranean rights crystallized in moments of upheaval—such as the juura closures—and through daily negotiations among orpailleurs, state officials, politicians, and the employees of mining and exploration firms. In Kédougou, orpailleurs assert their right to mine gold through four primary modes of redress. First are claims to discovery or precedence. Regional residents argue that they, not geologists, were the first to discover gold deposits now mined by corporations. Second, orpailleurs claim juuras as a subsistence right, a collective granary and famine resource that should remain available to future generations and to regional migrants. Third, orpailleurs argue that they are small and weak, capable of mining gold only at the surface, allowing corporations to mine gold at depth. Finally, orpailleurs argue they have a right to the region's gold because the colonial and postcolonial state marginalized Kédougou by failing to invest in its infrastructure while profiting from its natural resources. While orpailleurs are the primary authors of this language of subterranean rights, bureaucrats and mining company personnel also speak in its idioms, although they recognize some arguments as more legitimate than others. In Senegal's poorest region, both farmers and bureaucrats acknowledge the importance of juuras as subsistence resources. By contrast, orpailleurs' claims to gold based on the state's historical exploitation of Kédougou's natural resources are more controversial and thus more easily dismissed, as I show later.

Tracking this West African language of subterranean rights inserts new concerns into the scholarship on anti-mining protests in the global South, which have expanded in tandem with the internationalization of mining capital since the late 1980s.[8] Many conflicts around capital-intensive mining projects center on their nefarious effects on ecosystems and waterways, the marginalization of indigenous land claims, and the opacity of mining contract negotiations and environmental impact assessments.[9] Residents of Kédougou share these concerns. But they do not protest corporate mining altogether, as is common in Latin America. In fact, they concede that corporations have a right to some gold as sanctioned by the state. Orpailleurs seek entitlement to a share of gold, not its entirety. Consider the words of Neege Traoré, an elder of Duuta, a village where the mining firm, Bassari Resources, has operated its exploration camp for more than a decade. "When [Bassari Resources] came, they greeted us. It was the state who sold them this land. And we said, 'OK, we cannot say that we don't agree if the government said that you could have the land. We are all Senegalese. But you cannot come here and prevent us from surviving.'"[10]

The anthropologist Amiel Bize documents a similar dynamic of claims making in fuel siphoning along Kenya's northern trucking corridor. Truckers construct and claim an entitlement to a share of fuel—a "remainder" conserved by skilled driving—while recognizing the rights of truck owners to a much larger share of fuel. As Bize argues, the "right to the remainder" as a particular kind of share emerged "both from the contingencies of material [oil and driving] and through a preexisting social negotiation" that unfolded in an agrarian context marked by severe inequality.[11] Compared with fuel, which can be siphoned as it is moved across different access points and containers, orpailleurs lay claim to gold that remains lodged in its geological context underground. Orpailleurs thus negotiate with corporations for access to one of two kinds of gold shares: a parcel of the surface area of mining permits or a stratigraphic division of the underground, whereby orpailleurs work "on the surface" while companies work below. These two notions of rights—one segregated horizontally; the other, vertically—echo the two models of African customary mining rights codified in the fluctuating mining regimes of colonial French West Africa (see chapter 3).

Orpailleurs' claims to a share of Kédougou's gold do not emerge from a unified social group or central organization. In Ghana, many artisanal gold miners, known as *galamsey*, belong to unions.[12] But orpailleurs in Senegal rarely organize beyond the level of a single village or juura, which reflects the region's long history of political non-centralization.[13] Over the past two decades, however, conflicts with mining companies have given rise to new forms of collective affiliation. On one hand, a growing number of people in Kédougou identify their full-time profession as orpaillage. On the other hand, residents of Kédougou increasingly refer to themselves as "Kédovins," a portmanteau of Kédougou and the French verb *venir* (to come from). As a term that signals a pan-ethnic regional affiliation, *Kédovins* has gained political currency in the crucible of Senegal's gold-mining boom.

Senegal's Gold-Mining Boom

In the 1990s, rising gold prices and the depletion of more accessible deposits elsewhere on the globe inspired interest among mining investors in the gold of savanna West Africa. While geologists had spent decades mapping the region's gold-bearing Birimian rocks, it was only at the turn of the twenty-first century that exploration firms began marketing the idea of a West African "Birimian Greenstone Belt" as a regional geological formation with untapped mining potential.[14] In part, the marketing of the Birimian Greenstone Belt imposed an artificial unanimity on West Africa's diverse goldfields, each with distinctive histories of exploration. At the same time, it recognized the Birimian rocks that united these spaces, which had motivated the expansion of medieval West African empires and long-distance trading networks for gold across the savanna and the Sahel.

Most exploration and mining firms that ventured into savanna West Africa in the 1990s drew their expertise and capital from Anglophone countries with historical gold-mining industries that, in turn, grew out of nineteenth-century gold rushes and white settler-colonial projects. By decade's end, Australian, Canadian, South African, and British companies—including dozens of junior firms—held exploration permits across historical Bambuk, Buré, Poura, and Yaouré. Guinea opened the Léro mine in 1995, followed by Siguiri in 1998. In 1996, Mali entered a joint venture with a private firm for the Sadiola mine, with Luolo, Yatéla, and Tabakoto following suit. Senegal, comparatively late to the table, opened Sabodala in 2007.[15]

In part, these private mining investments were encouraged by the widespread adoption of pro-market mining codes by African states in the 1990s and 2000s, which offered massive tax breaks to foreign investors.[16] The region's mining boom was also built on earlier generations of scientific research—a fact often elided in media and scholarly coverage. The first wave of mines opened in Guinea, Mali, and Senegal were all "shelf projects": gold deposits that had been partially mapped in the colonial period or in the early decades of independence.[17] West African states jump-started their mining economies by tendering these shelf projects to competitive bidding by private investors who built on preexisting research. The geologists who staffed exploration firms working on West Africa's Birimian rocks in the late 1990s had techniques for mapping the subsurface that were unavailable to geologists of earlier decades. But they also consulted maps and reports from historical exploration missions held in state archives. As Sembou Danfakha, a Kédovin who worked for independence-era mineral missions, put it, "It is the old work that becomes the projects [Endeavor Mining, Resolute Mining, etc.] of today."[18]

The embrace of foreign mining capital by West African states reversed decades of policies aimed at nationalizing mining within the framework of African socialism. Economic decline weakened ideological investment in state-run industries. By the 1970s, most African states were operating on budget deficits. In Senegal, the declining price of peanuts, coupled with the Sahelian droughts of the 1970s and 1980s, stressed rural incomes, agricultural production, and state revenue.[19] In exchange for loan forgiveness, the World Bank and the International Monetary Fund pressured African states, and other states in the global South, to adopt budget austerity reforms known as structural adjustment programs (SAPs). Senegal was an early adopter of SAPs, which led to major cuts in state bureaucracy, agricultural subsidies, education, and health care.[20] The World Bank targeted the mining sector as a potential source of revenue and encouraged African states to shift their historical role from one of "owner-operator" of mines to "promoter-regulator" of private mining investments.[21]

In 1988, Senegal adopted a more "investor-friendly" mining code to promote the exploitation of its shelf projects in joint-venture arrangements.[22] Abdou Diouf, Senegal's second president, entertained two agreements to mine Sabodala with foreign partners. After they fell through, he authorized an agreement with a Senegalese company, Eeximcor, to mine a portion of Sabodala.[23] Eeximcor was financed exclusively by Senegalese capital and staffed by Senegalese technicians. In 1997, one year after it was opened, the state ordered Eeximcor's closure on the grounds that it had violated its permit. Suspiciously to some, this closure aligned with a renewed state-led campaign to promote private investments in Senegal's mineral sector with a focus on Kédougou's Birimian rocks.[24]

In 2000, Abdoulaye Wade, a long-term opposition candidate, became Senegal's third president running on a campaign of market liberalization. In 2003, he adopted a far more liberal mining code than that of 1988 and opened a bidding war for Sabodala. The Australian company Mineral Deposits Limited (MDL) won the bid in 2004.[25] Meanwhile, the state entered negotiations with Arcelor Mittal (then an Indian-based steel giant) to exploit another shelf project of the independence-era mineral missions: a massive iron-ore deposit along the Falémé River.[26] Kédougou's mining boom converged with a number of infrastructural and bureaucratic transformations. Construction began on a long-planned international highway between Dakar and Bamako that passed through southeastern Senegal. In 2008, Kédougou became an official region, which led to the opening of new state offices and the appointment of dozens of new bureaucrats to the region. Hundreds of geologists, mine managers, day laborers, merchants, truck drivers, and technicians moved to Kédougou. Orpailleurs from Mali, Guinea, and Burkina Faso also migrated to the region, drawn by juuras newly discovered by resident orpailleurs and by the exploration trenches of mining juniors. The influx of outsiders stoked concerns in Kédougou that coastal Senegalese and itinerant workers from abroad stood to benefit from the region's mining boom more than local residents. These grievances erupted in a protest in 2008, in which Kédovins accused government officials of overlooking regional residents for employment in mining camps—an event to which I return later.

Kédovins were not the only ones concerned that outsiders accrued the majority of the profits from gold mining. When Macky Sall became Senegal's fourth president in 2012, he criticized Wade for handing over too much revenue in the mining sector to foreign investors. Sall, a mining engineer by training, had spent time in Kédougou as Senegal's minister of mines from 2001 to 2003.[27] Shortly after entering office, Sall called for a review of all mining conventions and created pathways to partially legalize orpaillage, to which Wade had largely turned a blind eye.[28] In 2013, Sall introduced the couloirs d'orpaillage policy, which allowed Senegalese citizens, for a small fee, to mine as individuals or groups across multiple corridors. In 2016, Senegal's National Assembly ratified a new mining code that lowered fees for Senegalese entrepreneurs to access mining licenses.[29] Finally, in 2018, the state opened an official market board for gold in Kédougou, where for the first time orpailleurs could legally sell gold dust to the Senegalese state. Despite these pathways to legalization, most orpaillage in Kédougou remained illegal because it is conducted outside of state-defined corridors. In this context, orpailleurs defended their right to gold through a political and moral language, rather than one based on legal claims.

158 CHAPTER SIX

Claiming Discovery

> The tubabs [whites] did not show us the filon [lode-ore rock]. We learned the filon. The mining of filon in Kédougou started in Golouma; it was the year in which I was born. We call that the *kuru taki sono* [the year of breaking rocks].[30]

Moussa Tigana, the reader may recall, worked for several mineral missions in the 1960s and '70s. He was born in Mamakono—home of the Atlantic-era "slave king," Taubry Sidibé—in 1949, the year of kuru taki sono. At the time, Golouma was a juura mined by residents of Mamakono and other villages in historical Bélédougou. Alongside Tinkoto, Golouma was one of southeastern Senegal's most active juuras across the twentieth century. Today Golouma no longer exists: it is an open-pit mine excavated by Endeavor Mining. Tigana's declaration was part of a broad genre of arguments about precedence to gold discovery that I heard from orpailleurs during my fieldwork. Claims by Kédovins that they, or their ancestors, were "the first" to discover gold deposits now slated to be mined by corporations are core to the language of subterranean rights on Senegal's goldfields.

At first blush, the relationship between gold discovery and mining rights is a straightforward legal question. According to Senegal's current mining law, a person or corporation must be in possession of a state-issued gold exploration permit to be granted priority rights to mine a prospect they have documented.[31] But orpailleurs can neither afford the cost of exploration permits nor the geological staff required to legally prove the existence of a deposit within a permit (map 6.1). Senegal's mining law also allows the state to retract a permit if a deposit of greater value to the "public good" is discovered nearby.[32] In sum, even if rural residents acquire "artisanal" or "small mine" permits that align with a local gold discovery, they can lose the right to mine it if the holder of an exploration permit—a title far too expensive for village organizations in Kédougou—legally proves the existence of a prospect in the same zone. Further, none of the mining codes ratified in Senegal since independence legally recognize the contribution of orpailleurs, living or deceased to private or state-funded gold exploration. This is despite the fact that geologists working for private firms in Kédougou region today continue to sample local orpaillage shafts: a practice that dates to the colonial period (see chapters 1, 4, and 5).[33]

Because orpailleurs have virtually no legal protections for their—or their ancestors'—gold discoveries, they mobilize claims to precedence in negotiations with state officials and mining corporations that appeal to

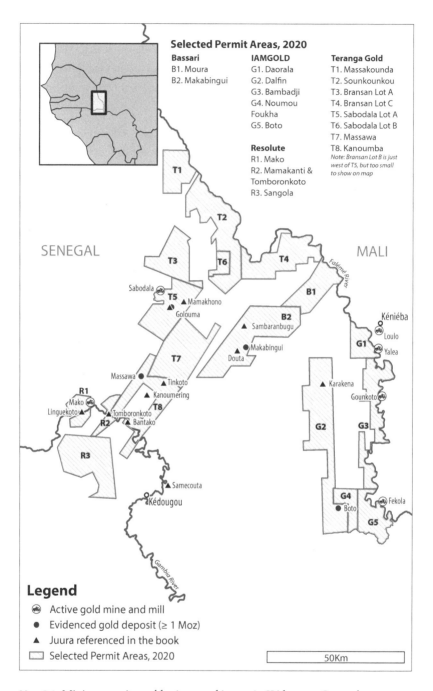

Map 6.1 Mining permits, gold mines, and juuras in Kédougou, Senegal, ca. 2020.

ethical, rather than legal, registers. When a gold deposit was "discovered" is a complex ontological problem that pries open space for debate shaped by multiple and competing versions of history. Each gold-bearing ore body has a distinct history of use and discovery by multiple actors: orpailleurs, private firms, and the state. These histories can be mobilized to defend a moral vision for why a group of orpailleurs or a mining firm should, or should not, have a right to mine a given deposit.

The discovery of Sabodala, Senegal's first open-pit mining operation, offers a compelling view on these issues. Residents of the historical province of Bélédougou, in which the villages of Sabodala and Mamakono are situated, place Sabodala's discovery within a deep genealogy of regional land settlement. However, the geography of Sabodala in oral histories is slippery. For some, Sabodala refers exclusively to the present-day village of the same name, while others use Sabodala as a gloss for a much larger gold-bearing geological formation in which a range of juuras and villages are located. According to oral histories of regional Soninke and Maninka lineages, their ancestors settled Bélédougou due to its rich agricultural soils and the presence of gold and iron, the latter for blacksmithing. By the dawn of the first millennium, gold flakes mined from the runoff of laterite plateaus surrounding Bélédougou may have been mined and sold to Soninke Wangara traders (chapter 2). Oral histories suggest that Sabodala was first established as a juura, mined seasonally by residents of Bélédougou. Like many villages in this zone, including Tinkoto, Sabodala later became a year-round agricultural hamlet. During the interwar gold boom, orpailleurs from Bélédougou discovered new juuras in the vicinity of Sabodala, including Bambaraya, Kerekounda, and Sékoto-kô. For them, their ancestors, some within living memory, unambiguously discovered Sabodala and adjacent juuras, including Golouma.[34]

State archives, by contrast, credit independence-era mineral missions with the discovery of Sabodala. Yet even these sources recognize the importance of preexisting orpaillage sites to the exploration activities that documented the Sabodala deposit, on one hand, and point to the multitude of different geologists involved in this discovery, on the other hand. In the 1960s, the United Nations (UN) sampled soils and dug trenches in the vicinity of Mamakono and Sabodala, largely in alluvial deposits mined by local orpailleurs. While orpaillage workings guided the UN's work, it also relied on the reports produced by colonial-era geologists who, in the 1950s, dug exploration trenches in abandoned orpaillage shafts. While the UN provided evidence of the Sabodala deposit on maps, future geologists deepened knowledge of the deposit. In the 1970s, Soviet geologists working for the Sénégalo-Sovietique mission dug diamond-drill holes in gold-bearing quartz rock of the prospect 2.5 kilometers to the north of the village named Sabodala and the juura of the same name. In 1973, a French parastatal, the Bureau de Recherches Géologiques et Minières (BRGM), perforated more than fifty-three diamond-drill holes in the surrounding soil. From the mid-1980s to the mid-1990s, the Senegalese state, in a joint partnership with an Australian firm, conducted diamond-drilling and reverse-circulation drilling on Sabodala. By the close of the 1990s, Sabodala's gold reserves were estimated at thirteen tons. In sum, each generation of geologists expanded the geography incorporated under the place name Sabodala.

The discovery of Sabodala continued when, in 2004, the Senegalese state accorded a mining concession to the Australian firm MDL, to mine the deposit. The company updated the reserves through additional exploration and commenced mining Sabodala in 2009. In 2010, the Canadian-owned Teranga Gold Corporation acquired MDL. Teranga also acquired exploitation licenses and residual exploration licenses from several firms working adjacent to Sabodala, expanding the territory glossed as part of the Sabodala project.[35] Teranga Gold (now Endeavor Mining) offered its own account of the discovery of Sabodala. Under a section titled "History" in a technical report from 2017, the report's authors—a consultancy hired by Teranga—argued that "a soil sampling program carried out by BRGM in 1961 resulted in the discovery of Sabodala, which had not previously been recognized by the local artisanal miners, as the gold was fine grained."[36] The attribution of discovery to the BRGM is a highly selective telling of the multilayered geological labor that went into mapping Sabodala in the 1960s and 1970s. More interesting yet was Teranga Gold's engagement with the history of "local artisanal miners." The company recognized that orpailleurs mined Sabodala's alluvial deposits, which are visible to the naked eye, but differentiates these from lode ore, which is more "fine grained." For Teranga Gold, Sabodala was only "discovered" when its lode ore, not its alluvials, were mapped. Even mining firms recognize that orpailleurs excavated portions of Sabodala before geologists ever explored for gold in the region. The question is what discovery means and whose discoveries count.

When did this messy compendium of silts, quartz carbonate, albite-pyrite veins, and alluvial sediments come into being as Sabodala, an objectified gold deposit that is constructed and claimed as property? Did women from Mamakono discover Sabodala when they panned alluvial silts along a stream on its surface? Or when local men dug shafts into the hillside north

Figure 6.1 Exploration trenches near Tambanoumouya, Senegal, 2014. Photograph by the author.

of Sabodala village? When a juurakuntigi spilled the blood of slaughtered chickens into the soil in the name of the patron spirit of Sabodala's gold? When Soviet or French geologists sunk exploration trenches into its quartz rock? Or is Sabodala rediscovered each time a new set of human hands or modeling techniques touches or projects the mineralization of this stretch of earth glossed as Sabodala (figure 6.1)?

In ontological terms, there was no single moment when Sabodala was discovered. Even the legal definition of a mineral deposit or reserve is historically contingent. In legal terms, a mineral reserve is defined by the classification schemes of the countries in which exploration and mining firms list their stock, such as Canada, Australia, and South Africa.[37] Classification schemes differ from one country to the next, but they generally define mineral reserves as deposits known to exist with a relative degree of certainty based on geological studies and that are economically exploitable with available technologies.[38] Shifting market prices for minerals, infrastructure development, and mining laws in countries that host exploitation (and in which companies list their stock) thus shape the legal definition of a mineral reserve, and this definition can shift rapidly over time.

During exploration, firms benefit from the gold discoveries of orpailleurs, current and past, within their permits and employ orpailleurs as semiskilled laborers. However, once a company legally proves the existence of an economically exploitable mineral reserve, companies lean into a classic Euro-American ownership strategy based on promoting rights on the basis of exclusion. They exclude orpailleurs from their permits by erecting electrified barbed-wire fences and lobbying the state to bulldoze orpaillage sites. In Senegal, state-issued mining concessions restrict the claims of orpailleurs to the discovery of a gold deposit by restricting ownership to the final segment in the geographically and temporally diffuse network that often contributes to the "discovery" of a given deposit—such as Sabodala. Mining companies limit competing claims to gold deposits by emphasizing their adherence to Senegalese law and their contribution to Senegal's economy through the payment of taxes and permit fees and through employment creation.[39] By contrast, orpailleurs attempt to enroll corporations in webs of responsibility and exchange that go far beyond the spatial and temporal bounds of the mining concession. They embed companies in the region's history of mineral exploration and mining, and seek recognition for their role in discovery in the form of permission to mine a portion of the deposit or by receiving returns (in the form of employment or investment in infrastructure) from the mining of deposits that they, and their ancestors, helped to discover. As companies move toward exploitation, they narrow the geography of the communities to which they claim contractual and moral responsibility. Orpailleurs insert an ensemble of individuals, living and dead; sociopolitical institutions; and occult forces of the underground into the beneficiaries of gold. In negotiations with the state, orpailleurs also argue that orpaillage confers far greater benefits to a much wider network of people—men and women, citizens and migrants—than corporate gold mines, which employ a small fleet of skilled workers, and machines, most of whom are not from Kédougou.

Claiming Small-Scale

We work with picks and shovels. We cannot touch what the mining companies search. They search hundreds of feet underground.... Those who search deep and those who search on the surface, is it the same thing?[40]

Mahamadi Cissokho, an elderly resident of Samaranbugu, articulates a common defense made by orpailleurs for mining gold within corporate permits. Orpailleurs construct themselves as small-scale and weak, often by emphasizing their use of "traditional" tools such as picks, shovels, and calabash gourds. Or, as Fadiyen Keita, the chief of Kharakenna put it, "When they came with the machines, we had the calabash."[41] Such descriptions set up scalar comparisons with mining companies: big versus little machinery, depth versus surface, and traditional versus modern technologies. By claiming a small-scale status, orpailleurs enroll corporations into moral obligations based on a patronage logic: those in power who monopolize most of a resource should give some of it to the less powerful.

Scales are not, however, fixed social realities. They are spatial and temporal categories, systems of observation and value, created by historical actors with divergent motivations and access to power. The production of scales—national, imperial, local, and geological—is emergent and relational. Scale can be created through discourse or produced materially through the movements, alliances, and activities of people and technologies.[42] But discursive and material scales do not necessarily align. On one hand, the scalar divergence of orpailleurs from mining corporations is self-evident. Orpailleurs work in ephemeral teams, rarely digging deeper than thirty meters; meanwhile bulldozers excavate open-pit mines up to two hundred meters in depth. However, while orpaillage is constrained in depth, it is geographically expansive. In a single dry season, orpailleurs often work across multiple juuras; recruit workers from Burkina Faso, Guinea and Mali; and use pneumatic pumps and jackhammers imported from Dubai and Shenzhen. Far from small-scale, the financial, social, and technical networks of orpaillage reach around the globe.

In advance of the state's closures of juuras in 2014, orpailleurs made scalar arguments in an attempt to assert some control over regional gold deposits. The closure of the juura of Golouma was particularly controversial because it served villages in historical Bélédougou, which had already lost several juuras to Teranga Gold. Aliou Diallo, the male head of a large Pular household in Mamakono, put it in the following terms: "We would like the mining companies to leave a small parcel so that people can survive, a little bit.... What we can work with our hands and what the mining company needs are not the same. The company has needs of tons, and we only need a few grams. We do not dig more than fifty meters, even if it is deep. And the companies dig up to one hundred meters or more."[43] Diallo proposed that companies either allocate a parcel of land for orpailleurs or allow orpailleurs to excavate the top fifty meters of a deposit, leaving companies to mine at depth. Bambo Cissokho, the chief of Tinkoto (chapter 1), made a similar proposition to Randgold in negotiating for access to a portion of its exploration permit. In his words, he asked company representatives to "let us work with the pick and shovel. We are small; we just want to dig the surface."[44] As the reader may recall, at the close of the nineteenth century, the first architect of French West Africa's mining laws imagined a similar demarcation of access to gold: Africans on the surface, with Europeans laboring below. This premise was challenged as early as the 1910s, when African orpailleurs proved capable of exploiting deposits the French initially thought were beyond the depth "they can reach with their current procedures" (see chapter 3).

Claims by orpailleurs that they work only at "the surface" are complicated by the shift, over the past two decades, toward orpailleurs exploiting more lode ore (*filon, sanukuru*). Mining companies are quick to point out that they have no problem with "traditional" orpaillage within their exploration permits, which they identify as the mining of alluvial deposits (*nara*) with traditional tools: a pickax and calabash. In their view, the problem is that orpailleurs now use industrial or semi-industrial tools to mine lode ore: the same deposits targeted by mining firms. In 2012, the Australian company Bassari Resources campaigned the Senegalese state to evict orpailleurs who they accused of invading Bassari's primary gold prospect at Makabingui. In letters and emails written to Senegalese authorities, Bassari emphasized the "industrial" character of the tools used by orpailleurs operating on their permits. This language is evident in a 2012 letter from the management of Bassari Resources to the Senegalese Ministry of the Interior: "It is clear that the illegal miners engaging in artisanal exploitation do not employ traditional methods, but, to the contrary, are sophisticated operators working with industrial mining equipment."[45] In January 2013, the managing director of Bassari wrote that the "illegal activities [of orpailleurs] are clearly reaching significant depth."[46] The emphasis on depth counters orpailleurs' claims that they dig "at the surface." As detailed in company correspondence, orpailleurs cut directly into Bassari's future profits by mining the lode ore of Makabingui.[47]

Senegalese officials also drew distinctions between "traditional" and "semi-industrial" orpaillage in permitting orpaillage in some contexts and not others. In the words of the prefect of Kédougou in 2014, "Orpaillage used to be in the image of other activities in the zone, such as agriculture and animal husbandry. But with the evolution of activities, it has become semi-industrial. It is no longer traditional. People use the same chemicals as the mining companies, such as cyanide and mercury."[48] Orpailleurs in Kédougou today clearly use tools that were unavailable to earlier generations of miners. At the same time, orpailleurs did mine lode ore prior to the region's corporate mining boom, as in Khossanto, Golouma, and Tinkoto in the 1940s–50s and again in the 1980s–90s (see chapter 5).

For state authorities and mining companies, the alleged transition of orpaillage from traditional to semi-industrial is also tied to the growing presence of migrants on Kédougou's juuras. In the words of a Senegalese coordinator of the environmental division for a British firm working in Kédougou in 2014, "We have no problem with orpaillage using traditional methods, like the calabash. The problem is strangers coming here with machines."[49] A 2012 letter from Bassari Resources also underscored the transition from "non-industrial small-scale traditional mining carried out by local Senegalese *orpeyeurs* [*sic*]" to a "professionally organized operation" managed by migrants from Mali and from coastal Senegal.[50] Bassari referred to these migrants as "illegal miners," differentiating them from "traditional *orpeuyers* [*sic*]."[51] For regional residents, however, regional migrants are crucial to the historical role of orpaillage as a collective drought resource.

Claiming Subsistence

> The juura is our granary [*kurukuro*]. It is how I nourish my family. What will I do if they take it? Wouldn't you rather risk death than let someone light your granary on fire?[52]

Boukari Kamara is the chief of Kerekonko, a small village along the Gambia. In February 2014, the village was negotiating with Torogold (now Resolute Mining) over where it could practice orpaillage within the firm's exploration permits. Arguably the most prevalent genre of arguments made by orpailleurs to Kédougou's gold consist of claims to subsistence. Juuras are described in Maninka either as a *kurukuro* (a granary used for storing harvested rice, sorghum, or millet) or a *feeto faate* (which translates roughly as "livelihood" in English).[53] In savanna West Africa, gold deposits have long been understood as a famine resource, a subterranean granary that can be tapped when drought or warfare depletes agricultural granaries. Within living memory, the discovery of gold in someone's agricultural field would convert a field, considered the property of a lineage, into a communal resource. "In the past," Moussa Tigana explained, "we would say, brother, our *feeto faate* [livelihood] has come out in your field, let us help you clear a new field so that we can get something out of this place."[54] When Senegalese officials informed villages of the juura closures in 2014, local residents argued that the state was depriving future generations of a granary. Such imagery was captured by a Senegalese journalist in the speech of an elderly woman from Sambaranbugu. She jeered at soldiers bulldozing the juura of Makabingui, exclaiming: "We live from this. We feed our children from this. Our grandparents lived from this. May Allah curse you and condemn you. This is our life. You come here and bring force and close our place of work. May Allah punish you. Next to this river, this is where we washed this gold. And you come here and take all of that by force."[55] Her condemnation frames the juura as an intergenerational subsistence resource.

This genre of claims making articulates with what James Scott described as a "moral economy of subsistence," drawing on E. P. Thompson's "moral economy" as one governed by forms of reciprocity and entitlements to resources that extend beyond financial transactions.[56] While there is not a unified agrarian ideology or "economy" on Kédougou's multiethnic goldfields, Scott's attention to entitlements to resources on which agrarian livelihoods depend shares a family resemblance to the claim of Kédovins to gold as a subsistence resource.[57] Mahamadi Cissokho deployed this idiom in recounting an exchange between village elders from Sambaranbugu and Bassari Resources. When the company first arrived in the zone, he said, "The chief ... said you are welcome here because all of the population here is searching for something. But you must know that since our grandparents, we are digging and looking for gold. You, you have your papers from the state. If you say that we have to leave here, we cannot support you. That will be difficult. . . . We will try to work together, but do not prevent us from working."[58] Cissokho recognizes the company's right to gold, as authorized by the state, but not at the expense of local livelihoods. Similar to the elderly woman at Sambaranbugu, he frames gold as an intergenerational resource through his temporal reference to grandparents.

Senegalese officials readily acknowledged the legitimacy of claims by orpailleurs to juuras as a subsistence resource. Lamine Touré, the regional director of mines in Tambacounda in 2014, put it in blunt terms: "We would like to close all of the juuras, but this is an impossible social problem. People are poor here. Mining has made life more expensive here than in Dakar. And you cannot take a granary from a starving child."[59] Agents of the state and mining companies were, however, less tolerant of the historical role of juuras as a subsistence resource that also welcomes long-distance migrants. They pegged the ills of the juura—crime, semi-industrialization, and chemical use—on migrant miners while upholding regional residents as traditional, childlike, and easily deceived by outsiders.

For Kédovins, by contrast, a crucial component of juuras as a subsistence resource is their openness to strangers. Migrants are valued as a source of wealth in people, machinery, and expertise. "We cannot prevent Guineans, Senegalese, Malians from coming here," said Moussa Cissokho, a tomboluma based in Duuta, "Anybody who wants to come has the right to come. The richness came out here for everyone. Everyone can try their luck in the juura. It is for everyone."[60] Historically, welcoming strangers to juuras was adaptive to the reliance on orpaillage during times of drought and other environmental upheaval. Gold dust could be sold to Muslim merchants, juulas, in exchange for grain on regional markets. Because a given juura is rarely productive for more than two or three seasons, the host of a juura one year might be a stranger on a juura the next. Senegalese officials and mining companies embrace a narrow vision of orpaillage as a local subsistence activity carried out by regional farmers, mostly women, who pan for gold with calabashes seasonally along regional riverways. This is an attempt to freeze-frame orpaillage in a static and bucolic notion of traditional village life, as did the colonial and early post-colonial state. For residents of the savanna's Birimian rocks, there is no distinction between juuras as a subsistence resource and the incorporative ethic of the juura. Orpailleurs see the expansion of their households with Guineans and rock-crushing machines as a novel articulation of a long-standing practice of incorporating migrants and their expertise into regional juuras.

Claiming Marginalization

On the morning of December 23, 2008, a group of Senegalese students, radio hosts, bakers, migrants repatriated from Spain, shop owners, mechanics, and retired soldiers assembled in Kédougou's public garden. They began a protest march down the town's main thoroughfare toward the marketplace. The self-named Mouvement Citoyen pour la Défense des Intérêts de Kédougou (Citizens' Movement for the Defense of Kédougou's Interests) organized the protest after the prefect of Kédougou ignored repeated requests to meet to discuss problems surrounding the region's corporate mining sector. In an open letter to regional state officials and to President Abdoulaye Wade, the Citizens' Movement voiced concerns that Kédougou was not receiving adequate returns from mining revenues. It demanded greater transparency in the management of funds allocated by mining companies for regional development; employment for army veterans as private security guards at mining camps; and a review of the environmental impact assessment for the Sabodala mine. The authors of the letter framed their grievances within the state's historical marginalization of Kédougou, evidenced by "endemic unemployment" and enduring "socio-economic conditions." The opening paragraph of the letter establishes this rhetoric of marginalization: "Mr. President, the truth is that our locality, since independence[,] has always lived in injustice and ... we estimate today that Kédougou, despite its visibility on the national level for its numerous riches, continues to see its population submitted to all types of injustice that are the deep causes of its poverty."[61]

Gendarmes deployed to stop the Citizens' Movement protest were quickly overwhelmed. They called on assistance from soldiers training at a local base. In the chaos that followed, a soldier fired on the crowd, killing a young man named Bana Sidibé. A riot ensued. While protestors carried Sidibé's lifeless body on their shoulders, they burned municipal buildings and gendarmes' vehicles. By nightfall, many protestors had fled to the remote villages of distant relatives. In Kédougou, gendarmes entered family compounds and beat suspected protestors until they identified the households of other participants. In total, thirty-three protestors were detained and jailed in Tambacounda. The riot, which became known in Kédougou as *les évènements de 2008* (the events of 2008), was part of a turbulent chapter of political protest in Senegal.[62] In the years to follow, hip-hop artists and activists launched a movement called Y'en a Marre (We've Had Enough in Wolof) that criticized economic stagnation and curbs on democratic practice during Wade's presidency.[63] While Y'en a Marre mobilized a broad-based urban constituency drawn from across the nation, the events of 2008 emerged from grievances distinct to Kédougou's history. Moreover, the protests articulated a modality of regional, not national, belonging. The riots marked the cumulation of tensions surrounding the growth of Kédougou's mining industry as it ran against the troubled history of the state's treatment of southeastern Senegal.

Early grievances in Kédougou centered on the role of state-appointed officials in the selection process for employment at Sabodala, then run by the Australian company MDL. In 2006, MDL began construction on the mine, mill, and camp facility—the most labor-intensive phase of open-pit mining. The company claimed to prioritize regional residents for unskilled labor and any skilled work for which they could be easily trained. Mineral Deposits Limited employed a rotation system for employment. Day laborers each worked for two weeks of the month, with the idea that some workers would transition into more permanent contracts over time. Every Saturday a committee met to organize unskilled labor recruitment at MDL. It was composed of representatives from the company, the chiefs of villages adjacent to the state-appointed subprefect of Saraya.[64] Each week chiefs presented to MDL a prioritized list of workers based on geographic repartition across villages.

Some Kédovins accused state-appointed officials involved in the committee of prioritizing their relatives from elsewhere in Senegal for positions as unskilled laborers at Sabodala. Rumors circulated that busloads of men from coastal Senegal were ushered through the gates of the Sabodala mine to fill positions reserved for regional residents. For many Kédovins, the favoring of outsiders for employment echoed a historical pattern of state bureaucrats and urban merchants profiting from Kédougou's natural resources while investing little in the region's infrastructure or people.[65] Residents of villages adjacent to the Sabodala mine compared the reportedly corrupt labor recruitment process to grievances against Senegal's Direction des Eaux et Forêt (Department of Water and Forests). Forestry guards are notorious for policing subsistence hunting, charcoal production, and timber use in Kédougou, home to Senegal's largest national forest—Niokolo-Koba National Park—and other protected lands. In the 1960s and 1970s, the forestry service carried out raids of villages near the park, searching women's cooking huts for illegal bush meat and arresting poor subsistence hunters. Adding insult to injury, for decades the forestry service accorded timber and charcoal licenses for southeastern Senegal primarily to wealthy merchants from the Muridiyya Islamic brotherhood.[66]

The governance of Senegal's gold-mining contracts further fueled suspicions that state officials were exploiting Kédougou for personal gain. Senegal's Mining Code of 2003 concentrated decision making in the hands of authorities in Dakar. Kédougou's residents and elected officials played no part in the mining contract negotiations between MDL and the state, represented by the Department of Mines and Geology. The only moment for local input was during the approval process for social and environmental impact studies (SEIS). According to Senegalese mining law, approval of the SEIS should always precede the granting of a mining concession. But for Sabodala, MDL conducted the SEIS after the state granted the company a mining permit. This effectively excluded regional residents from the one deliberative process associated with opening a mining project in Senegal.

The final chord of local discontent focused on the management of the so-called Fond Social Minière (Social Mining Fund).[67] Mining conventions and contracts signed between the state and mining and exploration firms in

Kédougou included provisions that these companies had to contribute set funds to social programs. However, in the mid-2000s, there was ongoing confusion as to where these funds resided within the state and how they were effectively spent. In November 2007, residents of twenty-four villages in the rural community of Khossanto, directly adjacent to the Sabodala concession, protested to demand greater transparency in the management of these funds. Roughly eight hundred men blocked the roads between Khossanto and Sabodala, the major access route for Sabodala, and set tires on fire in front of the gates of MDL's camp.[68] A year later, similar grievances animated the much larger and coordinated protests of the events of 2008.

In January 2009, the tribunal of Tambacounda tried twenty-nine of the original thirty-three detainees and condemned nineteen protestors to prison for sentences ranging from five to ten years.[69] The court's harsh sentencing inspired a political mobilization to "free" the protestors. Members of Kédougou's diaspora played a key role in the mobilization. They demonstrated before Senegalese consulates in Barcelona, Paris, and New York City and hired a lawyer to represent the accused protestors in the appeal process (figure 6.2).[70] Among its residents and its diaspora, the events of 2008 strengthened a sense of belonging to the region of Kédougou. Prior to 2008, most immigrants from Kédougou had convened in village- or ethnic-based organizations abroad.[71] For many immigrants, 2008 was the first time they self-identified as members of a Kédougou diaspora by referring to themselves as Kédovins. Members of diverse ethnolinguistic groups back in Kédougou also adopted the term *Kédovin* after 2008.

Senegalese officials challenged the claims to regional marginalization expressed by protestors in Kédougou and its diaspora. In contrast to claims to juuras as a subsistence resource, state bureaucrats were unsympathetic to appeals to regional exceptionalism. In part, Senegal has cultivated a sense of national belonging by violently policing regional political projects, such as the Casamançais separatist movement.[72] The events of 2008 were slotted into a similar narrative. Serigne Bassirou Guéye, the prosecutor who represented the state at the 2009 trial, challenged the claims of protestors that they and their ancestors were victims of state discrimination. Guéye inverted this logic to argue that the protestors, not the state, were "xenophobic" against citizens of other regions of Senegal. He reminded the court that Sabodala was supposed to benefit all of Senegal, not just Kédougou.[73] In March 2009, two months after the trial in Tambacounda, Wade issued a unilateral presidential pardon to release the nineteen detainees jailed for their participation in the protest.[74] The pardon was a bald political move, announced by Wade

Figure 6.2 March of Kédovins to liberate imprisoned protestors in Granollers, Spain, 2009. Photograph by the author.

while he was in Kédougou for the ribbon-cutting ceremony for the Sabodala mine and campaigning in support of candidates from his political party for upcoming regional elections.[75]

For roughly a decade following the presidential pardon, there was little activism or protest in Kédougou directed at the state or the mining sector. Rather, Kédovins retrenched their engagement in orpaillage. When I returned to Senegal for field research in 2013, many young people still sought employment at mining and exploration camps. But the locus of political debate had shifted from the loss of juuras to corporate encroachment. This shift was evidenced in the biographies of two men involved in the 2008 protests: Aliou Monékhata and Daouda Djiguiba. In 2008, Monékhata, known as "DJ Monex," was a popular host of a weekly reggae show on the region's most popular private radio station. On Wednesday evenings, DJ Monex took phone calls during his show, whose subjects ranged from dedications to sweethearts to commentary on regional politics.[76] During the summer of 2008, the show became a platform for exchanging information about employment in the mines. Monékhata traveled to Sabodala to investigate some of the claims from his callers, a trip that inspired him to join the 2008 protest. He was among the nineteen people sentenced to prison for his involvement. After receiving a presidential pardon, DJ Monex resigned from his radio show and left the public eye. He entered a business arrangement with a cousin in Spain who sent him gold detectors purchased from a hobbyist shop in Barcelona. Each morning, Monékhata sets out with a close friend by motorcycle to search for gold. He makes a better living as a self-employed gold prospector than he ever did as a radio DJ or in a previous job working for the state's economic control.

Djiguiba was born into a Jakhanke family in Kédougou and migrated to Spain in 2001 on a work visa. He found employment in the automotive industry in Barcelona but was laid off during the global financial crisis of 2008. He found part-time work in construction while volunteering for an organization that provides legal services to immigrants in Catalan. Djiguiba's brother was one of the protesters in Kédougou who was jailed and later freed by President Wade. Djiguiba was the lead organizer of a march to free the imprisoned protestors held in Granollers, Spain (see figure 6.2). In 2013, Djiguiba traveled from Spain to Kédougou to visit his family. Instead of purchasing a plane ticket, he bought a used car in Barcelona. He filled it with two-dozen gold detectors and drove across the Sahara Desert through western Morocco and Mauritania. He later returned to Spain, where he lives with his wife and young children. He invests in orpaillage teams managed by his relatives in Kédougou. Orpaillage generates a more reliable and regenerative source of income for Djiguiba's extended family than his remittances.

"A Region Abandoned by Senegal"

In April 2014, President Sall traveled to Kédougou for a special interministerial council on orpaillage. This meeting led to the state's decision to bulldoze a number of regional juuras. While the media coverage of this event focused on the juura closures, Sall legalized as many juuras as he closed during this visit by superimposing official orpaillage corridors onto a number of important regional juuras, including Tinkoto, Kharakenna, and Bantaco. Sall demonstrated his fluency in Kédougou's language of subterranean rights when, during an address broadcast on the regional public radio station, he acknowledged that Kédougou "was, in the past, a region abandoned by Senegal."[77] Sall framed the orpaillage corridors as one of several steps he was taking to address Kédougou's historical marginalization.

This chapter documents the language of subterranean rights innovated by orpailleurs—along with farmers, merchants, students, and radio hosts—in Kédougou, Senegal. Claims to discovery, scale, subsistence, and regional marginalization are the primary idioms in which this language was spoken during my research in the mid-2010s. Orpailleurs, state agents, and representatives of mining companies draw creatively on this language and different versions of the history of orpaillage to defend their claims to specific gold deposits. All sides omit inconvenient facts and embellish others. Like all forms of speech, this language is flexible and evolving. Some elements of this language are found on resource frontiers globally; others are unique to Kédougou. This language is distinctively West African, motivated by a historical notion of juuras as famine resources that should remain open to local residents, migrants, and future generations (see conclusion). It reveals how entitlements to the underground are constructed and defended in the face of corporate mining capital, which works to efface multiple and overlapping claims to gold.

Mining companies have developed their own language to defend their claims to subterranean resources in Senegal. When appealing to the state to expel orpailleurs from their permits, they reference their financial investments in Senegal through taxation and formal job creation while pointing out that orpaillage is largely illegal and generates little revenue for the state. The mining industry also makes moral appeals to its own legitimacy, pointing to its contributions to community development, environmental remediation, women's literacy programs, and antimalaria campaigns. For example, when requesting that Senegal's Ministry of Mines expel orpailleurs from the Makabingui deposit, the managing director of Bassari Resources carefully detailed the company's contributions to Senegal's economy; its investments in local infrastructure (a mosque, a school, grain mills, a clinic, and an ambulance), and the fact that nearly 100 percent of its employees were Senegalese. Kédovins appreciate corporate investments in public health and education, and they ask and expect mining companies to provide these services. But they do not see such expenditures as compensation for the loss of juuras for mining by future generations.

State-issued exploration permits, most of which are held by a few firms, now cover more than three-quarters of Kédougou region. Fresh gold discoveries present a range of possible outcomes for the Senegalese villages dotting the interior of these permits. The building of a new mine, or adding new pits to active mines and mills, could mean more formal employment opportunities for local residents or an increase in funding for regional development projects. But residents of villages adjacent to gold deposits are also at risk of displacement if the state deems the mining of a gold deposit in the interest of the "public good."[78] The discovery of the Niakafiri deposit, announced several years ago, could mean the eventual displacement of the entire village of Sabodala. One guaranteed outcome of the discovery of new deposits containing one million ounces or more of gold is that some juuras will be permanently closed. Whether or not any given juura will become the subject of corporate interest depends on the relative profitability of mining it compared with others maintained in the firm's pipeline. The destiny of many of Kédougou's juuras depends on global market prices and ever-evolving corporate strategy.

Orpailleurs are not powerless in negotiations with mining firms. State officials and mining companies are well aware of the potential for violence in densely populated juuras. Any visit to Sabodala by high-ranking officials in Senegal's Ministry of Mines is followed by meetings with leaders of the region's largest juuras. At the same time, because orpaillage remains illegal in many corridors, orpailleurs are constrained in what they can demand of the state. This chapter has concerned largely public-facing debates about mineral discovery and the law. Chapter 7 turns to intimate realms of concern unfolding in the households of orpailleurs and farmers in southeastern Senegal. In it, I return to another thread that winds through this book like the subterranean movements of Bida and Nininkala: how a centuries-old ritual geology shapes Senegal's contemporary mining boom.

7
Race, Islam, and Ethnicity in the Pits

In the late 1950s, on the eve of Senegal's independence from France, a re-spected Muslim diviner from Kéniéba, Mali, traveled to coastal Senegal to visit relatives. On the way, he stopped to visit a friend in "Jakha," the colloquial name for several Jakhanke villages that line the Gambia River in Kédougou. News of the diviner's arrival spread quickly. Using cowries and the Qur'an, the diviner consulted with clients seeking advice about infertility, business arrangements, and marriage. Every night, the compound of his host filled with visitors bearing kola nuts, chickens, and fonio as pay-ment for divination. The day before his departure, the diviner delivered a prophesy that affected all of his clients: Kédougou contained riches in gold that would attract people from Dakar, Bamako, and across the ocean. But to dispense these riches to human hands, the patron spirit of Kédougou's gold demanded the sacrifice of a light-skinned woman with a distended bellybutton. The description matched one person: the daughter of a chief of the Jakha. Outraged, Jakha's leaders admonished the diviner and prayed for Kédougou's gold to stay underground.

The story of the traveling diviner is widely recounted in southeastern Senegal as a folk theory for why gold appears in some places and not in others. This tale resonates with elements of West Africa's ritual geology dating to the medieval period: the annual sacrifice of a young woman to Bida, the spirit snake of Wagadu. Rumors of human sacrifice remain a key idiom through which Kédovins narrate the social costs of orpaillage, the intimate sacrifices required to generate wealth from the earth's subsurface.[1]

Concerns about the morality of wealth from minerals are found around the globe. In her ethnography of Mongolia's recent gold rush, Mette High observes that gold is "polluted money," unusable for many transactions. As High writes, while gold is considered a store of universal value—presumably exchangeable with all other objects—in many parts of the world, it is also a fraught material that is not easily commodified because it "retains strong ties to the landscape and its many spirit beings."[2] In Papua New Guinea, artisanal gold miners handle "wasted money."[3] In Burkina Faso, Mossi-speakers classify gold as "bitter," as do the Luo of Kenya.[4] Diamond mining in Congo-Zaire and in Sierra Leone produces "wild" or "fast" money.[5] In Kédougou, money derived from orpaillage is similarly "fast" or "quick" money (*wari teriya*).[6] Quick money—which is produced by activities based on luck, illicit enterprises, or nefarious engagements with the occult—is contrasted with clean money, wealth earned incrementally through hard work.[7] In contemporary Kédougou, clean money is also associated with following Islam: performing daily prayers and ablutions and paying the religious tax (*zakat* in Arabic) prescribed in the Qur'an.[8] While clean money can be invested in any domain, quick money should not be invested in sentient beings: cattle and bridewealth. Quick money is best used on consumables—clothing, motorcycles, gasoline—or in construction, which returns gold to the earth.

Scholars offer competing theories for the fraught moral status of mineral wealth. Laboring underground brings miners in proximity to death, human burials, and the underworld of the Abrahamic religious traditions. In agrarian societies, mining may threaten agricultural production and the forms of social reproduction bound to agrarian lifestyles. Compared with earning a set wage in an industrial mine, artisanal mining is often viewed as a game of chance because earnings are based in large part on luck—that is, the quantity of minerals one finds. Mining rushes invite cosmological upheaval, pulling the young into spaces of multiethnic mixture and violence far from the oversight of elders. Similar to street hawking and sex tourism—other domains associated with "short-cut" and "rushed" money—artisanal mining has grown with the rise of market liberalization and the casualization of labor. In such settings, as anthropologists working elsewhere in Africa document, notions of ill-gotten wealth are a commentary on growing economic inequality and antisocial wealth.[9]

These concerns animate moral anxieties about orpaillage in Kédougou. But rumors of human sacrifice and quick money also speak to a far older association of gold with occult forces on the West African savanna and Sahel. The most common concerns I heard expressed about gold wealth during my research were centered on the historic association of orpaillage with pagans. Of particular concern to my interlocutors was the contested transition of orpaillage from the primary domain of ancestral religious practitioners, putatively ethnic Maninka, to an activity pursued by Muslims and people from diverse ethnolinguistic backgrounds. Small groups of Muslims have lived and worked in Kédougou for centuries. But conversion to Islam among the majority of its rural residents has been slow compared with elsewhere in Senegal. This has changed in recent decades, however, as most of Kédougou's diverse residents have converted to Islam, including many of the Maninka lineages that historically presided over Kédougou's juuras.

Despite the growing presence of Muslims in orpaillage, it has been difficult to dislodge the centuries-old adage that "gold is in the hands of spirits" (*sanu ye jinne le bulu*). Patron spirits of gold disliked Muslim prayers and ablutions, which were prohibited on Kédougou's goldfields as late as the 1970s and are still discouraged on some juuras. Because spirits were thought to reward individuals who engage in ancestral religious practices, many in Kédougou accuse Muslims who become wealthy from orpaillage of engaging in non-Muslim rituals. Rumors often take on a racial character. Muslims are quick to assert the universalism of Islam with the phrase, "A Muslim is a Muslim." Behind closed doors, however, many Kédovins argue that conversion does not erase an individual's ethnolinguistic heritage.

In Kédougou, different ethnolinguistic groups are understood to sit on a spectrum between ancestral religious practices and Islam, based on the timing of the conversion of their ancestors to Islam.[10] Ancestral religious practices are associated with "firstcomer" groups, those who claim precedence to a given territory because they entered into exchange relationships with spirits upon their arrival. It is even rumored that subterranean spirits can detect the "soul" or "essence" (*ni*) of orpailleurs. As one orpailleur put it: "The jinne knows where you come from, and they know where you have been. They want a dirty body. You will never find a Muslim who gets rich off gold."[11] A "dirty body" refers to someone who either does not practice Muslim ablutions or is proximate, in hereditary terms, to firstcomer groups. Statements of this genre express "essentialism," what Susan Gelman defines as the "view that categories have an underlying reality or true nature that one cannot observe directly but that gives [category members] their identity."[12] The "underlying reality" in Kédougou is the notion that a person's ethnolinguistic origins are part of an embodied essence. Rumors that a person's success in orpaillage is due to their ethnolinguistic heritage is a means of morally ranking groups in terms of their perceived proximity to ancestral religious practices or Islam.[13] Essentialist notions are so widespread on Kédougou's goldfields that mining chiefs (*damantigi*) typically recruit at least one descendant of a firstcomer group, which is thought to enhance the team's prospects.

Essentialist notions of embodied ethnolinguistic difference are part of a racial language that has flourished on Kédougou's goldfields over the past two decades. It has developed in dialogue with the more public-facing language of subterranean rights described in chapter 6. My use of the term *racial* draws on the philosopher Kwame Anthony Appiah's definition of *racialism* as a notion that humankind is divided into different categories, each distinguished by inherited traits and characteristics. Racism—at least, one form of it—is the belief that categories of peoples, nations, or ethnicities can be ranked in a hierarchical fashion according to universal registers of moral inferiority or superiority.[14] Racial language draws attention to the fact that practices or stereotypes attached to groups of people evolve through debate among diverse parties. Most Kédovins claim to belong to one or more ethnolinguistic groups. These affiliations become imbued with racial meaning only when emphasis is placed on ideas about hierarchy and bodily descent across groups.

Corporate capital contours this racial language. For one, growing competition for access to juuras among orpailleurs, and between orpailleurs and corporations, has accelerated the formalization of land titles in a region where rural land ownership was once fluid.[15] With the corporate enclosure of large tracts of land, there has been a modest rise in nativist thinking in Kédougou. This is part of a continent-wide trend as growing land pressure has encouraged people to make claims to ethnic belonging bound to specific tracts of land.[16] For example, some ethnic Maninka argue that they have the exclusive right to manage juuras due to their heritage as ritual intermediaries with territorial spirits. But calling attention to ancestral ritual practices is a risky enterprise for recent converts to Islam who seek social legitimacy as practicing Muslims.

Scholars of capital-intensive mining in Africa attend to the ways in which migrant labor regimes and the segregation of work on mines create racialized divisions of work and skill between African workers and (mostly) white mine management and technicians.[17] I build on this critical literature to explore how categories of race and skill are forged among different segments of West African society.[18] These racial formations are shaped by Black-white binaries, but they also emerge from long-standing concerns in the West African savanna and Sahel about the perceived relationship among embodied difference, ethnolinguistic affiliation, firstcomer status to the land, and Islam. I present the landscape of rumor and racialization on Kédougou's goldfields first by surveying the ethnolinguistic spectrum along which debates about the relationship between gold and embodied difference are drawn in the region. Next, I examine how divergent histories of settlement and religion shape engagements with orpaillage in three villages. In closing, I consider how orpailleurs and other residents of Kédougou justify their intense concerns about the morality of gold wealth in the face of the corporate enclosure of gold-bearing land.

Ethnolinguistic "Origins" in Kédougou

During the rainy season, an aerial view of southeastern Senegal reveals a verdant green landscape dotted with bald brown patches of cleared land that are villages, juuras, and gold-exploration camps. While agrarian life appears uniform from a distance, on the ground Kédougou is characterized by ethnolinguistic and religious diversity. This is a legacy of the region's history as an Atlantic-era refuge for the enslaved and those fleeing enslavement by large-scale states. In most corridors, interethnic settlement is organized around dyadic relationships between putative firstcomers and incomers. Table 7.1 provides an overview of the ethnolinguistic and religious affiliations associated with firstcomer and incomer groups as commonly reported by Kédovins. The reader should keep in mind that individuals and entire lineages have moved across these groups over time and that the boundaries between groups is far more porous in practice than suggested by these typological categorizations. Yet many Kédovins remain invested in the notion that these categories are static, embodied, and hereditary. As the anthropologist Frederick Barth once pointed out, "categorical distinctions" are based not on the absence of mobility but on "social processes of exclusion and incorporation whereby discrete categories are maintained despite changing participation and membership in the course of individual life histories."

Firstcomers in Kédougou are typically from one of three ethnolinguistic groups: Maninka, Jallonke, and speakers of Tenda languages (Bedik, Beliyan-Bassari, Coniagui, and Badiaranke peoples).[19] Ethnic Maninka and Jallonke speak distinct languages of the broader Mande language family: they share many lexical features but are not mutually intelligible.

Firstcomers all claim autochthony of given zones in Kédougou—that their ancestors were the first inhabitants of the land. They claim their ancestors encountered territorial spirits, not humans, when they arrived. Speakers of Tenda languages, and ethnic Jallonke and Maninka people, claim precedence to land in different corridors in Kédougou. Bedik and Beliyan-Bassari are widely credited as the first known residents of the region. They trace their presence in the zone to the sixteenth century, although some

Table 7.1 Ethnolinguistic, religious affiliations, and settlement history in Kédougou

Ethnolinguistic Affiliation	Settlement History	Religious Affiliation
Jakhanke	Incomers	Muslim
Pular	Incomers	Muslim, ancestral religion
Maninka	Firstcomers, incomers	Muslim, ancestral religion
Soninke	Firstcomers, incomers	Muslim, ancestral religion
Bedik, Beliyan-Bassari, Coniagui, Badiaranke	Firstcomers	Christian, Muslim, ancestral religion
Jallonke	Firstcomers	Muslim, ancestral religion

scholars date their arrival to the thirteenth century or earlier.[20] During the Atlantic period, Beliyan-Bassari and Bedik—whom Muslim states targeted as potential captives—moved to Kédougou's upland massifs for protection, where they engaged in hunting, plant collection, and mountainside farming. Bedik ethnogenesis may also date to the Atlantic era, a product of alliances between speakers of Tenda and Manding language varieties who sought refuge in the highlands.[21] Jallonke claim to be the original inhabitants of the Fouta Djallon mountains, from which they derive their name: mountain (*jallon*) inhabitants (*ka*). In the seventeenth century, the Muslim Pular theocracy that rose to power in the Fouta Djallon pushed Jallonke to the edges of the plateau, including southeastern Senegal.[22] Ethnic Maninka in Kédougou claim their ancestors began settling the zone in the thirteenth century, having migrated from Manden during Sunjata's reign. It is also likely that refugees of diverse backgrounds, fleeing enslavement, integrated into Maninka lineages in Kédougou during the Atlantic period.[23] Some Maninka villages concede that Tenda-speakers preceded them on the land but moved voluntarily upon the arrival of Maninka settlers in the zone.

Incomers to Kédougou settled in the region at different times, but they all report having been practicing Muslims prior to their arrival in southeastern Senegal. Incomer groups include ethnic Soninke, Pular, and Jakhanke. Soninke, speakers of a Mande language variety of the same name, constitute a small minority in Kédougou. Tracing their ancestry to the medieval empire of Wagadu, they established several villages along the Falémé, suggestive of their influence on early gold mining in the region. In some settlement narratives, Soninke were glossed as pagan firstcomers, but they were Muslim in other cases. The Jakhanke trace their lineage to the Soninke but teach the Qur'an in Jakhanke, a Manding language variety. The Jakhanke established autonomous Muslim communities along the Gambia River in the Atlantic period—today's Jakha. Finally, Pular-speakers in Kédougou trace their ancestry to several waves of Pular migration to the zone associated with the rise of the Pular states of Bundu and Fouta Toro (both in Senegal) and the Fouta Djallon (Guinea) in the sixteenth and seventeenth centuries. Pular migration to Kédougou accelerated in the early twentieth century as large numbers of Pular-speakers from the Fouta Djallon fled a violent rubber tax regime in French Guinea. While searching for wild rubber vines, they settled villages in Senegal, where colonial officials accepted head taxes in cash or in kind through a range of products. In the 1960s and 1970s, thousands of ethnic Pulars fled persecution from Guinea's first president, Sékou Touré. Most refugees simply passed through Kédougou, but a number settled permanently.

Depending on the corridor and period in question, relationships between firstcomers and incomers in Kédougou ranged from complementary to violent. In many cases, Muslim incomers deferred to firstcomers as their hosts, recognizing their authority over the land and asking permission to settle autonomous villages. Such rights were often granted in a region where population density was low and wealth in people was valued. This dyadic relationship pertained on the gold-bearing Birimian rocks that stretch from Kédougou town toward the Malian border, home to the Maninka-dominated provinces of Bélédougou, Sirimana, and Dantila. Here, Jakhanke and some Pular incomers accessed land by deferring to Maninka chiefs. In other corridors, Muslim incomers conquered or displaced firstcomers by force. This transpired in some parts of historical Niokolo, populated today by ethnic Maninka, Bedik, and Pular; in the highlands of southwestern Kédougou, home to the Beliyan-Bassari; and in the foothills of the Fouta Djallon in southeastern Kédougou, home to the Jallonke. In these zones, Muslim Pular incomers, primarily originating from Guinea, entered into conflict with firstcomers. In the Atlantic era, Pular immigrants and mercenaries from the Fouta Djallon pillaged Jallonke, Beliyan-Bassari, Bedik, and Maninka for captives. These skirmishes pushed Jallonke and speakers of Tenda languages farther into the region's rock escarpments, and onto marginal farmland, as Pulars claimed fertile valleys for their livestock and villages.[24]

The legacies of slavery further complicate interethnic relations in Kédougou. During the Atlantic period, most firstcomer groups did not own slaves or owned very few. By contrast, Jakhanke and Pular incomers relied heavily on slave labor for agricultural production. Pular nobles and free farmers from the Fouta Djallon were heavily involved in the transatlantic slave trade and kept slaves of their own. They targeted pagans who refused to convert to Islam. Captives lived in separate villages, called *runde* in Pular. Large numbers of Pular-speakers of former slave descent—those with ethnic Maninka, Jallonke, and Tenda origins—populated southern Kédougou under colonial rule. They established separate villages from their former overlords and engaged in some intermarriage with ethnic Jallonke, Bedik, and Beliyan-Bassari.[25]

Today, as in the past, membership in different ethnolinguistic groups is fluid as individuals and entire lineages adopt new religions and languages. Conversion to Islam, in particular, occasioned transitions in status. For descendants of formerly enslaved people, becoming Muslim created distance from slave heritage. For example, since being Pular was synonymous with Islam, former captives often adopted the common Pular patronym Diallo when they converted.[26] Christianity offered an alternative path for some. In the 1960s, Senegal's President Léopold Senghor invited a French Catholic mission to open in Kédougou and Salemata. Hundreds of Tenda-speakers and ethnic Maninka adopted Catholicism, but by the late 1970s, Islam had gained a stronger foothold among these groups. Several descendants of respected Maninka Muslim lineages from Niokolo proselytized in Maninka and Jallonke villages, earning converts and establishing small outdoor mosques for communal prayer. In the 1990s, many Tenda-speakers, including some former Christians, adopted Islam. This trend continues today.

The multilayered history of interethnic settlement and religious conversion in Kédougou helps us understand the stakes in rumors about the relationship between success in orpaillage and one's ethnolinguistic "origins." Orpaillage invites commentary on ethnolinguistic difference because of its tightly bound association with territorial spirits, with whom firstcomer lineages cultivate relationships. The locus of controversy centers on two factors. The first is whether a person's ethnolinguistic background alone garners them favor with underground spirits or the authority to preside over juuras. The second concerns the ubiquitous practice of blood sacrifice on Senegal's goldfields. Both Muslim and non-Muslim orpailleurs slaughter chickens, goats, sheep, and cows to seek protection while working underground and to give thanks for a productive mining shaft. In southeastern

Senegal, these sacrifices are called *sadaxo*, a modification of the Arabic term for "alms giving" in the Qur'an. But blood sacrifices differ in their protocols and intended recipients. Historically, Maninka masters of the mines (*juurakuntigi*) and orpailleurs slaughtered domestic animals directly on the juura or on lineage shrines (*jalan*) in the name of territorial spirits, Nininkala, or a Supreme Being. Historically, Muslims view jalans as the most potent symbol of ancestral religious practices in Kédougou. Animals sacrificed on juuras or on jalans were often suffocated or buried. By contrast, Muslims following halal protocol severed the animal's jugular vein with a knife. They made sacrifices in the name of Allah in lineage compounds or mosques, never on shrines or in the bush.[27]

With the growing embrace of Islam by members of diverse ethnolinguistic groups in Kédougou, the degree to which individuals still engage in ancestral religious practices, or admit to doing so, varies. Today, some juurakuntigi openly sacrifice animals on juuras and jalans in the name of territorial spirits. But most are self-professing Muslims who perform sacrifices in lineage compounds by halal protocol while reciting prayers from the Qur'an. Some jalans have been abandoned; others are consulted in private. A few have generated a cult following with the recent expansion of orpaillage, frequented by those seeking the favor of local spirits. Regardless of what any individual does or does not practice, both Muslims and non-Muslims who succeed in orpaillage can be accused of "passing by the shrine [*jalan*]," a euphemism for engaging in ritual practices that run counter to Islam. Statements of this genre in Kédougou are often directed at people with shallow Muslim genealogies, although no one is safe from the accusation. Attempts to make orpaillage into a secular activity in which Muslims, regardless of their ethnolinguistic background, can derive morally regenerative wealth is challenged from multiple angles.

Tinkoto: A Maninka Ritual Territory

In 2014 I was living in the compound of Bambo Cissokho, the charismatic chief of Tinkoto village, when I witnessed the opening of a new juura. Roughly two miles from Tinkoto, gold detectors operated by two Guinean migrants illuminated in a thicket of bamboo. Guided by a quickening beep, the men dug a test pit and hit an alluvial gold seam four meters underground. They reported their discovery to the head of Tinkoto's tomboluma, the customary police force of the juura. The tomboluma called Cissokho, who was traveling at the time, to report the discovery. Cissokho authorized

Figure 7.1 Deepening a mining shaft. Tinkoto, Senegal, 2012. Photograph by Aliou Bakhoum.

the men to open the new juura.[28] Within a week, the bamboo thicket was puckered with mine shafts (figure 7.1).

Cissokho named the new juura Thiankoun Bassadié, after a small Beliyan-Bassari farming hamlet adjacent to the gold discovery. Residents of Thiankoun Bassadié sent a delegation to Cissokho's compound to declare that only they, not Tinkoto, had the right to open a juura found in their agricultural fields. In exchange for this breach, they demanded a share of gold from each mine shaft. Cissokho refused, arguing that any gold deposit discovered within ten kilometers of Tinkoto was within his jurisdiction. Cissokho justified this claim on the grounds that only those who follow "Maninka custom" (*Maningolu laado*) have the requisite ritual knowledge to manage juuras. Beliyan-Bassari are considered the firstcomer group in this zone and proximate to territorial spirits. But in the case of gold rights, Cissokho did not recognize their claim on the juura because Beliyan-Bassari did not historically mine for gold. Cissokho underscored the alliance between ethnic Maninka and gold as a justification for why Maninka should control orpaillage even on land occupied by other first-comers:

> Where there is a juura, there are Maninka behind it. Every juura you go to, you will hear the names *daman* [shaft], *soli* [pick], *tomboluma* [security force of the juura], *juurakuntigi* [master of the mines]. Are these Pullo [Pular] words? No, they are Maninka. The juura is for the Manden [people from the heart of the Malian empire]. From here as far

as you can see, this is the land of Manden. If I conduct a sacrifice here, its force will be felt in Bélédougou and Sirimana. Even Niokolo, they will know the benefits of our sacrifice.[29]

Cissokho references the fact that the words commonly used to describe the labor, tools, and political institutions on the mines derive from Maninka, not, as he argues, from Pular. Cissokho also credited the ritual labor of his ancestors, such as making blood sacrifices to territorial spirits, for loosening the grip of spirits on gold. This, he argued, accounted for the strength of Maninka juuras compared with those of Muslim Pulars. Cissokho himself is a self-proclaimed Muslim, but he openly admits to maintaining "one foot in Islam and one foot in tradition" (*A sin kilin be dino to, sin kilin don be laado to*).[30] While he attends prayers at mosque, he also displays Maninka ritual objects in his sleeping hut.

Cissokho was the target of frequent social commentary about the moral ambiguity of ritually blending Islam and Maninka ancestral practices. Like many chiefs of orpaillage villages, Cissokho often sacrificed sheep, chickens, and even cows in his lineage compound to secure the safety of orpailleurs and to keep Tinkoto's juuras fertile in gold. These sacrifices were public affairs, performed according to halal protocol and accompanied by Qur'anic recitations. One afternoon, shortly after the discovery of Thiankoun Bassadié, Cissokho organized a sacrifice of three white sheep in his compound to mark the ritual opening of the new juura. He divided the meat among his wives and a recent widow as a form of alms giving. Cissokho asked his wives to prepare the meat with rice and invited the male heads of Tinkoto's founding households to a communal meal. During the festivities, I shared a bowl of rice with Cissokho's youngest wife and several women whom I had never met before. They blessed Cissokho and praised the tenderness of the meat. Toward the end of the meal, an older woman commented in a hushed tone in Pular that the "real sacrifice took place in the bush" (*sadaxo fano be kela wulo to le*). This references the historical practice of sacrifices made to the spirits of gold-bearing land at lineage shrines or on the juura. The other women laughed, and the conversation moved on. Such a statement could be made in jest because Cissokho is proud of his Maninka ritual heritage. In other contexts, however, an accusation that an orpailleur "eats his sacrifice in the bush" is a public questioning of the person's authenticity as a Muslim, suggesting that he (or more rarely she) secretly engages in ancestral religious practices. Descendants of long-standing Muslim lineages, as we shall now see, face different challenges in navigating the moral landscape of orpaillage.

Making a Muslim Juura in Kanoumering

Kanoumering village is roughly six kilometers from Tinkoto, but its architecture and daily rhythms diverge remarkably from those of its neighbor. For almost twenty years, Kanoumering has hosted the exploration camp of Randgold (now Endeavor). Unlike the makeshift palm frond huts that characterize Tinkoto, most compounds in Kanoumering feature at least one concrete building encircled by concrete walls. A few boutiques border the mosque at the center of town, but commercial activity is minimal compared with that in Tinkoto's bustling marketplace. Today Kanoumering is majority-Pular, but it was initially founded as a Maninka agricultural hamlet more than a century ago. During the droughts of the late 1970s and early 1980s, Maninka firstcomers welcomed dozens of Pular families from villages in Bélédougou and Sirimana whose wells had run dry. Different Pular lineages in Kanoumering trace their heritage to the Muslim states of Fouta Toro, Bundu, and Fouta Djallon. By their account, their ancestors were Muslims when they migrated to Kédougou. They settled peaceably in Maninka villages, establishing separate neighborhoods or farming hamlets while conceding political authority to their Maninka hosts. Life in Kanoumering was historically centered on rainy season agriculture and raising cattle, sheep, and goats. During the dry season, children studied the Qur'an. Adult men, and occasionally women, migrated to Dakar or Tambacounda to seek wage labor, sell fruit in roadside stands, or work as domestic help in wealthy households. It was only during the droughts of the 1980s that Pular men from Kanoumering entered orpaillage (see chapter 5).

Men from Kanoumering also worked as bush guides and geological assistants of independence-era mineral research missions, including those of the United Nations and the French parastatal, the Bureau de Recherches Géologiques et Minières. In the 1990s, Anmericosa, a gold-exploration company, also employed guides and laborers from Kanoumering. In 2003, the Senegalese state granted Randgold (Endeavor) land to open an exploration camp adjacent to the village. Since then, residents of Kanoumering have worked as guardians, geological aides, and laborers in the exploration camp, financing the purchase of cattle, corrugated tin roofs, and a village mosque.[31] As the price of gold rose in the early 2000s, more of Kanoumering's residents entered orpaillage. They mined in Tinkoto and Bantaco, a Maninka village west of Kanoumering that competed with Tinkoto as Kédougou's most popular orpaillage site in the mid-2000s.[32]

In 2010, a young man from Kanoumering discovered gold in one of the village's agricultural fields. A council of elders assembled to discuss the discovery and decided they would open the village's first juura. The decision was controversial because, at the time, there were few Pular villages in southeastern Senegal that oversaw juuras. The village elected a juurakuntigi and a group of tomboluma, following historical Maninka practices. But they vowed to manage the ritual dimensions of the juura according to the Path of Islam (*Laawol Allah* in Pular). Torodo Diallo, the chief of Kanoumering, recounted the opening of the juura: "The tradition of the juura, people say, is based on the jinne. The jinne own the juura. Our juura is based on the tradition of the Qur'an. Gold is in the hands of God. It was God who put gold in the ground for humans, not jinne. God also created jinne, and some of them guard gold, but ... we asked God to let gold rise to the surface of the earth." Torodo reverses the common statement, "Gold is in the hands of jinne," insisting that the Almighty God of the Qur'an "put gold in the ground for humans, not jinne." Prior to opening the juura, the village recruited a Muslim cleric from the Fouta Djallon. He blessed the gold-bearing land and planted amulets—Qur'anic verses bound in leather bundles—in the juura's soil. These amulets draw on the power of the written word of the Qur'an to chase away spirits. Torodo contrasted Kanoumering's management of its juura with Tinkoto's ritual protocols: "There is the jalan in Tinkoto. We ... have studied the Qur'an, and our path is Islam. Before we dig in the earth and before we make our sacrifices, we say, 'Let this work be in the name of God.' They say this in Tinkoto, but they also take chickens to the juura. In Kanoumering, we do not make sacrifices in the bush. The Imam will tell us to make a sacrifice, and we will go and prepare the sacrifice for the people in the mosque. We eat the sacrifice."[33] The statement "We eat the sacrifice" refers to a historical practice carried out by some Maninka juurakuntigi in Kédougou, whereby the sacrificed animal was offered to spirits—rather than consumed by people—by burying the carcass in gold-bearing land.

Bambo Cissokho reportedly warned Kanoumering's elders that their juura would be unprofitable without Maninka oversight. The elders dismissed Cissokho's warning, but his prediction proved accurate. Kanoumering's juura produced little gold. A few months after it was opened, young men had left the juura in favor of employment with Randgold or to mine in Tinkoto. When I visited Kanoumering's juura in 2014, it was largely mined by women to meet daily food expenses. Cissokho argued that Kanoumering's juura produced poor returns because it was managed by ethnic Pular who did not know the traditions of orpaillage. Kanoumering's residents, by contrast, argued that the middling success of their juura was evidence of their piety as Muslims. Consider the words of Bana Sidibé, a tomboluma on Kanoumering's juura: "It is difficult to see a Muslim juura with lots of gold. It is always little by little that you will find gold in a Muslim juura. You will never find a true Muslim earn wealth quickly. It is always little by little, by the sweat of his brow. Because God gives those who practice the 'way of Islam' what they need…, not more."[34] Sidibé placed a positive valence on the "slow" wealth of Kanoumering's juura, contrasting it with the "quick" but dubious wealth of non-Muslim juuras. The ascription of different temporal qualities to Muslim and non-Muslim religious techniques used in orpaillage articulates with the notion, widespread in Kédougou, that wealth from gold is quick money. Indeed, most Muslims and non-Muslims in Kédougou agree that ancestral religious practices produce quick wealth that diminishes over time. By contrast, techniques based on Islam generate gradual but enduring profits. Kanoumering's residents point to Tinkoto as evidence for this principle. Despite the tons of gold pulled from Tinkoto's juuras over time, Kanoumering appears far more prosperous, with its concrete buildings, than Tinkoto.

Within this discursive framework, it is easy to see why a Muslim who becomes enriched by orpaillage can be accused of trafficking in occult forces. For this reason, many Muslims who work full time as orpailleurs reject the idea that rapid wealth creation from juuras is a sign of their engagement in non-Muslim ritual practices. When I met Ousmane Diallo in 2014, he was finishing construction of a multi-bedroom concrete home in Kanoumering that was financed by orpaillage. Then in his late twenties, Diallo had achieved financial success that was notable for a young man who grew up in a farming family. He first entered orpaillage by laboring on a mining team in Tinkoto and worked his way up to becoming a damantigi, overseeing several mining teams of his own. As he recounted to me, while gesturing to workers pouring concrete bricks for his house:

> I am a Muslim. My father raised me on the Qur'an. But I have had luck in gold. I work with the Qur'an; everything I do it is based on the Qur'an…. And you see this house I am building? You tell me that this house is not blessed? Because it is here my mother will age and I will raise my children. I will never have to replace my roof with thatch, like my father. And you tell me this work is not blessed? All work performed in the name of Allah is blessed.[35]

Diallo assigns gold to the category "All work performed in the name of Allah," rejecting the common accusation that gold money is not blessed with divine grace (*baraka* in Arabic) because of its historical association with ancestral religious practices.

Most of the Muslim leaders I interviewed in Kédougou town and other villages shared Diallo's perspective that orpaillage was like any income-generating activity: it could generate blessed money when carried out according to the precepts of Islam. They resisted the idea that gold or orpaillage was bound to ancestral (non-Muslim) ritual practices. Rather, they emphasized that the physical dimensions of mining made it difficult to follow Laawol Allâh. Thierno Sidi Bâ, the Imam of the neighborhood of Laawol Tamba in Kédougou, a vibrant Pular man, elegantly captured a range of talking points that emerged across my interviews:

> We cannot say that there is something forbidden (*haram* in Arabic) about orpaillage because Allah put gold in the earth for the benefit of humankind. What we can say is this: it is difficult for the man who searches for gold to practice Islam. In Islam, you must pray five times a day, facing Mecca. It is best if you can perform ablutions, to be clean before Allah. But if from sunrise to sunset you find yourself in the bush searching for gold, you can find yourself forgetting to pray. There is no water to pray, the people around you are not praying, so it becomes easy to stray. When you are digging underground, you do not see the sun moving across the sky. You can forget when you are supposed to pray. It is for this reason that we can say that gold mining does not go with Islam, but not because gold is forbidden.... We can also say that the juura is not a place of Islam because it is not a clean place. It is not a healthy place for people and for children. There is prostitution; there is drinking. And the Prophet, peace be upon him, instructed Muslims to avoid unclean places.[36]

The Imam relates the dangers of orpaillage to a constellation of practices that run counter to the daily practices of Islam: heeding the call to prayer, access to water for ablutions, and cleanliness. In addition, Muslims are counseled to avoid places where activities that are forbidden in the Qur'an—such as drinking alcohol and prostitution—are common. While none of these factors makes money from gold mining unclean, each makes it harder to follow Islam while mining.

For Muslims, the growing engagement of young people in orpaillage also threatens Qur'anic education, which is a dry season activity. Because orpaillage requires living at or near the juura, it is difficult to pursue complementary activities. Thus, it is far more disruptive to the rhythm of Qur'anic school than hunting, plant collection, and making charcoal. This point was brought home to me during a social visit to a friend in a Pular village near the border of Guinea. Then in his early thirties, he had spent much of the previous decade selling fruit on the streets of Dakar but had returned home to farm and care for his aging mother. While he had not attended Qur'anic school, he was eager for his children to do so. As we shelled peanuts, he gestured to a patch of bare earth adjacent to the village mosque, where children had once convened to learn the Qur'an. He lamented, "The Qur'anic school has fallen" (*Jande dudal Qur'an ronkaama*, in Pular), because the teacher, one of his agemates, had abandoned teaching the Qur'an to pursue orpaillage full time.[37]

Kédovins from across the ethnolinguistic spectrum raised another secular concern about orpaillage: its creep deeper into the rainy season. With some exceptions, orpaillage in Kédougou was historically practiced for a few months of the dry season. But rising gold prices—and new machines and chemicals—have enabled mining, and gold processing, well into the annual rains, when agricultural fields are seeded. State officials have raised alarm about attrition in agricultural production in Kédougou, where many households already experience food shortages for several months of the year. It is debatable whether orpaillage has worsened this problem, as many orpailleurs invest some of their earnings in farming enterprises. What is clear is that increased reliance on orpaillage makes more families dependent on the market for food on a resource frontier where inflation is high. If households opt out of farming together, a bad year on the juura could mean hunger.

Moralizing Geology in Samecouta

The Jakha—a cluster of Muslim Jakhanke villages flanking the Gambia River several kilometers east of Kédougou town—has enjoyed more material prosperity than many corridors in Kédougou. Building on a long history as successful farmers and Muslim clerics, the Jakhanke encouraged their sons to emigrate to Europe in the 1960s and 1970s. Families farmed collective fields of cotton to finance emigration to France and, later, Spain.[38] By the early 2000s, before cellphones were common, most compounds in the Jakha had a landline to call relatives in Europe. With remittances, families in the Jakha were among the first to construct concrete houses and mosques outside Kédougou town.

Jakhanke women occasionally panned for gold along the banks of the Gambia. When the river descended to its lowest point in April, women sank calabash gourds into the riverbed, drawing out silt and gold flakes. Most women stored this gold dust until they had a sufficient quantity to commission a goldsmith to make earrings for themselves or their daughters.

Jakhanke men dedicated the dry season to teaching at their famous Qur'anic schools, which attracted children of prominent Muslim families from Mali, Senegal, and the Gambia. For decades, the leaders of the Jakha considered the lack of juuras on their land—beyond the modest quantity of gold dust panned by women in the Gambia—as the outcome of their collective prayers to Allah to "keep the gold underground." As one elder from Samecouta recounted, in the past "gold would never come out in the Jakha because the land of the Jakha was blessed. A juura never comes out of blessed land."[39] For him, gold is not an accident of geology but the product of divergent human ritual engagements with the land. As I was told frequently in private conversations with Muslim Jakhanke and Pular friends, "Gold appears in abundance only in the land of pagans."[40] Such statements moralize geology, embedding the distribution of metals in the earth within ritual engagements: human-spirit exchanges or the power of Islamic prayer.

There is, in fact, a strong correlation in Kédougou between the settlements of ethnic Maninka and the region's gold-bearing Birimian rocks. By contrast, relatively few gold deposits have been discovered—by geologists or orpailleurs—in historical Pular and Jakhanke villages, with the exception of those directly adjacent to Maninka settlements. Kanoumering, which is located in a majority-Maninka area, is a case in point. There are historical reasons for the correlation of Maninka villages with Birimian rocks. For one, when Maninka lineages migrated to Kédougou from Guinea and Mali—perhaps as early as the thirteenth century, as oral narratives suggest—they settled landscapes that resembled the wooded savanna regions from which they had departed. Birimian rocks undergirded many of these weathered landscapes. In other cases, Maninka settlers—or those who later claimed Maninka cultural heritage—also settled land explicitly for its gold-bearing potential. Many Maninka villages in the provinces of Sirimana and Bélédougou were first settled as seasonal juuras and later converted into agricultural villages. This was the case of Sabodala, Sambarabugu, Duuta, and Kharakenna. By contrast, many Pulars settled landscapes that resembled the Fouta Djallon plateau, which consists of thick sandstone formations overlying granite basement rocks. These rocks contained rich iron deposits and were ideal for animal pasturage but contained few gold deposits. Jakhanke, in turn, settled fertile farmland along the Gambia, positioned along a key Atlantic-era caravan route. Jakhanke likely traded in gold dust at different junctures, but their primary occupation was agriculture and Qur'anic education. In sum, there are clear geophysical and cultural reasons that the villages of ethnic Maninka—firstcomers to the land—align with gold-bearing geological shear zones, while those of Muslim incomers do not. At the same time, the grafting of ethnolinguistic difference onto distinct geological landscapes fuels rumor and speculation about the ritual engagements of different groups with the land.

Since the late 1990s, however, Kédougou's gold boom has loosened the association of juuras with pagan villages as intensified gold exploration by corporations and orpailleurs alike has led to the discovery of new gold deposits outside historical Maninka territories. In 2013, the Jakha was thrown into tumult when a young man discovered gold on a stretch of land north of the Gambia River. While there are no permanent settlements on the road, the land is considered part of the traditional territory of Samecouta because the village has several fallow fields bisecting it. The young man discovered an alluvial gold deposit, one likely created by an ancient tributary of the Gambia that subsequently dried up and was covered by laterite rock thousands of years ago. Samecouta's elders prohibited opening a juura at the discovery site. In defending his opposition to the juura, the head Imam of Samecouta argued: "Gold can bring great benefit to people. But not in the Jakha. This is a land of Islam, and gold does not go with Islam."[41] Here we see another implication that gold and the juura reside in the land of pagans, not in the land of Islam.

Samecouta's younger generation rejected the advice of their elders and opened a juura north of the village.[42] In response, Muslim leaders from across the Jakha organized a series of *du'as*, Muslim prayers of supplication. In the words of one du'a participant, "We asked Allah to protect our village, with all our force. We asked him to not let gold rise to the surface to turn our children away from Islam."[43] Gold did emerge from the juura of Samecouta, but production was low compared with the massive quantities of gold rock and dust pulled from juuras run by Maninka authorities during the same time period in Kédougou. While many young men from the Jakha worked in Samecouta's juura, they distanced themselves physically and ideologically from the labor of orpaillage. Gold deposition in Samecouta's juura was not visible to the naked eye; it could be sensed only with the use of gold detectors. In the early 2010s, Jakhanke immigrants in Europe began sending gold detectors to their younger brothers and cousins in Senegal, facilitating a unique labor system. Young men from the Jakha operated the detectors while immigrants from Mali and Guinea dug out the gold. Proceeds from the mine were divided between the owner-operator of the detector and the workers. There was a moral valence to this system. By only operating detectors, and not physically digging for gold, youth from Jakha sidestepped concerns from elders about their interaction with underground spirits.

Claims to physical distance from the juura—and from the act of mining—echo a much older principle operative on the West African savanna and Sahel: the strict geographic separation of spaces controlled by Muslims and pagans (chapter 2). Indeed, many men and women I encountered in Kédougou who did not live in orpaillage villages boasted that they had "never stepped foot in the juura." Such statements staked out physical and, by extension, moral distance between the speaker and the space of the juura. Distancing oneself from the juura was largely a class privilege. In Kédougou, where half of regional residents older than sixteen derive at least part of their income from activities tied to orpaillage, it is only wealthy merchants, bureaucrats, and teachers who can separate themselves from the juura. But as orpailleurs argue, even state officials are "in the juura" because many of their wives own freezer chests—powered by their privileged continuous access to electricity—out of which they sell frozen ice blocks. Merchants purchase ice from their compounds. Loaded into Styrofoam coolers and strapped to the roof of bush taxis, this ice makes it way to juuras across Kédougou, where it is sold at double the price. Moral and physical distance from juuras is valued by those who can afford it. Even for this privileged few, it is difficult to resist the lucrative returns afforded by economies of orpaillage.

Tubabs, Sacrifices, and Inequality

For most Kédovins, orpaillage was not a neutral activity. Men and women who worked in juuras went to great lengths to convince their families, themselves, and me that money earned from gold was morally legitimate. Everyone I encountered agreed that there were clear limits on how much gold should be mined in a given place or by a given person. As I was told repeatedly, gold has a "price" (*songo*) that must be paid through sacrifices made in the name of Allah or territorial spirits (figure 7.2). There were stretches of the Gambia, the savanna, and hillsides where gold was not mined because the spirits of those territories asked for human sacrifices in exchange for gold. When the sacrifices were not met, spirits took revenge on human interlopers on the land: "There are places here that we do not touch.... Someone saw gold with his machine. He detected it. He became crazy. We spent two months treating him. The son of Sano Sy..., where he dug. Since he reached the gold, he became blind. He saw nothing. Those places are innumerable here."[44] This was the account of Sajoh Kamara of Linguekoto, a small Maninka village on the Gambia. I heard countless stories of this genre. The French colonial archive is also littered with accounts of people rendered blind and insane by

Figure 7.2 Preparing kola nuts for sacrifices on the juura. Tinkoto, Senegal, 2014. Photograph by the author.

handling gold nuggets (*sanubiro*). These stories operate as warnings against taking gold from spirits without making sacrificial payments.

Such intense moral concern about the mining of gold juxtaposed sharply with the fact that itinerant engineers—mostly white men of Euro-American descent—extracted millions of dollars of gold from Senegal's soil each year from gargantuan open-pit gold mines. I asked my interlocutors whether the white staff of mining corporations were subject to the same ritual constraints as African orpailleurs. Responses pivoted on two core interpretations—one rooted in a materialist and Afro-pessimist framework; the other, in affirmations that white itinerant workers did make ritual payments to spirits, but they differed from those of Africans.

One evening, I recounted a story I had recently heard on a juura to a close friend who runs a transportation company in Kédougou. Reportedly, there were rocks at the bottom of the Sabodala mine that could not be broken because the spirits refused it. "That is ridiculous," my friend retorted. "It is just a psychological problem. If you have the right machinery, you will find gold.

It is that simple. They have machines, and they will get out every piece of gold and rock that they see fit."[45] Such sentiments are common among Kédougou's college-educated class, state bureaucrats, and Senegalese geologists. No one I interviewed denied that differential access to capital and machinery affected how much orpailleurs or corporations could mine. The question was whether corporations, like orpailleurs, had to pay for the gold they mined with sacrificial exchanges. While educated men and women dismissed concerns about spirits as "psychological" justifications from the less educated, they often took ritual precautions when handling gold. My friend, for example, sought a protective amulet before accepting gold rock as payment for a service. He would not have taken such precautions to accept payment in sorghum or corn.

Others argued that foreign white workers, known by the Wolof term *tubab*, could mine large quantities of gold because they had privileged relationships with the occult, not an absence of such relationships. The affinity of tubabs with land spirits has a deep genealogy in Atlantic West Africa, where otherworldly forces are often associated with the color white.[46] Today in southeastern Senegal, land spirits are described as light-skinned creatures with long and straight "hair like a tubab." During a group interview with elderly residents of Mako, a village situated on the national highway and along the Gambia River, I was told a story about a colonial-era French mining engineer who held special sway over territorial spirits. The engineer was based in Mako in the late 1940s, where he oversaw the construction of a bridge across the Gambia. The female spirit who haunts this portion of the river repeatedly interrupted construction, cracking a portion of the bridge and causing several workers to fall ill. Frustrated with delays caused by the spirit, the engineer approached the construction site one day holding a glass jar. He announced he wanted to play a game with the jinne. As one resident of Mako recounted, the engineer said: "I am going to go into this bottle and come out, and then you will do the same. The jinne agreed. One morning, the tubab transformed and went into the bottle, and then came out. The jinne did the same and then he [the engineer] trapped him [the jinne]." This version of the classic 'genie in the bottle' story—a long-standing genre in the Muslim world—credits the French engineer with taming a powerful spirit of the Gambia River.[47]

Tubabs also made sacrifices to the spirited owners of gold. Prior to starting work on a new exploration permit or opening a mine, geologists sacrificed cows and sheep in ceremonies overseen by local imams or juurakuntigi. I witnessed two such ceremonies in Kédougou—one performed by a team of Senegalese and foreign geologists; the other carried out by the village of

Kerekonko with a Danish man, the owner of a small gold mining operation. In both cases, cows were slaughtered for the sacrifice following halal protocol.[48] For some Senegalese participants in these ceremonies, ritual animal slaughter was simply a polite gesture to local custom. Others viewed these ceremonies as essential to securing the ritual and physical safety of their mining operations. I also overheard rumors that tubabs performed human sacrifices on their mining permits under the cover of night.

At times, tubabs have suffered for their negligence of ritual sacrifices. One widely circulating story of this genre concerned the Compagnie de la Haute Gambie, a French firm that operated an alluvial gold-dredging boat on the Gambia River from 1911 until the eve of World War II. The company closed several times due to lack of capital and broken machinery. In oral histories I conducted near the Falémé River, I was told that inadequate sacrifices caused these equipment failures. In the 1920s, three Frenchmen working for the company were navigating a small canoe on the Falémé. When they were halfway across the river, the serpent spirit Nininkala emerged from the river and swallowed the canoe with the men inside. There are parallels in a more recent rumor concerning a Rotary Air Blast drill operated by a subcontractor working for Randgold. In the early 2000s, the drill reportedly punctured a giant snake as it perforated the ground, stopping a machine that uses a pneumatic piston-driven hammer to drive a heavy drill bit into rock. It was rumored that Randgold's mechanics could not repair the machine. A local juurakuntigi concluded that Nininkala, the Maninka spirit snake, had entrapped the machine. He advised the geologists to sacrifice a red cow, and the machine sprang back to life.[49]

Many of my interlocutors concluded that sacrifices carried out by the personnel of mining companies were only the public face of more elaborate ritual engagements carried out in private. Others argued that Africans were forced to conduct blood sacrifices because their poverty left them with little else to offer spirits in exchange for gold. As Soriba Keita, a former orpailleur and long-term resident of Tinkoto, mused at the end of a long evening of conversation: "We do not have materials; we do not have machines; we do not have detectors. We have only sacrifices. It is because we have so little else to offer that the jinne asks us for our children. But for tubabs, it can be different. They can offer the jinne something else it desires, other riches we cannot offer."[50] Kédougou's residents debated whether differential access to machinery or ritual expertise shaped success in gold mining. They all agreed, however, that the primary difference between orpailleurs and corporations was profoundly unequal access to capital.

Golden Bones

A month before I concluded my field research in Kédougou, I was escorted by a close friend to a shrine, a jalan, managed by Koumba Keita, near a village situated on the Gambia River. Most jalans in southeastern Senegal are strictly private affairs. But Keita, a Bedik woman, proudly leads visitors to her jalan for a fee. Keita and I approached the jalan on two motorcycles, which we leaned against two large trees at the edge of a dirt path. Several meters into the woods, I glimpsed a tangled heap of iron bicycle parts and agricultural hoes, glass bottles, batteries, and bundles of leaves and sticks smeared with chicken blood at the base of a tree. Keita erected this jalan after she suffered three miscarriages. Within a year she had given birth to her first child and a lifelong relationship with the jalan. For years, Keita visited the jalan on her own and with other women struggling with infertility. With the uptick in orpaillage in the 2000s, hundreds of clients came to her door, seeking favor with regional spirits. She began monetizing visits to the jalan.[51] This financed a concrete house for Keita and her son, who was handicapped by a car accident and can no longer work.

Keita's jalan is an example of how some descendants of firstcomer groups have valorized their ancestry to profit from new economic opportunities created by orpaillage. But in a region where Islam is increasingly hegemonic, most descendants of firstcomer groups distance themselves from jalans. Indeed, some Muslims decry the popularity of Keita's jalan as evidence of the moral corruption of orpaillage, which, they claim, has cultivated a resurgence of paganism in a region long stigmatized for its ties to ancestral religious practices. With the religious and economic upheaval propelled by the gold boom, rumors about success in orpaillage can also operate as accusations about the relationship of different individuals and entire ethnolinguistic groups to Islam or paganism, regardless of their own ascription of religious belief. This is one prong of a racial language that has thrived on the goldfields of twenty-first-century Kédougou.

This racial language was also on display in a rumor about golden bones that circulated in Kédougou during my research. "You will only know a true Muslim when he dies in the mines," an elder in Tinkoto relayed to me at the end of a long interview. "Those who say they are Muslims but perform sacrifices to the jinne, if they die underground, their bones turn to gold."[52] As the reader may recall, this metonymic link between the bones of pagan orpailleurs and gold riddles the archival record of Atlantic and colonial-era Bambuk. In 1855, Frédéric Carrère and Paul Holle, early French colonial officials based in Soudan (now Mali), visited alluvial gold mines near Kéniéba. They recorded a story, likely relayed by their African interpreter, about the bodies of miners who were buried alive by collapsed mining pits: "If a miner is surprised by a cave-in and is buried underneath, the space belongs to the relatives of the deceased. No one has the right to place a hand on it. It is not until after seven years that the family can unearth the cadaver. It is claimed that the pores of the bones are filled with gold dust."[53] A half-century later, André Arcin, a French official based in Guinea, recounted a similar story that was circulating on the goldfields of Siguiri during his stay there: "When one returns later to the abandoned shaft after the accident, one finds, it appears, much more gold, the genie having been satisfied by this immolation. The gold itself becomes lodged in the bones of the cadaver."[54] Stories of miner's bones turned to gold parallel the spiritual alchemy performed by Nininkala's consumption of iron deposits, which she converted into secreted gold veins. The stories trouble the boundary among spirits, humans, and gold—as did the payments made in gold dust and iron bars for human captives during the Atlantic era. They speak to the razor-thin line between earning a moral living from orpaillage and trafficking with occult forces and human greed.

Today, Muslims in Kédougou argue that gold is in the hands of God (*sanu ye Allah le bulu*), a mundane material that can be bought and sold like any other product. These arguments are framed, however, against a much older regional understanding: that gold is in the hands of the spirits (*sanu ye jinne le bulu*) who reward ancestral religious practices. Not everyone in Kédougou is trying to make juuras or orpaillage Muslim. Nor are all descendants of firstcomer lineages ashamed of their ties to the non-Islamic and to territorial spirits. Others challenge essentialized notions of ethnolinguistic difference, drawing on the universalizing principles of Islam or Christianity to argue for equality before Allah. At the same time, no Muslim who practices orpaillage is safe from accusations that they traffic in pagan rituals. Much is at stake in these debates in a region where conversion to Islam is fragile for many and where rumors about ethnolinguistic origins fuel racial arguments. The view from Kédougou's juuras offers one regional account of how orpailleurs are remaking the ritual geology of savanna West Africa to new circumstances. It speaks, moreover, to how corporate mining is shaped by histories of wealth and sacred engagements with the earth that predate and evolve alongside it.

Conclusion
Subterranean Granaries

After months of cloudless skies, the rains are coming. Pressure mounts against the temples; humidity creeps into aching joints. I shell peanuts with an old friend, Aissatou Keita, as she tends to rice porridge over an open flame. Aissatou is worried. Her friends have seeded corn, the first crop to mature to cut the "hunger months" that stretch before the harvest of sorghum and millet. Aissatou's husband, Mamadou, has not returned from the juura. The planting window will soon close. When we met fifteen years ago, Aissatou and Mamadou were, like me, in their early twenties. With modest savings from stocking fruit at a roadside stand in Dakar, Mamadou married Aissatou and built a concrete building that is now home to their four children. They are farmers, but two years ago, Mamadou decided to try his hand at orpaillage. He joined a mining team in Bantaco, a day's journey from their natal Pular village. Proceeds from the first mining season financed their eldest son's school fees and six months of rice. This year, in 2014, Mamadou's team failed to strike gold.

Shame gathers with storm clouds on the juura. Most migrants from Mali, Guinea, and Burkina Faso have returned home to prepare their fields. But men like Mamadou trail behind, hopeful they might still reach gold. Some will return indebted; others not at all, too ashamed to face hungry families. A few will get lucky, riding home on a new motorcycle stacked with cooking oil and children's clothes. Pointing to abandoned millet fields and fallen Qur'anic schools, elders will speak of orpaillage as the "work of the devil." Mamadou and Aissatou are not alone. Today, orpaillage is the occupation of roughly ten million in West Africa, more than one hundred million globally. The juura pulls many into its orbit.

West Africans, like their counterparts elsewhere on the globe, greet orpaillage with ambivalence. Concerns over gold wealth run deep on the savanna, where gold mining is predicated on sacrificial exchanges with subterranean spirits. Recall the annual sacrifice prepared by the population of medieval Wagadu for Bida, their guardian serpent who controlled rain and the fertility of goldfields. Or the story of miners, on the verge of famine in nineteenth-century Tinkoto, who buried a dozen young men to their necks in sand as an offering to the juura's patron spirit. Such violent stories of men and women sacrificing their own children for a share of gold speaks to the high price residents of the savanna paid for a metal that can, when bartered for grain, alleviate the suffering of extended families.

Whatever one thinks of orpaillage, or artisanal mining more broadly, it appears to be here to stay. The story of mining in the global South has not turned out as most analysts would have predicted. Since the large-scale "gold rushes" of the nineteenth century, mining appeared to be on a trajectory of increased capitalization, mechanization, and globalization. In the second half of the twentieth century, vertical integration in the mining industry and the rise of transnational corporations facilitated the expansion of gold-mining capital into the former Soviet Union, Latin America, Oceania, and Africa. More surprising has been the explosion of artisanal and small-scale mining across the formerly colonized world. The ubiquity of mobile, labor-intensive mining challenges a narrative heavily weighted in the direction of stable and linear accounts of industrial modernity.

Yet in savanna West Africa, capital-intensive mining is the historical exception to the rule. Even at the height of colonial rule, when European-owned mines mushroomed across the continent, gold mined by Africans was the most important export of French West Africa. The French colonial state, and its postcolonial successors, have variously criminalized and regulated orpaillage as a shadow economy, denigrating it as a premodern industry seemingly stuck in time. Far from a precolonial "survival," as this book shows, orpaillage developed in a direct, though asymmetrical, dialogue with industrial mining. Over centuries, the embodied praxis and gold discoveries of African miners have vitally informed exploration geology and the strategies of capitalist firms. Orpailleurs have given geologists insights into botany, mineralization, and regional geological formations while serving as a highly skilled reservoir of labor for mineral surveys and gold-prospecting missions. This book—one of the first historical accounts of exploration geology in Africa—approaches African miners as producers of subterranean knowledge, not just laborers. It invites us to consider how other African societies, in different time periods and regions, have constructed knowledge about the subsoil and defended claims to its resources.

Despite the historical entanglement of orpaillage with capitalist mining enterprises, orpaillage has retained distinct material practices and socio-cultural logics. Orpaillage is embedded in what I call West Africa's ritual geology—a set of practices, prohibitions, and cosmological engagements with the earth—tied to gold-bearing Birimian rock formations of the savanna. With roots in the medieval period, this ritual geology has evolved with the rise and fall of medieval empires; the transatlantic slave trade; European colonialism; narratives of the mystical snakes Bida and Nininkala; the emergence of novel ritual complexes; and ever shifting demands for gold on a global scale. Despite these changes, core idioms of this ritual geology reemerge in the historical record of orpaillage, a West African mining tradition that is as much a part of the region's religious history over the past millennium as Islam. By constructing a regional narrative of orpaillage, grounded in a broad spatial and temporal framework, this book centers geological structures as an entry into African history.

Orpaillage tells a story of the dark underbelly of productive life on the savanna. Juuras expand during times of drought and economic crisis, such as the violent transition to French colonial rule, the Great Depression, the Sahelian famines of the 1970s–80s, the financial crisis of 2008–9, and the COVID-19 pandemic.[1] Goldfields are famine resources, commonly described in Maninka as granaries (*kurukuro*): a communal store of grain that is drawn on by families or villages after the abundance of the harvest has been depleted. Those in need can take a share of this resource. People congregate at juuras, as they do at aquifers or big-game hunting grounds, to access a resource spread unevenly across the landscape. Strangers are welcome to try their hand at these point sources as long as they submit to the local ritual authorities who broker between humans and the sacred forces of trees, mountains, rivers, and minerals. Yet there have always been constraints on how much gold any individual can take from the earth. In southeastern Senegal, such limitations are expressed through the language of a share, also translated as an inheritance in Maninka (*niyoro*). Before starting their work, mining teams decide how the proceeds of the shaft will be divided among workers, investors, and authorities at the mines. Spirits claim a share of gold in the form of sacrifices, as do extended family members. Orpailleurs also talk about the need to leave a share of gold underground for future generations. Spirits reinforce this ethic by rendering orpailleurs blind or insane if they take more than their share or pocket a nugget without making adequate sacrifices in exchange.

It is not surprising that residents of the West African savanna, a zone long susceptible to periodic droughts, have innovated social and ritual mechanisms to conserve a famine resource. In the Atlantic age, European travelers to Bambuk criticized African miners for "wasting" gold by abandoning deposits before they were fully depleted. Centuries later, gold-mining firms deploy similar tropes. They argue that orpaillage "eats away" at surface gold that could be more efficiently mined with open-pit technologies.[2] But efficiency—like waste—is in the eye of the beholder. Orpaillage distributes benefits across a range of workers, migrants, and their dependents. For orpailleurs, gold mined from disparate juuras, processed, and sold locally is a far more efficient means of feeding and clothing extended families than employment in a corporate mine for a single person or relying on a distant state to redistribute tax receipts from foreign mining firms.

The moral of the story of orpaillage is not simple. The use of unregulated methylmercury and cyanide at orpaillage sites pollutes local waterways and bloodstreams. But orpaillage also enables rural dwellers to earn an income close to home, curbing migration to cities. For centuries juuras have also provided refuge for men and women fleeing states, enslavement, and religious persecution. The juura is a place where people can refashion their lives, innovate ritual forms, and engage in modes of cosmopolitan sociability that rival those of port cities. So long overlooked by the region's historians, and poorly understood by the states encompassing them, juuras are now at risk of erasure.

As I write, corporate mining firms are depleting West Africa's goldfields at a breakneck speed. Since I began this project, the number of open-pit mines and mills in Senegal has tripled, and dozens of new gold deposits have been excavated by companies based across the border in Mali. Every fiscal quarter, corporations listed on the stock exchanges of London, Toronto, and New York announce new discoveries of multimillion-ounce gold deposits on the savanna. Corporate selloffs and mergers quickly follow; the owners of exploration and concessionary permits shuffle. A single open-pit mining operation can efface dozens of juuras, each embedded in distinctive cosmologies of patron spirits, of multivocal histories of discovery and use rights. In southeastern Senegal, Teranga Gold (Endeavor Mining), which operates the Sabodala mill, bulldozed the juuras of Golouma, Sabodala, Kerekounda, Gora, and Diakhalin. Orpaillage sites across the savanna face similar fates. The Siguiri mine in Guinea took Fatoya mountain, where, in the 1910s, orpailleurs defended their customary rights to mine gold. In Mali, the Luolo mine has taken the placers of Kéniéba that, centuries ago, lured Portuguese ships to the shores of the West African coast. Because few juuras are legally recognized, states do not require mining companies to compensate for their loss, as they do for the destruction of farm and pasturage land.

204 CONCLUSION

Mining corporations are not just depleting gold. They are also destroying a way of life that is dependent on this resource. African states, nongovernmental organizations, and scholars engage in considerable debate over how mining corporations and artisanal miners can peaceably "coexist" on resource frontiers.[3] But coexistence is a temporary solution, at best, because gold is a nonrenewable resource. Corporations and orpailleurs compete for gold in a zero-sum game; thus, they also compete for different notions of time. Corporations curtail their temporal investment in the communities in which they operate. Most open-pit mines have estimated "lives" of five to fifteen years. After corporations deplete and "remediate" a mine—a contentious process that is anything but a straightforward replacement of topsoil— they exit the region and sever ties to the land. Meanwhile, the value of gold mined from West Africa accrues in the market shares of investors far from the continent: compounding the long-term exit of hard-metal wealth from West Africa that dates to the medieval period.[4] By contrast, to conceive of gold deposits as subterranean granaries, as many orpailleurs do, engages with a distant future-oriented temporal horizon. To leave a share of gold underground inscribes this resource in human and human-spirit relationships that stretch deep into the past and into the future.

I close with my personal view, one informed by years spent living and working in and around the juuras of southeastern Senegal. There is value to leaving some gold underground, to disaggregating this resource piecemeal over time rather than in a single generation. Mining corporations, whether run by the state or private companies, take more than their share of the earth. Once metal is dislodged from the "hands of the spirits," it cannot be returned. Drought will return to the savanna, as it will to many parts of the world. Stories of men buried to their necks in sand and vengeful spirits remind new generations to prepare for drought, to make sacrifices. Decades of developmentalist interventions have not remedied the problem of poor rain cycles, which are predicted to increase with the most existential of threats: global warming. Historians do not have a unique vantage point on the political and ecological issues facing communities on resource frontiers. But we can remind readers of viable alternatives to industrial modernity that have flourished in these spaces before they are gone.[5] Orpaillage is one such alternative.

I am brought back to a night in April 2014 when I joined the *kuru tala luno* (day of the division of rocks) at the base of a juura on the outskirts of Tinkoto. The central heap of gold-bearing rock, the proceeds of a single mine shaft, are distributed among each member of the mining team. At the end of the ceremony, each team member shovels their share into empty rice sacks. Before departing, they scoop out a bucket of their rock onto a new pile that does not correspond to a mining team member. This rock is for the destitute and feeble, who will claim their share later at night, without the shame of observation.

It is humbling to watch this share of rock grow at the expense of the proceeds of orpailleurs who labored for months underground. So often criminalized and denigrated as backward by states and corporations, these men and women, poor by any global measure, carefully ensure that their share of gold-bearing rock is distributed among spirits, dependents, and those in need. "On the day of the division of rock," explained Filé Keita, a long-term resident of Tinkoto, "a stranger can come to ask for rock—a stranger who has nothing to eat, who does not have a host. You cannot give him everything you have earned, but you can give him a rock. One day, you may go to another juura and find yourself in the same situation. Everyone has come here to search for something. In places where you seek wealth, you have to show people mercy, so they can also profit."[6] Keita, and the thousands of other orpailleurs who animate this book, call forth questions we can carry into other realms, other places where battles for the natural world unfold. What is our rightful share of the earth's subterranean granaries? What are we obliged to leave for the unborn and the otherworldly? What is the price, in this life or the next, for taking more than our share?

GLOSSARY

Alluvial deposit (English) eroded gold flakes deposited by running water (see *nara*)

Balandula (Maninka) placers of wood reinforcements in mining tunnels

Baraka (Arabic) divine grace, blessing, benediction

Birimian (English) geological term for Precambrian basement rocks in West Africa

Boli (Maninka) ritual objects in Manding-speaking cosmological worlds

Coopération (French) formal contracts signed between the French Republic and its former colonies for institutional and technical assistance

Daman (Maninka) mining shaft in Mali and Senegal; gold mine in Guinea

Damansinna (Maninka) digger of gold-mining shafts

Damantigi (Maninka) master of the mining shaft

Dugu (Maninka) land, village, ground

Dugutigi (Maninka) master of land; village chief

Eluvial deposit (English) deposits of eroded gold flakes created from geological weathering

Farafina londo (Maninka) African/Black knowledge

Fétiche (French) term used by colonial agents for Muslim ritual objects or shrines

Féticheur (French) term used by colonial agents for practitioner of ancestral religions

Filon (French) lode-ore rock (see also *sanukuru*)

Garanke (Maninka) leatherworkers, part of the artisan group known as *nyamakala*

Gendarmes (French) a branch of the Senegalese military that polices rural jurisdictions

Goto (Maninka) goblin, gnome

Indigène (French) term used by colonial agents for African subjects

Jalan (Maninka) shrine

Jalantigi (Maninka) master of the shrine

Jinne (Maninka) spirit, derived from the Arabic term *jinn*

Juula (Maninka, Soninke) long-distance Muslim merchant

Juulusabala (Maninka) operators of the pulley system of a mining shaft

Juura (Maninka, Soninke) gold mine

Juurakuntigi (Maninka, Soninke) master of the gold mine, a ritual office

Kalakuntigi (Maninka) master of ceremonies; often a child who selects a leader

Komo (Maninka) Manding male initiation society led by blacksmiths

Kuru (Maninka) rock

Kurukuro (Maninka) granary

Kuru taki (Maninka) pounders of rock

Kuru tala luno (Maninka) day of the division of rock

Lode ore (English) gold ore embedded in parent rock (see *filon* and *sanukuru*)

Marabout (French) derived from the Arabic term for Muslim religious leader or cleric

Nara (Maninka) deposits of alluvial or eluvial gold (see *alluvial deposit, eluvial deposit*)

Navétane (Wolof, French) term used in French West Africa for seasonal laborers, rainy season migration to Senegal's peanut farms

Numu (Maninka) blacksmith, part of the artisan group known as *nyamakala*

Nyafa (Maninka) temporary dwelling, often constructed of straw or palm leaves

Nyama (Maninka) life force contained by all sentient beings and natural substances

Nyamakala (Maninka) endogamous artisan groups

Orpaillage (French) gold panning or labor-intensive gold mining

Orpailleur (French) gendered male gold miner or panner

Orpailleuse (French) gendered female gold panner or washer (see also *sanukuula*)

Outcrop (English) a portion of basement rock protruding at the earth's surface

Placer (English, Spanish) eluvial or alluvial gold deposit (see *nara*)

Sadaxo (Maninka) derived from the Arabic term for voluntary alms, blood sacrifice

Sanu (Maninka) gold

Sanubaarala (Maninka) gold miner or panner (see also *orpailleur*)

Sanubiro (Maninka) gold nugget

Sanukuru (Maninka) gold-bearing rocks, lode ore, or *filon*

Sanukuula (Maninka) gendered female washer of gold (see also *orpailleuse*)

Sanumogola (Maninka) a person mystically allied with gold

Sanutigi (Maninka) master of gold; someone who is lucky in the mines

Sharia (Arabic) Islamic canonical law; vernacular laws on West African goldfields

Sluice (English) an elongated trough for washing gold-bearing earth

Soli (Maninka) locally forged pick-axe used to excavate mining shafts

Sukunbalila (Maninka) specialist in excavating abandoned mining shafts

Surga (Wolof? Pular?) migrant laborer (derogatory in some contexts)

Tana (Maninka) totem or taboo shared by a clan or tied to a place

Tata (Maninka) stone-wall fortification common in Atlantic-era West Africa

Tomboluma (Maninka) African security force on orpaillage sites

Tubab (Wolof) white person

Zakat (Arabic) charitable payment given to the poor, obligatory in Islam

NOTES

Introduction

1 Many mining firms operating in West Africa name themselves after places, ethnic groups, or phrases in regional languages. Bassari is the name of a minority ethnic group, concentrated in Kédougou region, who self-identify as Beliyan. In this book, I use the term *Beliyan-Bassari* to both reference the preferred term of self-address of Beliyan people and to signal scholarship and policy documents in which they are referred to as the Bassari.

2 "Artisanal mining" is also referred to as "artisanal and small-scale mining" or by the acronym ASM or ASGM. I use *artisanal mining* to encompass these diverse terms.

3 There are two civilian armed forces in Senegal, modeled on the French system: the police and the gendarme. The police are a civilian force primarily responsible for urban areas in Senegal. The gendarmerie is a branch of the Senegalese military that police rural jurisdictions, military installations, ports, and highways. Until 2014, there were no police assigned to Kédougou, only gendarmes.

4 "Toro Gold Mako Project," accessed October 1, 2018, https://www.youtube .com/watch? v=9c0Hgg9NuvY; "CNBC Africa: The Positive Impact of Teranga Gold's Sabodala Mine in Senegal," accessed October 1, 2018, https://www .youtube.com/watch? v=aouwo7jAC-0. On the fiscal, economic, and social work mining firms invest in distancing themselves from the sociopolitical worlds in which they operate, see Appel, *The Licit Life of Capitalism*, 25.

5 On the geology of the Kédougou-Kéniéba Inlier, see Gueye et al., "New Evidences for an Early Birimian."

6 This phrase alludes to the nineteenth-century European "scramble" for Africa that led to the colonization of much of the continent. For academic perspectives on the twenty-first-century scramble for African land, fuel, and mineral resources, see Carmody, *The New Scramble for Africa*; Klare, *The Race for What's Left*; Southall and Melber, *A New Scramble for Africa?* For policy approaches, see Africa Progress Panel, "Equity in Extractives"; "Africa Rising: A Hopeful Continent," *The Economist*, March 2, 2013; "Africa's Natural Resources: Blood Earth," *The Economist*, April 11, 2015; Roxburgh et al., *Lions on the Move*.

7   Bell, *Ritual Theory*, 74, 89–90, 100.

8   I owe this metaphor to James Scott, who suggested it at the Yale Agrarian Studies Program Colloquium in February 2020.

9   Gold-bearing Birimian rocks in West Africa are primarily found in two climatological zones: the savanna and the forest. The history of gold mining in these two regions diverges sharply. Goldfields on the savanna were in production by the eighth or ninth century, whereas gold was not mined at scale in the forest until the fourteenth or fifteenth century. Divergent colonial experiences deepened socioeconomic divides between the two regions. In the 1870s, the British gained control over the goldfields of the Akan-speaking forests (of modern Ghana), while the French army claimed gold-bearing lands in the western savanna (and some forested areas in Côte d'Ivoire). Gold in Ghana is also found in Tarkwaian rocks, which do not derive from Birimian terranes. On gold mining in Ghana, see Dumett, *El Dorado in West Africa*; Garrad, *Akan Weights and the Gold Trade*; Wilks, *Forests of Gold*.

10 In this book, the "medieval period" refers to the ninth to the fourteenth century. "Atlantic period" refers to the era of Afro-European coastal trade from the fifteenth through the mid-nineteenth century. In much of West Africa, the "colonial period" stretches from the late nineteenth century until the 1950s, although there were small European colonies along the Atlantic coast as early as the fifteenth century.

11 Two books on orpaillage in Senegal have recently appeared in French: Doucouré, *Des pierres dans les mortiers et non du maïs!*; Niang, *Dans les mines d'or du Sénégal Oriental*. Articles include Curtin, "The Lure of Bambuk Gold"; Jansen, "What Gold Mining Means for the Malinke"; Luning et al., "The *Mise en Valeur* of the Gold Mines in the Haut-Niger"; Moussa, "L'or des régions de Poura et de Gaoua"; Panella, *Worlds of Debts* and "L'éthique sociale du Damansen"; Samson, "Les 'trésors méconnus' l'Afrique subsaharienne françaises"; Werthmann, "Dans un monde masculin."

    In reconstructing the history of orpaillage, I draw on a rich literature on West Africa's agrarian economies: Berry, *No Condition Is Permanent* and *Fathers Work for Their Sons*; Fairhead and Leach, *Misreading the African Landscape*; Lentz, *Land, Mobility, and Belonging in West Africa*; McGovern, *Unmasking the State*; Philip, *Les navétanes*; Richards, *Indigenous Agricultural Revolution*; Sarr, *Islam, Power, and Dependency in the Gambia River Basin*; Sarró, *The Politics of Religious Change on the Upper Guinea Coast*.

12 Mavhunga, *Transient Workspaces*, 9–17; Serlin, "Confronting African Histories of Technology"; Twagira, "Introduction." On the role of technology in European imperialism, see Adas, *Machines as the Measure of Men*; Headrick, *The Tools of Empire*.

13 de Luna, *Collecting Food, Cultivating People*; Grace, *African Motors*; Hecht, *Being Nuclear*; Mike, *Africanizing Oncology*; Osseo-Asare, *Bitter Roots*; Park, "Human-ATMs"; Storey, *Guns, Race, and Power*.

14 Archeological work that shapes my approach to the history of technology in Africa includes Chirikure, *Indigenous Mining and Metallurgy in Africa*; Gokee,

Assembling the Village in Medieval Bambuk; Killick, "Iron Smelting Technology in the Middle Senegal Valley"; Logan, *The Scarcity Slot*; McIntosh, *Beyond Chiefdoms*; McIntosh, *Peoples of the Middle Niger*; Stahl, *African Archeology*; Thiaw, "Atlantic Impacts on Inland Senegambia."

15 Ferguson, *The Anti-Politics Machine*, and Mitchell, *Rule of Experts*, write, respectively, on "development" and "the economy" as categories with similar qualities.

16 Hilson and McQuilken, "Four Decades of Support for Artisanal and Small-scale Mining in Sub-Saharan Africa"; United Nations Economic Commission for Africa, *Artisanal and Small-scale Mining and Technology Challenges in Africa*; World Bank, *The Millennium Development Goals and Small-scale Mining*. The International Labour Organization (ILO), uses a scale-based nomenclature: ILO, "Social and Labour Issues in Small-scale Mines."

17 World Bank, *Mining Together*, 9. This definition was updated from a 1996 World Bank report that described artisanal mining as "the most primitive type of informal, small-scale mining, characterized by individuals or groups of individuals exploiting deposits—usually illegally—with the simplest equipment": Barry, *Regularizing Informal Mining*, 1.

18 d'Avignon, "Primitive Techniques."

19 On poaching as a form of criminality created by land enclosures, see Jacoby, *Crimes Against Nature*; Mavhunga, *Transient Workspaces*; Thompson, *Whigs and Hunters*.

20 Amnesty International, *This Is What We Die For*; OECD, *Due Diligence Guidance for Responsible Supply Chains of Minerals from Conflict-Affected and High-Risk Areas*. Globally since 1998, ASM has been responsible for one-third of all mercury released into the environment: Hentschel et al., *Global Report on Artisanal and Small-scale Mining*; Pure Earth, "Global Mercury Program"; Steckling et al., "Global Burden of Disease of Mercury Used in Artisanal Small-scale Gold Mining." On child labor in artisanal mines, see Human Rights Watch, "Precious Metals, Cheap Labor"; ILO, "Social and Labour Issues in Small-scale Mines."

21 Out of a vast literature, see Hilson, "Once a Miner, Always a Miner"; Hilson et al., "Going for Gold"; Maconachie, "Re-agrarianising Livelihoods in Post-conflict Sierra Leone?"

22 United Nations Economic Commission for Africa, *Recommendations from Artisanal Mining Workshop*; United Nations Environmental Programme, *Final Report*; World Bank, *Mining Together*.

23 "Jobs in Africa: In Praise of Small Miners," *The Economist*, May 7, 2017, 45. See also World Bank, "Shining a Light on a Hidden Sector."

24 Bryceson et al., *Mining and Social Transformation in Africa*; Tschakert, "Digging Deep for Justice."

25 For example, see Adunbi, *Oil Wealth and Insurgency in Nigeria*; Appel, *The Licit Life of Capitalism*; Ferguson, *Global Shadows*; Rajak, *In Good Company*; Watts, "Petro-violence."

26 De Boeck, "Domesticating Diamonds and Dollars"; Makori, "Mobilizing the Past"; Mantz, "Improvisational Economies"; Smith, "Tantalus in the Digital Age"; Smith and Mantz, "Do Cellular Phones Dream of Civil War?" 78; Walsh, "'Hot Money' and Daring Consumption in a Northern Malagasy Sapphire-Mining Town."

27 Lauren Coyle's *Fires of Gold* is an ethnographic exception to this rule. Also on Ghana, see Aubynn, "Sustainable Solution or Marriage of Inconvenience?"; Hilson and Yakovleva, "Strained Relations"; Luning and Pijpers, "Governing Access to Gold in Ghana." On the Democratic Republic of Congo, see Geenen and Classens, "Disputed Access to the Gold Sites in Luhwindja." On Guinea, see Bolay, "Artisanal Gold Miners Encountering Large-Scale Mining in Guinea."

28 Feierman, "Colonizers, Scholars, and the Creation of Invisible Histories," 206–7.

29 Vansina, *Paths in the Rainforest*, 258–60.

30 Vansina, *Paths in the Rainforest*.

31 In a comparative vein, for an exploration of African-derived healing traditions as a scientific tradition constitutive of the emergence of Enlightenment-era evidence-based healing practices, see Gómez, *The Experiential Caribbean*.

32 *Le Dictionnaire de l'Académie Française*, 8th ed. (Paris, 1932), s.v. "orpailleur."

33 I did consider the use of other terms. Many contemporary Maninka speakers use the term *sano baara*—"the work of gold"—as a gloss for orpaillage. However, they just as often referred to their work as orpaillage. While some Maninka terms relating to gold mining are universally used on the goldfields of the savanna, sano baara was not one of them—speakers of other languages used the equivalent phrase in Wolof, Pular, and so forth. Thus, *orpaillage* better captured the ethnic and linguistic heterogeneity of the goldfields, the regional legacy of French colonialism, and evolving linguistic norms. Many women referred to their work as orpaillage but rarely to themselves as *orpailleuses*. Some Maninka women referred to themselves as *sanukuula*—"washers of gold."

For the sake of consistency, I sometimes use the term *orpaillage* anachronistically to refer to gold mining by West Africans prior to colonialism. The term *orpaillage* is ubiquitous in French-language scholarship.

34 For a critical discussion of the classification of Manding language varieties, see Donaldson, "Orthography, Standardization, and Register" and "Clear Language."

35 The close association of Maninka institutions with gold mining in the Atlantic period is likely indicative of growing Maninka cultural hegemony after the sixteenth-century demise of the Malian empire rather than evidence that ethnic Maninka were the primary (or only) gold miners in earlier periods. For a detailed discussion, see chapter 2.

36 Devisse, "L'or"; Mauny, *Tableau géographique de l'Ouest africain au Moyen Age*, 293–306; Mayor et al., "Dynamiques techniques et environnementales dans la vallée de la Falémé (Sénégal)."

37 I thank Mike McGovern for underscoring the extensive character of orpaillage.

38 On stranger-host relationships in West African societies, see Brooks, *Landlords and Strangers*; Geschiere, *The Perils of Belonging*; Jansen, "The Younger Brother and the Stranger"; Lentz, *Land, Mobility, and Belonging in West Africa*. The supposed abundance of land in much of precolonial Africa (compared with Europe) has given rise to the influential thesis that "wealth in people" was a widespread political ideology: Guyer, "Wealth in People"; Herbst, *States and Power in Africa*; Kopytoff, *The African Frontier*; Miers and Kopytoff, *Slavery in Africa*.

39 On the importance of hospitality in the context of seasonal, and cyclical, shortages of rain and food in this part of the world, see Togola, "Memories, Abstractions, and Conceptualizations of Ecological Crisis in the Mande World"; Twagira, *Embodied Engineering*.

40 The exception to the inclusivity of orpaillage was a ritual taboo against mining by leatherworkers (see chapters 1 and 2).

41 I detail these technological exchanges in chapters 2 and 4. On the claims of states and transnational organizations to "vertical encompassment," see Ferguson, *Global Shadows*, 94; Gupta and Ferguson, "Spatializing States."

42 My approach to embodied ritual knowledge on the West African savanna and Sahel draws inspiration from Diagne, *The Ink of the Scholars*, and Ware, *The Walking Qur'an*.

43 Okeke-Agulu, *Postcolonial Modernism*, 15.

44 On how labor regimes and political claims making are shaped by the different material qualities of minerals see Barry, *Material Politics*; Hecht, *Being Nuclear*; Mitchell, *Carbon Democracy*; Rolston, "The Politics of the Pits and the Materiality of Mine Labor."

45 On global divergences in artisanal mining economies, see Lahiri-Dutt, *Between the Plough and the Pick*. On Indonesia, see Peluso, "Entangled Territories in Small-scale Gold Mining Frontiers." On Mongolia, see High, *Fear and Fortune*.

46 Makori, "Mobilizing the Past"; Morris, "Shadow and Impress," esp. 112, 117. Jaramillo, "Mining Leftovers," uses similar language in studies of postindustrial mining landscapes in South America.

47 On the latter in Africa, see Ferguson, *Expectations of Modernity*; Walsh, "After the Rush."

48 On the ethnography of mineral exploration, see d'Avignon, "Shelf Projects"; Kneas, "Subsoil Abundance and Surface Absence"; Özden-Schilling, "Trust in Ventures"; Weszkalnys, "Hope and Oil."

49 Dubow, "Earth History, Natural History, and Prehistory at the Cape," is an exception. On the relationship of geology to the production of historical knowledge in colonial India, see Chakrabarti, *Inscriptions of Nature* and "Gondwana and the Politics of Deep Past."

50 On "contact zones" in scientific encounters, see Raj, *Relocating Modern Science*, 10–13. See also Gómez, *The Experiential Caribbean*; Mukharji, *Doctoring Traditions*.

NOTES TO INTRODUCTION 215

51 Harries, "Field Sciences in Scientific Fields"; Jacobs, "The Intimate Politics of Ornithology in Colonial Africa"; Jézéquel, "Voices of Their Own?"; MacArthur, *Cartography and the Political Imagination*, 17, 19–20; Osseo-Asare, *Bitter Roots*; Schumaker, *Africanizing Anthropology*; Tilley, *Africa as a Living Laboratory*, 117.

On the occluded contributions of women and Black assistants to scientific authorship in Western contexts, see Des Jardins, *The Madame Curie Complex*; Lerman, "Categories of Difference, Categories of Power"; Timmermans, "A Black Technician and Blue Babies." On the uncredited contributions of local residents and assistants to field research in the United States, see Kohler, *All Creatures*, 156–62, 184–85; Schneider, "Local Knowledge, Environmental Politics, and the Founding of Ecology in the United States"; Vetter, "Cowboys, Scientists, and Fossils" and *Knowing Global Environments*.

52 Carney, *Black Rice*; Carney and Rosomoff, *In the Shadow of Slavery*; Fields-Black, *Deep Roots*; La Fleur, *Fusion Foodways of Africa's Gold Coast in the Atlantic Era*; Logan, *The Scarcity Slot*; Sluyter, *Black Ranching Frontiers*.

53 Gómez, *The Experiential Caribbean*; Hicks, *Captive Cosmopolitans*; Kananoja, "Infected by the Devil, Cured by Calundu"; Roberts, "To Heal and to Harm"; Sweet, *Domingos Álvares, African Healing, and the Intellectual History of the Atlantic World*.

54 Helen Tilley's 2021 edited volume in *Osiris*, "Therapeutic Properties: Global Medical Cultures, Knowledge, and the Law," asks this question for the history of medicine: Tilley, "Medical Cultures, Therapeutic Properties, and Laws in Global History."

55 Grove, *Green Imperialism*; Langwick, "Properties of (Dis)Posessions," Osseo-Asare, *Bitter Roots*; Schiebinger, *Plants and Empire*; Tilley, "Traditional Medicine Goes Global."

56 Osseo-Asare, *Bitter Roots*, 110.

57 For brief discussions of European "takeovers" of African mines, see Dumett, *El Dorado in West Africa*; Freund, *Capital and Labour in the Nigerian Tin Mines*, esp. 47; Van Onselen, *Chibaro*, 11–12.

58 On labor, land alienation, and migration to South Africa's gold mines, see Crush et al., *South Africa's Labor Empire*; Gordon, *Mines, Masters, and Migrants*; Harries, *Work, Culture, and Identity*; Moodie and Ndatshe, *Going for Gold*; Van Onselen, *Chibaro*; Wolpe, *Race, Class, and the Apartheid State*. On Nigeria, see Brown, *"We Were All Slaves"*; Freund, *Capital and Labour in the Nigerian Tin Mines*. On the Copperbelt of southeastern Africa, see Bates, *Rural Responses to Industrialization*; Buroway, *The Colour of Class on the Copper Mines*; Epstein, *Politics in an Urban African Community*; Ferguson, *Expectations of Modernity*, chap. 1; Gluckman, "Anthropological Problems Arising from the African Industrial Revolution"; Powdermaker, *Copper Town*.

59 See also d'Avignon, "Spirited Geobodies."

60 Huffman, "Snakes and Birds"; Wilks, *Forests of Gold*, chap. 6.

61 On cartography in Africa, see Gray, *Colonial Rule and Crisis in Equatorial Africa*; MacArthur, *Cartography and the Political Imagination*, 17, 19–20; Scott, *Seeing like a State*, chap. 7. On the role of borders in African political formations, see Boone, *Property and Political Order in Africa*; Herbst, *States and Power in Africa*; Nugent, *Boundaries, Communities, and State-Making in West Africa*.

62 Billé, *Voluminous States*; Bridge, "Territory, Now in 3D!"; Elden, "Secure the Volume"; Oguz, "Theorizing the Contemporary"; Weizman, *Hollow Land*.

63 On the mapping of vertical territory, see Braun, "Producing Vertical Territory"; Oreskes, "A Context of Motivation"; Rozwadowski, *Fathoming the Ocean*.

64 Yusoff, *A Billion Black Anthropocenes or None*, 7, 10, 12.

65 Berzock, *Caravans of Gold, Fragments in Time*; Fauvelle, *The Golden Rhinoceros*; Gomez, *African Dominion*; Green, *A Fistful of Shells*.

66 I use "pagan" as a gloss for several words derived from Arabic: non-believer or infidel (*kaafir*), idolator (*wathani*), and polytheist (*mushrik*). I thank Jeremy Dell for pointing out distinctions across these terms. I follow the anthropologist Benjamin Soares's definition of "religion" as "discourses and practices encompassing modalities of religious expression—as a heterogeneous field in which there is considerable debate, contestation, and transformation": Soares, "'Structural Adjustment Islam' and the Religious Economy in Neoliberal Mali," 138. This definition departs from outmoded notions of African "traditional" religion as a static system of thought. For critical discussions of the latter term, see Baum, "Indigenous African Religions"; Shaw, "The Invention of 'African Traditional Religion.'" Asad, *Genealogies*, 55, argues against using the abstract category of "religion" for places that do not share the term's discursive origins in Protestantism (see also Landau, "Religion," 19–20, 29–30). I share this critique, and whenever possible I use terms from Arabic, Maninka, and Pular to describe ritual practices in different historical settings. However, I retain the glosses of *pagan* and *ancestral religions* as useful abstractions to track and compare shifting practices and ideologies across broad temporal and spatial units and in dialogue with other global developments. I thank Paul Johnson and Robert Blunt for guiding me through some of these debates in religious studies.

67 Scott, *The Art of Not Being Governed*, 8, 22. Scott builds on the concept of "shatter zone" from Wright, *Middle Ground*, 14.

68 Zobel, "Les génies du Kòma," 628, makes this point for the Bandiagara massif in Mali. On Bedik settlements in southeastern Senegal, see Kroot and Gokee, "Histories and Material Manifestations of Slavery in the Upper Gambia River Region."

69 Work that explores the relationship between religion and the environment in Africa includes Giles-Vernick, *Cutting the Vines of the Past*; Mavhunga, *Transient Workspaces*; Ranger, *Voices from the Rocks*; Shetler, *Imagining Serengeti*.

70 Examples include Amrith, *Unruly Water*; Demuth, *Floating Coast*; Pritchard, *Confluence*; Zhang, *The River, the Plain, and the State*. Urban environmental historians have innovated regional frameworks by following the materials—charcoal, timber, coal, concrete—from which cities are built and sustained:

Cronon, *Nature's Metropolis*; Brownell, *Going to Ground*; and Needham, *Power Lines*.

71 Classic ethnographies by Nash (*We Eat the Mines and the Mines Eat Us*) and Taussig (*The Devil and Commodity Fetishism in South America*) address rituals in capitalist mines in South America. On the ritual worlds of artisanal mining sites, see chapter 2 and 7.

72 On "earth beings" in Andean mining contexts, see de la Cadena, "Indigenous Cosmopolitics in the Andes." In Western Europe, leprechauns (Ireland), gnomes (England), kobolds (Germany), and the petit mineur (France) are genres of earth beings that haunted subterranean mines. Resource extraction in high-risk environments—mining, deep-sea fishing, hunting large mammals— tends to be more ritualized than less risky activities such as farming. Bronislaw Malinowski, *Magic, Science and Religion, and Other Essays*, 30–31, famously compared the "extensive magical ritual" associated with deep-sea ocean fishing in the Trobriand Islands with the lack thereof in inland lagoon fishing.

73 Barry, *Senegambia and the Atlantic Slave Trade*; Rodney, *A History of the Upper Guinea Coast*. I am also inspired by the appeal to regional histories of Africa in Feierman, "African Histories and the Dissolution of World History," 186.

74 On this debate in African studies, see Baum, "Indigenous African Religions"; Baum, *Shrines of the Slave Trade*; Horton, "Stateless Societies in the History of West Africa"; Shaw, *Memories of the Slave Trade*.

75 Gomez, *African Dominion*; Hall, *A History of Race in Muslim West Africa*; Kane, *Beyond Timbuktu*; Lydon, *On Trans-Saharan Trails*; Scheele, *Smugglers and Saints of the Sahara*; Ware, *The Walking Qur'an*.

76 Allman and Parker, *Tongnaab*, 6–7.

77 Senegal borrows from a French model of regional organization (région, département, commune). Kédougou has gone by many names. Prior to colonial rule, a number of small chiefdoms—such as Sirimana, Bélédougou, Niokolo, and Dantila—dotted the landscape (see map 2.1). In the late nineteenth century, the French army named this territory Haute-Gambie (Upper Gambia). Between the wars, Upper Gambia was reconstituted as an administrative circle and, after World War II, renamed Kédougou. In 1960, Kédougou became a department of the region of Sénégal Oriental, later renamed Tambacounda. In 2008, Kédougou became an independent region. To minimize confusion for the reader, I often refer to Kédougou as a region even when this is anachronistic.

78 Amadou Bamba, the celebrated Muslim cleric, founded the Muridiyya in the late nineteenth century. There are three major Muslim Sufi orders in Senegal: the Qadiriyya, the Tijaniyya, and the Muridiyya. The Muridiyya and the Layene originated in Senegal.

79 Based on calculations from 2013 census data, the projection of Senegal's population in 2019 stood at roughly seventeen million, with Kédougou's population at 200,000: Agence Nationale de la Statisique et de la Démographie,

République du Sénégal, "Projections démographiques, 2019," https://www .ansd.sn/index.php? option=com_ansd&view=titrepublication&id=30. Based on national census data from 1988—the last time Senegal collected ethnic data on a census—the reported ethnic breakdown of Kédougou's 71,125 counted residents was 41 percent "Poular" (Pular), 34.2 percent "Mandingue" (Maninka), .8 percent "Bambara," 1.8 percent "Sarakhole" (Soninke), 1.4 percent "Wolof," .4 percent "Serer," and 20.4 percent "Other." The "Other" category included ethnic Jallonke, Jakhanke, Bedik, and Beliyan-Bassari and several hundred ethnic Coniagui and Bandiaranke: quoted from République du Sénégal, *Recensement général de la population et de l'habitat de 1988*, 21.

80 Diouf, *Histoire du Sénégal*, 15.

81 McLaughlin, "Dakar Wolof and the Configuration of an Urban Identity"; McLaughlin, "Senegal"; O'Brien, "The Shadow Politics of Wolofisation."

82 There is a growing literature on the impacts of orpaillage and corporate gold mining on Kédougou's economy and social and political life: Cartelli, "A Snake in the Hole"; Dia, "Activité minière et culture cotonnière"; Diallo, "Mine d'or et développement"; Diallo, "Mines et dynamiques spatiales dans le Sud-est du Sénégal"; Doucouré, *Des pierres dans les mortiers et non du maïs!*; Niang, "Mining as Development?"; Niang, *Dans les mines d'or du Sénégal Oriental*; Persaud et al., "Artisanal and Small-scale Gold Mining in Senegal"; Williams, "The Gold Standard of Governance."

83 This book is based on field research I conducted in Senegal in 2013–14 and 2017, in addition to archival research carried out in shorter trips to France, Senegal, and Guinea between 2010 and 2017.

84 The Sirba goldfields at the border of Niger and Burkina Faso are beyond the purview of this study. On Sirba, see Magnavita, "Sahelian Crossroads," and discussion in Nixon, "Trans-Saharan Gold Trade in Pre-modern Times," 169.

85 For overviews, see Murphy et al., *Anthrohistory*; Palmié and Stewart, "Introduction."

86 Models of historical anthropology that inform my approach include Cohen and Obdiambo, *Siaya*; Feierman, *Peasant Intellectuals*; Hunt, *A Colonial Lexicon*; Livingston, *Debility and the Moral Imagination*. Archeologists of West Africa, in particular, have been central to the practice of historical anthropology in African studies more broadly: see Logan, *The Scarcity Slot*; Richard, *Reluctant Landscapes*; Stahl, *Making History in Banda*.

87 Oral traditions, according to Vansina, are "reported statements from the past beyond the present generation" whereas oral histories are accounts based on a speaker's lived experience: Vansina, *Oral Tradition as History*, 13. Oral praise poems and proverbs are other genres of speaking about the past beyond the lives of their speakers.

88 Cooper, "Oral Sources and the Challenges of African History," 210. See also Cohen et al., "Introduction." For critical discussion of oral traditions research, see Cohen, "The Undefining of Oral Tradition"; Hofmeyer, *"We Spend Our Years as a Tale That Is Told"*; Kodesh, "History from the Healer's Shrine";

Tonkin, *Narrating Our Pasts*. Research on texts in African languages brings attention to the written (not just oral) historical production of African intellectuals: see Barber, *The Anthropology of Texts, Persons, and Publics*; Ngom, *Muslims beyond the Arab World*; Peterson and Macola, *Recasting the Past*.

89 On rumor as historical evidence, see White, *Speaking with Vampires*. On spirits as evidence for different historical temporalities, see Apter, "History in the Dungeon"; Johnson, *Spirited Things*; Palmié, "Historicist Knowledge and Its Conditions of Impossibility"; and Shaw, *Memories of the Slave Trade*.

90 On African landscapes as repositories of memory, see de Luna, *Collecting Food, Cultivating People*; Carney, *Black Rice*; Richard, *Reluctant Landscapes*; Fairhead and Leach, *Misreading the African Landscape*; Giles-Vernick, *Cutting the Vines of the Past*.

91 Cohen and Obhiambo, "Introduction."

Chapter One: A Tale of Two Miners

1 *Burkinabe* is a colloquial term used throughout Francophone West Africa for citizens of Burkina Faso.

2 Human African trypanosomiasis is the scientific name for sleeping sickness.

3 Telli Diallo, interview by the author, Kanoumering, February 9, 2014.

4 Orpaillage villages share features with refugee camps, where temporary dwellings often become permanent residences: see Siddiqi, "Ephemerality."

5 Since independence from France in 1960, the Senegalese state has not legally recognized village chiefs. Most independence-era leaders in West Africa abolished the chieftaincy, which they viewed as a form of despotism created by French colonialism.

6 Bambo Cissokho, interview by the author, Tinkoto, February 11, 2014.

7 Doucouré, *Des pierres dans les mortiers et non du maïs!*, 51–52, describes the tribunal in Bantaco, another important orpaillage village in the Kédougou region.

8 Established in 1995, Randgold opened two major gold mines in Kéniéba, Mali, in the 2000s. Randgold no longer operates in Kédougou. In 2021, Endeavor Mining, a multinational company with headquarters in the Cayman Islands, acquired the research and permits to mine Massawa, Randgold's primary prospect.

9 In contemporary Senegal, ethnic Maninka, Pular, and Wolof follow patrilineal descent. Children take their father's patronym (*jamu* in Maninka). A child's given or first name (*toxo*) is often taken after a family member, friend, or wealthy patron—a means of securing an alliance between the newborn's family and the namesake. On the politics of naming in Kédougou, see Sweet, *The Poetics of Relationality*, chap. 8.

10 Author's field notes, 2014.

11 Sabodala was renamed the Sabodala-Massawa complex. I continue to refer to it as "Sabodala" because this is what it was called during the resarech and writing of this book.

12 On the ephemerality of junior exploration firms, see Kneas, "Subsoil Abundance and Surface Absence"; Özden-Schilling, "Theorizing the Contemporary"; Tsing, "Inside the Economy of Appearances."

13 Ferguson, *Global Shadows*, esp. chap. 2. See also Appel, *The Licit Life of Capitalism*; Appel, "Offshore Work"; Watts, "Resource Curse?"

14 Residential and workplace segregation by race and ethnicity is common in the corporate mining industry: see Appel, *The Licit Life of Capital*, esp. chap. 2; Santiago, *The Ecology of Oil*; Touraj et al., *Working for Oil*; Vitalis, *America's Kingdom*, 22. Thanks to Zachary Davis Cuyler for pointing me to several of these works.

15 I follow the anthropologist Hannah Appel in using the term "itinerant" (and, depending on the context, "foreign") rather than "expatriate" to refer to the largely white high-level managers, engineers, and geologists who work in the global mining industry. As Appel, *The Licit Life of Capital*, 4fn4, argues, the term "itinerant" denaturalizes the racialized associations of the term "expatriate" with "white global mobility, based on the ongoing colonial advantage secured by European nations."

16 Bambo Cissokho interview.

17 Yaya Touré, interview by the author, Tinkoto, January 24, 2014.

18 Yaya Touré interview.

19 Gassimou Cissokho, interview by the author, Tinkoto, January 24, 2014.

20 Some elders I interviewed in Kédougou called these spirits "thing of the bush" (*wula fen*) or "thing of *nyama*" (*nyamadin*). For a discussion of the term *nyama*, see chapter 2.

21 Moussa Cissokho, interview by the author, Tomboroncoto, March 10, 2014.

22 Mamadou Sagna, interview by the author, Mamakono, March 30, 2014.

23 I discuss these oral traditions in chapter 2.

24 Fanta Madi Cissokho, interview by the author, Bambaraya, March 29, 2014.

25 Idi Diallo, interview by the author, Tinkoto, January 16, 2014. Diallo is no longer the juurakuntigi of Tinkoto.

26 On totems among Maninka societies in West Africa, see Brooks, *Landlords and Strangers*; Conrad and Frank, *"Nyamakalaw"*; McNaughton, *The Mande Blacksmiths*.

27 Author's field notes, 2014. Across much of West Africa, leatherworkers are classified as one of several endogamous craft specialists, known as *nyamakala*. I discuss this term in chapter 2.

28 Gassimou Cissokho interview.

29 Author's field notes, 2014.

30 Orpaillage villages cultivate a competitive "religious economy," similar to what Benjamin Soares describes for urban Mali: *Islam and the Prayer Economy*, 251–53.

31 Abdou Sangare, interview by the author, Tinkoto, February 8, 2014.

32 Sidi Gueye, interview by the author, Tinkoto, January 16, 2014.

33 Yonko Camara, interview by the author, Tinkoto, January 18, 2014. Many regional residents remember 1984 as the worst in the multiyear droughts in terms of access to food resources. It is also marked in regional memory by the death of Sékou Touré, who had been the president of Guinea since 1958. See also Bana Sidibé, interview by the author, Kanoumering, February 9, 2014.

34 Maninka households in Senegal, known as *lu*, are typically the residential unit of the lineage of an elder male, his wives, and descendants who share his patronym (*jamu*).

35 Coumba Keita, interview by the author, Kerekonko, February 18, 2014. See also Niamendi Keita, interview by author, Mako, February 24, 2014; Tenimbo Cissokho, interview by the author, Tambanoumouya, March 13, 2014; Ramatou Sadiakho, interview by the author, Kerekonko, February 18, 2014.

36 On the growth of orpaillage in Kédougou during the droughts, see de Lestrange et al., "Stratégies de lutte contre la disette au Sénégal Oriental." See also Koka Boukari Kamara, interview by the author, Kerekonko, February 16, 2014.

37 Yonko Camara interview.

38 On divisibility as a productive social feature of many currencies in Atlantic-era Africa, see Guyer, "Indigenous Currencies and the History of Marriage Payments," 593–94.

39 On wealth in people, see n. 38 in the introduction.

40 Coumbouna Camara, interview by the author, Tinkoto, January 20, 2014.

41 Sajoh Madi Kamara, interview by the author, Linguekoto, March 12, 2014.

42 Mariama Bâ, interview by the author, Kédougou, February 15, 2014.

43 Niang, "Impacts environnementaux liée à l'utilisation du mercure lors de l'exploitation artisanale de l'or dans la région de Kédougou"; Persaud, "Mercury Use and the Socio-economic Significance of Artisanal and Small-scale Gold (ASGM) Mining in Senegal"; Sow, "Risques de l'exposition au mercure liés à l'exploitation artisanale de l'or au Sénégal Oriental."

44 Mali created a formal commercial board for gold dust in the early 1990s, which encouraged the flow of gold sales from eastern Senegal to Mali. Gold sales on West African juuras are usually between 80–95 percent of "global prices" for gold, which are set in reference to the London Bullion Market Association. In 2016, orpaillage in Senegal alone produced an estimated 2.3–6.7 tons of gold per year, although only 1 ton of gold was officially exported. Industrial mines exported roughly 6.4 tons per year during this same period: Alvarez et al., "Supply Chains of Artisanal Gold in West Africa," 9.

45 This is a pseudonym. Interview by the author, March 10, 2014.

46 The CFA (Communauté Financière Africaine) franc is the currency used in most of France's former West African colonies.

47 Cyanide heap leaching was used in nineteenth-century mining operations in Scotland and Britain, but it was not until the 1970s that the use of cyanide

became widespread globally. Cyanide makes the recuperation of extremely low-grade ore possible, but it also creates enormous amounts of waste.

48 Anonymous, interview by the author, Kédougou, March 26, 2014.

49 Moussa Cissokho interview

50 Bambo Cissokho interview. See also Filé Keita, interview by the author, Tinkoto, February 11, 2014.

51 Yonko Camara interview.

52 Hamidou Sow, interview by the author, Dakar, July 21, 2017.

53 Lamine Sy, interview by the author, Kédougou, March 18, 2014; Hamidou Sow interview; author's field notes, 2014.

54 Hamidou Sow interview. Geologists working for juniors and multinational mining corporations in Senegal today continue to sample orpaillage sites (see chapter 6).

55 Comaroff and Comaroff, "Chiefs, Capital, and the State in Contemporary Africa," 13, write about the resurgence of customary power in Africa in the context of late liberalism.

56 The concept of the "social license" first emerged in the timber industry and was later adopted by the mining sector: see Business for Social Responsibility, *The Social License to Operate*; Moffat and Zhang, "The Paths to Social License to Operate."

57 On ethnographic approaches to CSR in the mining industry, see Rajak, *In Good Company*; Welker, *Enacting the Corporation*. For an overview of a management approach to CSR in Africa, see Hilson et al., "Corporate Social Responsibility at African Mines."

58 Makhan Keita, interview by the author, Kanoumering, February 10, 2014.

59 Sega Cissokho, interview by the author, Tinkoto, January 22, 2014.

60 Anonymous, interview by the author, Tinkoto, January 16, 2014.

Chapter Two: West Africa's Ritual Geology

1 Published versions of the Taubry (Tobri, Tobiri) narrative include: Altschul et al., *The Slave Who Would Be King*, 210; Aubert, "Légendes historiques et traditions orales recueillies en Haute-Gambie"; Chataigner, "Les populations du Cercle de Kédougou," 96. Aubert reports that Tobri's (*sic*) patronym was Kamara and that he was enslaved by the Soumaré clan. I adopted the convention of my interlocutors, who insisted Taubry's patronym was Sidibé: Bambo Cissokho, interview by the author, Tinkoto, February 11, 2014; Tumbi Cheikhou Cissokho, interview by the author, Mamakono, March 31, 2014; Makhan Keita, interview by the author, Kanoumering, February 10, 2014; Bambo Keita, interview by the author, Tomboroncoto, March 3, 2014; Toumanie Keita, interview by the author, Mako, February 23, 2014.

2 Makhan Keita interview.

3 Toumanie Keita interview.

4   Dan Mania's role in overcoming Taubry parallels that of women in the Sunjata Keita narrative (discussed later). On women as the providers (*sabuw*) of men's power in other Maninka oral narratives, see Conrad, "Mooning Armies and Mothering Heroes," 193.

5   Makhan Keita interview.

6   Aubert, "Légendes historiques et traditions orales recueillies en Haute-Gambie," 409.

7   Bélédougou largely aligns with the contemporary rural community (*communauté rurale*) of Khossanto. Bélédougou in Senegal is distinct from the province of Bélédougou/Beledugu in central Mali, though they both derive their name from the "land of gravel" (*bele*, gravel; *dugu*, land).

8   On this tension between state makers and orpailleurs in the medieval period, see Gomez, *African Dominion*, 107–8; Levtzion and Hopkins, *Corpus of Early Arabic Sources for West African History*, 70, 72; Ly-Tall, *Contribution à l'histoire de l'Empire du Mali*, 103. On the Atlantic era, see Bathily, *Les portes de l'or*; Curtin, "The Lure of Bambuk Gold"; Kiéthéga, *L'or de la Volta noire*; Perinbam, "The Political Organization of Traditional Gold Mining."

9   Scare quotes around the term *pagan* are hereafter implied. My use of the term *pagan* is intended to reflect the viewpoint of Muslim dynasts and chroniclers of non-Muslim populations in West Africa (see the introduction).

10 Berzock, *Caravans of Gold, Fragments in Time*; Fauvelle, *The Golden Rhinoceros*; Green, *A Fistful of Shells*.

11 Green, *A Fistful of Shells*, 14–15.

12 Green, *A Fistful of Shells*, 6.

13 Green, *A Fistful of Shells*, 41.

14 Bambuk is situated within two broader geographies common in regional historiography: "Upper Senegal Valley" and "Greater Senegambia." On the latter, see Barry, *Senegambia and the Atlantic Slave Trade*, 4–5.

15 Nixon, "Trans-Saharan Gold Trade in Pre-modern Times," 164.

16 Levtzion and Hopkins, *Corpus of Early Arabic Sources for West African History*, 21.

17 The Manding language continuum is a subset of the Mande language family that includes Soninke, Jallunke, Susu, Vai, Mende, and many others (see the orthographic notes). In the present day, many spoken varieties of the Manding language continuum are mutually intelligible, whereas Soninke (classified as Mande but not Manding) and Maninka are not.

18 McIntosh, *The Peoples of the Middle Niger*, 37, 255–56. On Wagadu's relationship with southern-lying regions, see Bathily, *Les portes de l'or*, 76; Gokee, *Assembling the Village in Medieval Bambuk*, 64.

19 Magnavita, "Sahelian Crossroads"; McIntosh, *Ancient Middle Niger*; Monroe, "Power and Agency in Precolonial African States."

20 There are few recent archeological studies of West African mines. But see Devisse, "L'or"; Mauny, *Tableau géographique de l'Ouest africain au Moyen Age*, 293–306.

21 On gold objects recovered from burials, see Garenne-Marot, "Archéologie d'un métal"; Joire, "Découvertes archéologiques dans la région de Rao"; Magnavita, "First Geophysical Exploration in the Tumuli Zone of Central Senegal"; Thiaw and Magnavita, "Nouvelles recherches archéologiques dans la zone des tumuli du Sénégal"; Thilmans and Descamps, "Fouille d'un tumulus á Ndalane."

On gold coin molds in Tadmekka (Mali), see Nixon, *Essouk Tadmekka*; Rehren and Nixon, "Refining Gold with Glass." Gold weights and numismatic systems are important sources of data: Garrard, *Akan Gold Weights*; Garrard, "Myth and Metrology." Magnavita and Magnavita, "All That Glitters Is Not Gold," surveys recent advances in the chemical analysis of gold provenance. On possible evidence for gold-working in Bambuk, see Mayor et al., "Dynamiques techniques et environnementales dans la vallée de la Falémé (Sénégal)."

22 Buré, situated at the headwaters of the Niger River in Guinea, likely furnished Wagadu with gold later than Bambuk: Nixon, "Trans-Saharan Gold Trade in Pre-modern Times," 169.

23 Beliyan-Bassari and Bedik are the earliest known inhabitants of auriferous land in southeastern Senegal and portions of western Mali, but there is no indication that they engaged in orpaillage: Altschul et al., *The Slave Who Would Be King*, 20; Aubert, "Légendes historiques et traditions orales recueillies en Haute-Gambie"; Bathily, *Les portes de l'or*; Ferry, "Pour une histoire des Bedik," 125–26; Gessain, *Les migrations des Coniagui et Bassari*, 47, 52.

24 Gokee, *Assembling the Village in Medieval Bambuk*, chap. 2; Thiaw, "Archeological Investigations of Long-Term Culture Change in the Lower Falemme," 40.

25 On Wangara (Wanghara, Wanqara, Wankara) trading networks, see McIntosh, "A Reconsideration of Wangāra/Palolus"; Perinbam, "Social Relations in the Trans-Saharan and Western Sudanese Trade"; Thiaw, "Archaeological Investigations of Long-Term Culture Change in the Lower Falemme"; Wilks, "Wangara, Akan and Portuguese."

26 Analysis of animal bone data shows that residents of medieval Diouboye, an archeological site in Bambuk, exploited animals for the export of ivory and hides: Dueppen and Gokee, "Hunting on the Margins of Medieval West African States."

27 On Saharan salt mines, see McDougall, "Salts of the Western Sahara," 253.

28 See Garenne-Marot, "Archéologie d'un métal," on copper grave goods in Senegambian burials. Copper was preferred over gold by many precolonial African societies: Herbert, *Red Gold of Africa*, esp. 105–6, 184–85.

29 McIntosh, "Reconceptualizing Early Ghana," 367.

30 My account of Bida is drawn from Bathily, "A Discussion of the Traditions of Wagadu with Some Reference to Ancient Ghāna"; de Zeltner, *Contes du Sénégal et du Niger*; Monteil, "La légende du Ougadou et l'histoire des Soninké"; Vidal, "Le mystère de Ghana." Elements of the Bida story resonate with a Hausa origin story of a prince who conquers a mystical serpent haunting a well in the town of Daura. He subsequently marries the town's queen, and their children become the founders of a number of Hausa-speaking states: Lange, *Ancient*

Kingdoms of West Africa, 161–62, 172–74. I thank Barbara Cooper for suggesting these parallels at a conference and directing me to Lange's work.

31 On climatic data, see McIntosh, *The Peoples of the Middle Niger*, 254–55. On the contested Almoravid invasion, see Conrad and Fisher, "The Conquest that Never Was." On Bida and reformist Islam, see Gomez, *African Dominion*, 38.

32 The dynasts of Takrur (a Pular polity near the Atlantic Ocean) were reportedly among the first to convert to Islam circa 1030: Levtzion, *Ancient Ghana and Mali*, 80.

33 Al-Bakrī never left Spain. He collected data from firsthand travelers to West Africa: Levtzion and Hopkins, *Corpus of Early Arabic Sources for West African History*, 80.

34 Killick, "Invention and Innovation in African Iron Smelting Technology"; Killick, "Iron Smelting Technology in the Middle Senegal Valley"; Dème and McIntosh, "Excavations at Walaldé"; Walmsley et al., "Variability of Early Iron Production in the Falémé Valley Region." On iron and fertility, see Herbert, *Iron, Gender, and Power*; Schmidt, "Tropes, Materiality; Schmidt, "Ritual Embodiment of African Iron Smelting Furnaces as Human Figures," and *Iron Technology in East Africa*.

35 Dieterlen, "The Mande Creation Myth," 127.

36 McIntosh, *Ancient Middle Niger*, 151–55.

37 Appia, "Notes sur le génie des eaux en Guinée"; Gamble, "Accounts of Supernatural Beings"; Kesteloot, "Les Mandingues de Casamance"; McIntosh, *The Peoples of the Middle Niger*, 168, 187–89.

38 Levtzion and Hopkins, *Corpus of Early Arabic Sources for West African History*, 78–79.

39 Bathily, *Les portes de l'or*, 39; Gomez, *African Dominion*, 44–45.

40 There is disagreement about the location of Mali's capital. An emergent hypothesis is that the capitals of Wagadu and Mali shifted across time: Roderick McIntosh, personal communication with the author, February 14, 2020.

41 I consulted the following versions: Camara, "The Epic of *Sunjata*"; Cissé and Kamissoko, *La grande geste du Mali*; Conrad and Condé, *Sunjata*; Innes et al., *Sunjata*; Johnson and Sisòkò, *The Epic of Son-Jara*; Niane, *Soundjata ou l'épopée mandingue*.

42 Niane, *Soundjataou l'épopée mandingue*, 39, 69. See also references in Gomez, *African Dominion*, 84n146.

43 A famous example is the "Jaa-Ogo" blacksmith dynasty that ruled over Takrur prior to the eleventh-century conversion of its leaders to Islam. Archeologists suspect that blacksmiths are featured among burial mounds, tumuli, that proliferated in the eighth century along the Niger and Senegal river basins. This period coincided with a rapid expansion in iron smelting and furnace production: Killick, "Iron Smelting Technology in the Middle Senegal Valley"; McIntosh, *Excavations at Jenné-jeno*, 278; McIntosh, *The Peoples of the Middle Niger*, 117–19, 186; McIntosh et al., *The Search for Takrur*.

44 Nyamakala is the "handle" (*kala*) of nyama. Tamari Tal dates the emergence *nyamakala* as a linguistic category to the thirteenth century: Tal, "The Development of Caste Systems in West Africa," and "Linguistic Evidence," 65.

45 McNaughton, *The Mande Blacksmiths*, 16.

46 Leather workers manipulate the nyama of wild animals. Blacksmiths encounter nyama when mining and smelting iron. Female smiths, specialists in pottery, handle the nyama in clay, fire, and water. Hunters and healers were also considered skilled manipulators of nyama, although they were not classified as nyamakala. Until recently, nyamakala putatively practiced endogamy. For critical overviews of nyamakala in Manding-speaking worlds, see Brett-Smith, *The Making of Bamana Sculpture*, 48–83; Cissé, "Notes sur les sociétés de chasseurs Malinke," 201, 207; Conrad and Frank, "*Nyamakalaw*"; Frank, *Mande Potters and Leatherworkers*; McNaughton, *The Mande Blacksmiths*, 15–21.

47 McIntosh, *Excavations at Jenné-jeno, Hambarketolo, and Kaniana*, 381; McIntosh, *Ancient Middle Niger*, 108fn151.

48 Smiths cultivated relationships with spirits of iron-bearing land: Appia, "Les forgerons du Fouta Djallon"; McNaughton, *The Mande Blacksmiths*, 15–21.

49 Al-Bakrī describes the city of Ghana as consisting of "two towns situated on a plain," one inhabited by Muslims and the other by non-Muslims: Levtzion and Hopkins, *Corpus of Early Arabic Sources for West African History*, 79–80. On the archeological footprint of this spatial distinction in Gao/Gao-Saney, see Cissé et al., "Excavations at Gao Saney."

50 Mussa's voyage is memorialized in the "Catalan Atlas" of 1375, which depicts the emperor of Mali wearing a golden crown and holding an orb of gold: Bibliothèque Nationale de France, Paris, Abraham Cresques (Majorcan, 1325–87), *Atlas of Maritime Charts* (*The Catalan Atlas*), 1375.

51 In Cairo at this time, Takrur was a geographic gloss for all territories to the west of Mali. As Michael Gomez suggests, since Christianity was not widespread in West Africa at the time, "the Christians" is likely a stand-in for pagans: Gomez, *African Dominion*, 107–8.

52 Levtzion and Hopkins, *Corpus of Early Arabic Sources for West African History*, 249.

53 Levtzion and Hopkins, *Corpus of Early Arabic Sources for West African History*, 262.

54 Levtzion and Hopkins, *Corpus of Early Arabic Sources for West African History*, 262. See also Mauny, *Tableau géographique de l'Ouest Africain au Moyen Age*.

55 Levtzion and Hopkins, *Corpus of Early Arabic Sources for West African History*, 80.

56 Levtzion and Hopkins, *Corpus of Early Arabic Sources for West African History*, 290–93.

57 These "gold rings of Wangara" were used as currency on Sahelian markets and are among the oldest known West African jewelry design. Arabic- and European-language accounts from later centuries describe women from groups

resident on the Sahel—speakers of Pular and Soninke language varieties—wearing conical gold beads, a design also indigenous to the region: Garrard, *Akan Weights*, and *African Gold*, 128.

58 Garrard, *African Gold*, 128; Herbert, *Red Gold of Africa*, 121–22.

59 The Rao Pectoral, which dates to the twelfth or thirteenth century, is the most prominent example of gold regalia found in a medieval tumulus: see Joire, "Découvertes archaeologiques dans la region de Rao (Bas-Sénégal)." Decades of archeological excavations at Jenné-Jeno, Mali, a town situated on a gold-trading route for nearly a millennium, has recovered only a single gold earring: McIntosh, *Excavations at Jenné-jeno, Hambarketolo, and Kaniana*. For an overview of gold and silver artifacts excavated from archeological sites in Western Africa, see Magnavita and Mertz-Kraus, "XRF and LA-ICP-MS Studies of Gold and Silver Artefacts from a 12–13th Century CE Tumulus in Senegal," 417.

60 Garenne-Marot and Mille, "Copper-based Metal in the Inland Niger Delta."

61 Magnavita and Mertz-Kraus, "XRF and LA-ICP-MS Studies of Gold and Silver Artefacts from a 12–13th Century CE Tumulus in Senegal," esp. 421–23. See also Thiaw and Magnavita, "Nouvelles recherches archéologiques dans la zone des tumuli du Sénégal"; Magnavita, "First Geophysical Exploration in the Tumuli Zone of Central Senegal."

62 Kiéthéga, *L'or de la Volta noire*, 158.

63 Green, *A Fistful of Shells*, chap. 3, surveys these developments.

64 On competing theories of Akan-Manding exchanges: see Konadu, *The Akan Diaspora in the Americas*, chap 2; Stewart and Wilks, "The Mande Loan Element in Twi"; Wilks, *Forests of Gold*, chap. 1.

65 Wright, "Beyond Migration and Conquest," makes this point for Mandinka-speakers in the Gambia.

66 On the komo in Mali, see Dieterlen and Cissé, *Les fondements de la société d'initiation du Komo*, 9–10, 15–20; Zobel, "Les génies du Kòma." On the *kánkourang* in eastern Senegal, see IFAN-UCAD, "Prospections, fouilles archéologiques et enquêtes ethnographiques dans le périmètre minier de ToroGold à Mako." George Brooks, *Landlords and Strangers*, 45–46, 75–76, proposes that Manding smiths may have settled to the south and west of Manden as they prospected for gold and iron, founding local chapters of power associations to protect trade routes and integrate their children into host societies.

67 Bâ and Dieterlen, *Koumen*, 21; Gamble, "Accounts of Supernatural Beings"; Kesteloot, "Les Mandingues de Casamance"; Sarr, *Islam, Power, and Dependency in the Gambia River Basin*, 35, 40–41, 91.

68 Bâ and Dieterlen, *Koumen*. See also Ligers, "Comment les Peuls de Koa castrent leurs taureaux," 201.

69 Béatrice Appia, a French ethnographer who worked in colonial Guinea, recorded use of the name "Niniganne" among Baga-speakers; "Ninger" and "Ningiri" among Pular-speakers of the Fouta Djallon; "Ninkinanka" in

Casamance (Senegal); and "Rianseeou" among speakers of Portuguese creole in Guinea-Bissau: Appia, "Notes sur le génie des eaux en Guinée." See also Appia, "Masques de Guinée Française et de Casamance," 161.

70 Archeological surveys along other West African paleo-channels, highly desirable due to their proximity to potable water, have revealed rich clusters of medieval settlement. By contrast, there is almost no evidence of settlement along the Vallée du Serpent for this time period. The nyama left in Bida's wake may have rendered the land dangerous for human settlement. This is the interpretation of McIntosh, *Ancient Middle Niger*, 49, McIntosh, *The Peoples of the Middle Niger*, 144–45; MacDonald and Allsworth-Jones, "A Reconsideration of the West African Macrolithic Conundrum."

71 Appia, "Notes sur le génie des eaux en Guinée"; Kesteloot, "Les Mandingues de Casamance."

72 Hair, "The Falls of Felou"; Wilks, *Forests of Gold*, chap. 1.

73 Niane, *Histoire des Mandingues de l'Ouest*, 49.

74 Curtin, "The Lure of Bambuk Gold." Examples of eighteenth-century French accounts of Bambuk include Boucard, "Relation de Bambouc"; David, *Journal d'un voyage fait en Bambouc en 1744*. See also the unpublished reports of André Brue and Michel de la Courbe, compiled in Labat, *Nouvelle relation de l'Afrique occidentale*, vol. 4, 39–56, 73–77.

75 Labat, *Nouvelle relation de l'Afrique occidentale*, 291–93. On these rumors, see Moore, *Travels into the Inland of Africa*, 41.

76 See also Altschul et al., *The Slave Who Would Be King*, 57–58. Kroot and Gokee, "Histories and Material Manifestations of Slavery in the Upper Gambia River Region," describe similar dynamics in western Kédougou.

77 Marooning was a defensive strategy of noncentralized societies in inhospitable terrains across West Africa: see Diouf, *Fighting the Slave Trade*, 86; Hawthorne, *Planting Rice and Harvesting Slaves*; Klein, "The Slave Trade and Decentralized Societies."

78 Mollien, *Travels in the Interior of Africa*, 80.

79 Raffenel, *Voyage dans l'Afrique occidentale*, 383.

80 Raffenel, *Voyage dans l'Afrique occidentale*, 385.

81 Sanneh, *The Jakhanke Muslim Clerics*, chaps. 2, 4.

82 David, *Journal d'un voyage fait en Bambouc en 1744*, 164; Raffenel, *Voyage dans l'Afrique occidentale*, 42. On the proliferation of *tatas* along the Upper Senegal Valley, see Thiaw, "Atlantic Impacts on Inland Senegambia."

83 Boucard, "Relation de Bambouc," 272. See also Golbéry, *Travels in Africa*, 321; Mollien, *Travels in the Interior of Africa*, 92; Raffenel, *Voyage dans l'Afrique occidentale*, 383–84.

84 Carrère and Holle, *De la Sénégambie française*, 170.

85 David, *Journal d'un voyage fait en Bambouc en 1744*, 107; Hecquard, *Voyage sur la côte et dans l'intérieur de l'Afrique occidentale*; Mollien, *Travels in the Interior of Africa*, 383. See Labat, *Nouvelle relation de l'Afrique occidentale*, vol. 4, 30–31.

On the reluctance of miners to sell gold directly to the French, see Boucard, "Relation de Bambouc," 254.

86 Park, *Travels in the Interior Districts of Africa Performed in the Years 1795, 1796 and 1797*, 158, 170.

87 Boucard, "Relation de Bambouc"; Carrère and Holle, *De la Sénégambie française*, 172.

88 See Sarró, *The Politics of Religious Change on the Upper Guinea Coast*, 58–59.

89 Carrère and Holle, *De la Sénégambie française*, 169, describe a *jalan* in nineteenth-century Bambuk. Sarr, *Islam, Power, and Dependency*, 90, reviews Atlantic-era British accounts of *jalang* on the Gambia River. For a discussion of the relationship of *jalans* to the African mahogany tree, *jala* in Maninka, see chapter 4.

90 Raffenel, *Voyage dans l'Afrique occidentale*, 42. First-comer rights could be contested, lost, or transferred: Kopytoff, *The African Frontier*, 52–61; Lentz, *Land, Mobility, and Belonging in West Africa*, 18. Claims to first-comer status may be fictive, but sacrifices to land spirits can naturalize this claim over time: McGovern, *Unmasking the State*, chap. 4.

91 Mady Sadiakho, interview by the author, Baraboye, June 15, 2014; Toumanie Keita interview.

92 On the construction of subterranean property claims by Maninka lineages in Atlantic-era Bambuk, see d'Avignon, "Spirited Geobodies"; Salioum Soaré, interview by the author, Kédougou, June 6, 2014.

93 On elephant hunting, see Carrère and Holle, *De la Sénégambie française*, 170–71.

94 For a discussion of this term, see chapter 1.

95 The antiquity of the office of the *juurakuntigi* is difficult to establish in the absence of historical linguistics. By the early nineteenth century, some juuras in Bambuk were overseen by a *juurakuntigi*, while others were managed by a more general ritual practitioner: a "master of the shrines" (*jalankuntigi* or *jalan nila*). On the term *jalan nila*, see Belan, "L'or dans le cercle de Kédougou"; Curtin, "The Lure of Bambuk Gold," 629. Abdoulaye Bathily, *Les portes de l'or*, 176, reported use of the term *jababalon* in Soninke oral narratives north of Bambuk.

96 I suspect the term *juura* is Soninke, although this question merits further research. *Juura* is used widely in Bambuk, and not on goldfields to the east. Bambuk was within the sphere of influence of Soninke traders known as Wangara and later as *juula*. The terms *juura* and *juula* may have been the same word in the deeper past as the "r/l" can be interchangeable in some Manding language varieties based on context. The term *juura* is likely derived from the Soninke word *juul*, which is used in "prayer" (*juulde*, *njuulu*), "to engage in commerce" (*juulade*), and "merchant" (*juula*). The root word *juul* forms the basis for *juula*, or trader. My interlocutors interpreted the meaning of the term *juura* as "place of ritual," which aligns with the etymology of the root word *juul*. On Soninke terms for prayer, see Kane, *La première hégémonie peule*, 336–37; Ware, *The Walking Qur'an*, 93.

97 The most important of these trees is known in Maninka as nyama (*Bauhinia reticulata*), so or "soso" (*Berlinia heudelotiana*), and sunsun (*Diospyros mespiliformis*). Nyama, as the name implies, is a tree favored by spirits. See also discussion in chapter 4.

98 Moussa Keita, interview by the author, Mako, March 20, 2014. Termite mounds are used to test agricultural soils in West Africa: see Fairhead, "Termites, Mud Daubers and Their Earths."

99 Mamadou Kamara, interview by the author, Kerekonko, February 18, 2014. See also Golbéry, *Travels in Africa*, 332. d'Avignon, "Spirited Geobodies."

100 Bambo Cissokho interview; Toumanie Keita interview; Makhan Keita interview.

101 Gokee, *Assembling the Village in Medieval Bambuk*, 176.

102 Golbéry, *Travels in Africa*, 317.

103 Boucard, "Relation de Bambouc," 260. See also Golbéry, *Travels in Africa*, 314; Mollien, *Travels in the Interior of Africa*, 192; Noirot, *À travers le Fouta-Diallon et le Bambouc*, 205.

104 Durand, *Voyage au Sénégal*, 363–64.

105 David, *Journal d'un voyage fait en Bambouc en 1744*, 165. See also Raffenel, *Voyage dans l'Afrique occidentale*, 381.

106 Carrère and Holle, *De la Sénégambie française*, 172.

107 Hecquard, *Voyage sur la côte et dans l'intérieur de l'Afrique occidentale*; Durand, *Voyage au Sénégal*, 348, 352; Golbéry, *Travels in Africa*, 316–17.

108 Gomez, *Pragmatism in the Age of Jihad*, 98; Robinson, *The Holy War of Umar Tal*, 153, 167.

109 Louis Faidherbe, "Mémoire sur les mines d'or du Bambouk, sur leur historie et sur la possibilité de les exploiter," July 12, 1856, SEN/XIII/55A, ANOM. See also Robinson, *The Holy War of Umar Tal*, 221, 241.

110 "Letter from Maritz to L. Faidherbe," March 18, 1860, SEN/XIII/55A, ANOM.

111 "Letter from Maritz to L. Faidherbe."

112 Heller, *Labour, Science and Technology in France*, 443–51; Sébillot, *Les travaux publics et les mines dans les traditions et les superstitions de tous les pays*, 390–418.

113 Adas, *Machines as the Measure of Men*, 112.

114 Porter, *The Making of Geology*; Rudwick, *Earth's Deep History*. On similar transformations across scientific disciplines in the early modern period, see Latour, *We Have Never Been Modern*, 27; Shapin and Schaffer, *Leviathan and the Air-Pump*.

115 Johnson, "Atlantic Genealogy of 'Spirit Possession,'" 400. See also Matory, *Black Atlantic Religion*, 243, 258.

116 Golbéry, *Travels in Africa*, 314; Hecquard, *Voyage sur la côte et dans l'intérieur de l'Afrique occidentale*, 381.

117 Golbéry, *Travels in Africa*, 293–94.

118 Golbéry, *Travels in Africa*, 322.

NOTES TO CHAPTER TWO   231

119 Carrère and Holle, *De la Sénégambie française*, 172.

120 Noirot, *À travers le Fouta-Djallon et le Bambouc*, 202–3. See also Rançon, *Dans la Haute-Gambie*.

121 Noirot, *À travers le Fouta-Djallon et le Bambouc*, 204–5.

122 Noirot, *À travers le Fouta-Djallon et le Bambouc*, 200–202.

123 L'administrateur du cercle de Matam à M. le Directeur des Affaires Politiques (St. Louis), "Missions Diverses, incursions des gens du Fouta Jallon (Alpha Yaya, Bocar Biro)," 1893, 10D1–006, ANS.

124 Bathily, "Mamadou Lamine Dramé et la résistance anti-impérialiste dans le Haut-Sénégal."

125 Makhan Keita interview.

Chapter Three: Making Customary Mining in French West Africa

1 Eduard Julian, Ingénieur Adjoint adressé à Pierre Legoux, Chef-Adjoint, Ingénieur Principal, Service des Mines de l'AOF, letter, January 11, 1934, ADMGS. The ADMGS files have no collection or box numbers.

2 Robequain, "Problèmes de l'économie rurale en AOF," 146.

3 I discuss this literature in the introduction.

4 The case was similar for colonial-era cash cropping: see Berry, *No Condition Is Permanent*, chap. 3.

5 Berry, *No Condition is Permanent*, chap 2.

6 Juula were barred from acquiring import and export licenses and from trading across imperial boundaries. Juula became reliant on French merchants for both credit and access to European imports. On the AOF's trade policies, see Boone, *Merchant Capital and the Roots of State Power in Senegal*; Coquery-Vidrovitch, *L'Afrique occidentale au temps des Français*, esp. chap. 5; Goerg, *Commerce et colonisation en Guinée*; Suret-Canale, *French Colonialism*.

7 Several articles treat the history of orpaillage in the AOF: Curtin, "The Lure of Bambuk Gold"; Jansen, "What Gold Mining Means for the Malinke"; Luning et al., "The *Mise en Valeur* of the Gold Mines in the Haut-Niger"; Moussa, "L'or des régions de Poura et de Gaoua"; Panella, "L'éthique sociale du Damansen"; Samson, "Les 'trésors méconnus' l'Afrique subsaharienne françaises." By contrast, there are dozens of monographs on peanut cultivation in colonial Senegal and Gambia: Babou, *Fighting the Greater Jihad*; David, *Les navétanes*; O'Brien, *The Mourides of Senegal*; Swindell and Jeng, *Migrants, Credit and Climate*.

8 *Navétane* is derived from *navète*, which translates as "rainy season" in Wolof. In 1939 alone, more than 65,000 "strangers" migrated to Guinea to mine gold. In the same year, more than 64,000 seasonal laborers cultivated peanuts in Senegal. See figures in David, *Les navétanes*, 464–65; Labouret, "L'Afrique-Occidentale Française en 1934," 289; Robequain, "Problèmes de l'économie rurale en AOF," 223.

9 Colonial officials and ethnographers characterized orpaillage as a "Malinké industry": Mathelin de Papigny, "Note sur les exploitations indigènes du

Satadougou," 396. Other examples include Keita, "Autour des placers du Cercle de Siguiri"; Méniaud, *Haut-Sénégal-Niger*, 175; Siossat, "Les coutumes des orpailleurs indigènes du Maramandougou."

10 Scare quotes around the terms *customary* and *traditional* are hereafter implied. Customary mining rights were not the sole mechanism by which Africans accessed rights to minerals under colonial rule. In South Africa, some African "chiefs" on tribal reserves acquired formal titles to land with mineral rights attached: Capps, "Tribal-Landed Property," 469–70. African authorities in the Gold Coast also retained some control over mineralized land through communal property known as stool land that was held in trust by Asante chiefs: Dumett, *El Dorado in West Africa*, 89, 272–77. On customary mining regimes in colonial Africa, see d'Avignon, "Primitive Techniques."

11 The *indigénat,* however, made no pretense to custom: Mann, "What Was the *Indigénat?*" 335.

12 All candidates for the French Assembly were French or métis until Blaise Diagne's election in 1914: Coquery-Vidrovitch, "Nationalité et citoyenneté en Afrique-Occidentale Française"; Diouf, "Assimilation colonial et identité religieuses de la civilité des originaires des Quatre Communes."

13 Robequain, "Problèmes de l'économie rurale en AOF."

14 Residents of the goldfields of Hiré (Côte d'Ivoire), and Poura and Gaoua (Haute-Volta), largely abandoned orpaillage during colonial rule. They found more lucrative work as migrant laborers on African-owned cocoa plantations in Ghana and on timber plantations in Côte d'Ivoire: Allman and Tashjian, *I Will Not Eat Stone*; Berry, *Fathers Work for Their Sons*; Rouch, "Migrations au Ghana."

15 On gold commerce, see Inspecteur Principal des Affaires Administrative Aubert, "Rapport: Sur la situation de commerce de l'or et sur l'exploitation des mines d'or de Siguiri par les indigenes," March 22–25, 1934, ADMGS. Reports on the "customs" of orpailleurs include: Colonie de la Guinée Française, "Étude des coutumes indigènes," n.d. [after 1945], ANG; Colonie de la Guinée Française, Service des Travaux Publics, Conakry, "Recueil de documents relatifs au droit coutumier," July 11, 1929, ADMGS; Hubert, "Coutumes indigènes"; Jean Malavoy, "Note sur l'amelioration de l'orpaillage indigenè," March 24, 1931, ADMGS; Siossat, "Les coutumes des orpailleurs indigènes du Maramandougou."

16 Balandier, "L'or de la Guinée Françaises [*sic*]." See also Denise Savineau, "Siguiri et les Placers d'or: Séjour à Siguiri et sur quelques placers du Cercle," Fieldwork report no. 14, presented to Governor-General Marcel de Coppet of the AOF, April 12–15, 1938.

17 Quoted in Gallieni, *Mission d'exploration du Haut-Niger*, 305–6, 512–13. See also Peroz, *Au Soudan français*, which makes numerous mentions of African gold workings in Buré. The accounts of indigenous gold mines, written by British officers returning from the Asante War of 1873–74, contributed to gold rushes in the colonial Gold Coast: Dumett, *El Dorado in West Africa*, 89.

18 Le Barbier, "Comment les noirs extraient l'or à la Côte d'Ivoire," 88–89; Serrant, *Les mines et gisements d'or de l'Afrique occidentale*. On the language of "primitive methods," see Méniaud, *Haut-Sénégal-Niger*, 203–4.

19 In 1894, France created the Colonial Ministry in Paris to establish civilian control over its African colonies. The AOF initially included Senegal, Soudan, Guinea, and Côte d'Ivoire. After World War I, Dahomey (Benin), Haute-Volta, Mauritania, and Niger were added to the federation. At that time, Togo, a former German colony, became a French mandate state. In 1902, the seat of the federation was transferred from St. Louis to Dakar: see Newbury, "The Formation of the Government General of French West Africa." On requests for gold permits, see Gouverneur Général de l'AOF à M. le Ministre des Colonies, St. Louis, letter, 1895, AOF/XIII/2, ANOM.

20 Maurice Barrat, "Note sur les mines du Soudan," October 21, 1895, P 464, ANS, 31–32.

21 Barrat's mineral regime (*régime minière*) was implemented by decree (*décret*): Maurice Barrat, "Régime minière," 1895, AOF/XIII/2/4, ANOM. See also Barrat, "Les mines d'or du basin du Senegal."

22 Barrat, "Note sur les mines du Soudan."

23 Barrat, "Note sur les mines du Soudan."

24 For this range in colonial customary law, see Berry, *No Condition Is Permanent*; Chanock, "Paradigms, Policies, and Property"; Roberts and Mann, "Law in Colonial Africa"; Spear, "Neo-traditionalism and the Limits of Invention in British Colonial Africa."

25 Goloubinow, "L'or en Guinée Française," 38; Hubert, "Coutumes indigènes."

26 Barrat, "Note sur les mines du Soudan," 31–32.

27 Mines, Fieux Lamartigny et Roux de Bethune, "Copie de rapports sur les mines d'or de Kéniéba, de la Falémé, et du Bambouk, 1879–80," P 463, ANS.

28 On Guinea's rubber boom, see Osborn, "'Rubber Fever,' Commerce and French Colonial Rule in Upper Guinea," 454. The Marseillaise merchant houses Peyrissac and Chavanel specialized in Guinea's gold trade. On Syrien merchants in colonial Guinea, see Condé, *Histoire de Siguiri*; Suret-Canale, *French Colonialism*, 12.

29 The mining code of 1896 annulled a number of treaties to exploit gold signed between French explorers and African authorities: Suret-Canale, *French Colonialism*, 50.

30 "Rapport du contrôleur des mines, M. Coussien, adressé au Lieutenant-Gouverneur de la Guinée Française," April 25, 1909, 3 Q 10, ANG.

31 "Rapport: Affaire de Vidal, Commandant de Cercle de Kéniéba (Soudan)," 1898, P 465, ANS.

32 "Rapport."

33 "Traduction d'un rapport de William Atherton à l'Ivory Coast Exploring Syndicate, Ingenieur, Province du Bouré," December 18, 1902, P 468, ANS. See also Condé, *Histoire de Siguiri*, 108–17.

34 "Rapport de M. l'Administrateur Bidiane," September 6, 1913, and "Procès-verbal d'une palabre tenue á Fatoya le 27 Janvier 1914," both in 3 Q 10, ANG.

35 "Procès-verbal d'une palabre tenue á Fatoya."

36 "Rapport de M. l'Administrateur Bidiane."

37 Maurice David, Ingénieur des Mines, "Extrait du Rapport du 3ème Trimestre 1913," Conakry, October 25, 1913, 3 Q 10, ANG.

38 Gouverneur Général de l'AOF à M. le Lieutenant-Gouverneur de la Guinée Française à Conakry, Dakar, letter, December 2, 1913, 3 Q 10, ANG.

39 "Rapport de M. l'Administrateur Bidiane."

40 "Decret du 22 Octobre 1924, fixant la régime des mines en AOF," *Journal Officiel de l'AOF*, December 6, 1924, 735.

41 Robequain, "Problèmes de l'économie rurale en AOF," 146; L. Baud, Ingénieur Géologue, "Rapport sur l'activité minière dans le Bassin de la Falémé en 1944," Dakar, August 29, 1944, ADMGS.

42 As early as 1912, millet and rice were sold for "famine prices" in Siguiri due to the large number of orpailleurs working there: Roberts, "The Emergence of a Grain Market in Bamako."

43 Labouret, "L'Afrique-Occidentale Française en 1934," 289.

44 Gouverneur Général de la Guinée Française, Joseph Vadier, adresse à M. l'Inspecteur Général des Travaux Publics, letter, July 4, 1934, ADMGS.

45 Pierre Legoux, Chef-Adjoint, Ingénieur Principal de la Service des Mines de l'AOF adressé à Fernand Blondel, Ingénieur en Chef des Mines, France d'Outre-mer, letter, February 29, 1934, 3 Q 10, ANG. On this "purely native industry," see also Blondel, "Études," 363.

46 Robequain, "Problèmes de l'économie rurale en AOF."

47 Tilley, *Africa as a Living Laboratory*, esp. chaps. 2–3.

48 Labouret, "L'Afrique-Occidentale Française en 1934," 45.

49 Coquery-Vidrovitch, "La politique économique colonial"; Delavignette, *Les paysans noirs*; Wilder, *The French Imperial Nation-State*, chap. 3.

50 Gilbert Arnaud, Directeur des Mines de l'AOF, "Rapport sur l'organisation administrative, technique, et coopérative d'orpaillage," Dakar, September 11, 1944, 3 Q 10, ANG. For colonial officials, placer mines presented the same concerns as cities: see Cooper, *Decolonization and African Society*.

51 The damantigi of Buré is the same office as the juurakuntigi of Bambuk. The distinction lies in the differential use of the term *daman* in the twentieth century. In Bambuk, *daman* denotes a single mining shaft; *juura* indicates a goldfield or mine. In Buré, *daman* indicates an entire goldfield—hence, the damantigi is the "master of the mines." In Bambuk, *damantigi* translates as "master of the [single] shaft."

52 Savineau, "Siguiri et les Placers d'or," 22. See also Baud, "Rapport sur l'activité minière dans le Bassin de la Falémé en 1944."

53 Colonie de la Guinée Française, "Étude des coutumes indigènes."

NOTES TO CHAPTER THREE 235

54 Siossat, "Les coutumes des orpailleurs indigènes du Maramandougou," 337.

55 Savineau, "Siguiri et les Placers d'or," 32–35.

56 Siossat, "Les coutumes des orpailleurs indigènes du Maramandougou," 339.

57 In "The Formation of an 'Islamic Sphere' in French Colonial West Africa," Robert Launay and Benjamin Soares argue that the acceleration of Islamization was an unintended consequence of colonial rule in the AOF. On conversion to Islam on the peanut fields of colonial Senegal, see Babou, *Fighting the Greater Jihad*; Copans, *Les marabouts de l'arachide*; Searing, *God Alone Is King*; Ware, *The Walking Qur'an*, esp. chap. 4. On the dynamics of conversion in agricultural villages in colonial Mali, see Peterson, *Islamization from Below*, esp. chap. 4.

58 Monday was also considered a day of rest among non-Muslim migrants to African-owned peanut farms in Senegal: David, *Les navétanes*, 256. The origins of this practice in Senegal may derive from Serer ancestral religious traditions in which Monday was a holy day of rest: Gravrand, *Pangool*, 66.

59 Colonie de la Guinée Française, "Étude des coutumes indigènes."

60 Laye, *The Dark Child*, 31–32.

61 Laye, *The Dark Child,* 35. The opening chapter of Laye's book also describes the presence of a mystical black snake in his father's workshop with whom Laye's father communicated—an allusion to the spirited totem of Maninka blacksmiths (see chapter 2).

62 Savineau, "Siguiri et les Placers d'or," 11.

63 Savineau, "Siguiri et les Placers d'or," 5–7, 24–27. See also Inspecteur Général, Travaux Publics, Section des Mines, "Note: Sur l'amélioration de l'orpaillage indigène," March 24, 1931, ANG.

64 Author's field notes, Siguiri, Guinea, 2011.

65 Rostilav Goloubinow, "Prospection aurifère en Guinée," Dakar, August 9, 1935, ADMGS; Siossat, "Les coutumes des orpailleurs indigènes du Maramandougou," 345.

66 Savineau, "Siguiri et les Placers d'or," 10–12.

67 In southeastern Senegal in the 1930s, male heads of household calculated colonial head taxes by their equivalent in tamarind seeds: Mamadou Danfakha, interview by the author, Kerekonko, February 18, 2014.

68 Condé, *Histoire de Siguiri*, 106–7, 128–30.

69 Humblot, "Kankan, métropole de la Haute-Guinée"; Kaba, "Islam, Society and Politics in Precolonial Baté"; Kaba and Charry, "Mamaya," 195–96.

70 Siossat, "Les coutumes des orpailleurs indigènes du Maramandougou."

71 Siossat, "Les coutumes des orpailleurs indigènes du Maramandougou," 341.

72 Author's field notes, Siguiri, July 2011.

73 Siossat, "Les coutumes des orpailleurs indigènes du Maramandougou," 346; Savineau, "Siguiri et les Placers d'or," 18.

74 Keita, "Autour des placers du Cercle de Siguiri." In 1957, Sékou Touré appointed Keita Guinea's minister of internal affairs and, later, minister of

defense: Kaba, "The Cultural Revolution, Artistic Creativity, and Freedom of Expression in Guinea."

75 Colonie de la Guinée Française, "Étude des coutumes indigènes."

76 Savineau, "Siguiri et les Placers d'or," 32.

77 Savineau, "Siguiri et les Placers d'or," 9.

78 On these developments, see Cooper, *Citizenship between Empire and Nation*.

79 Several of the Union du Mandé's founding members became prominent politicians, including Sékou Touré, the first president of independent Guinea. It was created in 1944 as a cultural dance association. On the union's activities in Siguiri, see Condé, *Histoire de Siguiri*, 211–23. Political parties in postwar Guinea were largely based on ethnoregional affinities: the Susu-majority Basse Côte (Union de la Basse Guinée), the Pular-majority Fouta Djallon (Amicale Gilbert Vieillard), and the Maninka-majority Upper Guinea (Union du Mandé): Morgenthau, *Political Parties in French-speaking West Africa*.

80 Mann, "Anti-colonialism and Social Science," 108.

81 Sékou Touré, Secrétaire Général, Union du Mandé, à M. le Gouverneur de la Guinée Française, letter, Conakry, March 28, 1947, 3 Q 23, ANG.

82 Framoi Bérété, Conseiller Général, à M. le Président de la Chambre de Commerce, letter, Conakry, July 9, 1947, ADMGS. Béréte began his political career in Guinea's Chamber of Commerce and served as the president of the Territorial Assembly of Guinea from 1954 to 1956.

83 Touré was then the secretary-general of a workers' union at the Postes, Télégraphes et Téléphones.

84 Sano served in the French National Assembly in 1946–58. According to Mann, "Anti-colonialism and Social Science," 108, Sano hoped to secure the patronage of juula traders and the Union du Mandé in campaigning to liberalize the gold trade. In the end, he lost the latter. Sano joined the RDA while the union split with the RDA after a brief alliance in 1948.

85 In Guinea, the RDA evolved into the Parti Démocratique de la Guinée (PDG), which was the party of Sékou Touré's presidency from 1958 until his death in 1984.

86 André Blouin, Ingénieur, Bureau Minier de la France d'Outre-mer, "Mission orpaillage de Siguiri," à Mr. Massoulard, Commandant le Cercle de Siguiri, June 22, 1950, 3 Q 23, ANG.

87 "L'octroi à des sociétés privées des permis de recherches et d'exploitation d'or dans le cercle de Siguiri signifie la suppression pure et simple de l'orpaillage des autochtones: Mise au point," *Voix de la Guinée*, 20 (June 1950): 3. The letter was not signed, but Béréte submitted the same signed statement to Guinea's General Council on May 22, 1950.

88 Framoi Bérété, Président, Commission Permanente du Conseil Général de la Guinée, "L'octroi à des sociétés privées...," Conakry, May 22, 1950, 3 Q 23, ANG.

89 Blouin, "Mission orpaillage de Siguiri."

90 M. Massoulard, Commandant le Cercle de Siguiri, à M. le Gouverneur de la Guinée Française, "Objet: Demande de permis de recherches CRAPEZ," letter, October 24, 1950, 3 Q 23, ANG.

91 See Berry, *No Condition Is Permanent*; Chanock, "Paradigms, Policies, and Property."

92 Bérété, "L'octroi á des sociétés privées," 3. In April 1949, Béréte compelled Guinea's General Council to reject a (French) permit request that would interfere with the "native reserves" of the Siguiri basin. Bérété argued, "There is above all the question of customary rights. The region under consideration should be reserved for those rights because the natives exploited deposits well before French occupation": Framoi Bérété, "Conseil Général, Session Ordinaire, Guinée Française, Avril 1, 1949," BIB, AOF/50451, ANOM.

93 Bérété, "L'octroi á des sociétés privées," 3.

94 Massoulard à M. le Gouverneur de la Guinée Française "Objet."

95 Gouverneur de la Guinée Française, Roland Pré, adressé au Gouverneur Général de L'AOF, Paul Béchard, Conakry, letter, April 25, 1950, 3 Q 23, ANG.

96 Pré adressé au Béchard, letter.

97 Diamonds (from Guinea and Côte d'Ivoire) and titanium also became important postwar exports.

98 "Décret no. 54-1110 du 13 novembre 1954 portant réforme du régime des substances minérales dans les territoires d'outre-mer, au Togo et au Cameroun," *Journal Officiel de la République Française*, November 14, 1954, 10713–18.

99 The 1954 decree was incorporated into the final mining decree of overseas France: "Décret no. 57-242 du 24 février 1957 relatif au régime des substances minérales dans les territoires d'outre-mer," *Journal Officiel de la République Française*, February 28, 1957, 2300–2.

100 Roberts, *Two Worlds of Cotton*, 16–17.

Chapter Four: Colonial Geology and African Gold Discoveries

1 Alexis Chermette, Ingénieur-Géologue, "Les filons de quartz aurifère de Hiré," Dakar, September 1934, ADMGS.

2 Analogous techniques were used in the Akan-speaking forests of Ghana and parts of Burkina Faso: Dumett, *El Dorado in West Africa*, 54–56; Kiéthéga, *L'or de la Volta noire*.

3 Chermette, "Les filons de quartz aurifère de Hiré."

4 Chermette, "Les filons de quartz aurifère de Hiré."

5 Tilley, *Africa as a Living Laboratory*, 117; Tilley, "Global Histories, Vernacular Science, and African Genealogies."

6 Hailey, *An African Survey*, chap. 22, compares imperial investments in mining and geology in Africa.

7 See discussion in chapter 2.

8 Breckenridge, *Biometric State*, introduction.

9 Dumett, *El Dorado in West Africa*, 29.

10 The terms *Birimian* and *Birrimien* appeared in French-language scientific publications (including the *Bulletin du Muséum National d'Histoire Naturelle* and the *Annales des Mines*) from the 1930s to the 1950s, as well as the Congrès International des Mines, held in Paris in 1935. I thank Hannah Leffingwell for tracking the use of the terms.

11 On the construction of regional scientific knowledge in dialogue with different environmental conditions, see De Bont and Lachmund, *Spatializing the History of Ecology*; Flores, "Place"; Naylor and Jones, "Writing Orderly Geographies from Distant Places"; Raby, *American Tropics*.

12 I draw on Abena Dove Osseo-Asare's use of the phrase "open access" in reference to the exchange and appropriation of botanical knowledge in colonial and postcolonial Africa: Osseo-Asare, *Bitter Roots*, 201, 205.

13 Geological insights were also gained from quarrying, the expansion of railways, and the construction of the earliest subways in Western Europe. In addition to its more practical applications, geology in Victorian Europe was considered a "gentleman's science" focused on developing theories of the earth's history. For overviews, see Knell, *The Culture of English Geology*; Porter, *The Making of Geology*; Rudwick, *Earth's Deep History*; Rudnick, *Worlds before Adam*; Winchester, *The Map That Changed the World*.

14 On these developments in geology, see Cohen, "Surveying Nature"; Lucier, "Commercial Interests and Scientific Disinterestedness"; Oldroyd, *Thinking about the Earth*, 115; Westerman, "Geology and World Politics."

15 For an overview, see Yusoff, *A Billion Black Anthropocenes or None*, 83. On Canada, see Braun, "Producing Vertical Territory." On India, see Chakrabarti, "Gondwana and the Politics of Deep Past"; Chakrabarti, *Inscriptions of Nature*.

16 Hubert's approach was eclectic. He studied the region's geological formations in relationship to metrology, physical geography, and what he described as the distribution of different "human races." *Mission scientifique au Dahomey*, 3, exemplifies Hubert's multidisciplinary approach. On his impact on geology in the AOF, see Legoux, "L'Afrique-Occidentale Française avant la Second Guerre mondiale," 10.

17 Fernand Blondel, "La richesse minière inconnue de la France d'outre-mer," *Bulletin de la Société Industrielle de l'Est* (1931): 5–20, quoted in Samson, "Fernand Blondel," 389. In "L'or en Afrique-Occidentale Française," 422, Georges Daumain writes that "it would be truly paradoxical that, in a country like [the] AOF," where the natives export more than two thousand kilograms of gold, "European companies could not achieve fruitful results."

18 Blondel, "Études," 362. See also Blondel, "Le problème minier aux colonies."

19 Gilbert Arnaud, Chef du Services des Mines de l'AOF, "Rapport du chef du services des mines de l'AOF sur sa mission au Soudan en Septembre 1940," Bagana, September 13, 1940, ADMGS. Many of the early recruits were the sons of "white Russians," those who fled post–Revolutionary Russia. This population was

highly represented in institutions of geological training in France. I translate the French word *brousse* as "bush" in English (*wula* in Maninka; *ladde* in Pular) to refer to uncultivated land beyond the bounds of villages.

20 Until 1944, the Service of Mines was administered as a branch of the Department of Public Works, whose budget was primarily allocated to road and bridge construction, not mining and geology.

21 Chermette, "Quelques réflexions sur la vie du géologue en brousse à Dakar," 133.

22 On the frequency of administrative transfers, see Osborn, "Interpreting Colonial Power in French Guinea," 65–66.

23 Coin, "Dakar, capitale de la géologie de l'ouest africain," 151.

24 Marelle, "L'Afrique-Occidentale Française de 1944 à 1960," 33.

25 Obermuller, "Difficultés d'un géologue inexpérimenté débutant en AOF," 127; Robin, "La vie dans un cercle de brousse," 159–61. See also Rostislav Goloubinow, Ingénieur-Géologue, "Rapport de prospection aurifère sur les cours du Lélé Guinée (1934–35)," Lélé-Dindinkoli, Siguiri, January 9, 1935, ADMGS.

26 See, e.g., Alexis Chermette, Géologue en Chef, "Note sur le filon Gobele (Cercle de Kouroussa, Haute Guinée)," Soubako, May 23, 1949, ANG.

27 Oldroyd, *Thinking about the Earth*, 115.

28 Legoux, "L'Afrique-Occidentale Française avant la Second Guerre mondiale," 16fn1.

29 Established as an independent territory in 1919, Haute-Volta was later absorbed into parts of Côte d'Ivoire, Soudan, and Niger in 1932. It was reconstituted along its previous boundaries in 1947 as part of the French Union of France's Fourth Republic.

30 Obermuller, "Difficultés d'un géologue inexpérimenté en AOF," 125–26.

31 Siossat, "Les coutumes des orpailleurs indigènes du Maramandougou," 339.

32 Colonie de la Guinée Française, "Étude des coutumes indigènes," n.d. [after 1945], ANG.

33 Keita, "Autour des placers du Cercle de Siguiri," 17. As reported in Colonie de la Guinée Française, "Étude des coutumes indigènes," "Gold in the form of a white ram rises and splits the earth: this is living gold." Living gold cannot be touched. Dead gold has "lost its soul," its power reduced from sacrifices and prayers.

34 Labouret, "L'or du Lobi." Labouret, one of the AOF's "administrator-ethnographers," conducted research among the Lobi of Haute-Volta/Côte d'Ivoire: Van Hoven, "Representing Social Hierarchy."

35 Labouret, "L'or du Lobi"; Labouret, *Les tribus du rameau Lobi*, 80–83; Schneider, "Extraction et traitement rituelle de l'or," 195.

36 Kiéthéga, *L'or de la Volta noire*, 135, 149.

37 Colonie de la Guinée Française, "Étude des coutumes indigènes."

38 The AOF's administrators also consulted geologists about the "customs" of African miners when crafting new customary mining rights legislation: "Recueil de

documents relatifs au droit coutumier," Colonie de la Guinée Française, Service des Travaux Publics, Conakry, July 11, 1929, ADMGS.

39 Méniaud, *Haut-Sénégal-Niger*, 174. Such positive evaluations of the "rationality" of African thought and practice resonated with the work of French ethnographers in West Africa between the wars: see, e.g., Griaule, *Masques Dogons*.

40 Rostislav Goloubinow, "La Prospection aurifère en Guinée," Dakar, August 9, 1935, ADMGS.

41 The Latin (binominal or scientific) names of tree species are indicated in parentheses: Siossat, "Les coutumes des orpailleurs indigènes du Maramandougou," 338. I could find no cross-referenced data indicating the scientific name for *congouroun*, also spelled *coungoun*.

42 The bark of so, also known as Soh Oigne, was used in fertility rites. See Colonie de la Guinée Française, "Étude des coutumes indigènes." On the importance of so and sounsoun in gold prospecting in Burkina Faso, see Kiéthéga, *L'or de la Volta noire*, 134, 141.

43 On nyama and gold prospecting in nineteenth-century Bambuk, see chapter 2.

44 On the medicinal and ritual uses of the African mahogany in West Africa, see Fortin et al., *Plantes médicinales du sahel*, 175; Malgras, *Arbres et arbustes guérisseurs des savanes maliennes*, 326–27; Pageard, "Plantes à brûler chez les Bambara," 114; Zahan, *La dialectique du verbe chez les Bambara*, 160–61.

45 For example, in Maninka villages in southeastern Senegal, some boys are named *fajala*, "father of the *jala*," and girls are named *bajala*, "mother of the *jala*": author's field notes, Kédougou, Senegal, 2014. See also El Hadji Alpha Diby Souaré, interview with author, Mako, March 22, 2014.

46 Koma could refer to the spirit attached to the komo association or to power objects held by local chapters of the komo in Guinea. See the discussion of komo in chapter 2.

47 Keita, "Autour des placers du Cercle de Siguiri," 17.

48 Sajoh Madi Kamara, interview with author, Linguekoto, March 12, 2014; Mamadou Kamara, interview with author, Kerekonko, February 18, 2014; Cheikou Traoré, interview with author, February 5, 2014.

49 Méniaud, *Haut-Sénégal-Niger*, 190–91. For other accounts of this genre, see Boucard, "Relation de Bambouc," 259; Carrère and Holle, *De la Sénégambie française*, 169; Colonie de la Guinée Française, "Étude des coutumes indigènes"; Raffenel, *Voyage dans l'Afrique occidentale*, 381. See also Aliou Diallo, interview with author, Mamakono, April 14, 2014; Fadiyen Keita, interview with author, Kharakhena, May 29, 2014.

50 Pierre Legoux, Chef-Adjoint, Ingénieur Principal, Service des Mines, à M. Marcel Bardin, Ingenieur des Travaux Public, Service des Mines, letter, July 23, 1939, ADMGS.

51 Goloubinow, "Géologie et ressources en or du nord-est de la Guinée Française"; Goloubinow, "L'or en Guinée Française" and "La prospection et les gisements d'or de demain."

NOTES TO CHAPTER FOUR **241**

52 Goloubinow, "La prospection et les gisements d'or de demain," 6.

53 Goloubinow, "La prospection et les gisements d'or de demain," 5. See also Blondel, "Études," 369.

54 Goloubinow, "Rapport de prospection aurifère sur le cours du Lélé."

55 Goloubinow, "L'or en Guinée Française," 35–36.

56 Mathelin de Papigny, "Note sur les exploitations indigènes du Satadougou," 394; Siossat, "Les coutumes des orpailleurs indigènes du Maramandougou."

57 Eduard Julian, Ingénieur Adjoint, "Rapport sur l'exercice du droit coutumier et l'amelioration des exploitations aurifères indigènes," Conakry, August 21, 1929, ADMGS.

58 Jean Malavoy, Chef du Service des Mines et de la Géologie de l'AOF, "Note sur l'amélioration de l'orpaillage indigène," March 24, 1931, ADMGS.

59 Blondel, "Études," 363–64.

60 Daumain, "L'or en Afrique-Occidentale Française," 409–10; Julian, "Rapport sur l'exercice du droit coutumier et l'amelioration des exploitations aurifères indigènes."

61 Inspecteur Principal des Affaires Administrative Aubert, "Rapport: Sur la situation de commerce de l'or et sur l'exploitation des mines d'or de Siguiri par les indigenes, 22–25, mars, 1934," ADMGS.

62 Eduard Julian, Ingénieur Adjoint, Colonie de la Guinée Française, Service des Mines, "Rapport: Sur le gisement aurifère de Bantabagne," February 22, 1933, ADMGS.

63 Pierre Seyer, Ingénieur, Chef du Service des Mines de l'AOF, "Rapport technique sur l'activité minière en AOF," Dakar, June 20, 1939, ANG.

64 Seyer, "Rapport technique sur l'activité minière en AOF." On Poura, see Kiéthéga, L'or de la Volta noire, 147; Moussa, "L'or des régions de Poura et de Gaoua," 569.

65 Chermette, "Le placer de la Perma," 154–55.

66 For details on the Fatoya controversy, see chapter 3.

67 Maurice Nicklès, Géologue en Tournée, "Observations sur l'or dans le Houré-Kaba et le Fitaba (Cercles de Mamou et de Dabola)," Labé, June 2, 1939, ADMGS. See also Robinson, The Holy War of Umar Tal, 221, 241.

68 Conseil Général du Soudan Français, Première Session Originaire de 1950, Procès-Verbal de la Séance du Samedi, April 1, 1950, BIB/50451, ANOM.

69 "Rapport de M. l'Administrateur Bidiane, 6 septembre 1913," 3 Q 10, ANG.

70 L. Baud, Ingénieur Géologue, "Rapport sur l'activité minière dans le Bassin de la Falémé en 1944," Dakar, August 29, 1944, ADMGS.

71 On the expansion of regional-level data on the AOF's mineral resources in the postwar years, see Marelle, "L'Afrique-Occidentale Française de 1944 à 1960," 86–87. Postwar studies of the AOF's regional Birimian formations include: Bolgarsky, Étude géologique et description pétrographique du Sud-Ouest de la Côte d'Ivoire; Sagatzky, La géologie et les ressources minières de la Haute-Volta meridionale.

72 On the AOF's postwar gold-prospecting strategy, see Arnaud, *Les ressources minières de l'Afrique occidentale.*

73 Alexis Chermette, "L'or filonien dans le Fitaba, Cercle de Dabola (Haute-Guinée)," Mamou, Service de Géologie et de Prospection Minière, June 1956, ADMGS; Paul Jochyms, Ingénieur Principal des Mines de la France d'outre-mer, Conakry, "Note sur les exploitations et gisements aurifères du Fitaba," August 21, 1951, ADMGS.

74 Gilbert Arnaud, Ingénieur Chef, Directeur des Mines de l'AOF, "Rapport sur l'organisation administrative, technique et cóoperative d'orpaillage," Dakar, September 11, 1944, ANG.

75 Arnaud, "Rapport sur l'organisation administrative, technique et cóoperative d'orpaillage."

76 Arnaud, "Rapport sur l'organisation administrative, technique et cóoperative d'orpaillage."

77 André Marelle, Ingénieur Principal au Corps des Mines, Directeur des Mines, "Rapport sur le développement minier de l'AOF," Dakar, December 1948, ADMGS.

78 Marelle, "Rapport sur le développement minier de l'AOF."

79 Robin, "La vie dans un cercle de brousse," 159.

80 I thank Fred Cooper for underscoring this distinction. On the development concept in postwar Africa, see Cooper, *Decolonization and African Society*; Cooper and Randall, *International Development and the Social Sciences.*

81 One of the stated goals of BUMIFOM when it was formed in 1948 was to incorporate more Africans into geological research. By 1958, the organization had given more than thirty-six scholarships to African students to pursue geological training in France: Rocci, "L'oeuvre des géologues français en AOF."

82 Marelle, "Rapport sur le développement minier de l'AOF."

83 Weszkalnys, "Geology, Potentiality, Speculation," 631.

Chapter Five: Mineral Mapping and the Global Cold War

1 El Hadj Mori Tigana, interview by the author, Saraya, May 29, 2014.

2 Senegal's postcolonial Direction des Mines et de la Géologie (DMG) is distinct from the Direction Fédérale des Mines de la Géologie (DFMG), which was a French colonial institution that worked in all of French West Africa.

3 There is a growing scholarship on the scientific and political work of African actors under sustained conditions of economic and material scarcity. See Livingston, *Improvising Medicine*; Mika, *Africanizing Oncology*, esp. introduction, chaps. 3–4; Park et al., "Intellectual and Cultural Work in Times of Austerity"; Grace, *African Motors*, esp. introduction, chaps. 1, 4; Quarshie, "Psychiatry on a Shoestring."

4 Lévi-Strauss, *La pensée sauvage*, 27. Joshua Grace writes of a form of technological bricolage in post-colonial Tanzanian car garages that he calls "unionizing," a

term taken from the name of a car made of 27 different makes and models, itself derived from the common Kiswahili word for "joining": Grace, *African Motors*, 133. On political bricolage by African "intermediaries" in colonial Guinea, see Osborn, "Interpreting Colonial Power in French Guinea."

5   Osseo-Asare, "Scientific Equity," esp. 714. See also Droney, "Ironies of Laboratory Work during Ghana's Second Age of Optimism"; Mika, *Africanizing Oncology*; Tousignant, "Broken Tempos"; Tousignant, *Edges of Exposure*.

6   On the continuity of a developmentalist ethos from the postwar period into the early decades of independence in Senegal, see Diouf, "Senegalese Development"; Kusiak, "'Tubab' Technologies and 'African' Ways of Knowing."

7   Osseo-Asare, *Atomic Junction*.

8   Lachenal, "The Intimate Rules of the French 'Coopération'"; Tousignant, *Edges of Exposure*. On these tensions in psychiatry in postcolonial Senegal, see Kilroy-Marac, *An Impossible Inheritance*, chaps. 1–2.

9   Ageron and Marc, *L'Afrique noire française*; Dozon, *Frères et sujets*; Seck, *Sénégal*.

10 Banks et al., "The African Soviet Modern"; Hecht, *Being Nuclear*; Hecht, *Entangled Geographies*, 6; Ivaska, *Cultured States*; Mavhunga, "A Plundering Tiger with Its Deadly Cubs?"; Osseo-Asare, *Atomic Junction*.

11 Chafer, "Chirac and 'la Françafrique'"; Chafer, *The End of Empire*.

12 Mali and Senegal initially became independent as a conjoined Mali Federation, which disbanded within a year.

13 Keita and Touré were leading politicians of the RDA. Senghor and Mamadou Dia led the Bloc Démocratique du Sénégal, which was renamed the Union Progressive Sénégalaise in 1958.

14 From the 1950s through the 1980s, no fewer than thirty-five out of fifty-three African nation-states proclaimed themselves socialist at one juncture or another. States pursued diverse forms of socialism, ranging from the scientific socialism of Karl Marx to more populist visions of African socialism. For an overview, see Pitcher and Askew. "African Socialisms and Postsocialisms"; and Sun, "Historicizing African Socialisms." On socialism in Francophone West Africa, see McGovern, *A Socialist Peace?*; McGovern, *Unmasking the State*; Schmidt, *The Global Cold War and Decolonization in Guinea*; On the transition to independence in AOF, see Chafer, *The End of Empire*; Person, "French West Africa and Decolonization."

15 Guinea left the French franc zone in 1961. Mali followed in 1962.

16 See Gellar, *Senegal*; Legvold, *Soviet Policy in West Africa*.

17 Land nationalization policies aimed to dismantle the hold of French colonists over large plantations and to dislodge unequal land access facilitated by colonial customary land law. The idea was that making the state the sole owner or trustee of land would enable all citizens to access use rights to land. In 1961, Sékou Touré declared all mining enterprises state property. In 1963, Modibo Keita outlawed private direct investment in Mali's subsoil, while leaving open the possibility for

state cooperation with private foreign companies. Senegal putatively national-ized phosphate mines in 1964. Former colonial and foreign firms continued to play a central role in bauxite (Guinea) and phosphate (Senegal) mining.

18 United Nations General Assembly Resolution 1515 (XV) of December 15, 1960, and United Nations General Assembly Resolution 1803 (XVII) of Decem-ber 14, 1962: Schrijver, *Sovereignty over Natural Resources*, chap 2.

19 See Touré, *L'Afrique en marche*, esp. 489.

20 Author's field notes, Siguiri, Guinea, June–August 2010.

21 Gary-Tounkara, *Migrants soudanais*, 55. See also Diarrah, *Le Mali de Modibo Keita*, 73, 110.

22 See Amin, *Trois expériences africaines de développement*; Diarrah, *Le Mali de Modibo Keita*, 81.

23 Diouf, *Histoire du Sénégal*. On the interplay between French colonialism and Wolof culture, see Diouf, *Le Kajoor au XIXe siècle*.

24 Diouf, *Histoire du Sénégal*.

25 Mady Cissokho was a descendant of Dan Siriman Cissokho, the founder of Sirimana (see chapter 2). On Mady Cissokho, see Filé Sadiakho, interview by the author, Kédougou, June 4, 2014; Salioum Soaré, interview by the author, Kédougou, June 6, 2014.

26 On colonial-era forced labor in the region, see Touré, "Le refus du travail forcé au Sénégal Oriental."

27 The BPS began as the Union des Fils Natifs de Kédougou. In 1956, the Ressor-tissants de la Vallée du Fleuve, a political party based in the Fouta Toro with a strong Pular base, also challenged the BPS.

28 Yousseph Diallo, interview by the author, Kédougou, June 5, 2014. See also Dupuy, *Soldat des Bêtes*, 72–73.

29 Boone, *Merchant Capital and the Roots of State Power in Senegal*, 93–95.

30 Ministère de l'Economie Rurale et de la Coopération, "Opération Kédougou, 29 février–4 mars," Dakar, March 15, 1960, ANS. The colonial-era reference is Commandant le Cercle du Kédougou, Administrateur Adjoint, "Rapport politique annuel, 1943," February 23, 1943, 2G, 44–82, ANS.

31 The department of Kédougou consisted of four arrondissements: Saraya, Ban-dafassi, Salemata, and Fongolimbi.

32 Bocar Sidibé was the first rural animator assigned to the department of Kédou-gou in the 1960s: Bocar Sidibé, interview by the author, Kédougou, March 25, 2014. On animation in Senegal, see Galvan, *The State Must Be Our Master of Fire*, chap. 4.

33 Sékou Touré and Modibo Keita implemented more communist-inspired col-lectivized farming schemes. On Mali's agrarian reforms, see Diarrah, *Le Mali de Modibo Keita*, 107. On Guinea, see Leach and Fairhead, *Misreading the African Landscape*, 252–57.

34 On the events leading up to Dia's imprisonment, see William Mbaye Ousmane, dir., *Président Dia*, DVD, Autoproduction, Paris, 2012; Dia, *Mémoires d'un*

militant du Tiers Monde; Documentation, Cheikh Faty Faye, Premières Journées Culturelles de Kédougou, "Résolution de Commission, No. 1, Kédougou: Histoire et culture," February 13–15, 1992, ANS.

35 Diouf, "Senegalese Development," 299.

36 On Niokolo-Koba National Park, see Dupuy, *Le Niokolo-Koba*; Dupuy, *Soldat des Bêtes*; Ece, "Conserving Nature, Transforming Authority"; Niang, "Développement du tourisme dans la région du Sénégal Oriental"; Roure, *La Haute Gambie et le Parc national du Niokolo-Koba*; Takforian, "Conservation et développement local au Niokolo-Koba." Ibrahima Niang was the first Senegalese governor of Sénégal Oriental.

37 From 1960 to 1966, roughly 40 percent of Senegal's budget came from foreign aid (85 percent from France, followed by the United States, West Germany, the USSR, and Canada): Diouf, "Senegalese Development."

38 Chiron, *Objectif terre*. The BRGM contracted out its laboratory services in Dakar for commercial purposes until it finally handed the building over to Senegal's Department of Mines in the 1980s.

39 Hecht, *Being Nuclear*, describes the case of uranium mining by French firms in former French colonies.

40 On former colonial lifestyles in Dakar, see O'Brien, *White Society in Black Africa*.

41 Rocci, "L'oeuvre des géologues français en AOF." Senghor encouraged French coopérants to leave the university in the 1980s by dramatically reducing their salaries.

42 Many of the first generation of Senegalese geologists to receive doctorates after independence chose to conduct research on Birimian formations. Prominent contributions include Dia, "Caractères et significations des complexes magmatiques et métamorphiques du secteur de Sandikounda-Laminia"; Diallo, "Contribution à l'étude géologique de la série du Dialé (Birimien) dans les Monts Bassaris,"; Dioh, "Étude des roches magmatiques birimiennes de la région de Sonfara-laminia-Médina Foulbé"; Ndiaye, "Étude géologique et métallogénique de la partie septentrionale du granite de Saraya"; Ngom, "Contribution à l'étude de la série birrimienne de Mako dans le secteur aurifère de Sabodala."

43 While employed by the AOF's Service of Mines in 1950 and 1951, Defossez sampled orpaillage shafts in Laminia, Samecouta, and Tomboroncoto, Tinkoto, Mamakono, and Khossanto: Michel Defossez, Ingénieur-Géologue, Directions des Mines de l'AOF, "Rapport géologique sur la Haute Gambie, Sénégal," October 1951, ADMGS. On French gold-prospecting activities in Kédougou through the early 1960s, see Bassot, *Compilation des études et prospection exécutés depuis 1945 sur les terrains anciens du Sénégal Oriental*"; Bassot, *Étude géologique du Sénégal Oriental et de ses confins guinéo-maliens*.

44 United Nations Department of Economic and Social Affairs, "Annex," esp. 69. In 1965, the Special Fund merged with the United Nations Development Programme.

45 Mehos and Moon, "The Uses of Portability"; Selcer, *The Postwar Origins of the Global Environment*.

46 From 1960 to 1965, the UN gave an estimated $13,320,000 to Senegal, which largely went to funding the development of peripheral regions lining the Senegal River.

47 Programme des Nations Unies pour le Développement, "Étude des ressources minières du Sénégal Oriental," DP/SF/UN-/21-Senegal, United Nations, New York, 1971, ADMGS, 2.

48 Not all of the scientists who worked for the BRGM were French citizens.

49 Programme des Nations Unies pour le Développement, "Étude des ressources minières du Sénégal Oriental," 2.

50 In 1981, Dia became the cofounder of the Institut des Sciences de la Terre (IST) at UCAD. Today, IST is among the top institutions for the training of engineers in the geosciences in Francophone West Africa.

51 The camp at Mako was later abandoned in favor of two smaller camps: one at Wassandara along the Falémé (focused on diamonds and gold) and one at Gabou near Bakel (copper and chromite).

52 Legvold, *Soviet Policy in West Africa*.

53 The USSR carried out two additional cooperative missions on Senegalese soil: a 1962 feasibility study for a pump-irrigation project on the Senegal River and a 1967 accord to assist Senegal's industrial tuna industry: Skurnik, *The Foreign Policy of Senegal*.

54 Sy also worked on the UN mission and received a scholarship to attend a year of university in Moscow, where he studied geochemistry with a focus on gold mineralization. Upon his return, Sy continued work with the UN, where he was the assistant to a Soviet geologist. Many Senegalese who pursued technical training with scholarships in the USSR were, on their return to Senegal, locked out of employment with French industries or forced to replicate their studies from the USSR in France to be eligible for employment: Banks et al., "The African Soviet Modern"; and Cheikh Diop, interview by the author, Kédougou, June 2014.

55 Projets de Recherches Minières Sénégalo-Sovietiques, "Rapport final sur les travaux de prospection pour la recherche de l'or filonien et alluvionnaire au Sénégal Oriental en 1971–1973," redigée par L. P. Chtocolov et V. V. Korj, Dakar, 1973.

56 Telli Diallo, interview by the author, Kanoumering, February 9, 2014.

57 Baka Cissokho, interview by the author, Sambaranbugu, April 12, 2014; Fonsa Danfakha, interview by the author, Saraya, June 7, 2014.

58 Toumanie Touré, interview by the author, Mamakono, April 14, 2014.

59 Sembou Danfakha, interview by the author, Saraya, June 7, 2014.

60 Projets de Recherches Minières Sénégalo-Sovietiques, "Rapport final sur les travaux de prospection pour la recherche de l'or filonien et alluvionnaire au Sénégal Oriental en 1971–1973," 145.

61 At this time, Tinkoto had never been a village, only a juura: Giraudon, "Étude d'indice de Plomb et de Molybdène a Tinkoto (Sud-est du Senegal)," rapport présenté par le BRGM, Dakar, 1962, ADMGS, 8.

62 Quoted in Programme des Nations Unies pour le Développement, "Étude des ressources minières du Sénégal Oriental," 187–88. On gold prospecting in the 1950s, see Defossez, "Rapport Géologique sur la Haute Gambie."

63 Mohamadou Sy, Projet du Gouvernement de la Republique du Senegal Aide par les Fonds Special des Nations Unies, "Rapport sur les travaux de prospection pour or exécutés dans le Bassin du Kouloun-Tabaly," Recherches Minières Sénégal Oriental, 1963–65, Dakar, October 1965, ADMGS, 13.

64 Programme des Nations Unies pour le Développement, "Étude des ressources minières du Sénégal Oriental," 19.

65 For commentary on *puits types orpailleurs*, see Jean Gravesteijn, "Mission Oussa-Sud Falémé (Rapport de fin campagne 1961–2)," rapport présenté par le BRGM, Dakar, 1962, ADMGS, 13; Robert Giraudon, "Étude d'indice de Plomb et de Molybdène a Tinkoto," 5.

66 Sembou Danfakha interview.

67 Projets de Recherches Minières Sénégalo-Sovietiques, "Rapport final sur les travaux de prospection pour la recherche de l'or filonien et alluvionnaire au Sénégal Oriental en 1971–1973," 12, see also 3.

68 Sembou Danfakha interview.

69 Toumanie Touré interview.

70 There were exceptions. Reportedly, two men from Kédougou received pensions for their work on the mineral missions.

71 Nations Unies, Projet Fonds Spécial Recherches Minières Sénégal, "Commentaire aux Rapports Mensuels—Mars 1964," Dakar, April 2, 1964, ADMGS.

72 Toumanie Touré interview.

73 Anonymous, interview by the author, Sambaranbugu, June 17, 2014.

74 The term *sudistes* became politicized in Casamance during a low-level civil war and separatist movement in the 1980s and 1990s that criticized the Senegalese state for marginalizing the region.

75 Moussa Tigana, interview by the author, Mamakono, June 6, 2014.

76 On postcolonial states as "gatekeepers" for foreign capital, including licenses for natural resource extraction, see Cooper, *Africa since 1940*, chap. 7.

77 Bonnecase, *La pauvreté au Sahel*; Mann, *From Empires to NGOs in the West African Sahel*, 3-8.

78 de Lestrange et al., "Stratégies de lutte contre la disette au Sénégal Oriental," esp. 46–47.

79 Bana Sidibé, interview by the author, Kanoumering, February 9, 2014. On embodied memories of the droughts in neighboring Mali, see Twagira, *Embodied Engineering*, chap. 5.

80 Cheikhou Traoré, interview by the author, Tinkoto, February 5, 2014; Fanta Madi Cissokho, interview by the author, Bambaraya, March 29, 2014.

81 An example includes the International Conference on the Future of Small-scale Mining held in Jurica, Mexico, in 1978: Gavin Hilson, personal communication with the author, 2015.

82 d'Avignon, "Primitive Techniques."

83 United Nations, *Small-scale Mining in Developing Countries*.

84 Berger, "The Importance of Small-scale Mining."

85 United Nations, *Small-scale Mining in the Developing Countries*, 80–85.

86 Projets de Recherches Minières Sénégalo-Sovietiques, "Rapport final sur les travaux de prospection pour la recherche de l'or filonien et alluvionnaire au Sénégal Oriental en 1971–1973."

87 Sy, "Rapport sur les travaux de prospection pour or executés dans le Bassin du Kouloun-Tabaly," 12.

88 Sy, "Rapport sur les travaux de prospection pour or executés dans le Bassin du Kouloun-Tabaly," 14.

89 République du Sénégal, Ministère du Développement, Industriel et de l'Environnement, Direction des Mines et de la Géologie, Matar Seck, Géologue à la Direction des Mines et de la Géologie, "Rapport de fin de mission 'Orpaillage' au Sénégal-Oriental," March 25, 1977, ADMGS.

90 Moussa Dieng, Directeur des Mines et de la Géologie, "Rapport de presentation du Project Orpaillage dans les secteurs de Moura, Wassangara, Moussala et Lingue, department de Kédougou," January 21, 1985, ADMGS.

91 Author's field notes, 2014.

92 Moussa Tigana interview.

Chapter Six: A West African Language of Subterranean Rights

1 Mahamadou L. Barro, "La déclaration du Président Macky Sall après sa visite a Sabodala (Kedougou)," *Sudestinfo.com*, April 17, 2014, accessed on April 17, 2016. Sall won Senegal's presidential campaign in April 2012 and was reelected during first-round voting in the February 2019 presidential election.

2 Soly Bourama Debo, "Les orpailleurs de Kédougou voteront sanction après la fermature des sites," *Radiodiffusion Télévision Sénégalaise*, May 18, 2014; "Les jeunes au coeur des DAC," *Radiodiffusion Télévision Sénégalaise*, November 10, 2014.

3 "Organisation des couloirs d'orpaillage traditionnel dans la région de Kédougou, *Radiodiffusion Télévision Sénégalaise*, June 2, 2014.

4 République du Sénégal, Ministère de l'Énergie et des Mines, "Arrête portant organisation de l'activité d'orpaillage," Dakar, June 14, 2013.

5 Alioune Diop, interview by the author, Kédougou, July 6, 2014.

6 Author's field notes, 2014. The "hunger season" is a two- to three-month period between July and September in Kédougou when grain stocks from the previous year are depleted but new crops have not yet matured.

7 Mann, *Native Sons*, 4. For related approaches to "political language" in African history, see Feierman, *Peasant Intellectuals*; Glassman, *Feasts and Riots*. My use

of "a," rather than "the," political language aims to capture the discursive terrain I encountered at a particular moment in time: during my research in 2013–14 and 2017.

8 Kirsch, *Mining Capitalism*, chap. 1, surveys these developments globally.

9 Many anti-mining movements in Latin America and Australasia center on environmental concerns. See Bebbington and Bury, "Political Ecologies of the Subsoil"; Fultz, "Economies of Representation"; Li, *Unearthing Conflict*. On indigenous land politics and mining protests, see de la Cadena, "Indigenous Cosmopolitics in the Andes"; Kirsch, "Indigenous Movements and the Risks of Counterglobalization"; Kirsch, *Reverse Anthropology*; Powell, *Landscapes of Power*. On environmental impact assessments, see Li, "Documenting Accountability."

10 Neege Traoré, interview by the author, Duuta, April 10, 2014.

11 Bize, "The Right to the Remainder," 474. I thank Kevin Donovan for pointing out synergies in our work.

12 Coyle, *Fires of Gold*, discusses political organizing among *galamsey* in Ghana.

13 Some orpailleurs belong to registered economic interest groups (*groupements d'interet economique* [GIE]). In the mid-2000s, the Programme d'Appui au Secteur Minier (PASMI), funded by the European Union, helped orpailleurs register as GIEs: PASMI, "Présentation des expériences pilotes. Objectifs et résultats," Dakar, Senegal, 2009. See also Mamadou Dramé, interview by the author, Tomboroncoto, March 5, 2014.

14 The corporate marketing of West Africa's Birimian Greenstone Belt parallels what Tom Özden-Schilling, "Theorizing the Contemporary," describes for the promotion of the "Rocky Mountain Rare Metal Belt" in North America as an underexplored geological region that was "only now being discovered" but whose "promise was there all along."

15 On Senegal's mining boom, see Diallo, "Mine d'or et développement durable"; Diallo, "Mines et dynamiques spatiales dans le Sud-est du Sénégal"; Mbodj, "Boom aurifère à l'est du Sénégal, l'ouest du Mali et au nord-est de la Guinée."

16 By 1997, Senegal had issued twenty-eight exploration permits for gold to twenty-four companies: "La ruée vers l'est," *Le Soleil*, April 8, 1997. On developments in Guinea and Mali, see Mbodj, "Boom aurifère et dynamiques économiques entre Sénégal, Mali et Guinée."

17 See d'Avignon, "Shelf Projects," and chapters 4 and 5 in this volume.

18 Sembou Danfakha, interview by the author, Saraya, June 7, 2014.

19 Mbodj, "La crise trentenaire de l'économie arachidière."

20 Sheldon, *Senegal*, esp. 55–83, surveys the effects of SAPs on Senegal's economy.

21 Campbell, *Modes of Governance and Revenue Flows in African Mining*; World Bank, *Strategy for African Mining*, esp. 10.

22 République du Sénégal, "Code minier du Sénégal, loi n 88-06 du 26 août 1988," Dakar, 1988.

23 Senegal created two state companies to promote partnerships for shelf projects on the Birimian: the Société Minière de Sabodala (SMS) and the Société des Mines de Fer du Sénégal Oriental (MIFERSO).

24 Critics accused the state of sabotaging Eeximcor to market the mining of Sabodala to a capital-rich foreign partner: Abdou Latif Coulibaly, "La Nébuleuse autour du Sabodala," *La Gazette*, 2003. On the state's relaunch of Senegal's gold sector in the late 1990s, see Mintech International, "Schème directeur sur le secteur minier du Sénégal pour la période 2001–2006," Ministère des Mines de l'Industrie et de l'Artisanat, Republique du Senegal, Dakar, September 2001; "L'or de Sabodala," *Le Soleil*, July 7, 1993.

25 République du Sénégal, "Code minier du Sénégal, loi n 2003-36 du 24 novembre 2003," Dakar, 2003; "Mines, plus d'attrait pour les investisseurs," *Le Soleil*, March 23, 2005. Mineral Deposits Limited began exploration drilling in 2005 and received permitting rights for exploitation in 2006. In 2009, MDL sold its shares to Teranga Gold.

26 Negotiations between the Senegalese state and Arcelor Mittal later fell apart.

27 Sall received his degree from the Institut des Sciences de la Terre at the Université de Cheikh Anta Diop in 1988.

28 Senegal's Mining Codes of 1988 and 2003 included a provision for artisanal mining (*exploitation artisanale*) permits, but the capital requirements were prohibitive for rural citizens: Title 5, "Exploitation Artisanale et Petite Mine," arts. 33–44, République du Sénégal, "Code minier du Sénégal, loi n 2003-36 du 24 novembre 2003."

29 République du Sénégal, "Code minier du Sénégal, loi n 2016-32 du 8 novembre 2016," Dakar, 2016.

30 Moussa Tigana, interview by the author, Mamakono, April 15, 2014. See also Juma Demba Cissokho, interview by the author, Sambaranbugu, May 27, 2014; Toumanie Touré, interview by the author, Mamakono, April 16, 2014. Some emphasized the discovery of lode ore in Golouma in the 1980s; others, in the 1940s. It seems likely that lode ore was mined intermittently in Golouma at different junctures over the past century, and perhaps far earlier.

31 République du Sénégal, "Code minier du Sénégal, loi n 2016-32 du 8 novembre 2016."

32 République du Sénégal, "Code minier du Sénégal, loi n 2016-32 du 8 novembre 2016."

33 For example, a technical report prepared by a consultancy for Teranga Gold in 2017 says that the "topographic surface" of the Gora deposit, now excavated by Teranga Gold, was "generated from surveyed drillhole collars and artisanal mined workings in 2012": Ling et al., "Technical Report on the Sabodala Project, Sénégal, West Africa," 14–11. Bassari Resources comments on its website (https://www.bassariresources.com/permits.html) that "artisanal activity within the Makabingui Gold Project area south of the existing resource has identified potential for multiple new areas of mineralization."

34 Author's field notes, 2014.

35 Teranga's acquisition of the Oromin Joint Venture Group in 2013 expanded the Sabodala Mining License to 291.2 square kilometers. Endeavor Mining acquired Teranga in 2021.

36 Ling et al., "Technical Report on the Sabodala Project, Sénégal, West Africa," 6-1.

37 Resource definition requirements are designed to protect investors. They were tightened after the "Bre-X" scandal of the mid 1990s, when a junior exploration company made false claims about massive gold discoveries in Indonesia: Tsing, "Inside the Economy of Appearances."

38 "Mineral resources" (which include mineral reserves) refers to the total known amount of a given material, regardless of mining costs. Widely used classification schemes include the Canadian Institute of Mining, Metallurgy, and Petroleum Classification; the Australian Joint Ore Reserves Committee Code; and the South African Code for the Reporting of Mineral Resources and Mineral Reserves.

39 My analysis of the competing notions of property promoted by mining companies and orpailleurs draws on Kirsch, "Property Effects," 147–48. As Kirsch points out, mining concessions share features with patents for scientific discoveries that often willfully ignore the preexisting and diffuse social networks of scientists, assistants, and non-institutionalized experts who contributed to discovery. On these issues for scientific discovery in Africa, see Osseo-Asare, *Bitter Roots*; Tilley, *Africa as a Living Laboratory*.

40 Mahamadi Cissokho, interview by the author, Sambaranbugu, March 13, 2014.

41 Fadiyen Keita, interview by the author, Kharakhenna, May 29, 2014. See also Neege Traoré interview.

42 Hecht, "Interscalar Vehicles for an African Anthropocene," esp. 111. On scale as the relational and emergent outcome of linguistic action, see Carr and Lempert, "Introduction."

43 Aliou Diallo, interview by the author, Mamakono, April 14, 2014. See also Moussa Cissokho, interview by the author, Tomboroncoto, March 10, 2014; Fonsa Danfakha, interview by the author, Saraya, June 7, 2014.

44 Bambo Cissokho, interview by the author, Tinkoto, February 11, 2014.

45 Bassari Resources to Minister of the Interior, "Exploitation illegal des gisements aurifères," letter, 2012. Alex MacKenzie kindly allowed me to review some printed copies of letters and emails written by Bassari Resources to different state agencies.

46 Bassari Resources to Minister of Mines, letter, January 14, 2013.

47 Advances in cyanide heap-leaching, in particular, have meant that mining companies can extract greater concentrations of gold from surface deposits than was feasible even fifteen to twenty years ago. Today, most companies calculate the mining of gold located in the first fifteen meters of excavation as part of their income stream.

48 Habib Léon Ndiaye, interview by the author, Kédougou, March 28, 2014. See also Lamine Sy, interview by author, Kédougou, March 18, 2014.

49 Author's field notes, 2014.

50 Bassari Resources to Minister of the Interior, "Exploitation illegal des gisements aurifères."

51 Bassari Resources to Ousmane Cisse, Director of Mines and Geology, "Re: Illegal Mining Status report," Dakar, August 7, 2012.

52 Koka Boukari Kamara, interview by the author, Kerekonko, February 16, 2014.

53 This terminology was used by Coumbouna Camara, interview by the author, Tinkoto, February 7, 2014; Baka Cissokho, interview by the author, Sambaranbugu, April 12, 2014; Bourahima Cissokho, interview by the author, Sambaranbugu, April 13, 2014; Juma Demba Cissokho, interview by the author, Sambaranbugu, May 27, 2014; Sajoh Madi Kamara, interview by the author, Linguekoto, March 12, 2014.

54 Moussa Tigana, interview by the author, Mamakono, April 15, 2014.

55 Recording in the author's possession.

56 Scott, *The Moral Economy of the Peasant*, 3–7; Thompson, *The Making of the English Working Class*.

57 As an alternative to the more static notion of a subsistence "ethic" upheld by some and not others, Kristin Philips attends to how "socially experienced and materially conditioned ideas about morality drive human experience and action" in rural Tanzania: Philips, *An Ethnography of Hunger*, 10. High, *Fear and Fortune*, 3, also describes the lack of a collective "moral economy" on mining frontiers with large migrant populations.

58 Mahamadi Cissokho interview.

59 Lamine Touré and Sadou Mody Kaba, interview by the author, Kédougou, February 15, 2014.

60 Moussa Cissokho interview.

61 A copy of the letter is in the author's possession.

62 On the events of 2008, see Khassoum Diallo, "Après Kédougou, à qui le tour?" *Le Quotidien*, December 12, 2009; Greig, "Le Sénégal Oriental à l'aube du développement minier"; Najib Sagna and Soly B. Dabo, "Sénégal: Après Guédiawaye, des émeutes éclatent a Kédougou!" *Walfadjiri*, December 24, 2008; USAID, *Democracy, Human Rights and Governance*; Williams, "The Gold Standard of Governance."

63 Fredericks, "The Old Man Is Dead"; Fredericks and Diouf, *Les arts de la citoyenneté au Sénégal*.

64 In 2007, Kédougou was still a department of Tambacounda, overseen by a prefect, and Saraya was an arrondissement within the department, overseen by a subprefect. When Kédougou became a region in 2008, Saraya became a department of Kédougou.

65 Ashley Fent's research on the now stalled Niafarang zircon mining sands project in Casamance reveals similar tensions to those I encountered in

NOTES TO CHAPTER SIX 253

Kédougou. Casamance lies to the west of Kédougou, although there is no road connecting the two regions due to the Niokolo-Koba National Park. Casamançais activists saw the Niafarang project as part of the state's historical exploitation of the region's unique natural resources to the benefit of bureaucrats and merchants based in Dakar: Fent, "Governing Alongside," 22.

66 On the forestry service in eastern Senegal, see Ece, "Conserving Nature, Transforming Authority"; Ribot, "Authority over Forests."

67 Coulibaly, "La Nébuleuse autour du Sabodala" and "Que cache t-on aux journalistes ayant effectué le déplacement ce Samedi sur Sabodala?" *Sud Quotidien*, July 9, 2007; Boubacar Dembo Tamba, "Kédougou: A une an de la fin du programme social minier: L'association Kédougou action s'interroge," *Quotidien*, July 14, 2012.

68 A. Seck, "Or de Sabodala, les populations menacent de mettre le feu aux installations des exploitants," *Le Populaire*, March 6, 2007; "24 villages se rebellent contre les sociétés aurifères à Kédougou, November 27, 2007" and "Rébellion contre les compagnies aurifères de Kédougou," November 30, 2007, both in *Sud Quotidien*.

69 Cheikh Tidiane Sy, then Senegal's minister of the interior, initially accused mercenaries from Guinea, Mali, Gambia, and even Ghana of inciting the riot in Kédougou. He later rescinded these remarks.

70 In January 2009, while I was working in Belgium, I conducted interviews with some of these activists in France and Spain: Daouda Djiguiba, interview by the author, Granollers, Spain, February 2009; Younkoun Kamara, interview by the author, Granollers, Spain, February 2009; Cheikhou Saouré, interview by the author, Paris, January 2009.

71 On the role of Senegal's diaspora in political organizing and development projects in Senegal, see Gueye, "The Colony Strikes Back"; Kane, "Senegal's Village Diaspora and the People Left Behind." The gold-mining boom on the Kédougou-Kéniéba Inlier forged new activist alliances among Malian and Senegalese immigrants in France: d'Avignon, "Theorizing the Contemporary"; Dell, "Undermining the 'Local.'"

72 There are close parallels to what the anthropologist Kristin Philips describes for the case of Tanzania, where the postcolonial state criminalized regional political affiliations and appeals to ethnoregional membership. In this context, Philips describes the emergence of a "subsistence citizenship" as a "particular form of political engagement, born in the context of widening wealth disparities" whereby poor farmers appeal to the Tanzanian state for resource distribution: Philips, *An Ethnography of Hunger*, 4–5.

73 Tamba, "Kédougou." See also "Evènements tragiques de Kédougou: Wade accorde grâce présidentielle et amnistie aux 19 personnes condamnées," *Nouvelle Horizon*, March 17, 2009.

74 Laurent Correau, "Émeutes de Kédougou: le Président Wade gracie 19 condamnés," *Radio France International*, March 18, 2009, accessed October 18, 2020, http://www1.rfi.fr/actufr/articles/111/article_79353.asp.

75 Amnesty International, *Mining and Human Rights in Senegal*; Herman Ulrich Ngoulou, "Sénégal: Emeutes de Kédougou—Amnesty contre 'les violations des droits humans,'" *Le Soleil*, December 30, 2008.

76 Aliou Monékhata, interview by the author, Kédougou, April 22, 2014, and June 23, 2014.

77 An audio recording of this broadcast is in the author's possession. See also Barro, "La déclaration du Président Macky Sall."

78 République du Sénégal, "Code minier du Sénégal, loi n 2016-32 du 8 novembre 2016." Several villages were relocated in the mid-2000s to accommodate the Sabodala mine: Amnesty International, *Mining and Human Rights in Senegal*.

Chapter Seven: Race, Islam, and Ethnicity in the Pits

1 Doucouré, *Des pierres dans les mortiers et non du maïs!*, 83–85, discusses rumors of sacrifice on Kédougou's goldfields.

2 High, "Polluted Money, Polluted Wealth" and *Fear and Fortune*, 2.

3 Clark, "Gold, Sex, and Pollution," 744.

4 Luning, "Gold, Cosmology, and Social Change in Burkina Faso," 325–29; Werthmann, "Cowries, Gold and 'Bitter Money.'" On Kenya, see Shipton, *Bitter Money*, 37.

5 D'Angelo, "Who Owns the Diamonds?" 277–88; De Boeck, "Domesticating Diamonds and Dollars," 786–87. Andrew Walsh makes similar observations for informal sapphire mining in Madagascar in "'Hot Money' and Daring Consumption in a Northern Malagasy Sapphire-Mining Town."

6 See also Niang, *Dans les mines d'or du Sénégal Oriental*, 46.

7 Fioratta, "States of Insecurity," describes concepts of clean money among Muslim Pular-speakers in the Fouta Djallon. On hardship money in Sierra Leone, see Bledsoe, "No Success without Struggle."

8 The italicized words here are in Maninka, unless noted otherwise.

9 Recent examples include Comaroff and Comaroff, "Millennial Capitalism," 3–9; Comaroff and Comaroff, "Occult Economies"; McIntosh, *The Edge of Islam*, 116; Meiu, *Ethno-erotic Economies*, 158; Smith, *Bewitching Development*, 105, 163. This scholarship builds upon a long-standing concern in Africanist anthropology with the relationship between capitalism and local forms of value: see Guyer, *Money Matters*; Hutchinson, *Nuer Dilemmas*, 108, 110, 115–16; Shipton, *Bitter Money*; Stoller, *Money Has No Smell*.

10 On my use of the term "ethnolinguistic group," see the introduction.

11 Fanta Madi Cissokho, interview by the author, Bambaraya, March 29, 2014.

12 Gelman, "Essentialism," 283.

13 I draw inspiration from the concept of an ethnolinguistic (and temporal) spectrum between Islam and "traditionalism" from Janet McIntosh's work on the Swahili coast: McIntosh, *The Edge of Islam*. In *A History of Race in Muslim West Africa*, Bruce Hall argues that the perceived proximity or distance of dif-

ferent ethnolinguistic groups to Islam was central to processes of racialization on the Sahel centuries prior to colonialism.

14 Appiah, *In My Father's House*, 13. See also Glassman, "Slower than a Massacre," 727.

15 Sweet, *The Poetics of Relationality*, 58–59, discusses the recent formalization of land claims in Kédougou. Most scholarship on land titling in West Africa focuses on the smallholder agricultural sector: see Boone, *Property and Political Order in Africa*; Lentz, *Land, Mobility, and Belonging in West Africa*.

16 For overviews, see Comaroff and Comaroff, *Ethnicity, Inc.*; Comaroff and Comaroff, *The Politics of Custom*. On the growing exclusion of "immigrants" from land in West Africa, see Berry, "Struggles over Land and Authority in Africa"; Gary-Tounkara, *Migrants soudanais*; McGovern, *Unmasking the State*; Geschiere, *The Perils of Belonging*.

17 Much of the literature on mining in South Africa examines these themes. Examples include Crush et al., *South Africa's Labor Empire*; Gordon, *Mines, Masters, and Migrants*; Harries, *Work, Culture, and Identity*; Moodie and Ndatshe, *Going for Gold*; Van Onselen, *Chibaro*; Wolpe, *Race, Class, and the Apartheid State*. On racial segregation on American oil rigs and residential enclaves in Equatorial Guinea, see Appel, *The Licit Life of Capital*.

18 Guy and Thabane's "Technology, Ethnicity, and Ideology" inspires my approach to the relationship between race and skill.

19 *Tenda* is a Pular term that translates roughly as "nonbeliever." Pulars applied it to non-Muslim inhabitants of the northern foothills of the Fouta Djallon. Today, this term is considered derogatory as an ethnic label, but linguists have retained it to refer to speakers of Tenda languages of the Atlantic family of Niger-Congo, including o-niyan (spoken by Beliyan-Bassari) and ménik (spoken by Bedik). On the term *Tenda*, see République du Sénégal, *Pays Bassari*, 58. In the 1960s, the Musée de l'Homme in Paris sponsored a multiyear anthropological mission in Kédougou focused on the language and culture of Tenda-speakers. See Delacour, "Les Tenda (Konigagui, Bassari, Badyaranké) de la Guinée Française"; de Lestrange, *Les Coniagui et les Bassari*; de Lestrange, "La piste Etyolo-Seguekho"; Ferry, "Pour une histoire des Bedik"; Gessain, *Actes du 2ème Colloque de Kédougou*; Gessain, *Les migrations des Coniagui et Bassari*; Gessain, "Introduction à l'étude du Sénégal Oriental"; Gomila and Ferry, "Notes sur l'ethnographie des Bedik"; Lalouel and Langaney, "Bedik and Niokholonko of Senegal."

20 Many Beliyan-Bassari claim their ancestors settled in Kédougou while accompanying the sixteenth-century Pular warrior Koly Tenguella on his pilgrimage to the Fouta Djallon: Aubert, "Legendes historiques et traditions orales receuillies en Haute-Gambie," 386. Chataigner, "Les populations du Cercle de Kédougou," and Gessain, *Les migrations des Coniagui et Bassari*, date Beliyan-Bassari settlement in Kédougou to the late first millennium CE.

21 This is the theory of Kroot and Gokee, "Histories and Material Manifestations of Slavery in the Upper Gambia River Region;" Gokee et al., "Le paysage historique de la Haute-Gambie."

22 On the Jalluonke, see Saidou Mohamed N'Daou, *Sangalan Oral Traditions*.

23 On Maninka settlement in Kédougou, see Aubert, "Legendes historiques et traditions orales recueillies en Haute-Gambie"; Chataigner, "Les populations du Cercle de Kédougou," 90–91, 100–101; Gérard, *Contes du pays malinké*.

24 Aubert, "Légendes historiques et traditions orales receuillies en Haute-Gambie"; Gessain, "Introduction à l'étude du Sénégal Oriental"; Roure, *La Haute Gambie et le Parc national du Niokolo-Koba*.

25 On the legacies of slavery among Pular-speakers in twentieth- and twenty-first-century Fouta Djallon, see Derman, *Serfs, Peasants, and Socialists*; Furth, "Marrying the Forbidden Other."

26 On slavery and the politics of naming in West Africa, see Mann, "What's in an Alias?"; Ware, *The Walking Qur'an*, 172f36.

27 Joseph Hellweg, *Hunting the Ethical State*, describes the shifting politics and practices of animal sacrifices among Jula-speaking hunters in Côte d'Ivoire.

28 Author's field notes, 2014.

29 Bambo Cissokho, interview by the author, Tinkoto, February 11, 2014.

30 Author's field notes, 2014.

31 Torodo Diallo, interview by the author, Kanoumering, February 9, 2014.

32 On orpaillage in Bantaco, see Cartelli, "A Snake in the Hole"; Doucouré, *Des pierres dans les mortiers et non du maïs!*

33 Oumar Sidibé, interview by the author, Kanoumering, February 10, 2014.

34 Bana Sidibé, interview by the author, Kanoumering, February 9, 2014.

35 Ousmane Diallo, interview by the author, Kanoumering, February 10, 2014.

36 Thierno Sidi Bâ, interview by the author, Kédougou, January 27, 2014.

37 Author's field notes, 2014.

38 The Senegalese state first introduced cotton cultivation to southeastern Senegal in the 1960s as a regional development program: see Hardin, "Developing the Periphery." The timeline of Jakhanke migration to France aligns with that of Soninke-speakers from the Senegal Valley: Manchuelle, *Willing Migrants*; Cheikhou Saouré, interviews by the author, Paris, January 2009, April 2013.

39 Kemokho Dansakho, interview by the author, Samecouta, March 6, 2014.

40 Author's field notes, 2014.

41 El Hadj Kemokho Touré, interview by the author, Samecouta, March 5, 2014.

42 Mamadou Diakhité, interview by the author, Samecouta, June 4, 2014.

43 Author's field notes, 2014.

44 Sajoh Madi Kamara, interview by the author, Linguekoto, March 12, 2014. See also Ibrahima Tounkara, interview by the author, Tambamounia, March 13, 2014; Bambo Cissokho interview.

45 Author's field notes, 2014.

46 In much of West Africa, white is associated both with the spirit world and with Arab or European origins. At times, the two have overlapped with the emergence of white spirits with foreign tastes or decorum: see Shaw, *Memories of*

the Slave Trade, 96, 106. Andrew Apter writes about the emergence of "white" gods and spirits, such as Nana Tabir in coastal Ghana, as a window into the Afro-European encounters associated with the rise of the Atlantic economy: "History in the Dungeon," 24, 32, 53.

47 Toumanie Keita, interview by the author, Mako, February 23, 2014.

48 Author's field notes, 2013–14.

49 Yonko Camara, interview by the author, Tinkoto, January 18, 2014.

50 Soriba Keita, interview by the author, Tinkoto, February 4, 2014.

51 Koumba Keita, interview by the author, Tinkoto, March 27, 2014.

52 Gassimou Cissokho, interview by the author, Tinkoto, January 24, 2014; Sidi Gueye, interview by the author, Tinkoto, January 16, 2014.

53 Carrère and Holle, *De la Sénégambie française*, 172.

54 Arcin, *La Guinée française*, 415–16.

Conclusion

1 In 2020, as the value of the US dollar fell, the gold price rose by more than 34 percent as panicked investors sought to secure their money in the metal that backs many of the world's currencies: Rupert Neate, "After COVID-19, Just How High Will Prices Go in the 2020 Gold Rush?" *The Guardian*, August 5, 2020, accessed October 15, 2020, https://www.theguardian.com/business/2020/aug/05/after-covid-19-just-how-high-will-prices-go-in-the-2020-gold-rush.

2 d'Avignon, "Minerals."

3 See, e.g., World Bank, *Mining Together*. For a critique of policies of cohabitation between artisanal and large-scale miners, see Hilson et al., "Large and Artisanal Scale Mine Development."

4 Green, *A Fistful of Shells*, esp. introduction.

5 Livingston, *Self-Devouring Growth*, explores similar questions in Botswana.

6 Filé Keita, interview by the author, Tinkoto, February 11, 2014.

BIBLIOGRAPHY

Archives

ADMGS Archives de la Direction des Mines et de la Géologie du Sénégal, Dakar
ANG Archives Nationales de la Guinée, Conakry, Guinea
ANOM Archives Nationales d'Outre-Mer, Aix-en-Provence, France
ANS Archives Nationales du Sénégal, Dakar

Interviews

Mariama Bâ, Kédougou, February 15, 2014
Thierno Sidi Bâ, Kédougou, January 27, 2014
Coumbouna Camara, Tinkoto, January 20, 2014, and February 7, 2014
Sajoh Madi Camara, Linguekoto, March 12, 2014
Yonko Camara, Tinkoto, January 18, 2014
Baka Cissokho, Sambaranbugu, April 12, 2014
Bambo Cissokho, Tinkoto, February 11, 2014
Bourahima Cissokho, Sambaranbugu, April 13, 2014
Fanta Madi Cissokho, Bambaraya, March 29, 2014
Gassimou Cissokho, Tinkoto, January 24, 2014
Juma Demba Cissokho, Sambaranbugu, May 27, 2014
Mahamadi Cissokho, Sambaranbugu, April 13, 2014
Moussa Cissokho, Tomboroncoto, March 10, 2014
Sega Cissokho, Tinkoto, January 22, 2014
Tenimbo Cissokho, Tambanoumouya, March 13, 2014
Tumbi Cheikhou Cissokho, Mamakono, March 31, 2014
Fonsa Danfakha, Saraya, June 7, 2014
Mamadou Danfakha, Kerekonko, February 18, 2014
Sembou Danfakha, Saraya, June 7, 2014
Kemokho Dansakho, Samecouta, March 6, 2014
Mamadou Diakhité, Samecouta, June 4, 2014
Aliou Diallo, Mamakono, April 14, 2014

Idi Diallo, Tinkoto, January 16, 2014

Ousmane Diallo, Kanoumering, February 10, 2014

Telli Diallo, Kanoumering, February 9, 2014

Torodo Diallo, Kanoumering, February 9, 2014

Yousseph Diallo, Kédougou, June 5, 2014

Alioune Diop, Kédougou, July 6, 2014

Cheikh Diop, Kédougou, June 2014

Daouda Djiguiba, Granollers, Spain, February 2009

Mamadou Dramé, Tomboroncoto, March 5, 2014

Sidi Gueye, Tinkoto, January 16, 2014

Koka Boukari Kamara, Kerekonko, February 16, 2014

Mamadou Kamara, Kerekonko, February 18, 2014

Sajoh Madi Kamara, Linguekoto, March 12, 2014

Younkoun Kamara, Granollers, Spain, February 2009

Bambo Keita, Tomboroncoto, March 3, 2014

Coumba Keita, Kerekonko, February 18, 2014

Fadiyen Keita, Kharakhena, May 29, 2014

Filé Keita, Tinkoto, February 11, 2014

Koumba Keita, Tenkoto, March 27, 2014

Makhan Keita, Kanoumering, February 10, 2014

Moussa Keita, Mako, March 20, 2014

Niamendi Keita, Mako, February 24, 2014

Soriba Keita, Tinkoto, February 4, 2014

Toumanie Keita, Mako, February 23, 2014

Aliou Monékhata, Kédougou, April 22, 2014, and June 23, 2014

Habib Léon Ndiaye, Kédougou, March 28, 2014

Filé Sadiakho, Kédougou, June 4, 2014

Mady Sadiakho, Baraboye, June 15, 2014

Ramatou Sadiakho, Kerekonko, February 18, 2014

Mamadou Sagna, Mamakono, March 30, 2014

Abdou Sangare, Tinkoto, February 8, 2014

Cheikhou Saouré, Paris, January 2009 and April 2013

Bana Sidibé, Kanoumering, February 9, 2014

Bocar Sidibé, Kédougou, March 25, 2014

Oumar Sidibé, Kanoumering, February 10, 2014

Salioum Soaré, Kédougou, June 6, 2014

El Hadji Alpha Diby Souaré, Mako, March 22, 2014

Hamidou Sow, Dakar, July 21, 2017

Lamine Sy, Kédougou, March 18, 2014

Moussa Tigana, Mamakono, April 15, 2014, and June 6, 2014

El Hadj Mori Tigana, Saraya, May 29, 2014

Ibrahima Tounkara, Tambanoumoya, March 13, 2014

El Hadj Kemokho Touré, Samecouta, March 5, 2014

Lamine Touré and Sadou Mody Kaba, Kédougou, February 15, 2014

Toumanie Touré, Mamakono, April 16, 2014

Yaya Touré, Tinkoto, January 24, 2014
Cheikhou Traoré, Tinkoto, February 5, 2014
Neege Traoré, Duuta, April 10, 2014

References

Adas, Michael. *Machines as the Measure of Men: Science, Technology and Ideologies of Western Dominance*. Ithaca, NY: Cornell University Press, 1989.

Adunbi, Omolade. *Oil Wealth and Insurgency in Nigeria*. Bloomington: Indiana University Press, 2015.

Africa Progress Panel. *Equity in Extractives: Stewarding Africa's Natural Resources for All*. Geneva: Africa Progress Report, 2013.

Ageron, Charles-Robert, and Michel Marc, eds. *L'Afrique noire française: L'heure des indépendances*. Paris: Centre National de la Recherche Scientifique, 2015.

Allman, Jean Marie, and John Parker. *Tongnaab: The History of a West African God*. Bloomington: Indiana University Press, 2005.

Allman, Jean Marie, and Victoria B. Tashjian. *I Will Not Eat Stone: A Women's History of Colonial Asante*. Portsmouth, NH: Heinemann, 2000.

Altschul, Jeffrey H., Ibrahima Thiaw, and Gerald A. Wait. *The Slave Who Would Be King: Oral Tradition and Archeology of the Recent Past in the Upper Senegal River Basin*. Oxford: Oxford Archaeopress, 2016.

Alvarez, Yves Bertran, Baptiste Coué, and Patrick Schein. "Supply Chains of Artisanal Gold in West Africa: A Study of the Supply Chain of Two Gold-producing Regions in Burkina Faso and Senegal." Alliance for Responsible Mining, October 2016. https://www.responsiblemines.org/wp-content/uploads/2018/04/Publication-supply-chains-artisanal-gold-west-africa_-ENGL_-baja.pdf.

Amin, Samir. *Trois expériences africaines de développement: Le Mali, La Guinée et la Ghana*. Paris: PUF, 1965.

Amnesty International. *Mining and Human Rights in Senegal: Closing the Gaps in Protection*. London: Amnesty International, 2014. Accessed December 22, 2021. https://www.amnesty.org/en/documents/afr49/002/2014/en.

Amnesty International. *"This Is What We Die For": Human Rights Abuses in the Democratic Republic of Congo Power the Global Trade in Cobalt*. London: Amnesty International, 2016. Accessed December 22, 2021. https://www.amnesty.org/en/wp-content/uploads/2021/05/AFR6231832016ENGLISH.pdf.

Amrith, Sunil. *Unruly Waters: How Rains, Rivers, Coasts, and Seas Have Shaped Asia's History*. New York: Basic, 2018.

Appel, Hannah. *The Licit Life of Capitalism: US Oil in Equatorial Guinea*. Durham, NC: Duke University Press, 2019.

Appel, Hannah. "Offshore Work: Oil, Modularity, and the How of Capitalism in Equatorial Guinea." *American Ethnologist* 39, no. 4 (2011): 692–709.

Appia, Béatrice. "Les forgerons du Fouta Djallon." *Journal de la Société des Africanistes* 35, no. 2 (1965): 317–52.

Appia, Béatrice. "Masques de Guinée Française et de Casamance." *Journal des Africanistes* 13 (1943): 153–82.

Appia, Béatrice. "Notes sur le génie des eaux en Guinée." *Journal de la Société des Africanistes*, 14 (1944): 33–41.

Appiah, Kwame Anthony. *In My Father's House: Africa in the Philosophy of Culture*. New York: Oxford University Press, 1992.

Apter, Andrew. "History in the Dungeon: Atlantic Slavery and the Spirit of Capitalism in Cape Coast Castle, Ghana." *American Historical Review* (February 2017): 23–54.

Arcin, André. *La Guinée Française: Races, religions, coutumes, production, commerce*. Paris: Challamel, 1907.

Arnaud, Gilbert. *Les ressources minières de l'Afrique occidentale*. Bulletin de la Direction des Mines, no. 8. Paris: Imprimerie Nationale, 1945.

Asad, Talal. *Genealogies of Religion: Discipline and Reasons of Power in Christianity and Islam*. Baltimore: Johns Hopkins University Press, 1993.

Aubert, Andrè. "Légendes historiques et traditions orales recueillies en Haute-Gambie." *Bulletin du Comité d'Études Historiques et Scientifiques de l'Afrique-Occidentale Française* 6 (1923): 384–428.

Aubynn, A. "Sustainable Solution or Marriage of Inconvenience? The Coexistence of Large-scale Mining and Artisanal Mining on the Abosso Gold Fields Concession in Western Ghana." *Resource Policy* 34 (2009): 64–70.

Bâ, Amadou Hampaté, and Germaine Dieterlen. *Koumen: Texte initiatique des pasteurs Peul*. Paris: Mouton, 1961.

Babou, Cheikh Anta. *Fighting the Greater Jihad: Amadou Bamba and the Founding of the Muridiyya of Senegal, 1853–1913*. Athens: Ohio University Press, 2010.

Balandier, George. "L'or de la Guinée Françaises [sic]." *Présence Africaine*, no. 4 (1947): 539–48.

Banks, Elizabeth, Robyn d'Avignon, and Asif Siddiqi. "The African Soviet Modern." *Comparative Studies of South Asia, Africa, and the Middle East* 41, no. 1 (2021): 2–10.

Barber, Karin. *The Anthropology of Texts, Persons, and Publics: Oral and Written Culture in Africa and Beyond*. Cambridge: Cambridge University Press, 2007.

Barrat, Maurice. "Les mines d'or du basin du Sénégal." *Revue Coloniale* (1896): 477–502.

Barry, Andrew. *Material Politics: Disputes along the Pipeline*. Chichester, UK: John Wiley, 2013

Barry, Boubacar. *Senegambia and the Atlantic Slave Trade*. Translated by Ayi Kwei Armay. Cambridge: Cambridge University Press, 1988.

Barry, Mamadou, ed. *Regularizing Informal Mining: A Summary of the Proceedings of the International Roundtable on Artisanal Mining*. Washington, DC: World Bank, 1996.

Barth, Frederick. *Ethnic Groups and Boundaries: The Social Organization of Cultural Difference*. Boston: Little Brown, 1969.

Bassot, Jean Pierre. *Compilation des études et prospection exécutés depuis 1945 sur les terrains anciens du Sénégal Oriental*. Paris: Éditions BRGM, 1964.

Bassot, Jean Pierre. *Étude géologique du Sénégal Oriental et de ses confins guinéo-maliens*. Bureau de Recherches Géologiques et Minières, no. 40. Paris: Éditions BRGM, 1966.

Bates, Robert. *Rural Responses to Industrialization: A Study of Village Zambia*. New Haven, CT: Yale University Press, 1976.

Bathily, Abdoulaye. "A Discussion of the Traditions of Wagadu with Some Reference to Ancient Ghāna." *Bulletin de l'Institut Fondamental d'Afrique Noire* (series B), no. 1 (1975): 1–94.

Bathily, Abdoulaye. "Mamadou Lamine Dramé et la résistance anti-impérialiste dans le Haut-Sénégal (1885–1887)." *Notes Africaines*, vol. 125, 1970, 20–32.

Bathily, Abdoulaye. *Les portes de l'or: Le royaume de Galam (Sénégal) de l'ère musulmane au temps de négriers (VIII–XVIIIe siècle)*. Paris: L'Harmattan, 1989.

Baum, Robert M. "Indigenous African Religions." In *The Oxford Handbook of Modern African History* [online], edited by John Parker and Richard Reid. Oxford: Oxford University Press, 2013. https://doi:10.1093/oxfordhb/9780199572472.013.0015.

Baum, Robert M. *Shrines of the Slave Trade: Diola Religion and Society in Pre-colonial Senegambia*. New York: Oxford University Press, 1999.

Bebbington, Anthony, and Jeffrey Bury. "Political Ecologies of the Subsoil." In *Subterranean Struggles: New Geographies of Extraction in Latin America*, edited by Anthony Bebbington and Jeffrey Bury, 1–26. Houston: University of Texas Press, 2013.

Belan, Alan. "L'or dans le cercle de Kédougou." *Notes Africaines*, vol. 31 (1946), 9–12.

Bell, Catherine. *Ritual Theory, Ritual Practice*. New York; Oxford: Oxford University Press, 1992.

Berger, A. R. "The Importance of Small-scale Mining: A General Review." In *Strategies for Small-scale Mining and Mineral Industries: Report of a Regional Workshop Held at Mombasa, Kenya, April 14–25, 1980*, edited by James M. Neilson, 1–12. Mombasa: Association of Geoscientists for International Development, 1982.

Berry, Sara. *Fathers Work for Their Sons: Accumulation, Mobility, and Class Formation in an Extended Yorùbá Community*. Berkeley: University of California Press, 1984.

Berry, Sara. *No Condition Is Permanent: The Social Dynamics of Agrarian Change in Sub-Saharan Africa*. Madison: University of Wisconsin Press, 1993.

Berry, Sara. "Struggles over Land and Authority in Africa." *African Studies Review* 60, no. 3 (2017): 1–21.

Berzock, Kathleen Bickford, ed. *Caravans of Gold, Fragments in Time: Art, Culture, and Exchange across Medieval Saharan Africa*. Princeton, NJ: Princeton University Press, 2019.

Billé, Franck, ed. *Voluminous States: Sovereignty, Materiality, and the Territorial Imagination*. Durham, NC: Duke University Press, 2020.

Bize, Amiel. "The Right to the Remainder: Gleaning in the Fuel Economies of East Africa's Northern Corridor." *Cultural Anthropology* 35, no. 3 (2020): 462–86.

Bledsoe, Caroline H. "'No Success without Struggle': Social Mobility and Hardship for Sierra Leone Children." *Man* 25, no. 1 (1990): 70–88.

Blondel, Fernand. "Études: Les recherches d'or en Afrique française." *La Chronique des Mines Coloniales* 33 (1934): 362–69.

Blondel, Fernand. "Le problème minier aux colonies." *Le Monde Colonial Illustré* (May 1930): 219–30.

Bolay, Matthieu. "Artisanal Gold Miners Encountering Large-scale Mining in Guinea. Expulsion, Tolerance and Interference." In *The Open Cut: Mining, Transnational Corporations and Local Populations*, edited by Thomas Niederberger, Tobias Haller, Helen Gambon, Madlen Kobi, and Irina Wenk, 187–204. Zurich: LIT, 2016.

Bolgarsky, Michel. *Étude géologique et description pétrographique du Sud-Ouest de la Côte d'Ivoire*. Bulletin de la Direction des Mines, no 9. Paris: Imprimerie Nationale, 1950.

Bonnecase, Vincent. *La pauvreté au Sahel: Du savoir colonial à la mesure internationale*. Paris: Karthala, 2011.

Boone, Catherine. *Merchant Capital and the Roots of State Power in Senegal 1930–1985*. Cambridge: Cambridge University Press, 1992.

Boone, Catherine. *Property and Political Order in Africa: Land Rights and the Structure of Politics*. Cambridge: Cambridge University Press, 2014.

Boucard, Claude. "Relation de Bambouc (1792)." *Bulletin de l'Institut Fondamental d'Afrique Noire* (series B) 36 (1974): 245–75.

Braun, Bruce. "Producing Vertical Territory: Geology and Governmentality in Late Victorian Canada." *Cultural Geographies* 7, no. 7 (2000): 7–46.

Breckenridge, Keith. *Biometric State: The Global Politics of Identification and Surveillance in South Africa, 1850 to the Present*. Cambridge: Cambridge University Press, 2014.

Brett-Smith, Sarah C. *The Making of Bamana Sculpture: Creativity and Gender*. Cambridge: Cambridge University Press, 1995.

Bridge, Gavin. "Territory, Now in 3D!" *Political Geography* 34 (2013): 55–57.

Brooks, George E. *Landlords and Strangers: Ecology, Society, and Trade in Western Africa, 1000–1630*. Boulder, CO: Westview, 1993.

Brown, Carolyn. *"We Were All Slaves": African Miners, Culture, and Resistance at the Enugu Government Colliery*. Portsmouth, NH: Heinemann, 2003.

Brownell, Emily. *Going to Ground: A History of Environment and Infrastructure in Dar es Salaam*. Pittsburgh: University of Pittsburgh Press, 2020.

Bryceson, Deborah Fahy, Eleanor Fisher, Jesper Bosse Jønsson, and Rosemarie Mwaipopo. *Mining and Social Transformation in Africa: Mineralizing and Democratizing Trends in Artisanal Production*. Hoboken, NJ: Taylor and Francis, 2013.

Buroway, Michael. *The Colour of Class on the Copper Mines: From African Advancement to Zambianization*. Manchester, UK: Manchester University Press, 1972.

Business for Social Responsibility. *The Social License to Operate*. Report, 2003. https://static1.squarespace.com/static/5bb24d3c9b8fe8421e87bbb6/t/5c3bd87340ec9ab9b9f3fdf9/1547425908683/file_BSR_Social_License_to_Operate.pdf.

Camara, Seydou. "The Epic of *Sunjata*: Structure, Preservation, and Transmission." In *In Search of Sunjata: The Mande Oral Epic as History, Literature, and Performance,* edited by Ralph A. Austen, 59–69. Bloomington: Indiana University Press, 1999.

Campbell, Bonnie K., ed. *Modes of Governance and Revenue Flows in African Mining*. Houndmills, UK: Palgrave, 2013.

Capps, Gavin. "Tribal-landed Property: The Value of the Chieftaincy in Contemporary Africa." *Journal of Agrarian Change* 16, no. 3 (2016): 452–77.

Carmody, Padraig. *The New Scramble for Africa*. Cambridge: Cambridge University Press, 2011.

Carney, Judith. *Black Rice: The African Origins of Rice Cultivation in the Americas*. Cambridge, MA: Harvard University Press, 2001.

Carney, Judith, and Richard Nicholas Rosomoff. *In the Shadow of Slavery: Africa's Botanical Legacy in the Atlantic World*. Berkeley: University of California Press, 2009.

Carr, E. Summerson, and Michael Lempert. "Introduction: Pragmatics of Scale." In *Scale: Discourse and Dimensions of Social Life*, edited by E. Summerson Carr and Michael Lempert, 1–21. Oakland: University of California Press, 2006.

Carrère, Frédéric, and Paul Holle. *De la Sénégambie Française*. Paris: Firmin Didot Frères, 1855.

Cartelli, Philip. "A Snake in the Hole: Possibilities and Risks of Artisanal Gold Mining in Southeastern Senegal." *Etnofoor* 25, no.1 (2013): 30–47.

Chafer, Tony. "Chirac and 'la Françafrique': No Longer a Family Affair." *Modern and Contemporary France* 13, no. 1 (2005): 7–23.

Chafer, Tony. *The End of Empire in French West Africa: France's Successful Decolonization?* Oxford: Berg, 2002.

Chakrabarti, Pratik. *Inscriptions of Nature: Geology and the Naturalization of Antiquity*. Baltimore: Johns Hopkins University Press, 2020.

Chanock, Martin. "Paradigms, Policies, and Property: A Review of the Customary Law of Land Tenure." In *Law in Colonial Africa*, edited by Kristin Mann and Richard Roberts, 61–84. Portsmouth, NH: Heinemann, 2011.

Chataigner, Abel. "Les populations du Cercle de Kédougou." *Cahiers du Centre de Recherches Anthropologiques* (series 11) 5, nos. 1–2 (1963): 87–111.

Chermette, Alexis. "Le placer de la Perma." In *Les mines et la recherche minière en Afrique-Occidentale Française*, edited by Jean Servant, Pierre Legoux, and André Marelle, 154–57. Paris: L'Harmattan, 1991.

Chermette, Alexis. "Quelques réflexions sur la vie du géologue en brousse à Dakar." In *Les mines et la recherche minière en Afrique-Occidentale Française*, edited by Jean Servant, Pierre Legoux, and André Marelle, 133–38. Paris: L'Harmattan, 1991.

Chirikure, Shadreck. *Indigenous Mining and Metallurgy in Africa*. Cape Town: Cambridge University Press, 2010.

Chiron, Jean-Claude, ed. *Objectif terre: 50 ans d'histoire du BRGM*. Orleans, France: Éditions BRGM, 2009.

Cissé, Mamadou, Susan Keech McIntosh, Laure Dussubieux, Thomas Fenn, Daphne Gallagher, and Abigail Chipps Smith. "Excavations at Gao Saney: New Evidence for Settlement Growth, Trade, and Interaction on the Niger Bend in the First Millennium CE." *Journal of Archeology* 11, no. 1 (2013): 9–37.

Cissé, Youssouf Tata. "Notes sur les sociétés de chasseurs Malinké." *Journal de la Société des Africanistes* 34, no. 2 (1964): 175–226.

Cissé, Youssouf Tata, and Wâ Kamissoko. *La grande geste du Mali: Des origines à la fondation de l'empire*. 2d ed. Paris: Karthala, 2007.

Clark, Jeffrey. "Gold, Sex, and Pollution: Male Illness and Myth at Mt. Kare, Papua New Guinea." *American Ethnologist* 20, no. 4 (1993): 742–57.

Cohen, Benjamin R. "Surveying Nature: Environmental Dimensions of Virginia's First Scientific Survey, 1835–1842." *Environmental History* 11 (2006): 37–69.

Cohen, David William. "The Undefining of Oral Tradition." *Ethnohistory* 36, no. 1 (1989): 9–18.

Cohen, David William, Stephan F. Miescher, and Luise White. "Introduction: Voices, Words, and African History." In *African Words, African Voices: Critical Practices in Oral History*, edited by Luise White, Stephan F. Miescher, and David William Cohen, 1–30. Bloomington: Indiana University Press, 2001.

Cohen, David William, and E. S. Atieno Obhiambo. "Introduction." In *The Risks of Knowledge: Investigations into the Death of the Hon. Minister John Robert Ouko in Kenya, 1990*, edited by David William Cohen and E. S. Atieno Obhiambo, 1–32. Athens: Ohio University Press, 2004.

Cohen, David William, and E. S. Atieno Obhiambo. *Siaya: The Historical Anthropology of an African Landscape*. Athens: Ohio University Press, 1989.

Coin, Casimir. "Dakar, capitale de la géologie de l'ouest africain, 1945–1960." In *Les mines et la recherche minière en Afrique-Occidentale Française*, edited by Jean Servant, Pierre Legoux, and André Marelle, 147–53. Paris: L'Harmattan, 1991.

Comaroff, Jean, and John L. Comaroff. "Millennial Capitalism: First Thoughts on a Second Coming." In *Millennial Capitalism and the Culture of Neoliberalism*, edited by John L. Comaroff, Jean Comaroff, and Robert P. Weller, 1–56. Durham, NC: Duke University Press, 2001.

Comaroff, Jean, and John L. Comaroff. "Occult Economies and the Violence of Abstraction: Notes from the South African Postcolony." *American Ethnologist* 26, no. 2 (1999): 279–303.

Comaroff, John L., and Jean Comaroff. "Chiefs, Capital, and the State in Contemporary Africa." In *The Politics of Custom, Chiefship, Capital, and the State in Contemporary Africa*, edited by John L. Comaroff and Jean Comaroff, 1–39. Chicago: University of Chicago Press, 2018.

Comaroff, John L., and Jean Comaroff. *Ethnicity, Inc.* Chicago: University of Chicago Press, 2009.

Comaroff, John L., and Jean Comaroff, eds. *The Politics of Custom, Chiefship, Capital, and the State in Contemporary Africa*. Chicago: University of Chicago Press, 2018.

Condé, Cheick Fantamady. *Histoire de Siguiri: De l'implémentation coloniale à l'indépendance (1888–1958)*. Paris: L'Harmattan, 2017.

Conrad, David C. "Mooning Armies and Mothering Heroes: Female Power in Mande Epic Tradition." In *Search for Sunjata: The Mande Oral Epic as History, Literature, and Performance*, edited by Ralph A. Austen, 189–222. Bloomington: Indiana University Press, 1999.

Conrad, David C., and Djanka Tassey Condé. *Sunjata: A West African Epic of the Mande Peoples*. Indianapolis: Hackett, 2004.

Conrad, David C., and Humphrey Fisher. "The Conquest That Never Was: Ghana and the Almoravids, 1076." *History in Africa* 9 (1982): 21–59.

Conrad, David C., and Barbara E. Frank. "*Nyamakalaw:* Contradiction and Ambiguity in Mande Society." In *Status and Identity in West Africa: Nyamakalaw of Mande*, edited by David C. Conrad and Barbara E. Frank, 1–23. Bloomington: Indiana University Press, 1995.

Cooper, Barbara M. "Oral Sources and the Challenges of African History." In *Writing African History*, edited by John Edward Phillips, 191–215. Rochester, NY: University of Rochester Press, 2005.

Cooper, Frederick. *Citizenship between Empire and Nation: Remaking France and French Africa, 1945–1960*. Princeton, NJ: Princeton University Press, 2014.

Cooper, Frederick. *Decolonization and African Society: The Labor Question in French and British Africa*. New York: Cambridge University Press, 1996.

Cooper, Frederick, and Randall Packard, eds. *International Development and the Social Sciences*. Berkeley: University of California Press, 1997.

Copans, Jean. *Les marabouts de l'arachide: La confrérie mouride et les paysans du Sénégal*. Paris: Le Sycomore, 1980.

Coquery-Vidrovitch, Catherine. *L'Afrique occidentale au temps des Français: Colonisateurs et colonisés, circa 1860–1960*. Paris: La Découverte, 1992.

Coquery-Vidrovitch, Catherine. "Nationalité et citoyenneté en Afrique-Occidentale Française: Originaires et citoyens dans le Sénégal colonial." *Journal of African History* 42 (2001): 285–305.

Coquery-Vidrovitch, Catherine. "La politique économique colonial." In *L'Afrique occidentale au temps des Français: Colonisateurs et colonisés, circa 1860–1960*, edited by Catherine Coquery-Vidrovitch and Odile Goerg, 105–40. Paris: La Découverte, 1992.

Coyle, Lauren. *Fires of Gold: Law, Spirit, and Sacrificial Labor in Ghana*. Berkeley: University of California Press, 2020.

Cronon, William. *Nature's Metropolis: Chicago and the Great West*. New York: W. W. Norton, 1991.

Crush, Jonathan, Alan Jeeves, and David Yudelman. *South Africa's Labor Empire: A History of Black Migrancy to the Gold Mines*. Boulder, CO: Westview, 1991.

Curtin, Philip. "The Lure of Bambuk Gold." *Journal of African History* 14, no. 4 (1973): 623–32.

D'Angelo, Lorenzo. "Who Owns the Diamonds? The Occult Economy of Diamond Mining in Sierra Leone." *Africa* 84, no. 2 (2014): 269–93.

Daumain, Georges. "L'or en Afrique-Occidentale Française." *La Chronique des Mines Coloniales*, no. 18 (1933): 404–22.

David, Philippe. *Les navétanes: Histoire des migrants saisonnier de l'arachide en Sénégambie des origines à nos jours*. Dakar: Nouvelles Éditions Africaines, 1980.

David, Pierre-Felix-Barthélemy. *Journal d'un voyage fait en Bambouc en 1744*. Paris: Société Française d'Histoire d'Outre-mer et Librairie Orientaliste Paul Geuthner, 1974.

d'Avignon, Robyn. "Primitive Techniques: From 'Customary' to 'Artisanal' Mining in French West Africa." *Journal of African History* 59, no. 2 (2018): 179–97.

d'Avignon, Robyn. "Shelf Projects: The Political Life of Exploration Geology in Senegal." *Engaging Science, Technology, and Society* 4 (2018): 111–30.

d'Avignon, Robyn. "Spirited Geobodies: Producing Subterranean Property in Nineteenth Century Bambuk, West Africa." *Technology and Culture* 61, no. 2 (April 2020): S20–48.

d'Avignon, Robyn. "Theorizing the Contemporary: Protest Geologies." *Fieldsights*, September 22, 2020. https://culanth.org/fieldsights/protest-geologies.

De Boeck, Filip. "Domesticating Diamonds and Dollars: Identity, Expenditure and Sharing in Southwestern Zaire (1984–1997)." *Development and Change* 29, no. 4 (1998): 777–810.

De Bont, Raf, and Jens Lachmund, eds. *Spatializing the History of Ecology: Sites, Journeys, Mappings*. New York: Routledge, 2017.

de la Cadena, Marisol. "Indigenous Cosmopolitics in the Andes: Conceptual Reflections beyond 'Politics.'" *Cultural Anthropology* 25, no. 2 (2010): 334–70.

Delacour, M. A. "Les Tenda (Konigagui, Bassari, Badyaranké) de la Guinée Française." *Revue d'Ethnographie et de Sociologie* 3 (1912): 287–96, 370–81.

Delavignette, Robert. *Les paysans noirs: Récit soudanais en douze mois*. Paris: Librairie Stock, 1931.

de Lestrange, Marie-Thérèse, Monique Gessain, Danielle Fouchier, and G. Crépy-Montal. "Stratégies de lutte contre la disette au Sénégal Oriental." *Journal des Africanistes* 56, no. 1 (1986): 35–50.

de Lestrange, Monique. *Les Coniagui et les Bassari (Guinée Française)*. Paris: Presses Universitaires de France, 1955.

de Lestrange, Monique. "La piste Etyolo-Seguekho: Document pour servir à l'histoire des Bassari." *Cahiers du Centre de Recherches Anthropologiques* (series 12) 2, nos. 1–2 (1967): 176–81.

Dell, Matthew. "Undermining the 'Local': Migration, Development and Gold in Southern Mali." *Journal of Intercultural Studies* 34, no. 5 (2013): 584–603.

de Luna, Kathryn M. 2016. *Collecting Food, Cultivating People: Subsistence and Society in Central Africa*. New Haven, CT: Yale University Press.

Dème, Alioune, and Susan Keech McIntosh. "Excavations at Walaldé: New Light on the Settlement of the Middle Senegal Valley by Iron-Using People." *Journal of African Archeology* 4, no. 2 (2006): 317–47.

Demuth, Bathsheba. *Floating Coast: An Environmental History of the Bering Strait*. New York: W. W. Norton, 2019.

Derman, William. *Serfs, Peasants, and Socialists*. Berkeley: University of California Press, 1973.

Des Jardins, Julie. *The Madame Curie Complex: The Hidden History of Women in Science*. New York: Feminist Press, 2010.

Devisse, Jean. "L'or." In *Vallées du Niger*, edited by Jean Devisse, 344–57. Paris: Éditions de la Réunions des Musées Nationaux, 1993.

de Zeltner, Franz. *Contes du Sénégal et du Niger*. Paris: Ernest Leroux, 1913.

Dia, Abdoulaye. "Caractères et significations des complexes magmatiques et métamorphiques du secteur de Sandikounda-Laminia, Nord de la boutonnière de

Kédougou, Est du Sénégal: Un modèle géodynamique du Birimien de l'Afrique de l'Ouest." PhD diss., Université Cheikh Anta Diop, Dakar, 1988.

Dia, Mamadou. *Mémoires d'un militant du Tiers Monde: Si mémoire ne ment*. Paris: Publisud, 1985.

Dia, Néné. "Activité minière et culture cotonnière: L'exemple de la mine d'or de Sabodala au Sud-est du Sénégal." Master's thesis, Université Gaston Berger de Saint-Louis, St. Louis, Senegal, 2006.

Diallo, Dinna Pathé. "Contribution à l'étude géologique de la série du Dialé (Birimien) dans les Monts Bassaris, Sénégal Oriental (secteur de Bandafassi-Ibel-Ndébou-Landiéné)." PhD diss., Université Cheikh Anta Diop, Dakar, 1983.

Diallo, Mouhamadou Lamine. "Mine d'or et développement durable: Quelques réflexions sur le site de Sabodala (Sénégal Oriental)." *EchoGeo* 8 (2009). https://doi.org/10/4000/echogeo.11103.

Diallo, Mouhamadou Lamine. "Mines et dynamiques spatiales dans le Sud-est du Sénégal: L'exemple de la communauté rurale de Khossanto." Mémoire, Géographie, Université Gaston Berger de Saint-Louis, St. Louis, Senegal, 2006.

Diarrah, Cheikh Oumar. *Le Mali de Modibo Keita*. Paris: L'Harmattan, 2000.

Dieterlen, Germaine. "The Mande Creation Myth." *Africa*, no. 27 (1957): 124–38.

Dieterlen, Germaine, and Youssouf Cissé. *Les fondements de la société d'initiation du Komo*. Paris: Mouton, 1972.

Dioh, Edmond. 1986. "Étude des roches magmatiques birimiennes de la région de Sonfara-laminia-Médina Foulbé (Sénégal Oriental)." PhD diss., Université de Nancy I, France, 1986.

Diouf, Mamadou. "Assimilation colonial et identité religieuses de la civilité des originaires des Quatre Communes (Sénégal)." *Canadian Journal of African Studies* 34 (1999): 565–87.

Diouf, Mamadou. *Histoire du Sénégal: Le modèle islamo-wolof et ses périphéries*. Paris: Maisonneuve et Larose, 2001.

Diouf, Mamadou. *Le Kajoor au XIXe siècle: Pouvoir ceddo et conquête coloniale*. Paris: Karthala, 1990.

Diouf, Mamadou. "Senegalese Development: From Mass Mobilization to Technocratic Elitism." In *International Development and the Social Sciences*, edited by Frederick Cooper and Randall Packard, 291–319. Berkeley: University of California Press, 1997.

Diouf, Sylviane Anna, ed. *Fighting the Slave Trade: West African Strategies*. Oxford: James Currey, 2003.

Donaldson, Coleman, "Orthography, Standardization and Register: The Case of Standardizing Minority Languages." In *Competing Ideologies of Authority and Authenticity in the Global Periphery*, edited by Pia Lane, James Costa, and Haley de Korne, 175–99. New York: Routledge, 2017.

Donaldson, Coleman. "Clear Language: Script, Register, and the N'ko Movement of Manding-Speaking West Africaa" PhD diss., University of Pennsylvania, Philadelphia, 2017.

Doucoure, Bakary. *Des pierres dans les mortiers et non du mais! Mutations dans les villages aurifères du sud-est du Sénégal.* Dakar: Council for the Development of Social Science Research in Africa, 2015.

Dozon, Jean-Pierre. *Frères et sujets. La France et l'Afrique en perspective.* Paris: Flammarion, 2003.

Droney, Damien. "Ironies of Laboratory Work during Ghana's Second Age of Optimism." *Cultural Anthropology* 29, no. 4 (2014): 363–84.

Dubow, Saul. "Earth History, Natural History, and Prehistory at the Cape, 1860–1875." *Comparative Studies in Society and History* 46, no. 1 (2004): 107–33.

Dueppen, Stephen A., and Cameron Gokee. "Hunting on the Margins of Medieval West African States: A Preliminary Study of the Zooarcheological Record at Diouboye, Senegal." *Azania* 49, no. 3 (2014): 354–85.

Dumett, Raymond E. *El Dorado in West Africa: The Gold-Mining Frontier, African Labor, and Colonial Capitalism on the Gold Coast, 1875–1900.* Athens: Ohio University Press, 1998.

Dupuy, André-Roger, ed. *Le Niokolo-Koba: Premier Grand Parc National de la République du Sénégal.* Dakar: GIA, 1971.

Dupuy, André-Roger. *Soldat des Bêtes: Vingt ans de lutte pour la défense de la faune africaine.* Rennes, France: Ouest-France, 1991.

Durand, Jean-Baptiste-Léonard. *Voyage au Sénégal: Fait dans les années 1785 et 1786.* Paris: Dentu, 1802.

Ece, Melis. "Conserving Nature, Transforming Authority: Eviction and Development at the Margins of the State: The Niokolo-Koba National Park, Senegal." PhD diss., Graduate School and University Center, City University of New York, 2012.

Elden, Stuart. "Secure the Volume: Vertical Geopolitics and the Depth of Power." *Political Geography* 34 (2013): 35–51.

Epstein, A. L. *Politics in an Urban African Community.* Manchester, UK: Manchester University Press, 1958.

Fairhead, James. "Termites, Mud Daubers and Their Earths: A Multispecies Approach to Fertility and Power in West Africa." *Conservation and Society* 14, no. 4 (2016): 359–67.

Fairhead, James, and Melissa Leach. *Misreading the African Landscape: Society and Ecology in a Forest-Savanna Mosaic.* Cambridge: Cambridge University Press, 1996.

Fauvelle, François-Xavier. *The Golden Rhinoceros: Histories of the African Middle Ages.* Translated by Troy Trice. Princeton, NJ: Princeton University Press, 2018.

Feierman, Steven. "African Histories and the Dissolution of World History." In *Africa and the Disciplines: The Contributions of Research in Africa to the Social Sciences and Humanities,* edited by Robert H. Bates, V. Y. Mudimbe, and Jean F. O'Barr, 167–212. Chicago: University of Chicago Press, 1993.

Feierman, Steven. "Colonizers, Scholars, and the Creation of Invisible Histories." In *Beyond the Cultural Turn,* edited by Victoria E. Bonnell and Lynn Hunt, 182–216. Berkeley: University of California Press, 1999.

Feierman, Steven. *Peasant Intellectuals: Anthropology and History in Tanzania.* Madison: University of Wisconsin Press, 1990.

Fent, Ashley. "Governing Alongside: Lateral State Spatiality and Unmet Expectations amid Mining Negotiations in Casamance, Senegal." *American Ethnologist* 46, no. 1 (2019): 20–33.

Ferguson, James. *Expectations of Modernity: Myths and Meanings of Urban Life on the Zambian Copperbelt*. Berkeley: University of California Press, 1999.

Ferguson, James. *Global Shadows: Africa in the Neoliberal World Order*. Durham, NC: Duke University Press, 2006.

Ferguson, James. *The Anti-politics Machine: Development, Depoliticization, and Bureaucratic Power in Lesotho*. Minneapolis: University of Minnesota Press, 1994.

Ferry, Marie-Paule. "Pour une histoire des Bedik (Sénégal Oriental)." *Cahiers du Centre de Recherches Anthropologiques* 12, no. 2 (1967): 125–48.

Fields-Black, Edda. *Deep Roots: Rice Farmers in West Africa and the African Diaspora*. Bloomington: Indiana University Press, 2008.

Fioratta, Susanna. "States of Insecurity: Migration, Remittances, and Islamic Reform in Guinea, West Africa." PhD diss., Yale University, New Haven, CT, 2013.

Flores, Daniel L. "Place: An Argument for Bioregional History." *Environmental History Review* 18, no. 4 (1994): 1–18.

Fortin, Daniel, Modou Lô, and Guy Maynart. *Plantes médicinales du sahel*. Dakar: Enda-Editions, 1997.

Frank, Barbara E. *Mande Potters and Leatherworkers: Art and Heritage in West Africa*. Washington, DC: Smithsonian Institution Press, 1998.

Fredericks, Rosalind. "'The Old Man Is Dead': Hip Hop and the Arts of Citizenship of Senegalese Youth." *Antipode* 46, no. 1 (2014): 130–48.

Fredericks, Rosalind, and Mamadou Diouf. *Les arts de la citoyenneté au Sénégal: Espaces contestés et civilités urbaines*. Paris: Karthala, 2013.

Freund, Bill. *Capital and Labour in the Nigerian Tin Mines*. London: Longman, 1981.

Fultz, Katherine. "Economies of Representation: Communication, Conflict, and Mining in Guatemala." PhD diss., University of Michigan, Ann Arbor, 2015.

Furth, Rebecca. "Marrying the Forbidden Other: Marriage, Status and Social Change in the Futa Jallon Highlands of Guinea." PhD diss., University of Wisconsin, Madison, 2005.

Gallieni, Joseph. *Mission d'exploration du Haut-Niger: Voyage au Soudan français (Haut-Niger et pays de Ségou), 1879–1881*. Paris: Hachette, 1885.

Galvan, Dennis. *The State Must Be Our Master of Fire: How Peasants Craft Culturally Sustainable Development in Senegal*. Berkeley: University of California Press, 2004.

Gamble, David P. "Accounts of Supernatural Beings: Spirits, Witches, Werewolves, Ninkinanko, etc. from the Mandinka Newspaper, Kibaro." *Gambian Studies*, no. 4 (November 1976): 1–11.

Garenne-Marot, Laurence. "Archéologie d'un métal: Le cuivre en Sénégambie (Afrique de l'Ouest) entre le Xe et le XIVe siècle." PhD diss., Université de Paris I, Panthéon-Sorbonne, 1993.

Garenne-Marot, Laurence, and Benoit Mille. "Copper-based Metal in the Inland Niger Delta: Metal and Technology at the Time of the Empire of Mali." In *Metals and Mines: Studies in Archeometallurgy*, edited by Susan La Niece, Duncan Hook, and Paul Craddock, 159–68. London: Archetype, 2007.

Garrard, Timothy F. *African Gold: Jewellery and Ornaments from Ghana, Côte d'Ivoire, Mali and Senegal in the Collection of the Gold of Africa Barbier-Mueller Museum in Cape Town.* Munich: Prestal, 2011.

Garrard, Timothy F. *Akan Weights and the Gold Trade.* London: Longman, 1980.

Garrard, Timothy F. "Myth and Metrology: The Early Trans-Saharan Gold Trade." *Journal of African History* 23 (1982): 443–61.

Gary-Tounkara, Daouda. *Migrants soudanais/Maliens et conscience ivoirienne: Les étrangers en Côte d'Ivoire, 1903–1980.* Paris: L'Harmattan, 2003.

Geenen, S., and K. Classens. "Disputed Access to the Gold Sites in Luhwindja, Eastern Democratic Republic of Congo." *Journal of Modern African Studies* 51, no. 1 (2013): 85–108.

Gellar, Sheldon. *Senegal: An African Nation between Islam and the West.* Boulder: University of Colorado Press, 1982.

Gelman, Susan. "Essentialism." In *The MIT Encyclopedia of Cognitive Science*, edited by Robert A. Wilson and Frank C. Keil, 282–84. Cambridge, MA: MIT Press, 1999.

Geschiere, Peter. *The Perils of Belonging: Autochthony, Citizenship and Exclusion in Africa and Europe.* Chicago: University of Chicago Press, 2009.

Gessain, Monique. *Actes du 2ème Colloque de Kédougou, Dakar, 18–22 février 1985.* Paris: Laboratoire d'Anthropologie du Musée National d'Histoire Naturelle, 1987.

Gessain, Monique. *Les migrations des Coniagui et Bassari.* Paris: Société des Africanistes, Musée de l'Homme, 1967.

Gessain, Robert. "Introduction à l'étude du Sénégal Oriental (cercle de Kédougou)." *Cahiers du Centre de Recherches Anthropologiques* 1 (1963): 5–85.

Giles-Vernick, Tamara. *Cutting the Vines of the Past: Environmental Histories of the Central African Rainforest.* Charlottesville: University Press of Virginia, 2002.

Glassman, Jonathan. *Feasts and Riots: Revelry, Rebellion, and Popular Consciousness on the Swahili Coast, 1856–1888.* Portsmouth, NH: James Currey, 1995.

Glassman, Jonathan. "Slower than a Massacre: The Multiple Sources of Racial Thought in Colonial Africa." *American Historical Review* 109, no. 3: (2004): 720–54.

Gluckman, Max. "Anthropological Problems Arising from the African Industrial Revolution." In *Social Change in Modern Africa*, edited by Aidan Southall, 68–82. London: Routledge, 1961.

Goerg, Odile. *Commerce et colonisation en Guinée, 1850–1913.* Paris: L'Harmattan, 1986.

Gokee, Cameron. *Assembling the Village in Medieval Bambuk: An Archaeology of Interaction at Diouboye, Senegal.* Sheffield, UK: Equinox, 2016.

Gokee, Cameron, Matthew Kroot, Aimé Kantoussan, Adama Harouna Athie, Djiby Tamba, and Massar Sarr. "Le paysage historique de la Haute-Gambie: Résultats des reconnaissances archéologiques en 2013 et 2015." *Nyame Akuma* 84 (2015): 27–40.

Golbéry, Sylvain Meinrad Xavier de. *Travels in Africa*, vol. 2, 2d ed. Translated by W. Mudford. London: Jones and Bumford, 1808.

Goloubinow, Rostislav. "Géologie et ressources en or du nord-est de la Guinée Française." PhD diss., Université de Nancy, France, 1936.

Goloubinow, Rostislav. "L'or en Guinée Française." In *Extrait du Congrès International des Mines, de la Métallurgie et de la Géologie Appliquée, VIIe session, Paris, 20–26 octobre 1935*, 2 vols. Paris: Secrétariat de la Section de Géologie Appliquée, 1937.

Goloubinow, Rostislav. "La prospection et les gisements d'or de demain." *Publications du Bureau d'Études Géologiques et Minières Coloniales* 15 (1940): 5–11.

Gomez, Michael A. *African Dominion: A New History of Empire in Early and Medieval West Africa*. Princeton, NJ: Princeton University Press, 2018.

Gomez, Michael A. *Pragmatism in the Age of Jihad: The Precolonial State of Bundu*. Cambridge: Cambridge University Press, 1992.

Gómez, Pablo F. *The Experiential Caribbean: Creating Knowledge and Healing in the Early Modern Atlantic*. Chapel Hill: University of North Carolina Press, 2011.

Gomila, Jacques, and Marie-Paule Ferry. "Notes sur l'ethnographie des Bedik (Sénégal Oriental)." *Journal des Africanistes* 36, no. 2 (1966): 209–49.

Gordon, Robert J. *Mines, Masters, and Migrants: Life in a Namibian Mine Compound*. Johannesburg: Ravan, 1977.

Grace, Joshua. *African Motors: Technology, Gender, and the History of Development*. Durham, NC: Duke University Press, 2021.

Gravrand, Henry. *Pangool: Le génie religieux sereer*. Dakar: Nouvelles Éditions Africaines, 1990.

Gray, Christopher. *Colonial Rule and Crisis in Equatorial Africa: Southern Gabon, ca. 1850–1940*. Rochester, NY: University of Rochester Press, 2002.

Green, Toby. *A Fistful of Shells: West Africa from the Rise of the Slave Trade to the Age of Revolution*. Chicago: University of Chicago Press, 2019.

Greig, Isabelle. "Le Sénégal Oriental à l'aube du développement minier: Quels enjeux pour les collectivités locales?" Master's thesis, École Normale Supérieure de Lettres et Sciences Humaines de Lyon, France, 2006.

Griaule, Marcel. *Masques Dogons*. Paris: Institut d'Ethnologie, 1938.

Grove, Richard H. *Green Imperialism: Colonial Expansion, Tropical Island Edens, and the Origin of Environmentalism, 1600–1860*. New York: Cambridge University Press, 1995.

Gueye, Abdoulaye. "The Colony Strikes Back: African Protest Movements in Postcolonial France." *Comparative Studies of Asia, Africa, and the Middle East* 26, no. 2 (2006): 225–42.

Gueye, Mamadou, Siegfried Siegesmund, and Klaus Wemmer. "New Evidences for an Early Birimian Evolution in the West African Craton: An Example from the Kédougou-Kéniéba Inlier, Southeast Senegal." *South African Journal of Geology* 110, no. 3 (2007): 511–34.

Gupta, Akhil, and James Ferguson. "Spatializing States: Toward an Ethnography of Neoliberal Governmentality." *American Ethnologist* 29, no. 4 (2002): 981–1002.

Guy, Jeff, and Motlasti Thabane. "Technology, Ethnicity, and Ideology: Basotho Mines and Shaft-Sinking on the South African Gold Mines." *Journal of Southern African Studies* 14, no. 2 (1988): 257–78.

Guyer, Jane. "Indigenous Currencies and the History of Marriage Payments: A Case Study from Cameroon." *Cahiers d'Études Africaines* 26, no. 104 (1986): 577–610.

Guyer, Jane, ed. *Money Matters: Instability, Values, and Social Payments in the Modern History of West African Communities.* Portsmouth, NH: Heinemann, 1995.

Guyer, Jane. "Wealth in People and Self-realization in Equatorial Africa." *Man* 28 (1993): 243–65.

Hailey, William Malcolm. *An African Survey: A Study of Problems Arising in Africa South of the Sahara,* rev. ed. London: Oxford University Press, 1957.

Hair, Paul. "The Falls of Felou: A Bibliographical Exploration." *History in Africa* 11 (1984): 113–30.

Hall, Bruce. *A History of Race in Muslim West Africa, 1600–1960.* Cambridge: Cambridge University Press, 2011.

Hardin, Sarah. "Developing the Periphery: Cotton Production, Pesticide, and the Marginalization of the Fulbe of Southeastern Senegal over the Twentieth Century." PhD diss., University of Wisconsin, Madison, 2013.

Harries, Patrick. "Field Sciences in Scientific Fields: Ethnology, Botany, and the Early Ethnographic Monograph in the Work of H.-A. Junod." In *Science and Society in Southern Africa,* edited by Saul Dubow, 11–41. Manchester, UK: Manchester University Press, 2000.

Harries, Patrick. *Work, Culture, and Identity: Migrant Laborers in Mozambique and South Africa, ca. 1860–1910.* Portsmouth, NH: Heinemann, 1994.

Hawthorne, Walter. *Planting Rice and Harvesting Slaves: Transformations along the Guinea-Bissau Coast, 1400–1900.* Portsmouth, NH: Heinemann, 2003.

Headrick, Daniel. *The Tools of Empire: Technology and European Imperialism in the Nineteenth Century.* Oxford: Oxford University Press, 1981.

Hecht, Gabrielle. *Being Nuclear: Africans and the Global Uranium Trade.* Cambridge, MA: MIT Press 2012.

Hecht, Gabrielle, ed. *Entangled Geographies: Empire and Technopolitics in the Global Cold War.* Cambridge, MA: MIT Press, 2011.

Hecht, Gabrielle. "Interscalar Vehicles for an African Anthropocene: On Waste, Temporality, and Violence." *Cultural Anthropology* 33, no. 1 (2018): 109–41.

Hecquard, Hyacinte. *Voyage sur la côte et dans l'intérieur de l'Afrique occidentale.* Paris: Bénard, 1855.

Heller, Henry. *Labour, Science and Technology in France: 1500–1620.* Cambridge: Cambridge University Press, 2002.

Hellweg, Joseph. *Hunting the Ethical State: The Benkadi Movement of Côte d'Ivoire.* Chicago: University of Chicago Press, 2011.

Hentschel, Thomas, Felix Hruschka, and Michael Priester. *Global Report on Artisanal and Small-scale Mining.* Mining, Minerals and Sustainable Development report no. 70. London: International Institute for Environmental Development, 2002.

Herbert, Eugenia W. *Iron, Gender, and Power: Rituals of Transformation in African Societies*. Bloomington: Indiana University Press, 1993.

Herbert, Eugenia W. *Red Gold of Africa: Copper in Precolonial History and Culture*. Madison: University of Wisconsin Press, 1984.

Herbst, Jeffrey. *States and Power in Africa: Comparative Lessons in Authority and Control*. Princeton, NJ: Princeton University Press, 2017.

Hicks, Mary E. *Captive Cosmopolitans: Black Mariners and the World of South Atlantic Slavery, 1721–1835*. Chapel Hill: University of North Carolina Press, forthcoming.

High, Mette M. *Fear and Fortune: Spirit Worlds and Emerging Economies in the Mongolian Gold Rush*. Ithaca, NY: Cornell University Press, 2017.

High, Mette M. "Polluted Money, Polluted Wealth: Emerging Regimes of Value in the Mongolian Gold Rush." *American Ethnologist* 40, no. 4 (2013): 676–88.

Hilson, Abigail, Gavin Hilson, and Dauda Suleman. "Corporate Social Responsibility at African Mines: Linking the Past to the Present." *Journal of Environmental Management* 241 (2019): 340–52.

Hilson, Gavin. "'Once a Miner, Always a Miner': Poverty and Livelihood Diversification in Akwatia, Ghana." *Journal of Rural Studies* 26 (2010): 296–307.

Hilson, Gavin, Richard Amankwah, and Grace Ofori-Sarpong. "Going for Gold: Transitional Livelihoods in Northern Ghana." *Journal of Modern African Studies* 51, no. 1 (2013): 109–37.

Hilson, Gavin, and James McQuilken. "Four Decades of Support for Artisanal and Small-scale Mining in Sub-Saharan Africa." *Extractive Industries and Society* 1 (2014): 104–18.

Hilson, Gavin, Titus Sauerwein, and John Owen. "Large and Artisanal Scale Mine Development: The Case for Autonomous Co-existence." *World Development* 130 (2020): 104919.

Hilson, Gavin, and Natalia Yakovleva. "Strained Relations: A Critical Analysis of the Mining Conflict in Prestea, Ghana." *Political Geography* 26, no. 1 (2007): 98–119.

Hofmeyer, Isabel. *"We Spend Our Years as a Tale That Is Told": Oral Historical Narratives in a South African Chiefdom*. Portsmouth, NH: Heinemann, 1994.

Horton, Robin. "Stateless Societies in the History of West Africa." In *History of West Africa*, vol. 1, edited by J. F. Ade Ajayi and Michael Crowder, 78–119. New York: Columbia University Press, 1972.

Hubert, Henry. "Coutumes indigénes en matière d'exploitation de gîtes aurifères en Afrique occidentale." *Annuaire et mémoires du Comité d'Études Historiques et Scientifiques de l'Afrique Occidentale Française* (1917): 226–43.

Hubert, Henry. *Mission scientifique au Dahomey*. Paris: Émile Larose, 1908.

Huffman, Thomas N. "Snakes and Birds: Expressive Space at Great Zimbabwe." *African Studies* 40, no. 2 (1981): 131–50.

Human Rights Watch. "Precious Metals, Cheap Labor: Child Labor and Corporate Social Responsibility in Ghana's Artisanal Gold Mines." Human Rights Watch website, June 10, 2015. https://www.hrw.org/report/2015/06/10/precious-metal-cheap-labor/child-labor-and-corporate-responsibility-ghanas#.

Humblot, P. "Kankan, métropole de la Haute-Guinée." *L'Afrique Française* (1921): 129–40, 153–61.

Hunt, Nancy Rose. *A Colonial Lexicon: Of Birth, Ritual, Medicalization, and Mobility in the Congo.* Durham, NC: Duke University Press, 1999.

Hutchinson, Sharon E. *Nuer Dilemmas: Coping with Money, War, and the State.* Berkeley: University of California Press, 1996.

Innes, Gordon, Bamba Suso, and Banna Kanute. *Sunjata: Three Mandinka Versions.* London: School of Oriental and African Studies, University of London, 1974.

Institut Fondamental d'Afrique Noire-Université Cheik Anta Diop (IFAN-UCAD). "Prospections, fouilles archéologiques et enquêtes ethnographiques dans le périmètre minier de ToroGold à Mako, région de Kédougou." Unpublished report, Dakar, 2014.

International Labour Organization (ILO). "Social and Labour Issues in Small-scale Mine." Geneva: ILO, 1999.

Ivaska, Andrew. *Cultured States: Youth, Gender, and Modern Style in 1960s Dar es Salaam.* Durham, NC: Duke University Press, 2011.

Jacobs, Nancy. "The Intimate Politics of Ornithology in Colonial Africa." *Comparative Studies in Society and History* 48, no. 3 (2006): 564–603.

Jacoby, Karl. *Crimes against Nature: Squatters, Poachers, Thieves, and the Hidden History of American Conservation.* Berkeley: University of California Press, 2003.

Jansen, Jan. "What Gold Mining Means for the Malinke, and How It Was Misunderstood by the French Colonial Administration." In *Worlds of Debts: Interdisciplinary Perspectives on Gold Mining in West Africa*, edited by Christiana Panella, 95–110. Amsterdam: Rozenberg, 2010.

Jansen, Jan. "The Younger Brother and the Stranger: In Search of a Status Discourse for Mande." *Cahiers d'Études Africaines* 36, no. 4 (1996): 659–88.

Jaramillo, Pablo. "Mining Leftovers: Making Futures on the Margins of Capitalism." *Cultural Anthropology* 35, no. 1 (2020): 48–73.

Jézéquel, Jean-Hervé. "Voices of Their Own? African Participation in the Production of Colonial Knowledge in French West Africa, 1900–50." In *Ordering Africa: Anthropology, European Imperialism, and the Politics of Knowledge*, edited by Helen Tilley and Robert Gordon, 145–172. Manchester, UK: Manchester University Press, 2010.

Johnson, John William, and Fa-Digi Sisòkò. *The Epic of Son-Jara: A West African Tradition.* Bloomington: Indiana University Press, 1986.

Johnson, Paul. "Atlantic Genealogy of 'Spirit Possession.'" *Comparative Studies in Society and History* 53, no. 2 (2011): 393–425.

Johnson, Paul, ed. *Spirited Things: The Work of "Possession" in Afro-Atlantic Religions.* Chicago: University of Chicago Press, 2014.

Joire, Jean M. "Découvertes archéologiques dans la région de Rao (Bas Sénégal)." *Bulletin de l'Institut Français d'Afrique Noire* (series B) 17, nos. 3–4 (1955): 249–333.

Kaba, Lansiné. "The Cultural Revolution, Artistic Creativity, and Freedom of Expression in Guinea." *Journal of Modern African Studies* 14 (1976): 201–18.

Kaba, Lansiné. "Islam, Society and Politics in Precolonial Baté (Guinea)." *Bulletin de l'Institut Fondamental d'Afrique Noire* (series B) 35, no. 2 (1973): 323–44.

Kaba, Lansiné, and Eric Charry. "Mamaya: Renewal and Tradition in Maninnka Music of Kankan, Guinea, 1935–45." In *African Diaspora: A Musical Perspective*, edited by Ingrid Monson, 187–206. London: Psychology Press, 2003.

Kananoja, Kalle. "'Infected by the Devil, Cured by Calundu': African Healers in Eighteenth-Century Minas Gerais, Brazil." *Social History of Medicine* 29, no. 3 (2016): 490–511.

Kane, Abdoulaye. "Senegal's Village Diaspora and the People Left Behind." In *The Transnational Family: New European Frontiers and Global Networks*, edited by Deborah Bryceson and Ulla Vuorella, 245–63. London: Berg, 2002.

Kane, Oumar. *La première hégémonie peule: Le Fuuta Tooro de Koli Teŋella à Al-maami Abdul*. Paris: Karthala, 2004.

Kane, Ousmane. *Beyond Timbuktu: An Intellectual History of Muslim West Africa*. Cambridge, MA: Harvard University Press, 2016.

Keita, Fodeba. "Autour des placers du Cercle de Siguiri." *Notes Africaines*, vol. 27 (1945), 16–18.

Kesteloot, Lilyan. "Les Mandingues de Casamance: Kankourang, castes et kora." In *Comprendre la Casamance: Chronique d'une intégration contrastée*, edited by François-George Barbier-Wiesser, 97–117. Paris: Karthala, 1994.

Kiéthéga, Jean-Baptiste. *L'or de la Volta noire: Archéologie et histoire de l'exploitation traditionnelle, région de Poura, Haute-Volta*. Paris: Karthala, 1983.

Killick, David. "Invention and Innovation in African Iron Smelting Technology." *Cambridge Archeological Journal* 25, no. 1 (2015): 307–19.

Killick, David. "Iron Smelting Technology in the Middle Senegal Valley, ca. 550 BCE–1500 CE." In *The Search for Takrur: Archaeological Excavations and Reconnaissance along the Middle Senegal River Valley*, edited by Roderick J. McIntosh, Susan Keech McIntosh, and Hamady Bocoum, 191–280. New Haven, CT: Yale University Press, 2016.

Kilroy-Marac, Katie. *An Impossible Inheritance: Postcolonial Psychiatry and the Work of Memory in a West African Clinic*. Berkeley: University of California Press, 2019.

Kirsch, Stuart. "Indigenous Movements and the Risks of Counterglobalization: Tracking the Campaign against Papua New Guinea's OK Tedi mine." *American Ethnologist* 34, no. 2 (2007): 303–21.

Kirsch, Stuart. *Mining Capitalism: The Relationship between Corporations and Their Critics*. Berkeley: University of California Press, 2014.

Kirsch, Stuart. "Property Effects: Social Networks and Compensation Claims in Melanesia." *Social Anthropology* 9, no. 2 (2001): 147–63.

Kirsch, Stuart. *Reverse Anthropology: Indigenous Analysis of Social and Environmental Relations in New Guinea*. Stanford, CA: Stanford University Press, 2006.

Klare, Michael T. *The Race for What's Left: The Global Scramble for the World's Resources*. New York: Metropolitan, 2001.

Klein, Martin. "The Slave Trade and Decentralized Societies." *Journal of African History* 42 (2001): 49–65.

Kneas, David. "Subsoil Abundance and Surface Absence: A Junior Mining Company and Its Performance of Prognosis in Northwestern Ecuador." *Journal of the Royal Anthropological Institute* (series 1) 22 (2016): 67–86.

Knell, Simon. *The Culture of English Geology, 1815–1851*. Aldershot, UK: Ashgate, 2000.

Kodesh, Neil. "History from the Healer's Shrine: Genre, Historical Imagination and Early Ganda History." *Comparative Studies in Society and HIstory* 2007, no. 3 (2007): 527–52.

Kohler, Robert. *All Creatures: Naturalists, Collectors, and Biodiversity, 1850–1950*. Princeton, NJ: Princeton University Press, 2006.

Konadu, Kwasi. *The Akan Diaspora in the Americas*. Oxford: Oxford University Press, 2010.

Kopytoff, Igor. *The African Frontier: The Reproduction of Traditional African Societies*. Bloomington: Indiana University Press, 1987.

Kroot, Matthew V., and Cameron Gokee. "Histories and Material Manifestations of Slavery in the Upper Gambia River Region: Preliminary Results of the Bandafassi Regional Archeological Project." *Journal of African Diaspora Archaeology and Heritage* 7, no. 2 (2019): 74–104.

Kusiak, Pauline. "'Tubab' Technologies and 'African' Ways of Knowing: Nationalist Techno-politics in Senegal." *History and Technology* 26, no. 3 (2010): 225–49.

Labat, Jean-Baptiste. *Nouvelle relation de l'Afrique occidentale*. Paris: G. Cavelier, 1728.

Labouret, Henri. "L'Afrique-Occidentale Française en 1934." In *Afrique française, Comité de l'Afrique Française et du Comité du Maroc*. Paris: Imprimerie Nationale, 1936.

Labouret, Henri. "L'or du Lobi." *Afrique Française* (suppl.), no. 3 (March 1925): 68–73.

Labouret, Henri. *Les tribus du rameau Lobi*. Paris: Institut d'Ethnologie, 1931.

Lachenal, Guillaume. "The Intimate Rules of the French 'Coopération': Morality, Race and the Post-colonial Division of Scientific Work at the Pasteur Institute of Cameroon." In *Evidence, Ethos and Experiment: The Anthropology and History of Medical Research in Africa*, edited by Wenzel Geissler and Sassy Molyneux, 373–402. Oxford: Berghahn, 2011.

La Fleur, James D. *Fusion Foodways of Africa's Gold Coast in the Atlantic Era*. Leiden: Brill, 2012.

Lahiri-Dutt, Kuntala, ed. *Between the Plough and the Pick: Informal, Artisanal, and Small-scale Mining in the Contemporary World*. Acton: Australian National University Press, 2018.

Lalouel, J., and A. Langaney. "Bedik and Niokholonko of Senegal: Inter-village Relationship Inferred from Migration Data." *American Journal of Human Genetics* 45 (1976): 453–66.

Landau, Paul. "'Religion and Christian Conversion in African History: A New Model." *Journal of Religious History* 23, no. 1 (1999): 8–30.

Lange, Dierk. *Ancient Kingdoms of West Africa: African-centered and Canaanite-Israelite Perspectives: A Collection of Published and Unpublished Studies in English and French*. Dettelbach, Germany: Röll, 2004.

Langwick, Stacey. "Properties of (Dis)Posessions: Therapeutic Plants, Intellectual Property, and Questions of Justice in Tanzania." *Osiris* 36, no. 1 (2021): 284–305.

Latour, Bruno. *We Have Never Been Modern*. Cambridge, MA: Harvard University Press, 1993.

Launay, Robert, and Benjamin F. Soares. "The Formation of an 'Islamic Sphere' in French Colonial West Africa." *Economy and Society* 28, no. 4 (1999): 497–519.

Laye, Camara. *The Dark Child*. Translated by James Kirkup and Ernest Jones. New York: Farrar, Straus and Giroux, [1954] 1994.

Le Barbier, L. "Comment les noirs extraient l'or à la Côte d'Ivoire." *Tour du Monde* 25 (1903): 88–89.

Legoux, Pierre. "L'Afrique-Occidentale Française avant la Second Guerre mondiale." In *Les mines et la recherche minière en Afrique-Occidentale Française*, edited by Jean Servant, Pierre Legoux, and André Marelle, 9–29. Paris: L'Harmattan, 1991.

Legvold, Robert. *Soviet Policy in West Africa*. Cambridge, MA: Harvard University Press, 1972.

Lentz, Carola. *Land, Mobility, and Belonging in West Africa*. Bloomington: Indiana University Press, 2013.

Lerman, Nina E. "Categories of Difference, Categories of Power: Bringing Gender and Race to the History of Technology." *Technology and Culture* 51, no. 4 (2010): 893–918.

Lévi-Strauss, Claude. *La pensée sauvage*. Paris: Librairie Plon, 1962.

Levtzion, Nehemia. *Ancient Ghana and Mali*. London: Metheun, 1981.

Levtzion, Nehemia, and J. F. P. Hopkins, eds. *Corpus of Early Arabic Sources for West African History*. Cambridge: Cambridge University Press, 1981.

Li, Fabiana. "Documenting Accountability: Environmental Impact Assessment in a Peruvian Mining Project." *Political and Legal Anthropology Review* 32, no. 2 (2009): 218–36.

Li, Fabiana. *Unearthing Conflict: Corporate Mining, Activism, and Expertise in Peru*. Durham, NC: Duke University Press, 2015.

Ligers, Ziedonis. "Comment les Peuls de Koa castrent leurs taureaux." *Bulletin de l'Institut Fondamental d'Afrique Noire* (series B) 20, nos. 1–2 (1958): 191–204.

Ling, Stephen, Patti Nakai-Lajoie, Peter L. Mann, Kathleen Ann Altman, and Jeff Sepp. "Technical Report on the Sabodala Project, Sénégal, West Africa." NI 43-101. Roscoe Postle Associates, Toronto, August 30, 2017.

Livingston, Julie. *Debility and the Moral Imagination in Botswana*. Bloomington: Indiana University Press, 2005.

Livingston, Julie. *Improvising Medicine: An African Oncology Ward in an Emerging Cancer Epidemic*. Durham, NC: Duke University Press, 2012.

Livingston, Julie. *Self-devouring Growth: A Planetary Parable as Told from Southern Africa*. Durham, NC: Duke University Press, 2019.

Logan, Amanda. *The Scarcity Slot: Excavating Histories of African Food Security*. Berkeley: University of California Press, 2020.

Lucier, Paul. "Commercial Interests and Scientific Disinterestedness: Consulting Geologists in Antebellum America." *Isis* 86, no. 2 (1995): 245–67.

Luning, Sabine. "Gold, Cosmology, and Social Change in Burkina Faso." In *Lives in Motion, Indeed: Interdisciplinary Perspectives on Social Change in Honor of Danielle de Lame*, edited by Christiana Panella, 323–40. Tervuren, Belgium: Koninklijk Museum voor Midden-Afrika, 2012.

Luning, Sabine, Jan Jansen, and Christiana Panella. "The *Mise en Valeur* of the Gold Mines in the Haut-Niger, 1918–1939." *French Colonial History* 15 (2014): 67–86.

Luning, Sabine, and Robert J. Pijpers. "Governing Access to Gold in Ghana: In-depth Geopolitics on Mining Concessions." *Africa* 87, no. 4 (2017): 758–79.

Lydon, Ghislaine. *On Trans-Saharan Trails: Islamic Law, Trade Networks and Cross-Cultural Exchange in Nineteenth-Century Western Africa*. Cambridge: Cambridge University Press, 2009.

Ly-Tall, Madina. *Contribution à l'histoire de l'Empire du Mali (XIII à XVI siècles): Limites, principales provinces, institutions politiques*. Dakar: Nouvelles Éditions Africaines, 1977.

MacArthur, Julie. *Cartography and the Political Imagination: Mapping Community in Colonial Kenya*. Athens: Ohio University Press, 2016.

MacDonald, Kevin C., and P. Allsworth-Jones. "A Reconsideration of the West African Macrolithic Conundrum: New Factory Sites and an Associated Settlement in the Vallée du Serpent, Mali." *African Archaeological Review* 12, no. 1 (1994): 73–104.

Maconachie, Roy. "Re-agrarianising Livelihoods in Post-conflict Sierra Leone? Mineral Wealth and Rural Challenges in Artisanal and Small-scale Mining Communities." *Journal of International Development* 23 (2011): 1054–67.

Magnavita, Sonja. "First Geophysical Exploration in the Tumuli Zone of Central Senegal: A Multidimensional Approach." *Azania* 52, no. 1 (2017): 100–22.

Magnavita, Sonja. "Sahelian Crossroads: Some Aspects on the Iron Age Sites of Kissi, Burkina Faso." In *Crossroads/ Carrefour Sahel: Cultural and Technological Developments in First Millennium BC/AD West Africa*, edited by Sonja Magnavita, Lassina Koté, Peter Breunig, and Oumarou A. Idé, 79–104. Frankfurt: Africa Magna, 2009.

Magnavita, Sonja, and Carlos Magnavita. "All That Glitters Is Not Gold: Facing the Myths of Ancient Trade between North and Western Africa." In *Landscapes, Sources and Intellectual Projects of the West African Past: Essays in Honour of Paulo Fernando de Moraes Farias*, edited by Toby Green and Benedetta Rossi, 25–45. Leiden: Brill, 2018.

Magnavita, Sonja, and Regina Mertz-Kraus. "XRF and LA- ICP-MS Studies of Gold and Silver Artefacts from a 12–13th Century CE Tumulus in Senegal: Implications for the Medieval African Gold Trade." *Journal of Archeological Science: Reports* 23 (2019): 416–25.

Makori, Timothy. "Mobilizing the Past: *Creuseurs*, Precarity, and the Colonizing Structure in the Congo Copperbelt." *Africa* 87, no. 4 (2017): 780–805.

Malgras, Denis. *Arbres et arbustes guérisseurs des savanes maliennes*. Paris: Karthala, 1992.

Malinowski, Bronislaw. *Magic, Science and Religion, and Other Essays*. Boston: Beacon, 1948.

Manchuelle, François. *Willing Migrants: Soninke Labor Diasporas, 1848–1960*. Athens: Ohio University Press, 1997.

Mann, Gregory. "Anti-colonialism and Social Science: Georges Balandier, Madeira Keita, and 'the Colonial Situation' in French Africa." *Comparative Studies in Society and History* 55, no. 1 (2013): 92–119.

Mann, Gregory. *From Empires to NGOs in the West African Sahel: The Road to Non-governmentality*. Cambridge: Cambridge University Press, 2014.

Mann, Gregory. *Native Sons: West African Veterans and France in the Twentieth Century*. Durham, NC: Duke University Press, 2006.

Mann, Gregory. "What's in an Alias? Family Names, Individual Histories, and Historical Method in the Western Sudan." *History of Africa* 29 (2002): 309–20.

Mann, Gregory. "What Was the *Indigénat*? The 'Empire of Law' in French West Africa." *Journal of African History* 50 (2009): 331–53.

Mantz, Jeffrey. "Improvisational Economies: Coltan Production in Eastern Congo." *Social Anthropology* 16, no. 1 (2008): 34–50.

Marelle, André. "L'Afrique-Occidentale Française de 1944 à 1960." In *Les Mines et la recherche minière en Afrique-Occidentale Française*, edited by Jean Servant, Pierre Legoux, and André Marelle, 31–122. Paris: L'Harmattan, 1991.

Mathelin de Papigny, Hippolyte Marie. "Note sur les exploitations indigènes du Satadougou." *Bulletin du Comité d'Études Historiques et Scientifiques de l'Afrique-Occidentale Française* 8, no. 3 (1925): 394–404.

Matory, J. Lorand. *Black Atlantic Religion: Tradition, Transnationalism, and Matriarchy in the Afro-Brazilian Candomblé*. Princeton, NJ: Princeton University Press, 2009.

Mauny, Raymond. *Tableau géographique de l'Ouest africain au Moyen Age*. Dakar: Institut Fondamental d'Afrique Noire, 1961.

Mavhunga, Clapperton Chakanesta. "A Plundering Tiger with Its Deadly Cubs? The USSR and China as Weapons in the Engineering of a Zimbabwean Nation, 1945–2009." In *Entangled Geographies: Empire and Technopolitics in the Global Cold War*, edited by Gabrielle Hecht, 231–66. Cambridge, MA: MIT Press, 2011.

Mavhunga, Clapperton Chakanesta. *Transient Workspaces: Technologies of Everyday Innovation in Zimbabwe*. Cambridge, MA: MIT Press, 2014.

Mbodj, Faty. "Boom aurifère à l'est du Sénégal, l'ouest du Mali et au nord-est de la Guinée: Mutations socio-économiques et spatiales d'anciennes marges géographiques et économiques." PhD thesis, Université Gaston Berger, St. Louis, Sénégal, 2011.

Mbodj, Faty. "Boom aurifère et dynamiques économiques entre Sénégal, Mali et Guinée." *EchoGéo* 8 (2009). https://doi.org/10/4000/echogeo.11034.

Mbodj, Mohamed. "La crise trentenaire de l'économie arachidière." In *Sénégal: Trajectoires d'un état*, edited by Momar-Coumba Diop, 431–77. Dakar: Council for the Development of Social Science Research, 1992.

McDougall, Ann E. "Salts of the Western Sahara: Myths, Mysteries, and Historical Significance." *International Journal of African Historical Studies* 23, no. 2 (1990): 231–57.

McGovern, Mike. *A Socialist Peace? Explaining the Absence of War in a West African Country*. Chicago: University of Chicago Press, 2018.

McGovern, Mike. *Unmasking the State: Making Guinea Modern*. Chicago: University of Chicago Press, 2013.

McIntosh, Janet. *The Edge of Islam: Power, Personhood, and Ethno-religious Boundaries on the Kenya Coast*. Durham, NC: Duke University Press, 2009.

McIntosh, Roderick J. *Ancient Middle Niger: Urbanism and the Self-organizing Landscape*. Cambridge: Cambridge University Press, 2005.

McIntosh, Roderick J. *The Peoples of the Middle Niger: The Island of Gold*. Oxford: Blackwell Publishers, 1988.

McIntosh, Roderick J., Susan Keech McIntosh, and Hamady Bocoum. *The Search for Takrur: Archaeological Excavations and Reconnaissance along the Middle Senegal Valley*. New Haven, CT: Yale University Press, 2017.

McIntosh, Susan Keech, ed. *Beyond Chiefdoms: Pathways to Complexity in Africa*. Cambridge: Cambridge University Press, 2009.

McIntosh, Susan Keech. *Excavations at Jenné-jeno, Hambarketolo, and Kaniana (Inland Niger Delta, Mali), the 1981 Season*. Berkeley: University of California Press, 1995.

McIntosh, Susan Keech. "Reconceptualizing Early Ghana." *Canadian Journal of African Studies* 42, nos. 2–3 (2008): 347–73.

McIntosh, Susan Keech. "A Reconsideration of Wangāra/Palolus, Island of Gold." *Journal of African History* 22 (1981): 145–58.

McLaughlin, Fiona. "Dakar Wolof and the Configuration of an Urban Identity." *Journal of African Cultural Studies* 14, no. 2 (2001): 153–172.

McLaughlin, Fiona. "Senegal: The Emergence of a National Lingua Franca." In *Language and National Identity in Africa*, edited by Andrew Simpson, 79–97. Oxford: Oxford University Press, 2008.

McNaughton, Patrick. *The Mande Blacksmiths: Knowledge, Power, and Art in West Africa*. Bloomington: Indiana University Press, 1988.

Mehos, Donna, and Suzanne Moon. "The Uses of Portability: Circulating Experts and the Technopolitics of Cold War and Decolonization." In *Entangled Geographies: Empire and Technopolitics in the Global Cold War*, edited by Gabrielle Hecht, 43–74. Cambridge, MA: MIT Press, 2011.

Meiu, George Paul. *Ethno-erotic Economies: Sexuality, Money and Belonging in Kenya*. Chicago: University of Chicago Press, 2017.

Méniaud, Jacques. *Haut-Sénégal-Niger (Soudan français): Géographie économique*. Paris: Émile Larose, 1912.

Meyer, Gérard. *Contes du pays malinké: Contes malinkes du Sénégal Oriental*. Kédougou: Mission Catholique, 1983.

Miers, Suzanne, and Igor Kopytoff, eds. *Slavery in Africa: Historical and Anthropological Perspectives*. Madison: University of Wisconsin Press, 1977.

Mika, Marissa. *Africanizing Oncology: Creativity, Crisis, and Cancer in Uganda*. Athens: Ohio University Press, 2021.

Mitchell, Timothy. *Carbon Democracy: Political Power in the Age of Oil*. London: Verso, 2011.

Mitchell, Timothy. *Rule of Experts: Egypt, Techno-politics, Modernity*. Berkeley: University of California Press, 2002.

Moffat, Kieren, and Airong Zhang. "The Paths to Social License to Operate: An Integrative Model Explaining Community Acceptance of Mining." *Resources Policy* 39 (March 2014): 61–70.

Mollien, Gaspard Théodore, Comte de. *Travels in the Interior of Africa, to the Sources of the Senegal and Gambia, in 1818*. London: Sir R. Phillips, 1820.

Monroe, J. Cameron. "Power and Agency in Precolonial African States." *Annual Review of Anthropology* 42 (2013): 17–35.

Monteil, Charles. "La légende du Ougadou et l'histoire des Soninké." *Mélanges Ethnologiques* (1953): 362–408.

Moodie, Dunbar T., and Vivienne Ndatshe. *Going for Gold: Men, Mines, and Migration*. Berkeley: University of California Press, 1994.

Moore, Francis. *Travels into the Inland Parts of Africa*. London: Edward Cave, 1738.

Morgenthau, Ruth Schachter. *Political Parties in French-speaking West Africa*. Oxford: Clarendon, 1964.

Morris, Rosalind C. "Shadow and Impress: Ethnography, Film, and the Task of Writing History in the Space of South Africa's Deindustrialization." *History and Theory* 56 (December 2018): 102–25.

Moussa, Bantenga. "L'or des régions de Poura et de Gaoua: Les vicissitudes de l'exploitation coloniale, 1925–1960." *International Journal of African Historical Studies* 28, no. 3 (1995): 563–76.

Mukharji, Projit Bihari. *Doctoring Traditions: Ayurveda, Small Technologies, and Braided Sciences*. Chicago: University of Chicago Press, 2016.

Murphy, Edward, David Cohen, Chandra Bhimull, Fernando Coronil, Monica Patterson, and Julie Skurski, eds. *Anthrohistory: Unsettling Knowledge, Questioning Discipline*. Ann Arbor: University of Michigan Press, 2011.

Nash, June. *We Eat the Mines and the Mines Eat Us: Dependency and Exploitation in Bolivian Tin Mines*. New York: Columbia University Press, 1993.

Naylor, Simon, and Gareth A. Jones. "Writing Orderly Geographies of Distant Places: The Regional Survey Movement and Latin America." *Ecumene* 4, no. 3 (1997): 273–99.

N'Daou, Saidou Mohamed. *Sangalan Oral Traditions: History, Memories, and Social Differentiation*. Durham, NC: Carolina Academic Press, 2005.

Ndiaye, Papa Moussa. "Étude géologique et métallogénique de la partie septentrionale du granite de Saraya (Sénégal Oriental)." PhD diss., Université Cheikh Anta Diop, Dakar, 1986.

Needham, Andrew. *Power Lines: Phoenix and the Making of the Modern Southwest*. Princeton, NJ: Princeton University Press, 2014.

Newbury, Catherine W. "The Formation of the Government General of French West Africa." *Journal of African History* 1 (1960): 111–28.

Ngom, Fallou. *Muslims beyond the Arab World: The Odyssey of Ajamī and the Murīdiyya*. New York: Oxford University Press, 2016.

Ngom, Papa Malick. "Contribution à l'étude de la série birrimienne de Mako dans le secteur aurifère de Sabodala (Sénégal Oriental)." PhD diss., Université de Nancy I, France, 1995.

Niane, Djibril Tamsir. *Histoire des Mandingues de l'Ouest*. Paris: Karthala, 2018.

Niane, Djibril Tamsir. *Soundjata ou l'épopée mandingue*. Paris: Présence Africaine, 1960.

Niang, Aminata. "Mining as Development? Corporate/Community Relationships in the New Gold Mining Sector of West Africa: The Case of Sabodala, Senegal." PhD diss., University of Arizona, Tucson, 2012.

Niang, Biraime. "Impacts environnementaux liée à l'utilisation du mercure lors de l'exploitation artisanale de l'or dans la région de Kédougou (Sénégal Oriental)." PhD diss., Université de Genève, Geneva, Switzerland, 2014.

Niang, Ibrahima. "Développement du tourisme dans la région du Sénégal Oriental." *Cahiers du Centre de Recherches Anthropologiques* (22d series) 2, nos. 1–2 (1967): 174–76.

Niang, Kaly. *Dans les mines d'or du Sénégal Oriental: La fin de l'orpaillage?* Paris: L'Harmattan, 2014.

Nixon, Sam, ed. *Essouk Tadmekka: An Early Islamic Trans-Saharan Market Town.* Leiden: Brill, 2017.

Nixon, Sam. "Trans-Saharan Gold Trade in Pre-modern Times: Available Evidence and Research Agendas." In *Trade in the Ancient Sahara and Beyond*, edited by D. J. Mattingly, V. Leitch, C. N. Duckworth, A. Cuénod, M. Sterry, and F. Cole, 156–88. Cambridge: Cambridge University Press, 2017.

Noirot, Ernest. *À travers le Fouta-Diallon et le Bambouc (Soudan occidental): Souvenirs de voyage.* Paris: Maurice Drefous, 1884.

Nugent, Paul. *Boundaries, Communities, and State-making in West Africa: The Centrality of the Margins.* Cambridge: Cambridge University Press, 2019.

Obermuller, Alphonse. "Difficultés d'un géologue inexpérimenté débutant en AOF." In *Les mines et la recherche minière en Afrique-Occidentale Française*, edited by Jean Servant, Pierre Legoux, and André Marelle, 125–32. Paris: L'Harmattan, 1991.

O'Brien, Donald Cruise. *The Mourides of Senegal: The Political and Economic Organization of an Islamic Brotherhood.* Oxford: Clarendon, 1971.

O'Brien, Donald Cruise. "The Shadow Politics of Wolofisation." *Journal of Modern African Studies* 36, no. 1 (1995): 25–46.

O'Brien, Rita Cruise. *White Society in Black Africa: The French of Senegal.* Evanston, IL: Northwestern University Press, 1972.

Oguz, Zeynep. "Theorizing the Contemporary: Geological Anthropology." *Fieldsights*, September 22, 2020. https://culanth.org/fieldsights/series/geological-anthropology.

Oldroyd, David R. *Thinking about the Earth: A History of Ideas in Geology.* Cambridge, MA: Harvard University Press, 1996.

Oreskes, Naomi. "A Context of Motivation: US Navy Oceanographic Research and the Discovery of Sea-Floor Hydrothermal Vents." *Social Studies of Science* 33 (2003): 697–742.

Organization for Economic Cooperation and Development (OECD). *Due Diligence Guidance for Responsible Supply Chains of Minerals from Conflict-Affected and High-Risk Areas.* Paris: OECD, 2017.

Osborn, Emily. "Interpreting Colonial Power in French Guinea: The Boubou Penda-Ernest Noirot Affair of 1905." In *Intermediaries, Interpreters, and Clerks: African Employees in the Making of Colonial Africa*, edited by Benjamin N. Lawrance, Emily Lynn Osborn, and Richard L. Roberts, 56–76. Madison: University of Wisconsin Press, 2006.

Osborn, Emily. "'Rubber Fever,' Commerce and French Colonial Rule in Upper Guinea, 1890–1913." *Journal of African History* 45 (2004): 445–65.

Osseo-Asare, Abena Dove. *Atomic Junction: Nuclear Power in Africa after Independence*. Cambridge: Cambridge University Press, 2019.

Osseo-Asare, Abena Dove. *Bitter Roots: The Search for Healing Plants in Africa*. Chicago: University of Chicago Press, 2014.

Osseo-Asare, Abena Dove. "Scientific Equity: Experiments in Laboratory Education in Ghana." *Isis* 104, no. 4 (2013): 713–41.

Özden-Schilling, Tom. "Theorizing the Contemporary: Regions, in Theory." *Fieldsights*, September 22, 2020. https://culanth.org/fieldsights/regions-in -theory.

Özden-Schilling, Tom. "Trust in Ventures: Serious Numbers and Speculative Fictions in Rare Earth Elements." Unpublished ms.

Pageard, R. "Plantes à brûler chez les Bambara." *Journal de la Société des Africanistes* 37, no. 1 (1967): 87–130.

Palmié, Stephan. "Historicist Knowledge and Its Conditions of Impossibility." In *The Social Life of Spirits*, edited by Ruy Blanes and Diana Espírito Santo, 218–39. Chicago: University of Chicago Press, 2013.

Palmié, Stephan, and Charles Stewart. "Introduction: For an Anthropology of History." *HAU: Journal of Ethnographic Theory* 6, no. 1 (2016): 207–36.

Panella, Christiana. "L'éthique sociale du Damansen: Education familiale et orpaillage artisanal dans le Basidibe (Wasolon, Mali)." *Cahiers d'Études Africaines* 186 (2007): 345–70.

Panella, Christiana, ed. *Worlds of Debts: Interdisciplinary Perspectives on Gold Mining in West Africa*. Amsterdam: Rozenberg, 2010.

Park, Emma. "'Human-ATMs': M-Pesa and the Expropriation of Affective Work in Safaricom's Kenya." *Africa* 90, no. 5 (2020): 914–33.

Park, Emma, Derek R. Peterson, Anne Pitcher, and Keith Breckenridge. "Intellectual and Cultural Work in Times of Austerity: Introduction." *Africa* 91, no. 4 (2021): 517–31.

Park, Mungo. *Travels in the Interior Districts of Africa Performed in the Years 1795, 1796, and 1797*. London: John Murray, 1816.

Peluso, Nancy Lee. "Entangled Territories in Small-scale Gold Mining Frontiers: Labor Practices, Property, and Secrets in Indonesian Gold Country." *World Development* 101 (2018): 400–416.

Perinbam, Marie B. "The Political Organization of Traditional Gold Mining: The Western Loby, c. 1850 to c. 1910." *Journal of African History* 29, no. 3 (1988): 437–62.

Perinbam, Marie B. "Social Relations in the Trans-Saharan and Western Sudanese Trade: An Overview." *Comparative Studies in Society and History* 15, no. 4 (1973): 416–36.

Peroz, Etienne. *Au Soudan français: Souvenirs de guerre et de mission*. Paris: Calmann Lévy, 1889.

Persaud, Anthony W. "Mercury Use and the Socio-economic Significance of Artisanal and Small-scale Gold (ASGM) Mining in Senegal: A Mixed-Methods Approach to Understanding ASGM." Master's thesis, University of Victoria, British Columbia, 2015.

Persaud, Anthony W., Kevin H. Telmer, Maycira Costa, and Michele-Lee Moore. "Artisanal and Small-scale Gold Mining in Senegal: Livelihoods, Customary Authority, and Formalization." *Society and Natural Resources* 30, no. 8 (2017): 980–93.

Person, Yves. "French West Africa and Decolonization' In *The Transfer of Power in Africa: Decolonization 1940–1960*, edited by Prosser Gifford and William Roger Louis 141–72. New Haven, CT: Yale University Press, 1982.

Peterson, Brian J. *Islamization from Below: The Making of Muslim Communities in Rural French Sudan, 1880–1960*. New Haven, CT: Yale University Press, 2011.

Peterson, Derek R., and Giacomo Macola. *Recasting the Past: History Writing and Political Work in Modern Africa*. Athens: Ohio University Press, 2009.

Philips, Kristin D. *An Ethnography of Hunger: Politics, Subsistence, and the Unpredictable Grace of the Sun*. Bloomington: Indiana University Press, 2018.

Pitcher, Anne, and Kelly M. Askew. "African Socialisms and Postsocialisms." *Africa* 76, no. 1 (2006): 1–14.

Porter, Roy. *The Making of Geology: Earth Science in Britain, 1660–1815*. Cambridge: Cambridge University Press, 1977.

Powdermaker, Hortense. *Copper Town: Changing Africa: The Human Situation on the Rhodesian Copperbelt*. New York: Harper and Row, 1962.

Powell, Dana. *Landscapes of Power: Politics of Energy in the Navajo Nation*. Durham, NC: Duke University Press, 2017.

Pritchard, Sara B. *Confluence: The Nature of Technology and the Remaking of the Rhône*. Cambridge, MA: Harvard University Press, 2011.

Pure Earth. "Global Mercury Program." Blacksmith Institute. Accessed September 10, 2020. http://www.pureearth.org/global-mercury-program.

Quarshie, Nana Osei. "Psychiatry on a Shoestring: West Africa and the Global Movements of Deinstitutionalization." *Bulletin of the History of Medicine*, 96, no. 2 (forthcoming summer 2022).

Raby, Megan. *American Tropics: The Caribbean Roots of Biodiversity Science*. Chapel Hill: University of North Carolina Press, 2017.

Raffenel, Anne. *Voyage dans l'Afrique occidentale*. Paris: A. Bertrand, 1846.

Raj, Kapil. *Relocating Modern Science: Circulation and the Construction of Knowledge in South Asia and Europe, 1650–1900*. New York: Palgrave Macmillan, 2007.

Rajak, Dinah. *In Good Company: An Anatomy of Corporate Social Responsibility*. Stanford, CA: Stanford University Press, 2011.

Rançon, André. *Dans la Haute-Gambie: Voyage d'exploration scientifique, 1891–1892*. Paris: Société d'Éditions Scientifiques, 1895.

Ranger, Terrence O. *Voices from the Rocks: Nature, Culture and History in the Matopos Hills of Zimbabwe*. Harare: Baobab, 1999.

Rehren, Thilo, and Sam Nixon. "Refining Gold with Glass—An Early Islamic Technology at Tadmekka, Mali." *Journal of Archeological Science* 49 (2014): 33–41.

République du Sénégal. *Pays Bassari: Paysages culturels Bassari, Peul, et Bédik. Proposition d'inscription sur la liste du patrimoine mondial*, January 2011. https://whc.unesco.org/uploads/nominations/1407.pdf.

République du Sénégal. *Recensement général de la population et de l'habitat de 1988, rapport régional Tambacounda.* Dakar: Ministère de l'Economie, des Finances et du Plan, 1992.

Ribot, Jesse C. "Authority over Forests: Empowerment and Subordination in Senegal's Democratic Decentralization." *Development and Change* 40, no. 1 (2009): 105–29.

Richard, François G. *Reluctant Landscapes: Historical Anthropologies of Political Experience in Siin, Senegal.* Chicago: University of Chicago Press, 2018.

Richards, Paul. *Indigenous Agricultural Revolution: Ecology and Food Production in West Africa.* London: Hutchinson, 1985.

Robequain, Charles. "Problèmes de l'économie rurale en AOF." *Annales de Géographie* 46 (1937): 137–63.

Roberts, Carolyn E. "To Heal and to Harm: Medicine, Knowledge, and Power in the Atlantic Slave Trade." PhD. diss., Harvard University, Cambridge, MA, 2017.

Roberts, Richard. "The Emergence of a Grain Market in Bamako, 1883–1908." *Canadian Journal of African Studies* 14, no. 1 (1980): 37–54.

Roberts, Richard. *Two Worlds of Cotton: Colonialism and the Regional Economy in the French Soudan.* Stanford, CA: Stanford University Press, 1996.

Roberts, Richard, and Kristin Mann. "Law in Colonial Africa." In *Law in Colonial Africa*, edited by Richard Roberts and Kristin Mann, 3–58. Portsmouth, NH: Heinemann, 1991.

Robin, Hervé. "La vie dans un cercle de brousse. Mission d'exploration et de prospection dans la région du Bas-Cavally." In *Les mines et la recherche minière en Afrique-Occidentale Française*, edited by Jean Servant, Pierre Legoux, and André Marelle, 158–63. Paris: L'Harmattan, 1991.

Robinson, David. *The Holy War of Umar Tal.* Oxford: Oxford University Press, 1985.

Rocci, Georges. "L'oeuvre des géologues français en AOF." *Travaux du Comité Français d'Histoire de la Géologie* (26th series) 3, no. 2 (2012): 25–54.

Rodney, Walter. *A History of the Upper Guinea Coast: 1545–1800.* New York: Monthly Review, 1970.

Rolston, Jessica Smith. "The Politics of the Pits and the Materiality of Mine Labor: Making Natural Resources in the American West." *American Anthropologist* 115, no. 4 (2013): 582–94.

Rouch, Jean. "Migrations au Ghana (Gold Coast): Enquête 1953–55." *Journal de la Société des Africainistes* 36 (1956): 33–193.

Roure, Georges. *La Haute Gambie et le Parc national du Niokolo-Koba.* Dakar: Grande, 1956.

Roxburgh, Charles, Norbert Dörr, Acha Leke, and Amine Tazi-Riffi et al. *Lions on the Move: The Progress and Potential of African Economies.* Report, McKinsey Global Institute. June 2010.

Rozwadowski, Helen. *Fathoming the Ocean: The Discovery and Exploration of the Deep Sea.* Cambridge, MA: Harvard University Press, 2005.

Rudwick, Martin. *Earth's Deep History: How It Was Discovered and Why It Matters.* Chicago: University of Chicago Press, 2017.

Rudwick, Martin. *Worlds before Adam: The Reconstruction of Geohistory in the Age of Reform.* Chicago: University of Chicago Press, 2008.

Sagatzky, Jean. *La géologie et les ressources minières de la Haute-Volta méridionale.* Bulletin de la Direction des Mines, no. 13. Paris: Gouvernement Général de l'Afrique-Occidentale Française, 1954.

Samson, Stephanie. "Fernand Blondel: Réforme administrative et reconnaissance géologique en Afrique subsaharienne française dans les années 1930." In *Les ingénieurs des mines: Cultures, pouvoirs, pratiques: Colloque des 7 et 8 octobre 2010,* edited by Anne-Françoise Garçon and Bruno Belhoste, 387–402. Paris: Institut de la Gestion Publique et du Développement Économique, 2012.

Samson, Stephanie. "Les 'trésors méconnus' de l'Afrique subsaharienne françaises." In *L'économie faite l'homme: Hommage à Alain Plessie,* edited by Olivier Feiertag and Isabelle Lespinet-Moret, 385–91. Geneva: Librairie Droz, 2010.

Sanneh, Lamin O. *The Jakhanke Muslim Clerics: A Religious and Historical Study of Islam in Senegambia.* London: International African Institute, 1979.

Santiago, Myrna. *The Ecology of Oil: Environment, Labor, and Mexican Revolution, 1900–1938.* Cambridge: Cambridge University Press, 2006.

Sarr, Assan. *Islam, Power, and Dependency in the Gambia River Basin: The Politics of Land Control, 1790–1940.* Rochester, NY: University of Rochester Press, 2016.

Sarró, Ramon. *The Politics of Religious Change on the Upper Guinea Coast: Iconoclasm Done and Undone.* Edinburgh: Edinburgh University Press, 2009.

Scheele, Judith. *Smugglers and Saints of the Sahara: Regional Connectivity in the Twentieth Century.* Cambridge: Cambridge University Press, 2015.

Schiebinger, Londa. *Plants and Empire: Colonial Bioprospecting in the Atlantic World.* Cambridge, MA: Harvard University Press, 2004.

Schmidt, Elizabeth. *The Global Cold War and Decolonization in Guinea, 1946–1958.* Athens: Ohio University Press, 2007.

Schmidt, Peter R. *Iron Technology in East Africa: Symbolism, Science, and Archeology.* Bloomington: Indiana University Press, 1997.

Schmidt, Peter R. "Tropes, Materiality, and Ritual Embodiment of African Iron Smelting Furnaces as Human Figures." *Journal of Archaeological Method and Theory* 16, no. 3 (2009): 262–82.

Schneider, Daniel W. "Local Knowledge, Environmental Politics, and the Founding of Ecology in the United States: Stephen Forbes and 'The Lake as a Microcosm' (1887)." *Isis* 91 (2000): 681–705.

Schneider, Klaus. "Extraction et traitement rituelle de l'or." In *Images d'Afrique et sciences sociales: Les pays Lobi, Birifor et Dagara,* edited by Michèle Fiéloux, Jacques Lombard, and Jean-Marie Kambou-Ferrand, 190–97. Paris: Karthala, 1993.

Schrijver, Nico. *Sovereignty over Natural Resources: Balancing Rights and Duties.* Cambridge: Cambridge University Press, 1997.

Schumaker, Lyn. *Africanizing Anthropology: Fieldwork, Networks, and the Making of Cultural Knowledge in Central Africa.* Durham, NC: Duke University Press, 2001.

Scott, James. *The Art of Not Being Governed: An Anarchist History of Upland Southeast Asia.* New Haven, CT: Yale University Press, 2010.

Scott, James. *The Moral Economy of the Peasant: Rebellion and Subsistence in Southeast Asia*. New Haven, CT: Yale University Press, 1977.

Scott, James. *Seeing like a State: How Certain Schemes to Improve the Human Condition Have Failed*. New Haven, CT: Yale University Press, 1998.

Searing, James. *God Alone Is King: Islam and Emancipation in Senegal: The Wolof Kingdoms of Kajoor and Bawol, 1859–1914*. Portsmouth, NH: Heinemann, 2002.

Sébillot, Paul. *Les travaux publics et les mines dans les traditions et les superstitions de tous les pays: Les routes, les ponts, les chemins de fer, les digues, les canaux, l'hydraulique, les ports, les phares, les mines et les mineurs*. Paris: J. Rothschild, 1894.

Seck, Assane. *Sénégal. Émergence d'une démocratie moderne (1945–2005): Un itinéraire politique*. Paris: Karthala, 2005.

Selcer, Perrin. *The Postwar Origins of the Global Environment: How the United Nations Built Spaceship Earth*. New York: Columbia University Press, 2018.

Serlin, David. "Confronting African Histories of Technology: A Conversation with Keith Breckenridge and Gabrielle Hecht." *Radical History Review* 2017, no. 127 (2017): 87–102.

Serrant, Émile. *Les mines et gisements d'or de l'Afrique occidentale*. Paris: Nadaud et Cie, 1889.

Servant, Jean, Pierre Legoux, and André Marelle, eds. *Les mines et la recherche minière en Afrique-Occidentale Française*. Paris: L'Harmattan, 1991.

Shapin, Steven, and Simon Schaffer. *Leviathan and the Air-Pump: Hobbes, Boyle, and the Experimental Life*. Princeton, NJ: Princeton University Press, 2017.

Shaw, Rosalind. "The Invention of 'African Traditional Religion.'" *Religion* 20 (1990): 339–53.

Shaw, Rosalind. *Memories of the Slave Trade: Ritual and the Historical Imagination in Sierra Leone*. Chicago: University of Chicago Press, 2002.

Sheldon, Gellar. *Senegal: An African Nation between Islam and the West*. Boulder, CO: Westview, 1995.

Shetler, Jan. *Imagining Serengeti: A History of Landscape Memory in Tanzania from Earliest Times to the Present*. Athens: Ohio University Press, 2007.

Shipton, Parker. *Bitter Money: Cultural Economy and Some African Meanings of Forbidden Commodities*. Washington, DC: American Anthropological Association, 1989.

Siddiqi, Anooradha Iyer. "Ephemerality." *Comparative Studies of South Asia, Africa and the Middle East* 40, no. 1 (2020): 24–34.

Siossat, J. "Les coutumes des orpailleurs indigènes du Maramandougou." *Bulletin du Comité d'Études Historiques et Scientifiques de l'Afrique-Occidentale Française* 20 (1937): 336–49.

Skurnik, W. A. E. *The Foreign Policy of Senegal*. Evanston, IL: Northwestern University Press, 1972.

Sluyter, Andrew. *Black Ranching Frontiers: African Cattle Herders of the Atlantic World, 1500–1900*. New Haven, CT: Yale University Press, 2012.

Smith, James. *Bewitching Development: Witchcraft and the Reinvention of Development in Neoliberal Kenya*. Chicago: University of Chicago Press, 2008.

Smith, James. "Tantalus in the Digital Age: Coltan Ore, Temporal Dispossession, and 'Movement' in the Eastern Democratic Republic of the Congo." *American Ethnologist* 38, no. 1 (2011): 17–35.

Smith, James H., and Jeffrey Mantz. "Do Cellular Phones Dream of Civil War? The Mystification of Production and the Consequences of Technology Fetishism in the Eastern Congo." In *Inclusion and Exclusion in the Global Arena*, edited by Max Kirsch, 71–93. New York: Routledge, 2006.

Soares, Benjamin F. *Islam and the Prayer Economy: History and Authority in a Malian Town*. Ann Arbor: University of Michigan Press, 2005.

Soares, Benjamin F. "'Structural Adjustment Islam' and the Religious Economy in Neoliberal Mali." In *Religion and the Morality of the Market*, edited by Filippo Osella and Daromir Rudnyckyj, 138–59. Cambridge: Cambridge University Press.

Southall, Roger, and Henning Melber, eds. *A New Scramble for Africa? Imperialism, Investment, and Development*. Kwa-Zulu Natal: University of KwaZulu-Natal Press, 2009.

Sow, Khadre. "Risques de l'exposition au mercure liés à l'exploitation artisanale de l'or au Sénégal Oriental." Thèse de pharmacie, Université de Cheikh Anta Diop, Dakar, 2010.

Spear, Thomas. "Neo-traditionalism and the Limits of Invention in British Colonial Africa." *Journal of African History* 44, no. 1 (2003): 3–27.

Stahl, Ann, ed. *African Archeology: A Critical Introduction*. Malden, MA: Blackwell, 2005.

Stahl, Ann. *Making History in Banda: Anthropological Visions of Africa's Past*. Cambridge: Cambridge University Press, 2009.

Steckling, Nadine, Myriam Tobollik, Dietrich Plass, and Claudia Hornberg et al. "Global Burden of Disease of Mercury Used in Artisanal Small-scale Gold Mining." *Annals of Global Health* 83, no. 2 (2017): 234–47.

Stewart, John, and Ivor Wilks. "The Mande Loan Element in Twi." *Ghana Notes and Queries* 4 (1962): 26–28.

Stoller, Paul. *Money Has No Smell: The Africanization of New York City*. Chicago: University of Chicago Press, 2002.

Storey, William Kelleher. *Guns, Race, and Power in Colonial South Africa*. Cambridge: Cambridge University Press, 2008.

Sun, Jodie Yuzhou. "Historicizing African Socialisms: Kenyan African Socialism, Zambian Humanism, and Communist China's Entanglements." *International Journal of African Historical Studies* 52, no. 3 (2019): 349–74.

Suret-Canale, Jean. *French Colonialism in Tropical Africa, 1900–1945*. New York: Pica, 1971.

Sweet, James. *Domingos Álvares, African Healing, and the Intellectual History of the Atlantic World*. Chapel Hill: University of North Carolina Press, 2011.

Sweet, Nikolas. "The Poetics of Relationality: Mobility, Naming, and Sociability in Southeastern Senegal." PhD diss., University of Michigan, Ann Arbor, 2019.

Swindell, Kenneth, and Alieu Jeng. *Migrants, Credit and Climate: The Gambian Groundnut Trade, 1834–1934*. Leiden: Brill, 2006.

Takforian, A. "Conservation et développement local au Niokolo-Koba." *Politique Africaine* 53 (1994): 52–63.

Tamari, Tal. "The Development of Caste Systems in West Africa." *Journal of African History* 32 (1991): 221–50.

Tamari, Tal. "Linguistic Evidence for the History of West African 'Castes.'" In *Status and Identity in West Africa: Nyamakalaw of Mande*, edited by David C. Conrad and Barbara E. Frank, 61–85. Bloomington: Indiana University Press, 1995.

Taussig, Michael T. *The Devil and Commodity Fetishism in South America*. Chapel Hill: University of North Carolina Press, 1980.

Thiaw, Ibrahima. "Archeological Investigations of Long-Term Culture Change in the Lower Falemme (Upper Senegal River) AD 500–1900." PhD diss., University of Texas, Houston, 1999.

Thiaw, Ibrahima. "Atlantic Impacts on Inland Senegambia: French Penetration and African Initiatives in Eighteenth- and Nineteenth-Century Gajaaga and Bundu (Upper Senegal River)." In *Power and Landscape in Atlantic West Africa*, edited by Cameron J. Monroe and Akinwumi Ogundiran, 49–77. Cambridge: Cambridge University Press, 2012.

Thiaw, Ibrahima, and Sonja Magnavita. "Nouvelles recherches archéologiques dans la zone des tumuli du Sénégal." *Nyame Akuma* 83 (2015): 3–10.

Thilmans, Guy, and Cyr Descamps, "Fouille d'un tumulus à Ndalane (région de Kaloack, Sénégal)." In *Senegalia, études sur le patrimoine ouest-africain. Hommage à Guy Thilmans*, edited by Cyr Descamps and Abdoulaye Camara, 235–38. Saint-Maur-des-Fosses, France: Sépia, 2007.

Thompson, E. P. *The Making of the English Working Class*. London: Victor Gollancz, 1963.

Thompson, E. P. *Whigs and Hunters: The Origins of the Black Act*. New York: Pantheon, 1975.

Tilley, Helen. *Africa as a Living Laboratory: Empire, Development, and the Problem of Scientific Knowledge, 1870–1950*. Chicago: University of Chicago Press, 2011.

Tilley, Helen. "Global Histories, Vernacular Science, and African Genealogies: Or, Is the History of Science Ready for the World?" *Isis* 101, no. 1 (2020): 110–19.

Tilley, Helen. "Medical Cultures, Therapeutic Properties, and Laws in Global History." *Osiris* 36, no. 1 (2021): 1–24.

Tilley, Helen. "Traditional Medicine Goes Global: Pan-African Precedents, Cultural Decolonization, and Cold War Rights/Properties." *Osiris* 36, no. 1 (2021): 132–59.

Timmermans, Stefan. "A Black Technician and Blue Babies." *Social Studies of Science* 33, no. 2 (2003): 197–229.

Togola, Téréba. "Memories, Abstractions, and Conceptualization of Ecological Crisis in the Mande World." In *The Way the Wind Blows: Climate, History, and Human Action*, edited by Roderick J. McIntosh, Joseph A. Tainter, and Susan Keech McIntosh, 187–89. New York: Columbia University Press, 2000.

Tonkin, Elizabeth. *Narrating Our Pasts: The Social Construction of Oral History*. Cambridge: Cambridge University Press, 1992.

Touraj, Atabaki, Elisabetta Bini, and Kaven Ehsani, eds. *Working for Oil: Comparative Social Histories of Labor in the Global Oil Industry*. Cham, Switzerland: Palgrave Macmillan, 2017.

Touré, Ahmed Sékou. *L'Afrique en marche*, vol. 10, 4th ed. Conakry: Imprimerie du Gouvernement, 1967.

Touré, Oussouby. "Le refus du travail forcé au Sénégal Oriental." *Cahiers d'Études Africaines* 93 (1984): 25–38.

Tousignant, Noémi. "Broken Tempos: Of Means and Memory in a Senegalese University Laboratory." *Social Studies of Science* 43, no. 5 (2013): 729–53.

Tousignant, Noémi. *Edges of Exposure: Toxicology and the Problem of Capacity in Postcolonial Senegal*. Durham, NC: Duke University Press, 2018.

Tschakert, Petra. "Digging Deep for Justice: A Radical Re-imagination of the Artisanal Gold Mining Sector in Ghana." *Antipode* 41, no. 4 (2009): 706–40.

Tsing, Anna. "Inside the Economy of Appearances." *Public Culture* 12, no. 1 (2000): 115–44.

Twagira, Laura Ann. *Embodied Engineering: Gendered Labor, Food Security, and Taste in Twentieth-Century Mali*. Athens: Ohio University Press, 2021.

Twagira, Laura Ann. "Introduction: Africanizing the History of Technology." *Technology and Culture* 61, no. 2 (2019): S1–19.

United Nations. *Small-scale Mining in Developing Countries*. New York: United Nations, 1972.

United Nations Department of Economic and Social Affairs. "Annex: International Co-operation in Mineral Development." In *Mineral Resources Development with Particular Reference to the Developing Countries*, 66–74. New York: United Nations Department of Economic and Social Affairs, 1970.

United Nations Economic Commission for Africa. *Artisanal and Small-scale Mining and Technology Challenges in Africa*. Addis Ababa: United Nations Economic Commission for Africa, 2003.

United Nations Economic Commission for Africa. *Recommendations from Artisanal Mining Workshop: Drive the Sector Forward*. Addis Ababa: United Nations Economic Commission for Africa, 2016.

United Nations Environmental Programme. *Final Report: Second Global Forum on Artisanal and Small-scale Gold Mining, 3–5 September 2013*. Lima: United Nations Environmental Programme, 2013.

US Agency for International Development (USAID). *Democracy, Human Rights and Governance: Assessment of Senegal*. Washington, DC: USAID, 2003.

Van Hoven, Ed. "Representing Social Hierarchy: Administrators-Ethnographers in the French Sudan: Delafosse, Monteil, and Labouret." *Cahiers d'Études Africaines* 30, no. 118 (1990): 179–98.

Van Onselen, Charles. *Chibaro: African Mine Labour in Southern Rhodesia, 1900–1933*. London: Pluto, 1976.

Vansina, Jan. *Oral Tradition as History*. Madison: University of Wisconsin Press, 1985.

Vansina, Jan. *Paths in the Rainforest: Toward a History of Political Tradition in Equatorial Africa*. Madison: University of Wisconsin Press, 1990.

Vetter, Jeremy. "Cowboys, Scientists, and Fossils: The Field Site and Local Collaboration in the American West." *Isis* 99 (2008): 273–303.

Vetter, Jeremy, ed. *Knowing Global Environments: New Historical Perspectives on the Field Sciences*. New Brunswick, NJ: Rutgers University Press, 2011.

Vidal, J. "Le mystère de Ghana." *Bulletin d'Études Historiques et Scientifiques de l'Afrique-Occidentale Française* 7 (1924): 317–28.

Vitalis, Robert. *America's Kingdom: Mythmaking on the Saudi Oil Frontier*. London: Verso, 2009.

Walmsley, Alexander, Vincent Serneels, Irka Hajdas, and Anne Mayor. "Variability of Early Iron Production in the Falémé Valley Region, Eastern Senegal." *African Archaeological Review* 37, no. 2 (2020): 225–50.

Walsh, Andrew. "After the Rush: Living with Uncertainty in a Malagasy Town." *Africa* 82, no. 2 (2012): 235–51.

Walsh, Andrew. "'Hot Money' and Daring Consumption in a Northern Malagasy Sapphire-Mining Town." *American Ethnologist* 30, no. 2 (2003): 290–305.

Ware, Rudolph, III. *The Walking Qur'an: Islamic Education, Embodied Knowledge, and History in West Africa*. Chapel Hill: University of North Caroline Press, 2014.

Watts, Michael. "Petro-violence: Community, Extraction, and Political Ecology of a Mythic Commodity." In *Violent Environments*, edited by Nancy L. Peluso and Michael Watts, 189–212. Ithaca, NY: Cornell University Press, 2001.

Watts, Michael. "Resource Curse? Governmentality, Oil and Power in the Niger Delta, Nigeria." *Geopolitics* 9, no. 1 (2004): 50–80.

Weizman, Eyal. *Hollow Land: Israel's Architecture of Occupation*. New York: Verso, 2007.

Welker, Marina. *Enacting the Corporation: An American Mining Firm in Post-authoritarian Indonesia*. Berkeley: University of California Press, 2014.

Werthmann, Katja. "Cowries, Gold and 'Bitter Money': Gold-Mining and Notions of Ill-Gotten Wealth in Burkina Faso." *Paideuma* 49 (2003): 105–24.

Werthmann, Katja. "Dans un monde masculin: Le travail des femmes dans un camp de chercheurs d'or au Burkina Faso." In *Les nouveaux urbains dans l'espace Sahara-Sahel: Un cosmopolitisme par le bas*, edited by Elisabeth Boesen and Laurence Marfaing, 295–322. Paris: Karthala, 2007.

Westerman, Andrea. "Geology and World Politics: Mineral Resource Appraisals as Tools of Geopolitical Calculation, 1919–1939." *Historical Social Research* 40, no. 2 (2015): 151–73.

Weszkalnys, Gisa. "Geology, Potentiality, Speculation: On the Indeterminacy of First Oil." *Cultural Anthropology* 30, no. 4 (2015): 611–39.

Weszkalnys, Gisa. "Hope and Oil: Expectations in São Tomé e Principe." *Review of African Political Economy* 35, no. 117 (2008): 473–82.

White, Luise. *Speaking with Vampires: Rumor and History in Colonial Africa*. Berkeley: University of California Press, 2000.

Wilder, Gary. *The French Imperial Nation-State: Negritude and Colonial Humanism between the Two World Wars*. Chicago: University of Chicago Press, 2005.

Wilks, Ivor. *Forests of Gold: Essays on the Akan and the Kingdom of Asante*. Athens: Ohio University Press, 1993.

Wilks, Ivor. "Wangara, Akan and Portuguese in the Fifteenth and Sixteenth Centuries, II. The Struggle for Trade." *Journal of African History* 23 (1982): 463–72.

Williams, Martin. "The Gold Standard of Governance: Mining, Decentralization, and State Power in Africa." *Politique Africaine* 17 (2010): 127–48.

Winchester, Simon. *The Map That Changed the World: William Smith and the Birth of Modern Geology*. New York: HarperCollins, 1999.

Wolpe, Harold. *Race, Class, and the Apartheid State*. Paris: UNESCO Press, 1988.

World Bank. *The Millennium Development Goals and Small-scale Mining*. Washington, DC: World Bank, 2005.

World Bank. *Mining Together: Large-Scale Mining Meets Artisanal Mining: A Guide for Action*. Washington, DC: World Bank, 2009.

World Bank. "Shining a Light on a Hidden Sector." WorldBank.org, June 19, 2019. Accessed August 31, 2020. https://www.worldbank.org/en/news/feature/2019/06/19/shining-a-light-on-a-hidden-sector.

World Bank. *Strategy for African Mining*. Technical paper no. 181. Washington, DC: World Bank, 1992.

Wright, Donald R. "Beyond Migration and Conquest: Oral Traditions and Mandinka Ethnicity in Senegambia." *History in Africa* 12 (1985): 335–48.

Wright, Richard. *Middle Ground: Indians, Empires, and Republics in the Great Lakes Region, 1650–1815*. Cambridge: Cambridge University Press, 2012.

Yusoff, Kathryn. *A Billion Black Anthropocenes or None*. Minneapolis: University of Minnesota Press, 2018.

Zahan, Dominique. *La dialectique du verbe chez les Bambara*. Paris: Mouton, 1963.

Zhang, Ling. *The River, the Plain, and the State: An Environmental Drama in Northern Song China, 1048–1128*. Cambridge: Cambridge University Press, 2016.

Zobel, Clemens. "Les génies du Kòma: Identités locales, logiques religieuses et enjeux socio-politiques dans les monts Manding du Mali." *Cahiers d'Études Africaines* 36, no. 144 (1996): 625–58.

INDEX

Afrique-Occidentale Française (AOF). *See* French West Africa; prospecting and geological exploration

Al-Bakrī, 66, 67, 70

Al-Dawādārī, 69–70

Allman, Jean, 19–20

alluvial gold deposits. See *nara*

Al-'Umarī, 70

Al-Ya'qūbī, 63

ancestral religious traditions: ethnogenesis and, 182*t*; goldfields as dominions of, 18; jihad against, 75–76; nonlocalized, 19–20; "pagan" label, 18, 67–68, 77, 217n66; quick wealth and, 190; refugees from Islam and, 47–48; spectrum between Islam and, 179. *See also* ethnolinguistic and religious affiliation and embodied difference in Kédougou; *jinne*; ritual geology; sacrifices; shrines

Angola model, 34

Anmericosa, 188

Appel, Hannah, 221n15

Appiah, Kwame Anthony, 180

Arcelor Mittal, 158, 251n26

Arcin, André, 200

Arnaud, Gilbert, 124–25

artisanal mining: birth of, 149–51; defined, 6–7; terms for, 211n2. See also *orpaillage*

Atlantic era, 29–30, 74–83

Bâ, Mariama, 46

Balandier, George, 89

balandulas (placers of wood), 37–38

Bamba, Amadou, 97, 218n78

Bambuk: Atlantic era and European contact, 74–83; Bida and, 66; in colonial period, 91–92; as inland maroon society, 76; KKI as aligning with, 3; maps, 59*f*, 64*f*, 71*f*; slave trade in, 82; Tinkoto and, 32–33; village foundation narratives, 77–78; Wagadu and, 64. *See also* French West Africa

Bandung Conference (1955), 133

Bantaco, 45

Baoulé, 108

Bardin, Marcel, 118

Barrat, Maurice, 90–91

Barrick Gold, 33

Barry, Boubacar, 19

Barth, Frederick, 180

Bassari ethnicity. *See* Beliyan-Bassari ethnicity

Bassari Resources, 1–2, 36*f*, 155, 160*f*, 166–68, 175

battle for Makabingui, 1–2

bauxite mines, 123–24

Bedik, 181–82, 182*t*, 225n23

Bélédougou: about, 224n7; Alpha Yaya and, 84; Cissokho clan as *dugutigi*, 60; French army and, 84–85; map, 59*f*; Ningiri and, 40; Noirot account, 83; settlement of, 161; Taubry Sidibé as "slave king," 58–60, 67. *See also* Sabodala

Beliyan-Bassari ethnicity: about, 211n1, 225n23; ethnogenesis and settlement, 181–82, 182*t*; Thiankoun Bassadié *juura* and, 186–87
Bell, Catherine, 5
Bérété, Framoi, 103–6, 121, 237n82, 238n92
Bida, 65–66, 73–74, 79, 83, 115, 177, 225n30
bioprospecting, 15–16
Birimian Greenstone Belt, 2, 18*f*, 156, 250n14
Birimian rocks: French geologists and, 110; gold-mining boom, 2–3; Maninka villages, correlation with, 193–94; primary and secondary deposits, 12–13; savanna and forest zones, 212n9
Bize, Amiel, 155
blacksmiths: in colonial period, 96; as kings, 69, 226n43; as *nyamakala*, 69; spirits and, 67
blacksmith shrines, 67
Bloc Populaire Sénégalais (BPS), 135
Blondel, Fernand, 111–12, 121
blood sacrifices. *See* sacrifices
Blouin, André, 103–5
boosterism, 89–90
botanical knowledge, 116–17
Boucard, Claude, 79
bricolage, 130, 136, 142, 243n4
Brooks, George, 228n66
Bundu, 59*f*, 75–76, 83
Buré, 64*f*, 66, 68, 70, 71*f*, 89–92, 225n22
Bureau de Recherches Géologiques et Minières (BRGM), 137, 140–44, 162, 188, 246n38
Bureau Minier de la France d'Outre-mer (BUMIFOM), 103–4, 123, 137, 243n81
Burkinabe migrants, 29, 31, 43, 47

Camara, Coumbouna, 42–47
Camara, Yonko, 42–47
capital, unequal access to, 197, 198
Carrère, Frédéric, 199
Casamançais separatist movement, 172, 254n65
Catholicism, 184

Chermette, Alexis, 108
Christianity, 184
Cissokho, Bambo: division of rocks ceremony and, 55; as *dugutigi*, 60; household of, 25; Kanoumering and, 189; Malians and, 49; Rangold and, 36, 166; sharia of, 53–54; Thiankoun Bassadié *juura*, opening of, 185–87; tribunal of, 31–33, 52
Cissokho, Fanta Madi, 40
Cissokho, Gassimou, 39, 41, 55
Cissokho, Mady, 134–35, 145–46, 245n25
Cissokho, Mahamadi, 164–65, 168–69
Cissokho, Moussa, 40, 49, 59–60
Cissokho, Siriman, 59–60
Cissokho, Soro, 59
Cohen, David William, 27
Cold War politics, 131. *See also* independence-era mineral missions in Sénégal Oriental
colonialism, French. *See* French West Africa; prospecting and geological exploration
Commissariat à l'Énergie Atomique (CEA), 144
Compagnie de la Haute-Gambie, 198
Compagnie des Indes (later Compagnie du Sénégal), 75, 79
Compagnie des Mines de Siguiri, 92–93
coopérants, 130–31, 137–38, 246n41
cooperatives, 150
copper, 65, 70–72
corporate/industrial mining: artisanal–industrial binary, 7–9; battle for Makabingui, 1–2; cyanide and, 48; delay between mapping and expansion of, 109, 127–28; depletion by, 204–5; *juuras* bulldozed for, 153, 164, 168, 174; Mamakono and, 58; open-pit mines, 2–3, 34, 50, 118–19, 159, 161, 165, 170–71, 196, 204–5; protests against, 169–74; racialization and, 7, 180; share entitlement and, 155; shelf projects, 129–30, 156–58, 251n23; social licenses, sharia of the *juura*, and, 52–55. *See also* geologists;

296   INDEX

prospecting and geological exploration; rights claims in Senegal, language of; *specific companies by name*

Corporate Social Responsibility (CSR) programs, 52, 152

couloirs d'orpaillage (orpaillage corridors), 153, 158, 174

customary mining, colonial. *See* French West Africa

customary mining rights, 88–91, 104–6, 238n92. *See also* rights claims in Senegal, language of

cyanide heap-leaching, 48, 49f, 204, 222n47, 252n47

damansinna (diggers), 37–38

damantigi (masters of the mining shaft), 37–42, 96–97

damming techniques, 122

Danfakha, Falaye, 26

Danfakha, Wali, 44

Danfkaha, Sembou, 143–45, 157

Dankaran Tuman, 68

Dan Mania, 59–60

Daumain, Georges, 239n17

dead gold vs. living gold, 115, 240n33

decolonization, 131, 134–36. *See also* independence-era mineral missions in Sénégal Oriental

de Gaulle, Charles, 102, 142

"development," 123

Dia, Mamadou, 134–35, 244n13

Dia, Ousseynou, 137–38

Diabé, 65

Diadhiou, Pierre, 146, 152

Diallo, Aliou, 165–66

Diallo, Idi, 40–41

Diallo, Mountaga, 146

Diallo, Ousmane, 190–91

Diallo, Telli, 30, 142

Diallo, Torodo, 189

Diba, Moussa, 15f

diggers (*damansinna*), 37–38

Dinga, 65

Diouf, Abdou, 157

Diouf, Mamadou, 22

Direction des Eaux et Forêt, 171

Direction des Mines et de la Géologie (DMG), 129–30, 136–42, 150, 243n2

Direction Fédérale des Mines de la Géologie (DFMG), 123–24, 137, 243n2

discovery, claims of, 159–64

diviners, 41–42, 177

division of rocks ceremony (*kuru tala luno*), 55–57, 205–6

Djiguiba, Daouda, 173–74

Dramé, Mamadou Lamine, 84

dreams, 117

droit coutumier (customary rights) legal clause, 88–89

droughts, 148–49

dugutigi (masters of the land), 31, 54, 55, 60, 78. *See also* Cissokho, Bambo

Durand, Jean-Baptiste, 79

École des Moniteurs des Mines, 125

Eeximcor, 157, 251n24

Elmina fort, 74–75

embodied difference. *See* ethnolinguistic and religious affiliation and embodied difference in Kédougou

Endeavor Mining, 33, 58, 157, 159, 162, 188, 204, 252n35. *See also* Randgold; Teranga Gold Corporation

ethnolinguistic and religious affiliation and embodied difference in Kédougou: essentialist notions of ethnolinguistic difference, 179–80; ethnogenesis, first-comers vs. incomers, and, 181–84, 182t; golden bones narratives and, 199–200; monetized *jalan* and, 199; moral anxieties about mineral wealth and, 177–78, 195; moralizing geology in Samecouta, 192–95; Muslim *juura* in Kanoumering and, 188–92; religious conversion and, 179, 184; sacrificial practices of Maninka vs. Muslims, 184–85, 187; story of the traveling diviner, 177; Tinkoto as Maninka ritual territory, 185–87; *tubabs* (white miners), occult relationships, and inequality, 195–98

exploration. *See* prospecting and geological exploration

Faidherbe, Louis, 80

"family" mining units in colonial period, 98

famine resources ("granaries"), *juuras* as, 49–50, 203–6

farafin londo (African/Black knowledge), 41–42

Feierman, Steven, 9

Fent, Ashley, 254n65

Ferguson, James, 34

firstcomer groups, 78, 179, 180–81, 182t, 230n90

Fonds d'Aide et de Coopération (FAC), 137, 139

Fond Social Minière, 171–72

foreign aid and assistance, 136–42, 246n37

Fouta Djallon, 75–76, 83, 84, 182–83

French Union, membership in, 104–5

French West Africa (Afrique-Occidentale Française; AOF): army conquest, 84–85, 90; centrality of profit from *orpaillage*, 106–7; conflicts over customary rights, 92–94; customary mining rights, 88–91, 104–6, 238n92; gold boosters, 89–90; interwar gold boom and *orpaillage* in Siguiri, 94–102; list of colonies in, 234n19; map, 87f; mining codes and decrees, 90–91, 94, 106, 234n29; neo-mercantile economy, 87–88; overview, 86–87; postwar politics of, 102–6; racialization of customary mining, 7; taxation, 85, 91–92. *See also* prospecting and geological exploration

garanke (leatherworkers), 41, 69, 79, 227n44

Gelman, Susan, 179

gender: in colonial period, 98–99; division of labor, persistence of, 99; division of proceeds and, 45; gold-washing and, 46; independence-era mineral missions and, 131, 146; *juuras* as women's work sites in 1960s, 131; new specialties and, 101–2

geologists: exploration camps, 33–36; geological teams, 112–13; history of, 14; at Makabingui, 1; Maninka and, 50–51; relationship with *orpailleurs*, 51; ritual

geology, reports of, 113–18; slow work of, 13–14

geology: meanings of, 17; professionalization of, 111; "superstitions" vs. "science" of, 81. *See also* prospecting and geological exploration

Giraudon, Robert, 143–44

Golbéry, Sylvain de, 82

gold detectors, 194

gold merchants. See *juulas*

gold mining. *See specific topics, such as* prospecting and geological exploration

Goloubinow, Rostislav, 116, 119–20

Golouma, 159, 160f, 251n30

Gomez, Michael, 227n51

goto (goblins), 78

Grace, Joshua, 243n4

Green, Toby, 62

groupements d'interet economique (GIE), 250n13

guardians, 38, 38f

guardian spirits, 117

Guéye, Serigne Bassirou, 172

Guinea: bauxite in, 124; gold campaign (*campagne de l'or*), 95; gold production in, 3; Goloubinow on, 119; independence of, 132; Julian's model mine, 120–21; Laye's *L'enfant noir*, 97–98; maps, 18f, 21f, 87f; migrants from, 39, 42, 55, 88, 96, 194; in oral history of mining, 49; *orpaillage* and Union du Mandé (postwar period), 102–6; Siguiri, 89, 92–102, 103–6, 120–21, 204; spirit snakes in, 73; Syriens in, 92; Touré and, 84, 130, 133, 183

"Gulf Wars," 53

Hall, Bruce, 256n13

High, Mette, 177–78

Holle, Paul, 199

horizontal vs. vertical division of rights, 90–91, 94, 155

hospitality, tradition of, 11

Hubert, Henry, 111, 239n16

IAMGOLD, 160f

Ibn Battūta, 70

incomers, 182–83, 182*t*

independence-era mineral missions in Sénégal Oriental: African socialism and *orpaillage*, 132–34; *coopérants* and, 130–31; decolonization and development, 134–36; drought and birth of artisanal mining, 147–51; economic marginalization of the region, 147; foreign aid and international missions, 129, 136–42; gender and, 131; scientific ambitions, 130; Sénégal Oriental designated as region, 135; "shelf projects," 129–30; worker narratives, 142–47

industrialization: colonial opposition to, 95–96, 109; postwar vision of, 124–25

industrial mining. *See* corporate/industrial mining

infant mortality, 29–30

Institut des Sciences de la Terre (IST), 247n50

International Monetary Fund (IMF), 150, 157

iron smelting, 66–67

Islam: conversion to, 97, 179, 184; "gold is in the hands of spirits," 200; ideological opposition with gold mining, 17–18, 61, 67, 69–70, 178–79; making a Muslim *juura* in Kanoumering, 188–92; Muridiyya, 20, 22, 97, 133–34, 218n78; quick wealth and, 190–91; in Senegal, 22. *See also* ethnolinguistic and religious affiliation and embodied difference in Kédougou

Islamo-Wolof model, 22

Jaa-Ogo blacksmith dynasty, 226n43

Jakhanke, 76–77, 84, 148–49, 182*t*, 183–84, 192–95

jalan (lineage shrines), 77–78, 79, 117, 185, 199

Jallonke, 182, 182*t*

Jenne-Jeno, Mali, 67, 69, 228n59

jewelry and regalia, 70–71, 227n57, 228n59

jinne: division of rocks ceremony and, 56; "genie in the bottle" story, 197; "gold is in the hands of spirits," 39, 179, 200; in medieval period, 78–79; as owners of gold, 39, 81; sacrifices to, 39–42, 43, 79;

soul or essence (*ni*) detected by, 179; spirits in French mines compared to, 81

jinn saa. See spirit snakes

Julian, Eduard, 120–21

juulas (gold merchants): about, 46; colonial state and, 88, 232n6; Europeans and, 75; Mali empire and expansion of, 72; in medieval period, 76; at Siguiri, 99–100, 100*f*; socialism and, 133; Wangara as predecessors to, 64–65. *See also* traders

juulusabala (pulley operators), 38, 55, 98, 148–49

Juuraba, 36–39

juurafuru (mine marriage), 98

juurakuntigi (masters of the mines), 40–42, 57, 60, 78–79, 185

juuras (dry season mining sites): about, 29–33, 230n99; closures of, 153–54, 174; *damantigi* (master of the mining shaft), role of, 37–39; as famine resource, 49–50, 203–6; geologists and the Maninka, 50–51; *juurakuntigi* (master of the mines) and sacrifices to *jinne*, 40–42; *kuru tala luno* (division of rocks ceremony), 55–57; mercy poisoning on, 46; physical and moral distancing from, 195; social licenses and sharia, 52–55; strangers, wealth of, 47–50; as subsistence, 167–69; *tanas* (ritual taboos), 41; as term, 78; washing of gold by women, 30*f*, 42–47, 96. *See also* prospecting and geological exploration; rights claims in Senegal, language of; ritual geology; sacrifices; Tinkoto

Kael, Senegal, 72

Kamar, Sajoh Madi, 46

Kamara, Boukari, 167

Kanoumering, 53, 160*f*, 188–92

Kédougou-Kéniéba Inlier (KKI), 3

Kédougou region: about, 20–24; closures of *juuras*, 153–54; human sacrifice rumors, 148; maps, 4*f*, 21*f*; names for, 218n77; Opération Kédougou, 135; permits, mines, and *juuras*, 160*f*; population of, 218n79. *See also* ethnolinguistic and religious affiliation and embodied difference in Kédougou

Kédougou town, 22–23
Kédovin protests, 168–74, 173f
Keita, Aissatou, 201
Keita, Coumba, 43
Keita, Fadiyen, 165
Keita, Filé, 206
Keïta, Fodéba, 101
Keita, Koumba, 199
Keita, Makhan, 85
Keita, Modibo, 132–33, 244n13, 244n17, 245n33
Keita, Soriba, 198
ken bulu ("rocks in hand"), 37
Kéniéba, 4f, 80, 160f, 220n8
Khossanto, 144, 172
knowledge, African/Black (*farafin londo*), 41–42
knowledge, subterranean: about, 13–17; embodied, 12; foreign assistance and, 136; geological exploration and, 109, 111, 122–26; search for, 42. *See also* independence-era mineral missions in Sénégal Oriental; prospecting and geological exploration
Koï Gourrey, Mali, 71–72
komo power associations, 73, 117, 228n66
Kone, Siaba, 117
Konkodougou, 83
Koumba, Naman, 101–2
Koyo, 115
kuru taki sono (the year of breaking rocks), 159
kuru tala luno (division of rocks ceremony), 55–57, 205–6

Labouret, Henri, 95
Lachenal, Guillaume, 130–31
land-nationalization policies, 133, 244n17
language of subterranean rights. *See* rights claims in Senegal, language of
Laye, Camara, 97–98, 236n61
leatherworkers. *See garanke*
Lévi-Strauss, Claude, 130
living gold vs. dead gold, 115, 240n33

Magan Kon Fatta, 68
Makabingui, 1–2, 4f, 168

Malavoy, Jean, 112
Mali: Beliyan-Bassari and Bedik in, 225n23; commercial gold dust board, 222n44; gold production in, 3; independence of, 132; Luolo mine, 204; Mali Federation, 244n12; map, 21f; migrants from, 39, 42; "professional" migrants from, 167; Sadiola joint-venture project, 156
Malian empire, 68–74
Malinowski, Bronislaw, 218n72
Mamakhono: map, 59f, 160f; Noirot account, 83; Soviets at, 129; Taubry "slave king" over, 58–60
Manden, 48–49, 68–69, 72–73
Manding, 72–73, 224n17
Maninka ethnicity: about, 10; Birimian rocks correlated with villages of, 193–94; ethnogenesis, 182, 182t; geologists and, 50–51; in medieval period, 64; patrilineal descent, 220n9; population in Kédougou, 219n79; as prospecting specialists, 116; Taubry narrative and, 60; Thiankoun Bassadié *juura* and, 186–87. *See also* ethnolinguistic and religious affiliation and embodied difference in Kédougou
Maninka language, 10
Mann, Gregory, 154
marabouts, 41–42, 75, 96–97
Marelle, André, 125
marginalization claims, 169–74
Massawa, 4f, 33, 160f
masters of the land (*dugutigi*), 31, 54, 55, 60, 78. *See also* Cissokho, Bambo
masters of the mines (*juurakuntigi*), 40–42, 57, 60, 78–79, 185
masters of the mining shaft (*damantigi*), 37–42, 96–97
McIntosh, Susan Keech, 65
medieval period, 63–68, 64f
Méniaud, Jean, 115–17
mercantilism, 87–88
mercury, 46, 204
migrants: Burkinabe, 29, 31, 43, 47; industrialization and fear of, 95–96; *navétane*, 22, 88, 134, 233n8; official targeting of, 48
Mineral Deposits Limited (MDL), 158, 162, 170–72, 251n25

mineral mapping. *See* independence-era mineral missions in Sénégal Oriental; prospecting and geological exploration

mineral "reserves," 163–64

mineral resource classification schemes, 163, 252n38

mining codes and decrees, colonial, 90–91, 94, 106

mining rights, customary, 88–91, 104–6, 238n92

mining tradition, concept of, 9–10

Ministry of Cooperation ("La Coopération"), 137

Monékhata, Aliou ("DJ Monex"), 173–74

money, clean vs. quick, 178, 190

moral anxieties about mineral wealth, 177–78, 195

Mouvement Citoyen pour la Défense des Intérêts de Kédougou, 169–70

Muridiyya, 20, 22, 97, 133–34, 218n78

Muslims. *See* ethnolinguistic and religious affiliation and embodied difference in Kédougou; Islam

Mussa, Mansa, 69–70

nara (alluvial gold deposits): gender and, 45–46; geological exploration and, 119; panning, 43, 45, 76; *sanukuru* vs., 44; *sanukuula* (washers of gold sand), 30*f*, 42–47, 96

native reserves (*réserves indigènes*) system, 94, 104, 238n92

navétane migrants, 22, 88, 134, 233n8

Ndiaye, Abdoulaye, 147

Niafarang project, 254n65

Nininkala (Ningiri), 40, 73–74, 79, 83, 115, 198, 200

Niokolo-Koba National Park, 136, 151, 171

Nkrumah, Kwame, 130

Noirot, Ernest, 83

Non-Aligned Movement, 133

nordistes, 147

nyafa (seasonal huts), 30, 96

nyama (life force), 69, 118

nyamakala (techno-ritual specialists), 69, 227n44

nyama trees, 116

Obermuller, Alphonse, 114

Obhiambo, E. S. Atieno, 27

Okeke-Agulu, Chika, 12

old campaign (*campagne de l'or*), 95

open-pit mines, 2–3, 34, 50, 118–19, 159, 161, 165, 170–71, 196, 204–5

Opération Kédougou, 135

Oromin Joint Venture Group, 252n35

orpaillage: about, 6–13; artisanal–industrial binary, 7–8; battle for Makabingui, 1–2; cooperatives of, 150; criminalization of, 132, 133, 149; decline of, 146; drought and ethnic reconfiguration of, 148–49; efficiency vs. waste and, 204; impacts of (Kédougou), 23–24; as largest mining industry in French West Africa, 87; *orpailleurs*, as term, 10; postwar contraction of, 124; as term, 10; traditional vs. semi-industrial, 166–67. See also *specific topics*

Osseo-Asare, Abena Dove, 15–16

Özden-Schilling, Tom, 250n14

"pagan" label, 18, 67–68, 77, 217n66

panning for gold, 43, 45, 76. See also *nara*

Park, Mungo, 77

Parker, John, 19–20

Parti Démocratique de la Guinée (PDG), 237n85

patrilineal descent, 220n9

Pétain, Philippe, 121

Petowal/Mako mine, 50–51

petroleum prospecting, 123

Philips, Kristin, 254n72

placer mines: closures and reopenings of, 122, 124, 133–34, 149; in colonial period, 86, 88, 93*f*, 95–103, 99*f*, 106; names of, 117; prospecting and, 113, 113*f*, 117, 127, 128*f*; women and, 76

placers of wood (*balandulas*), 37–38

political language. *See* rights claims in Senegal, language of

political parties and unions, 102–6, 134–35, 237nn84–85

Ponty, William, 93–94

Poura mining project, 122, 128

Pré, Roland, 105–6

INDEX 301

prices for gold, 12*f*, 54

prospecting and geological exploration: erasure of *orpaillage*, 126–28; exploration camps, 33–36; exploration trenches, 37–38, 45, 51, 53, 112–13, 113*f*, 122, 142–44, 161–63; future focus and temporal delays, 109, 127–28; geologists and geological teams, 111–13; interwar, 118–21; Kentinian model mine, 120–21; knowledge exchange, 109, 111, 116–17, 122–23; mapping, 108–10, 119–20, 120*f*, 126–27; postwar, 123–26; ritual geology, reports of, 113–18; Siguiri and, 105–6; slow work of, 13–14; Vichy regime and, 121. *See also* geologists; independence-era mineral missions in Sénégal Oriental

protests, 169–74

Pular ethnicity: ethnic composition of *orpaillage* and, 148–49; ethnogenesis, 182*t*, 183–84; in Kanoumering, 188; landscapes settled by, 193–94; patrilineal descent, 220n9; population in Kédougou, 219n79

pulley operators. See *juulusabala*

racialization and racism: artisanal–industrial mining binary and, 7; in colonial period, 88–89; "customary" mining and, 7; French *coopération* and, 131; industrialization and, 95–96; racial language, racialism, and racism, 180; "White geology," 17. *See also* ethnolinguistic and religious affiliation and embodied difference in Kédougou

Raffenel, Anne, 76

Randgold, 32–33, 52–53, 188, 198, 220n8. *See also* Endeavor Mining

Rao Pectoral, 228n59

Rassemblement Démocratique Africain (RDA), 103, 237nn84–85

religion. *See* ancestral religious traditions; ethnolinguistic and religious affiliation and embodied difference in Kédougou; Islam

réserves indigènes (native reserves) system, 94, 104, 238n92

Resolute Mining, 50–51, 157, 160*f*. *See also* ToroGold

rights claims in Senegal, language of: discovery claims, 159–64; entitlement to a share, 155; ethnic belonging and, 180; gold-mining boom and, 156–58; *juura* closures and, 153–54, 174; marginalization claims and protests, 169–74; political language, 154; small-scale claims, 164–67; subsistence claims, 167–69

rights of customary mining, 88–91, 104–6, 238n92

ritual geology: about, 5, 17–20; Atlantic-era Bambuk and European contact, 74–83; cosmology of *orpaillage*, 115–16; defined, 5, 17, 61; French colonial conquest and, 84–85; geologists' reports of, 113–18; Malian empire and, 68–74; rock outcrops as shrines, 113–14; sale of gold and ritual concerns, 62; spirit world, exchange relationship with, 42; Taubry narrative, 58–60; three elements of, 61; *tubabs* (white miners) and, 196–98. *See also* ethnolinguistic and religious affiliation and embodied difference in Kédougou; *jinne*; sacrifices; spirit snakes

Roberts, Richard, 107

rock-crushing, 43–44, 47, 92, 146, 169

rock outcrops, 113–14

Rodney, Walter, 19

Royal African Company, 75

royal ideology, 65

rubber boom, 92

Sabodala: airstrip at, 35*f*; construction of, 23; corporate partnerships, 157–58; discovery of, 142, 161–64; exploration, 33–34; map, 4*f*, 160*f*; ribbon-cutting ceremony, 33

sacrifices: blindness and insanity from not respecting, 117, 195–96, 203; European accounts, 79–80; human, 65–66, 74, 85, 148, 195, 198; to *jinne*, 39–42, 43, 79; kola nuts for, 196*f*; on placer mines, 97; practices, Maninka vs. Muslim, 184–85, 187; to snake spirits, 40, 65–66, 74; ter-

302   INDEX

ritories not mined due to, 195; by *tubabs* (white geologists), 197–98

Sagna, Mamadou, 40

Sall, Macky, 153, 158, 174, 249n1

Samecouta, 192–95

Sangare, Abdou, 42

Sano, Mamba, 103, 237n84

sano baara ("the work of gold"), 214n33

sanukuula (gold washers), 30f, 42–47, 96

Savineau, Denise, 98, 99, 101

scale, claims based on, 164–67

Scott, James, 18, 168

security force. See *tombuluma*

Senegal: foreign aid budget, 246n37; gold dust sales board, 46; gold-mining boom, 156–58; independence of, 132; Islam in, 22; map, 21f; mining codes, 133–34, 157–59, 171; population of, 218n79. *See also* independence-era mineral missions in Sénégal Oriental; rights claims in Senegal, language of

Sénégalo-Sovietique mission, 141–47, 162

Senghor, Léopold Sédar, 130, 132–36, 148, 184, 244n13

serpents. See spirit snakes

Service of Mines, 109, 112, 121–26, 240n20

sharia of the *juura*, 53–55

shelf projects, 129–30, 156–58, 251n23

shrines: *jalan* (lineage shrines), 77–78, 79, 117, 185; outcrops as, 113–14; "passing by the shrine" accusation, 185

Sidibé, Bana, 149, 170, 189–90

Sidibé, Bocar, 245n32

Sidibé, Taubry, 58–60, 67, 83, 129

Siguiri, 89, 92–102, 103–6, 120–21, 204

Siossat, J., 115

slavery and interethnic relations, 184

slave trade, 74–77, 82, 83

Small-scale Mining in the Developing Countries (UN), 149

Soares, Benjamin, 217n66

social and environmental impact studies (SEIs), 171

socialism, African, 132–34, 157, 244n14

social licenses, 52, 54–55

Société des Mines de Fer du Sénégal Oriental (MIFERSO), 251n23

Société Minière de Sabodala (SMS), 251n23

Sogolon Kejou, 68–69

Soninke people: ethnogenesis, 161, 182–83, 182t; Jakhanke and, 76–77; population in Kédougou, 219n79; Wagadu and, 63–66

South Africa, 87, 88, 232n4

Soviet missions, 129, 141–47, 162, 247n53

Sow, Hamidou, 50–51

spirits. See *jinne*

spirit snakes (*jinn saa*): Bida, 65–66, 73–74, 79, 83, 115, 177, 225n30; geologist reports of, 115; iron smelting and, 66–67; Nininkala, 40, 73–74, 79, 83, 115, 198, 200; Tyanaba, 73; Wagadu and, in medieval period, 63–68

strangers, welcoming of, 11, 47–50, 233n8

structural adjustment programs (SAPs), 157

subsistence claims, 167–69

sudistes, 248n74

sukunbalila (excavators of abandoned shafts), 100–101

Sumanguru Kante, 68–69

Sunjata Keita, 68–69

Sy, Mouhamadou, 141, 150, 247n54

Taal, Al-Hajj Umar, 80

Takrur, 64f, 226n43, 227n51

tanas (ritual taboos), 41, 79

taxation, colonial, 85, 91–92

technological innovation: African, 6; geological exploration and, 122–23; new specialists at Siguiri, 100–101; strangers credited for, 49

Tenda languages, 181, 182t, 256n19

Teranga Gold Corporation, 33, 160f, 162, 165, 204, 251n33, 252n35

termite mounds, 78–79

Thompson, E. P., 168

Tigana, El Hadj Mori, 129

Tigana, Moussa, 147, 152, 159, 167–68

Tilley, Helen, 109

Tinkoto: about, 29–31; Bambuk and, 32–33; Cissokho's tribunal, 31–33; established as year-round village, 43–44; exploration camps and, 33–36; French

Tinkoto (continued)
colonialism and, 85; geomorphological sketch of, 138*f*; Giraudon mission, 143–44; "Gulf Wars," 53; *kuru tala luno* (division of rocks ceremony), 55–57, 205–6; lode-ore techniques, introduction of, 49; map, 160*f*; population growth during drought, 148; ritual protocols compared to Kanoumering, 189; selection of *juurakuntigi*, 57; social licenses and sharia, 52–55; Thiankoun Bassadié *juura,* opening of, 185–87; washing of gold by women, 30*f*, 42–47
tombuluma (security force), 31–32, 54, 79, 96, 115
ToroGold, 50–51, 167. *See also* Resolute Mining
Touré, Lamine, 168
Touré, Samori, 84, 94
Touré, Sékou, 103, 130, 132–33, 149, 183, 222n33, 237n83, 237n85, 244n17, 245n33
Touré, Toumanie, 143, 146, 152
Touré, Yaya, 37
Tousignant, Noémi, 131
traders, Wangara, 64–65. See also *juula;* slave trade
tradition, concept of, 9
Traoré, Moussa, 149
Traoré, Neege, 155
tubabs (white miners) and ritual geology, 196–98
Tyanaba, 73

Union Démocratique des Ressortissants du Sénégal Oriental (UDRSO), 134–35
Union du Mandé, 102–3, 237n84

United Nations (UN), 133, 139–44, 141*f*, 149, 188, 247n46, 247n54
uranium prospecting, 123

Vallée du Serpent, Mali, 73–74, 229n70
Vansina, Jan, 9, 219n87
vertical geopolitics, 16
vertical vs. horizontal division of rights, 90–91, 94, 155
Vichy regime, 102, 121

Wade, Abdoulaye, 157–58, 169–74
Wagadu, 63–66, 64*f*, 70
Walila Filon, 44
Wangara, 64–65
washers of gold (*sanukuula*), 30*f*, 42–47, 96
West African Craton, 110
Weszkalnys, Gisa, 128
white spirits, 197, 258n46
Wolof ethnicity: colonial bias toward, 134, 147; Islamo-Wolof model, 22; patrilineal descent, 220n9; population in Kédougou, 219n79; traveling merchants, 23
Wolof language, 22, 134, 147
World Bank, 149, 150, 157
World War II, 102

Yaya, Alpha, 84
year of breaking rocks (*kuru taki sono*), 159
Y'en a Marre (We've Had Enough) movement, 170
Yusoff, Kathryn, 17

zakat (almsgiving), 56